D1285496

DEPRESSION POST OFFICE MURALS AND SOUTHERN CULTURE

SUE BRIDWELL BECKHAM / DEPRESSIO

POST OFFICE MURALS AND SOUTHERN CULTURE

A GENTLE RECONSTRUCTION

Louisiana State University Press
Baton Rouge and London

WITHDRAWN
Tennessee Tech. Library
Cookeville, Tenn.

Copyright © 1989 by Louisiana State University Press
All rights reserved
Manufactured in the United States of America

98 97 96 95 94 93 92 91 90 89   5 4 3 2 1

Designer: Laura Roubique Gleason
Typeface: Trump Mediaeval
Typesetter: G & S Typesetters, Inc.
Printer: Thomson-Shore, Inc.
Binder: John H. Dekker & Sons, Inc.

Library of Congress Cataloging-in-Publication Data
Beckham, Sue Bridwell.
  Depression post office murals and southern culture : a gentle
reconstruction / Sue Bridwell Beckham.
     p.   cm.
  Includes index.
  ISBN 0-8071-1447-2 (alk. paper)
  1. Mural painting and decoration, American—Southern States.
2. Mural painting and decoration—20th century—Southern States.
3. Postal service—Southern States—Buildings.   4. Federal Art
Project.   5. Southern States in art.   I. Title.
ND2611.B4   1989
751.7'3'0975—dc19   88-22031
                                                         CIP

The photographs appearing herein as Figures 1–6, 9–28, 30–32, 37–43, 45,
46, 48–49, 51–55, 57–61, 63–82, 84, and 87–93 are courtesy of the National
Archives.

The paper in this book meets the guidelines for permanence and durability of the
Committee on Production Guidelines for Book Longevity of the Council on
Library Resources. ∞

For Dick
and for Rich, Jeni, and Jay

CONTENTS

ILLUSTRATIONS

PREFACE

Thirty-five years ago, sixth graders in Cynthiana, Kentucky, were taught a peculiarly "border state" version of American history. A "civil" war had never been fought in the United States. A war among loosely confederated "sovereign" states was merely a "War Between the States." Some children farther south were taught that it was a "War of Northern Aggression" and a few farther north that it was a "War of Southern Secession," but in Kentucky we needed a neutral term. We also learned that the war was not fought over slavery—despite the fact that every time we drove country roads, we passed "slave-built stone fences," artifacts of which we learned to be proud. Those who fought for the South in the state where Abraham Lincoln was born could not have condoned slavery. The War Between the States had been fought over the sacred principle of states' rights—still a lively issue in the decade after World War II. And our native son, Honest Abe, had been the greatest American president, even though he had the poor taste to grow up in Illinois. He had, after all, saved the Union, which had not precisely existed before the states fought among themselves.

Not only did I grow up with that schizoid interpretation of my state's history; ancestors on both sides of my family were wounded at Shiloh—one fought for the North, the other for the South. I heard my grandmother claim that Lincoln took arms against the South only because he was jealous that he could not have slaves of his own. I took that with the proverbial grain of salt, but I found tales of family wealth lost in the war more alluring. And knowing that a skirmish of the Battle of Shiloh had been fought on "our" land was an endless source of romantic fantasy. Still I could find no evidence that her side of the family—Tennessee yeoman farmers—was fallen aristocracy. I early learned to scorn social pretense, of which there was much in Cynthiana. My family background left me with only one certainty. I knew that, as a daughter of a border state, I could choose which side I would have supported in that war. And I spent much time in my youth trying to convince myself that I belonged on the side that opposed slavery and favored a united nation and that, therefore, I was not a "southerner."

Not until I moved to the Midwest did I realize that there was more to being southern than race prejudice and an abstraction called states' rights. Perhaps more important, southernness included more than one geographic region, more than a single mind-set, and a whole conglomeration of local histories. I was free then to recognize that, however much I might disagree with certain ideas perceived to be "southern," I am southern. I was convinced by the cultural alienation I felt from those second- and third-generation Americans about me and by my instant rapport with anybody from any part of the South and any southern social level. Even with those who disagreed with me on politics and social issues, I could communicate more effectively than I could with citizens of my new home.

For years, as a student and an instructor of English language and literature, I read southern fiction as the best America had to offer; as a budding Americanist, I began reading classic studies of the South and the southern character. But though I made my peace with being southern and though I found bits of southern truth in each of those published works, nowhere could I find myself. Nor could I find the people I grew up among or my fellow expatriate southerners. We were not among Flannery O'Connor's grotesques or Eudora Welty's absurd characters. We were not of Katherine Anne Porter's decayed aristocracy or William Faulkner's comically profound people of the earth. And we certainly were not Snopeses, though we knew them well. We shared neither W. J. Cash's guilt-ridden southern mind nor C. Vann Woodward's burden of southern history. We were neither black nor sharecroppers; nor were we committed to an agrarian way of life—at least, no more than our midwestern neighbors were, and we certainly had no aristocratic pretensions. The religions we grew up in—Southern Baptist, Methodist, and Presbyterian—were only mildly fundamental by today's Moral Majority standards. We were not "hillbillies," and we neither made not drank moonshine. And yet we were as southern as any of these southerners characterized in fiction and scholarship and quite a bit less visible.

Then I wrote my first paper on a post office mural—one in northern Mississippi—and made my first trip to the National Archives to read the correspondence related to it. There, on yellowing paper dating from the decade before I was born, were the southerners I knew best. Letters to the Treasury Department's Section of Fine Arts (the agency responsible for those murals) were from small-town mayors and postmasters, politicians elected by the constituency of which I was a part or appointed to serve that constituency—people with their fingers on the pulse of southern voters. Others who wrote were leaders of the service clubs, the garden clubs, the book clubs, the chambers of commerce—organizations whose members were those white southerners who are rarely studied. Articles in the Section files had been clipped from the small-town newspapers that counted for their existence on sales to those who earned a decent living in the trades and in lower-echelon white-collar occupations. Here, finally, was a way to gain some insight into the least-studied and possibly the most influential group of southerners.

Here I found southerners who wanted first of all to be American, for whom the nineteenth-century war that made the South a special case was only history. Here I found the same southerners to be proud of southern regional traits and equally proud of the traits that distinguished their particular corner of the South from the South at large.

Section records revealed the South I knew because the Section had set itself up both to please and to edify its constituency throughout the nation. Thus, people felt it their right to air reactions to the murals placed in their post offices. And air them they did—especially southerners. When, a few years later, I began similar research into Wisconsin post office murals, I stumbled upon one of the traits that make me and my compatriots southern. The people of depression Wisconsin seldom wrote their government about the murals. They were almost uniformly either mildly pleased or too busy with other concerns to voice their judgments on such inconsequential events as the installation of art in their post offices. It became clear that the records about murals in states considered southern were a particularly fine lode of information on what made the South southern. When a mural failed to please citizens in a southern community, the government was sure to hear very specifically about what was objectionable. When, on the other hand, a community was delighted with the way it had been interpreted, the response was equally eloquent. In some cases, there was no response. Precisely because of the vehemence of southerners' objections, I could assume that the people who used the post office every day and found no reason to comment on the mural had been depicted as they saw themselves. Thus, even when correspondence was sparse, the iconography itself was invaluable to me in finding out about my South.

The fact that the murals were "art" of the 1930s and that composition was therefore important added another dimension to the study. Regionalism has been so thoroughly examined that some points about it have become axiomatic. To begin with, studies of regionalism assume it to be a manifestation of high art. Thus, when we study regional literature, we study southern literature, which is assumed to be the best. Regional art is invariably associated with the Midwest, where the best-known of its proponents—Thomas Hart Benton, John Steuart Curry, and Grant Wood—flourished. Just as midwesterners can find examples of regional literature, however, so we of the South have our own brand of regional art. Because southern art was seldom recognized by the establishment, only recently have experts begun to look at it. And only now do they do so in terms of its audience.

Perhaps the most important tenet of regionalism in art—at least as Benton, Curry, and Wood expressed it—is that its audience was not the art establishment, but rather the American public. In trying to please the people as represented by postmasters, mayors, club chairmen, and weekly newspapers—in trying to please the South I knew—the Section attempted to set up a truly regional art, the first art recognized as such in the South. Unfortunately, the art the government sponsored was often not regional at all. The Section assumed, with some justification, southern art to be underdeveloped at best. It frequently gave up too soon on finding southern artists to paint the southern scene and appointed artists from the eastern establishment. Too often, these artists did not look at the South and paint the South they saw. They painted instead the South of myth and fantasy. And they did not share southerners' mythology; theirs was some exoteric vision of the South. Thus in comparing the murals that worked and those that did not, I was able to tell much that was southern about southern art.

My quest, however, is not finally about southern art; it is about southern culture and its interaction with the federal government. In discovering my segment of southern culture, I would inevitably learn a lot about America. In 1937, John Dollard published *Caste and Class in a Southern Town,* which he began as a study of blacks in the South. As he did his research Dollard had to alter the focus of his book because he found that studying southern blacks was possible only in the context of a ruling southern white culture. Likewise, I have found that studying southern whites is possible only in a context that is largely black. I could not write of southern whites without writing of southern perceptions of blacks. And I could not write of acceptable southern images of blacks without discovering much about American racism. Only in the South do blacks appear in the murals, because Americans in the 1930s only "saw" blacks in the South. They were blind to blacks elsewhere. The racism for which the South has too often been held solely responsible is an American problem, and a great part of the southern effort to be recognized as American is an effort to see American racism acknowledged.

During the research for and the writing of this book, I have grown increasingly defensive as a southerner. The South is indeed a special case in American culture, but the frequent assumption that southerners are southern first and Americans second is questionable, and it is certainly anathema to the segment of southern culture in which I grew up. Also, I have found it difficult to view the material with scholarly detachment. More and more, I understand why southerners are suspicious of outsiders who come to study conditions in the South. And I am convinced that the United States must finally come to grips with the fact that the South, no less than the Midwest, the West, and the East, is America and that ultimately we must stop reconstructing the South and begin reconstructing America. None of that is new, but the post office murals provide a new way of examining and documenting it.

ACKNOWLEDGMENTS

Writing this book has been a labor of love, but the course of true love never did run smooth, and neither has the course of this labor. The fact that it is finished at all and much of whatever merit it has I owe to a number of people and agencies who have given me support. For the chance to make expensive trips to Washington to read voluminous records in the National Archives, I am grateful to the University of Minnesota for a Doctoral Dissertation Special Grant. For the chance to return to Washington and visit Madison, Wisconsin, to view 1930s movies set in the South, I thank the University of Minnesota Film Study Fund. A University of Minnesota Dissertation Fellowship provided me the time to do the extensive research both at home and in the field. Without the knowledgeable and cheerful help of the staff of the National Archives, the research would have been far more strenuous; without the Archives' open-door policy, it would have been impossible. I am particularly indebted to the Interlibrary Loan Department of the University of Minnesota's O. Meredith Wilson Library for friendly, dependable, and efficient help beyond the call of duty in locating obscure periodicals and long-out-of-print books. Thanks are also due the University of Wisconsin-Stout, where I have tenure, for allowing me to take four consecutive years of leave to complete the manuscript. I also thank Research Promotion Services at that institution.

Without all that institutional support, the project would have taken more years than I care to imagine, but personal support has perhaps been even more important. Karal Ann Marling deserves a special note of appreciation for writing the model for this type of research, for long hours discussing the topic, for reading and rereading the manuscript and commenting on it, for encouragement when the going got rough, and for seeing to it that I did not get complacent when things went well. Clarke Chambers performed beyond expectation both as an astute, often critical reader and as a friend. From David W. Noble, my teacher first and now my friend, I learned new ways of thinking about the South, about America, and about life. Jack Temple Kirby has moved from anonymous reader to indispensable advisor. Betty Agee, Secretary of American Studies at the University of Minnesota, has always been a supportive professional—even more, she is a close friend. And I owe special thanks to Jens Gunelson, who converted pictures of murals in a variety of forms into glossies suitable for mounting, occasionally at a moment's notice, and remained cheerful through it all. I hope all the others who, like Marjorie, Pat, Cris, and Betty, read and advised on bits and pieces will realize that while they may not appear in this list, they are neither forgotten nor unappreciated.

Jeni, Jay, and Rich deserve medals for tolerating all the late meals and missed social opportunities occasioned by an overextended mother—and particularly for all the vacation time they spent standing around in southern post office lobbies. And my husband Dick I thank most of all for help ranging from allowing me to bluster about the lack of logic in the universe to proofreading to doing dishes when it wasn't his turn, but mostly for being there.

DEPRESSION POST OFFICE MURALS AND SOUTHERN CULTURE

INTRODUCTION

For a very brief time, between April of 1861 and April of 1865, eleven states of the American South along with sympathetic sections and individuals of several others formed themselves into a separate, loosely constructed nation. During the Civil War and since, those who fought on the side of the Confederacy or sympathized with it have been called "Rebels." Perhaps, however, the nickname is a misnomer. The Rebels were fighting for the status quo, and there are many indications that most southern leaders, slaveholders included, felt forced into the position of fighting a war they could not wholly condone.[1] Whatever the truth of the causes— and they will be debated for years to come—the war was followed by anywhere from less than a year to over a decade of military reconstruction. In the century since, the period when one part of the nation supposedly forced its will on another has frequently been labeled one of the bleakest in American history. At least until the 1960s, the white southern view of Radical Reconstruction prevailed in most history textbooks.[2]

Whether Reconstruction was as unconscionable as it has been labeled, and current thinking suggests that Reconstruction was not

1. Two recent scholarly works on Civil War history demonstrate that most southern leaders in the 1850s and well into the war had at best mixed emotions about creating a new nation of the South and misgivings even about the sacredness of states' rights. In *The Ruling Race: A History of American Slaveholders* (New York, 1982), James Oakes powerfully demonstrates that through the 1850s most southern leaders opposed secession and were willing time and again to compromise to save the Union. During the war, they supported constitutions patterned on the Constitution they were rejecting and espoused, as did most Americans, capitalism, democracy, and evangelical Protestantism. Richard A. Beringer *et al.*, *Why the South Lost the Civil War* (Athens, Ga., 1986), show that a deficient nationalism resulting in a lack of commitment was the underlying cause of Confederate failure.

2. Roger L. Ransom and Richard Sutch, *One Kind of Freedom* (London, 1977), and David Herbert Donald, *Liberty and Union* (Lexington, Mass., 1978), suggest that the agrarian economy in the South was vital when the war began, but the germs of its decay were already in evidence. Oakes and Donald also suggest that most southern leaders wished to retain slavery and felt disagreeably forced into forming a separate nation in order to protect the "peculiar institution."

so bleak as folklore makes it, white southerners in the 1930s re-membered and resented a time when their land was occupied by men in uniform from other regions—and they remembered twelve years of it. In the preface to his respected and conciliatory history, *The Road to Reunion* (1937), Paul H. Buck ignored the early with-drawal of Union forces from some states and said, "For twelve years the North endeavored to build a policy upon force." The memory was so cherished that an Atlanta *Constitution* columnist review-ing *Tar Heel Editor* by Josephus Daniels was moved to fear that it could be forgotten: "We have got into such a hurry that we forget our background in seeking to interpret the present. We forget that the south was once occupied by an army of occupation and that in some sections that army remained for 11 years. In this day of mili-tary dictatorships we forget that for a decade or more the south lived under one. We are likely to forget, too, that the south during this period endured a government which was as fantastic and often as cruel in its aspect as any which has ever existed." He further ob-served, in his review of a book by a southerner who was so thor-oughly reconstructed that he served in Woodrow Wilson's cabinet, the South had been undaunted by federal efforts to reconstruct it. The South "accepted the verdict of the war, went to work under an oppressive military dictatorship and began to solve the problems left it by the issue of the war." Despite all efforts, poverty, depleted soil, and oppressed people were still facts of life for the South. At the same time, however, another Atlanta *Constitution* editor, Clark Howell, endorsed an "important little book" that rendered in everyday language the findings of a study showing that cotton ten-ancy, for blacks and whites, was an insidious waste of human po-tential and, worse, un-American as well. Reconstruction had done nothing to prevent the South from developing a system of poverty and dependency from which it had not recovered. The book, *The Collapse of Cotton Tenancy*, was a southern book published by a southern press and the study a southern study.[3] White southerners

3. Paul H. Buck, *The Road to Reunion: 1865–1900* (Boston, 1937), vii; "South's Transition Period Pictured in Editor's Story," Atlanta *Constitution*, December 10, 1939, Magazine section, 3; Charles S. Johnson *et al.*, *The Collapse of Cotton Ten-ancy: Summary of Field Studies & Statistical Surveys, 1933–35* (Chapel Hill, 1935). The preface was a collaboration in which seventeen northern and southern leaders from industry, academia, labor, agriculture, and journalism endorsed the book's message and its implications.

of the 1930s knew that the only way the South would climb out of its economic morass was through reclamation of its subsistence-level citizens, black and white. At the same time, they felt it imperative to remember that the national government had dictated their affairs for a time. That memory, however exaggerated, was important because of the impetus it gave the South to solve its own problems.

The Civil War and Reconstruction, which occurred when potential economic decay in the southeastern states could already be predicted, were only the beginning of a series of attempts to "reconstruct" the South in the American image in one way or other. Since that time, white southern resentment of the Reconstruction period has led many southerners to distrust well-intentioned projects emanating from the federal government. One of those projects was the United States Treasury Department program that sought to embellish new federal buildings with excellent American art. Those who administered this program hoped to please the communities in which buildings would be so decorated. At times, they even consulted residents of those communities about subject matter. Their plan was to "reconstruct" not only the South but all American regions by awakening the people to the possibilities of a national mural art. This effort seemed as innocuous as federal efforts at reformation could be. It was indeed a Gentle Reconstruction.

From 1934 to 1943, the United States government engaged in a massive program to decorate new federal buildings with a mural art of the American people. Not until late 1937 did murals and sculptures in any great number appear in southern federal buildings or in any other remote rural area of the country. Even so, between 1937 and the demise of the program, southeastern post offices and courthouses were embellished with approximately three hundred decorations, most of them murals—nearly one-fourth of the whole nine-year output of this New Deal program.[4]

4. There is as yet no complete and accurate collation of murals. "Geographical Directory of Murals and Sculptures Commissioned by Section of Fine Arts, Public Buildings Administration, Federal Works Agency," *American Art Annual,* XXXV (1941–42), 623–58, provides a reasonably complete list of Section artworks through 1939 and into 1940. No such compilation was attempted for 1940 and 1941. After World War II resulted in significant budget cuts for arts agencies, official records were carelessly kept. In the National Archives records for projects in 1942 and after

This is the story of that agency's efforts to decorate federal buildings in the South with mural art that would both please and edify
the people who patronized those buildings. It is the story of the interaction between the Section of Fine Arts, the muralists it employed, and the southern people it served—the frustrations, the
standoffs, and the resounding successes. The story of this gentle
reconstruction cannot be told without tales of the artists and the
federal agency that hired them. Most of all, however, this is a
southern story.

It is the story of the South as revealed in those murals and in the
mostly white southern interaction with the people responsible for
them. It is the story of a region and a people eager to recover past
glory—real or imagined—and to regain their rightful position as a
powerful and respected part of a powerful and respected nation in
the face of a beneficent government eager, apparently all too often,
to immortalize present suffering. It is the story of one region's
struggle to regain economic prosperity after seventy years of deprivation in the midst of a nation's struggle to regain prosperity
after less than a decade of want. It is the story of a society besieged
by images of itself that bore small relation to southern life as
southerners perceived it. It is the story of a culture striving to im-
part its own image within a greater culture that would rather deal
in popular stereotypes.

It is also the story of the South that neither suffered the hunger
and humiliation of the sharecroppers nor experienced the nostalgia
of displaced aristocrats. Over the past fifty years, the South has
been examined from every perspective except that of the largest

are often incomplete and poorly filed. Karel Yasko, Fine Arts Counselor for the General Services Administration until his death in 1985, began compiling a list of Section art projects and their present locations, but his list, "Final Report: Section of
Fine Arts, Public Buildings Administration, October 16, 1934 to July, 1943," was
never completed and the counselor's position has been abolished. Marlene Park and
Gerald E. Markowitz, *Democratic Vistas: Post Offices and Public Art in the New
Deal* (Philadelphia, 1984), compiled the fullest published list to date (pp. 201–35),
but through no fault of the authors, even that is incomplete and not entirely accurate. One would have to visit every community in which the Section placed a work
of art, and even then it would be impossible to locate the artworks that have been
"removed," sold to private collectors, retained by the United States Postal Service,
donated to local museums where they were stored, etc. When I have located a Section mural that is no longer on its original wall, I indicate its whereabouts in the
Appendix.

single group of southerners, the whites who developed skills and had jobs that enabled them to enjoy an economic life similar to that of most Americans. These southern Americans tilled productive land, operated small businesses, worked in offices, in schools, and in sales. They were the railroad men, the electricians, the house painters, and the housewives—those who delivered services that had no particular social esteem. I examine the prevailing culture of the American South during the late 1930s and early 1940s, when all too often the nation obfuscated questions about causes of the Great Depression with questions and suggested answers about the poverty of the American South. I take as a given the South's well-known xenophobia and seek to explain why southerners might be xenophobic. And I differentiate between events wherein that xenophobia was an actual force and events in which xenophobic reactions were merely conjectured by those who would study or serve the South.

Since the story is mostly about working-class white southerners and those in marginal white-collar occupations, the words *South,* *southern,* and *southerner* usually refer here to that largest single segment of southern society. When those words must refer to the whole South, that will be clear from the context. Other groups are designated specifically by such terms as *black southerners, planters,* and *sharecroppers.* As this is a story, the form and the organization are narrative and informal. And in narrating particular tales, I may resort to occasional hyperbole. One of the southern bequests to the nation is an oral, narrative tradition laced with exaggeration and colorful diction. The influence of that tradition on such southern writers of fiction as William Faulkner and Eudora Welty is well known. As it is an appropriate medium for southern fictional stories, so it is for this story of a modern, gentle reconstruction.

It would be well to clarify at the outset the terms *Reconstruction* and *reconstruction.* Capitalized, the word refers collectively to the organized actions taken by the federal government between 1865 and 1877 in various parts of the South to ensure that the nation would not again be split in twain and, to a lesser extent, to ensure that the newly freed blacks had a place in the region. Those actions were viewed by southerners in the 1930s as malicious and damaging overreactions. Unfortunately, many citizens of the South in that decade did not see reconstruction as stopping with those organized political actions. In my study of the murals, of local reactions to them, and of other cultural artifacts of the period, I hope to reveal that almost any government, journalistic, or academic action from outside the South, suggesting that the South could not handle its own problems, was perceived as an effort at reconstruction and regarded with a hostility similar to that reserved for organized Reconstruction. Such external actions and ideas are herein frequently referred to as *reconstruction*.

During the 1930s, national attention frequently focused on the South. The rhetoric of the 1920s that emphasized depravity and guilt in the South was replaced with well-meant but condescending rhetoric about how southern social problems might be solved.[5] Even before 1937, when a government-commissioned economic study labeled the South the "Nation's Number One Economic Problem," journalists, photographers, sociologists, and folklorists had begun to treat the South as a sort of investigative paradise. Such prominent examiners of culture as John Dollard, Gunnar Myrdal, Zora Neale Hurston, James Agee, and Walker Evans investigated the white tenant farmer, the black and the white sharecropper, and blacks from every conceivable vantage point.[6] Most of their published studies depicted a South in need of help or, even more objectionable to white southerners, a South with reprehensible social values.

When government agencies and such institutions as Encyclopedia Britannica Films set out to show the "real South" to the nation in the new medium of documentary film, their efforts did little to counteract the prevailing notion that the South was surviving only

5. Fred Hobson (ed.), *South-Watching: Selected Essays by Gerald W. Johnson* (Chapel Hill, 1983), vii–viii.

6. In the 1930s a veritable army of social scientists and humanists invaded the South to investigate its problems. Those cited here were selected to indicate the wide variety of studies that were done. John Dollard investigated black problems in *Caste and Class in a Southern Town* (New Haven, 1937) and discovered that he had to study the white culture as well. Gunnar Myrdal came from Sweden to study the race problem in the South with Richard Sterner and Arnold Rose in *An American Dilemma: The Negro Problem and Modern Democracy* (New York, 1944) and found it a dilemma in a democracy. Black writer Zora Neale Hurston returned from studies in anthropology at Columbia to gather black folktales and wisdom for *Mules and Men* (Philadelphia, 1935). James Agee and Walker Evans lived for several months with a white tenant family in order to record their lives in words and pictures for *Let Us Now Praise Famous Men* (Boston, 1941).

with the help of a generous and forgiving national family. Such "educational" films as Eastman's *The New South*, Erpi's *The Southeastern States*, and the Farm Security Administration's much-acclaimed *The River* showed a South recovering from poverty and destructive use of its land with the assistance of northern capital and a paternalistic government—being, as it were, reconstructed. Eastman's *The Old South* and numerous National Park Service films about the glories of such southern cities as Charleston and Montgomery dwelt on a past lost to all except tourists who in their recreation would be content with re-creations.[7] Even while government and educational films sought in this seemingly condescending way to rectify images of the South, moviegoing southerners beyond school age seldom saw their region in newsreels. Southern states appeared in movie news only when a tornado, flood, or crop failure once again revealed the South as inept and unable to provide for itself or when stories of demagogic politicians suggested that southern voters were incapable of making intelligent choices.[8]

Despite the fact that during the 1930s such writers as William Faulkner, Elizabeth Madox Roberts, and Robert Penn Warren continued the southern Renaissance born in the 1920s, they were popular only among academics and literary critics.[9] Their presentation of southern life was usually only a vehicle by which they could transmit more universal messages. The southern writers

7. *The New South* (Eastman Classroom Film, 1932); *The Southeastern States* (Erpi Educational Film, in collaboration with Howard W. Odum, 1936); *The River* (written and directed by Pare Lorentz under the auspices of the Farm Security Administration, 1937); *Virginia: The Old Dominion* (Eastman Classroom Film, 1932); *The Old South* (Eastman Teaching Film, 1932), and *The Heart of the Confederacy* (National Park Service Division of Motion Pictures, Series CCC in State Parks, 1939) depict an idyllic "Old South" and then dwell on the economic problems of the contemporary South.

8. Concentrated viewing in the National Archives collection of 1930s newsreels reveals that *Universal News* and *Paramount News* found only southern disaster newsworthy. *March of Time* segments dwelt on southern curiosities, as in the clip "Demagogues and Do Gooders." A segment of the Vitaphone series *Over the United States* entitled "Curious Industries" features twelve such, all located in the South.

9. Origins of the term *southern Renaissance* to refer to the great literary outpouring from the South in the 1920s, 1930s, and 1940s are dim. C. Vann Woodward, however, popularized it in "Why the Southern Renaissance," *Virginia Quarterly Review*, LI (Spring, 1975), 222–39. See also Richard H. King, *A Southern Renaissance: The Cultural Awakening of the American South, 1930–1955* (New York, 1980).

whose prose was widely read created of the southeastern United States a sort of curiosity upon which fantasies, both elegant and squalid, are built. Margaret Mitchell presented a fairy-tale South of gentility and nobility such as the world has never known outside the covers of a book, and Erskine Caldwell created an equally fantastic world of squalor, insensitivity, and depravity. These are the writers known to Middle America both within the South and without. And theirs are the images that southerners sought to counteract when they responded to the paintings on post office walls.

At the same time, southerners were faced with Hollywood's visual fantasy of a southern soil upon which only insensitive aristocrats and the exploited and the ignorant of two races had ever set foot. Moviegoers who saw only *So Red the Rose, Jezebel,* and *Gone With the Wind,* on the one hand, and *Swamp Water, I Am a Fugitive from a Chain Gang,* and *They Won't Forget,* on the other, could well have concluded that the South had lost whatever grace and dignity it had ever had nearly a century before and replaced it with squalor, injustice, and unfounded suspicion. Certainly, southerners could not have been blamed if they suspected that all outsiders saw the contemporary South not only in negative terms but as having no real place in America.

It is no wonder that Jonathan Daniels, son of Josephus Daniels and editor of the same prominent southern newspaper, set out on a pilgrimage of several months to discover the South for himself and write about it. And it is little wonder that the social science textbook adopted by the state of Alabama in 1937 was written and published in that state.[10] Southerners had little faith that nonsoutherners would represent them as they saw themselves.

And then, quietly at first, the federal government—which had begun Civilian Conservation Corps (CCC) projects to reclaim eroded southern soil and the massive Tennessee Valley Authority (TVA) effort to control the floods that regularly ravaged the South and to bring southern households into technical parity with those in the rest of the nation, and which hired thousands of southern workers through the Works Progress Administration (WPA)—began decorating southern post offices with murals in which the subject

10. Jonathan Daniels, *A Southerner Discovers the South* (New York, 1938); Samuel Lee Chestnut, *The Rural South: Background—Problems—Outlook* (Montgomery, Ala., 1937).

matter should be appropriate to the particular locale.[11] Thus, finally, the South perceived a tacit assumption in the New Deal that they had some say in how they were represented and in how government largesse was to be used. The agency responsible for this massive murals project was the Treasury Section of Fine Arts.[12] The Section, as it was called by those who did not confuse it with WPA arts projects, was the dream of Edward Bruce, who was its head from the beginning until he died in 1942. The public manifestation of that dream was the Treasury Department order that organized the Section in October, 1934. According to that order, the agency was to secure fine artwork to embellish public buildings and thus encourage the development of art in the United States; it was to seek the cooperation of the art world in selecting artists and, whenever possible, to employ local talent; it was to choose artists through objective competitions wherever practicable, though certain established artists could be commissioned on the basis of their reputations. Bruce was eager to disassociate the Section from such government efforts to employ needy artists as the WPA's Federal Art Project. Although needy artists did apply and often were com-

11. In chapters on his visit to Norris, Tennessee, the government's TVA new town, Jonathan Daniels shows that in spite of conscientious efforts to keep TVA political power, like its electric power, in the South, some of the highest-ranking officials were new-wave "carpetbaggers" sent from Washington to supervise the work there. He also found that Tennessee citizens were ambivalent toward the project. Few saw it as an exclusively altruistic endeavor on the government's part. Most, of course, did not deny the benefits.

12. Information on the workings of the Section comes from multiple sources: Karal Ann Marling, *Wall-to-Wall America* (Minneapolis, 1982); Belisario Ramon Contreras, "The New Deal Treasury Department Art Programs and the American Artist: 1933–1943" (Ph.D. dissertation, American University, 1967); Richard D. McKinzie, *The New Deal for Artists* (Princeton, 1973); and Francis Van O'Connor, *Federal Art Patronage, 1933–1943* (College Park, Md., 1966). More recent is Park and Markowitz, *Democratic Vistas.* The most important source, however, and the only one regarding Section dealings specifically with the South, remains the massive and meticulously kept records of the Section of Fine Arts, now in the National Archives, Division of Natural Resources, Record Group 121, "Records of the Public Buildings Service," Entries 104–59. Among these records are copies of the quarterly *Bulletin,* correspondence with other government agencies, and annual reports. More revealing, however, are the individual files on every community for which an artwork was ever proposed. These contain correspondence with artists, postmasters, citizens, and organizations of the individual communities; records of competitions; the various forms required for approval of an artwork; and clippings from local newspapers. An essay in Marling, *Wall-to-Wall America,* 329–36, outlines the organization of these records and tells how to find material in them.

missioned, the Section intended that employment be based on merit alone. And the artists were to "embellish Federal buildings with the best contemporary American art."

Artists to paint the murals were usually selected through competitions. When federal buildings that were nationally significant, such as the Justice and Post Office buildings in Washington, were to be decorated, the national competitions were open to all American artists. Most competitions, however, sought to reinforce the Section's goal of employing local talent whenever possible by limiting entries to those who had some knowledge of that region. The competition for Petersburg, Virginia, for example, was open to artists of the southeastern and mid-Atlantic states. For Jackson, Mississippi, the area from which artists were invited to compete extended farther north (Kentucky was included) and west (Texas and Arkansas), but artists from Maryland and Delaware were not eligible. To qualify to enter a regional competition, an artist had to live in that region or to have grown up in it. In the South, where entries were usually few in number, qualifications often included artists who had lived at least a given number of years in the area (five, for example, in fairly populous regions; two in areas where few artists were likely to reside).

Ideally, competitions were conducted by local citizens cognizant of good art. That in itself presented a problem for southern cities. Since the South of the 1930s had few art schools and since art museums were fewer still, even appointing a knowledgeable committee was difficult. With considerable effort, the Section accumulated enough names of people qualified to serve on the Petersburg competition committee, only to find all but one too busy and the one unwilling to serve if the others would not. The Section itself conducted that competition. In Jackson, Mississippi, where a committee was more easily appointed, the competition was so beset with mishaps—two members died suddenly, and there was a general disagreement with the Section on what constituted good art—that a Connecticut artist who had completed several satisfactory Section murals was finally appointed.

Competitions usually took place only when commissions were $1,500 or more and sometimes not even then. For most small-town post offices, where commissions averaged less than $700, artists would ideally be selected from the legions who entered competitions, did competent designs, but did not win. In the South, how-

ever, the number of entries was frequently small and often included people with no mural experience and little training. Thus,
the Section frequently had to resort to its third possibility for selecting a muralist: appointing an artist on the basis of "competent
work for the Section."

Once an artist was asked to "submit designs" for a particular
mural—Section language for appointing an artist to a project—the
Section routinely advised the artist to visit the community and
the building he was to decorate. In the case of the South, however,
the Section frequently found it necessary or at least convenient to
invoke the words "whenever practicable" at the end of its stated
aim to employ local talent. Artists appointed to decorate southern
post offices on the basis of "competent work" were often from New
York and New England art colonies, or they might be from the only
other sizable concentrations of artists who had proven their merit
with the Section—in and around Taos, New Mexico, in California,
and in Washington. And when the Section appointed artists from
distant places to paint southern murals, there was a risk that southerners would object to the appropriateness of the decoration.

Not only were the murals seldom painted on the walls on which
they were to be displayed, the work was only infrequently done in
the same city. Traditionally, an artist painted a mural on canvas or
gesso-treated masonite in his studio; then, if he could, he took the
finished product to the post office to install it. Often with southern
commissions, however, even this final trip was impossible. A New
York firm would take several murals to the South and move from
community to community installing them.

One can easily imagine the problems of a New York artist expected to design a mural appropriate for Okolona, Mississippi. He
probably had never heard of Okolona, and he certainly could not
make the trip to become acquainted. If he was out of work, he
hadn't the money; if he was employed, he hadn't the time. So, assured by the Section that he need not visit the post office if it was
too inconvenient and advised to look at a similar building in his
vicinity—small-town post offices in the 1930s were built from
three floor-plans, regardless of their location—he went to his public library and found out what Mississippi's main industries or
crops were. Then he designed a mural, using the information he
had found and perhaps a picture or two from a botany journal.

In a South that must have felt too much examined, characterized, and judged from without, being faced with a mural conceived and executed by a northerner must have seemed one more in a long string of insults to southern efforts at self-sufficiency. On the other hand, a muralist in need of work and wishing for important commissions with which to build a reputation must have found an appointment to paint a federal mural, however little he knew about the locale, irresistible. Thus, when a Michigan muralist painted a tobacco-growing scene for Mullins, South Carolina, he got his information from an encyclopedia. His rendering misrepresented the process of growing and curing tobacco from early weeks after planting until the leaves were ready for market.[13] Residents of Mullins, whose post office would be eternally graced with a mural so inaccurate and who were aware of the government's vague admonition that artists design a picture appropriate to the locale, likely felt that once again their government had disregarded their wishes and repudiated their autonomy.

The Section of Fine Arts grew from Edward Bruce's dream, but Bruce seldom dealt with the communities it served and the artists who served it. Most of the meticulously filed Section correspondence consists of letters to and from Bruce's assistant, Edward Rowan. Although the assumption was that an approved design had been accepted by the five-member Section staff, it was Rowan who relayed virtually all messages about appropriate subject matter as well as acceptability of design to Section artists. One suspects that he often made the judgments, since interoffice correspondence revealing communal effort is rare.

During his years with the Section, Edward Rowan lived in Arlington, Virginia, but his address in a southern state made him in no wise conversant with southern concerns. Arlington was and is a suburb of the nation's capital; most of its residents are people attached to Washington, D.C., often with roots in distant regions. So it was with Rowan. Well-known as a watercolorist by the time he came to help run the Section in his thirties, Rowan was associated

13. Mullins, South Carolina, file, in RG 121, Entry 133, NA. Section of Fine Arts Community Case files are kept in boxes within Entry 133. They are arranged alphabetically by state and, within a state, alphabetically by community. Although the boxes in which these files are stored are numbered (Mullins, South Carolina, is in Box 100), archivists prefer to pull boxes by community name rather than box number. Citations of these files will refer to Entry 133, unless otherwise noted.

with the midwestern regionalists. After he completed his formal education in art and art history at Miami University and Harvard, Rowan served as director of a Cedar Rapids, Iowa, art center and spent time at Grant Wood's Stone City art colony. Steeped in the aesthetic of Wood, Curry, and Benton, Rowan was the first to receive proposed designs, and, guided by that aesthetic, he transmitted the Section's response to them to the artists. Rowan was the most important government figure wth whom artists and communities would deal about a mural, but he was not the only Treasury official charged with actually approving the artwork.

When an artist received a letter inviting him to submit designs for a particular mural, he was informed that his design would have to be approved by the Section, by the Director of Procurement, and by the Supervising Architect. Usually, these approvals were rubberstamped. If Rowan faced a particularly recalcitrant artist, he could summon their help to make his disapproval more authoritative. To an artist struggling to maintain individuality and artistic integrity, the array of five Section officials and two Treasury administrators, all seemingly eager to tell him what to paint, must have seemed formidable indeed.

What the order creating the Section did not state was that Bruce and Rowan had a very narrow idea about what constituted excellence in art. To be good, it could not look like the old masters' works, with regal classical figures robed as Greeks might have been robed or in improbable symbolic poses. It could not, in other words, be in the "academic" artistic tradition. Neither could it be "modern" in the sense that abstract art was modern. To be appropriate for post office walls, art had to be intelligible to the masses as only representational art is intelligible. Bruce and his colleagues had at heart the ambition to develop a vital American mural art, which therefore had to reflect the American scene. Bruce and Rowan, however, had particular ideas about what that meant. Whereas Benton, Curry, and Wood could imbue their paintings with caricature, with humor, with individuality, and with specific scenery, good Section art had to be so innocuous that it offended no one, so realistic that every post office patron could identify with its figures, so general that murals painted for one post office could be installed in another one. These restrictions, though unstated, were apparently familiar to virtually all successful Section artists. If they were not revealed in Section suggestions for improving a design, the artist had learned from other artists how to "paint Section."[14]

In addition to this formidable array of restrictions, the Section artist often faced one further demand: that subject matter be appropriate to the locale in which the mural was to be placed. Washington, the prospective recipient of the mural, or both often interpreted this as meaning that the subject matter had to please community leaders. Although, strictly speaking, only Treasury officials had to approve a mural subject and its design, artists advised to visit a community also received the tacit suggestion that citizens be consulted about subjects. Sometimes it was even explicit, particularly when an artist could not visit and was therefore advised to consult the postmaster.

Postmasters faced with the formidable responsibility to suggest appropriate subject matter reacted with various degrees of seriousness. Some merely ignored letters; others said that they really didn't know or, in extreme cases, that there was nothing interesting about their community; still others convened local committees to suggest topics; and others turned the whole problem over to a local historian or a community do-gooder. Whatever the postmaster's and the community's response, they felt betrayed if the artist did not follow their advice, especially if he used their subject but his rendering did not match their preconceived notions. In Salisbury, Maryland, for instance, artist Jacob Getlar Smith painted exactly the subject outlined by community historian J. William Slemons, but he used artistic license to interpret the scene. The barrage of prose directed at Smith disclaimed any relationship between his interpretation and nineteenth-century Salisbury and described exactly how the black bell-ringer should be dressed, how people in Salisbury streets behaved, and what trees grew on what avenues.

On the other hand, when artists hired to paint southern murals assumed their responsibility to be only to the Section, which hired them, and consulted only Washington, the response was often worse. Southern towns, already aware that sociological arbiters from around the world but especially from Washington and the Northeast were judging them as deficient in American virtues,

---

14. Marling, *Wall-to-Wall America*, 84–85, discusses what it meant to "paint Section."

faced with a completed mural to whose subject they had had no opportunity to contribute, were likely to magnify the slightest fault, taking great umbrage. In Livingston, Texas, the "Southeast Texas" postmaster was distraught about what he considered a "western mural" until the Section apologized and offered him a more appropriate mural for another spot in the post office lobby. The new mural was singularly unattractive. But once the postmaster and his community were recognized as authorities on what was suitable for Livingston, they became complimentary about even the original despised cowboy and Indian picture.[15] The biggest furor of all over a post office mural, the one in Aiken, South Carolina, came about when artist Stefan Hirsch arrived to install a finished mural in the courtroom of a judge who had not even been notified that his courtroom was to be decorated.[16]

When an artist actually came from an area, got himself known in the community before designing his mural or, better still, painted the mural in the community, then the project was successful. With rare exceptions, the community included in the process was a happy community.[17] And almost as often the artist was rewarded for his effort. One New York artist sent to Oneonta, Alabama, complaining all the way of his lack of knowledge of southern culture and his wariness of the difficulty of working with southern people, actually moved to the little Alabama town to do the job. It wasn't long before he was writing the Section that he was "really nuts" about this little town and painting baptistry murals for local churches.

At the time the government was decorating new federal buildings with murals, southern artists struggled for patronage in their region. Few southern universities had active art departments; few southern communities had art museums; even fewer had galleries

15. Theodore Van Soelen to Edward Rowan, n.d. [mid-1941], in Livingston, Texas, file, RG 121, NA. Within a community file in Section records, documents are arranged in reverse chronological order. Thus, by listing the correspondent, the recipient, and the date of a letter, I identify its precise location. In cases such as this, approximate dates can be determined by a letter's location within the file. In this letter and in all quoted unpublished correspondence, obvious spelling errors have been corrected. Punctuation and grammar have been left as they were, however, because in many places the original intent is difficult to interpret.

16. Marling, *Wall-to-Wall America*, 62–71, thoroughly recounts and analyzes this controversy.

17. Two significant exceptions are Harold Egan at the Okolona, Mississippi, Post Office and Julien Binford at the Saunders Branch of the Richmond, Virginia, Post Office.

where contemporary artists might display their wares. Even so, there was an art community in New Orleans, and a few southern artists such as Edmund Archer, Julien Binford, and John McCrady studied in New York, then fled to their homeland to paint what they knew, much as Benton, Curry, and Wood were to return to the Midwest. Whereas the midwestern regionalists received national attention and could try to earn their living with their art, artists in the South were isolated and largely unrecognized. Such museums as there were, in Atlanta and Richmond, for example, specialized in the old masters, greater and lesser. Comments one student of southern art, "And yet in the South, there has been historically a curious absence of the collecting instinct which, even when it has surfaced, has tended to prefer anything but the art of its own region."[18] The only artworks most southerners saw in their daily lives were baptistry murals. These were, like the old masters, chiefly in the grand style and resplendent with academic poses, formal iconography, and often on sentimental themes, all of which were anathema to Section ideas of good art. Consequently, the southern mural artist found himself caught between a constituency who thought of art in terms of grandeur and an employer that found grandeur distasteful.

In this situation, the artist stood at the apex of a triangle; the other two rigid angles were the Section of Fine Arts and the southern community. In the interaction among these three agents, we have an ideal vehicle for the study of southern middle- and working-class consciousness during the late 1930s as well as of attitudes toward the South that perhaps informed that consciousness. Small-town postmasters, locally elected officials, local business leaders and newspaper editors—all from the lower middle class and all dependent on grass-roots, working-class support—were often willing to express their opinions on behalf of their constituency. Because they were led to believe they had some voice and because both Edward Rowan and many artists were equally willing to carry on lengthy correspondence with them, we have a record that provides valuable insight into opinions and attitudes.

This carefully kept correspondence reveals much about how south-

18. Bruce W. Chambers, *Art and Artists of the South: The Robert P. Coggins Collection* (Columbia, S.C., 1984), 1. This catalog for the only documented exhibition of a private collection of southern art makes clear the sorry state of southern art collecting, particularly in the past.

erners perceived themselves and their relationship to the nation. Even more revealing, however, are the murals themselves. Through a careful examination of the style and content of these pictorial records of the South in the 1930s—what the people accepted without question, what they lauded, and what they disliked—we can see when a painting represented the South as the South saw itself and when, like the movies, literature, and news media of the period, a mural presented a fantasy South known only to outsiders.

Thus far, I have refrained from a specific definition of "The South," and for good reason. The South, in the minds of southerners and nonsoutherners, is not so much a geographic, historic, social, or political entity as it is a concept. It is not the same concept for everyone because the South is not one region but a collection of subregions allied mostly by mercurial geographic boundaries and the accident of having once been inhabited by slave owners. Even so, a few cultural characteristics can be applied to most of those regions, and they are revealed through the murals and various reactions to them. Not only were particular subjects and treatments deemed appropriate for the southeastern states, there is a distinctive southern regional style as well. In the South, class is a more palpable reality than it is in other parts of the United States, and the classes are rigidly defined in murals by lines and horizontal planes that separate them. The desire for self-sufficiency and southerners' conviction that the South's position in the nation is precarious at best are indicated by mural figures protected from the outside and from the horizon. At the same time, the paradoxical need to be recognized as a fully equal part of the nation is invariably suggested by some link to the outside—a locomotive, perhaps, or a TVA electric tower.

A mural reflecting a community's consciousness was possible only if the Section of Fine Arts was successful in appointing an appropriate artist. And the match only worked when an artist could accommodate himself to another paradox of the South. In a poem addressed to whites who wish to share friendships with blacks, "The first thing you do is to forget that i'm Black / Second, you must never forget that i'm Black."[19] So it is with the South. The only way for an outsider or a government appointee to be accepted

---

19. Pat Parker, "For the white person who wants to know how to be my friend," *WomanSlaughter* (Oakland, Calif., 1978), 13.

by southerners is to remember that the South is different—that it has suffered more than and differently from the rest of the country, has been cast out and reconstructed by it, has had economic difficulties such as the nation has not known, and has a tradition inscrutable to outsiders. At the same time, the outsider must also be aware that American tradition, at least as southerners see it, emanates from the South in the influence of such luminaries as Thomas Jefferson and George Washington, that the South is and has always been a part of American culture, and that southerners are no different from other Americans in their beliefs, their experiences, and their ability to meet national challenges.

Southern newspaper editor and self-appointed seeker of southern verity Jonathan Daniels wrote that the relationship of the South to the nation was much like that of the southern black to the southern white.[20] However, the South resisted such a depiction and resented suggestions of that relationship on its post office walls. Erskine Caldwell's *Tobacco Road* was exceedingly popular in the 1930s, and the play based on it broke long-standing attendance records. Southerners, however, felt, with some justification, that the play and the book weakened their claims to full national citizenship and to a full share in the bounty that was America. Socially conscious artists felt it their duty, on the other hand, to point out the work that needed doing in the South, and those with less social conscience felt obliged to depict what they saw in the South, and perhaps sometimes they saw what popular culture in the 1930s led them to expect. Consequently, southerners, struggling with contour plowing, crop rotation, and reforestation, often saw themselves depicted using nineteenth-century farm methods among eroded hills and tumbledown shacks. And they didn't like it.

What southerners preferred were presentations of themselves as hardworking, prosperous, industrial, and agricultural Americans. In the 1930s, when work was scarce for all Americans, southerners shared the national plight. At no other time in American history, perhaps, was the role of labor in America considered from more points of view and, perhaps, at no other time were laboring Americans treated with more respect. Even so, if laborers in the South were white females or black males, they were regarded with suspi-

20. Daniels, *A Southerner Discovers the South,* 344.

cion, since they might be occupying jobs that could better be held by white heads of household.

The South has been the home of three races, and, in the murals, the third one seldom labors. Indians are virtually invisible in the South today, and so they were in the 1930s. Most of them had been driven west by the influx of whites and blacks. But in southern post office murals, they appear repeatedly—only, of course, in historical situations and usually posing as Cherokee, North Carolina, Indians do, so that pictures of them can be made. In the murals, they sign treaties with advance parties of scouts and representatives of the federal army, they welcome settlers who will deprive them of their homes, and occasionally they fight bloody wars with whites. But always, they are depicted with an artificial dignity much less satisfying than that accorded the working blacks, and seldom are they seen involved in productive labor. Just as Scarlett O'Hara's trusted and efficient half-Indian slave was expunged from the movie version of *Gone With the Wind*, so Indians in the murals are excluded from the business of building the South.

Southern mural Indians exist only in very early southern history in part, it seems, because southerners are partial to their very early history. One of the most revealing clues to modern southern attitudes could well be that the national concept of southern history often seems to extend into the past only so far as the decades before the Civil War. Americans tend to forget that the first European colony on American soil was in the South, that a southerner led revolutionary forces to victory against the English, and that a southerner wrote the Declaration of Independence. We tend to ignore the fact that both Thomas Jefferson and George Washington owned slaves. Most important, we tend to forget that the rest of the nation has condoned the racism for which it now condemns the South. Instead, by truncating southern history, we seem to remember only that which makes America look good and the South look bad. We congratulate ourselves on the nation's latter-day disapproval of slavery and its recent brief efforts to make first-class citizenship possible for the majority of blacks.

Despite surface evidence, it seems not to be the Civil War that the South continues to fight but rather "reconstruction"—the efforts of the federal government and others from the outside to remake the South into something suitable for other regions. There are murals that depict a South capable of solving its own problems, a productive, happy South that looks to a future that promises all the wealth and technology for which the United States has become an international symbol—a South, in short, which has no need of reconstruction from the outside. The most successful of all southern murals were the ones whose themes were the ordinary daily life of contemporary southerners—the American scene in the South. These murals in no way suggested reconstruction, harsh or gentle. Their South is just another part of a unified nation, and its pursuits are virtually indistinguishable from those elsewhere in America. This South was, in its desire to build itself, ambivalent at best about the New Deal's gentle reconstruction.

I / GOD'S LITTLE ACRE: THE SOUTH AS CONCEPT

When Beulah Bettersworth was asked to design a mural for the Columbus, Mississippi, Post Office, without much ado she chose agricultural work with cotton as the theme (Figure 1). So did Arthur Covey for Anderson, South Carolina; Arnold Friedman for Warrenton, Georgia; and F. Luis Mora for Clarksville, Tennessee. So, as a matter of fact, did about fifty other artists commissioned to design murals for southern communities. And so did Joan Cunningham for Poteau, Oklahoma, and Warren Hunter for Alice, Texas—but with a difference. Whereas those fifty artists drew southern designs with a cotton theme, the murals for Poteau and Alice were western (Figures 2, 3).

Regionalism in art history circles is invariably linked to Wood, Benton, and Curry and thus, in the popular mind, to the Midwest. Linking regionalism exclusively with one section of the nation is reductive, however, because these midwesterners share the very traits that distinguish them with painters from other regions: a passion for painting from their roots; a style appropriate to the geography and history of the section in which they painted; a tendency to romanticize the characteristics of their section; and, most apparent, a choice of subject matter typical of a given region. All of these add up to the most important trait shared by regional artists: their perception of the audience for whom they painted. Unlike other modern artists, regional artists painted to be understood by the lay population. They wanted to be popular in the sense that they chose to speak to the populace, even when they hung their representational designs on cubist scaffolding.[1] It is, of course, each

1. Karal Ann Marling, *Wall-to-Wall America* (Minneapolis, 1982), 81–127, demonstrates that the unifying principle in Regionalism is the artist's conception of his audience. She devotes most of Chapter 2, "De Gustibus Non Est Disputandum," much of Chapter 1, "The Patron, the Painter and the Public," and brief portions of several other chapters to a thorough consideration of "Regionalism," the aesthetic, as opposed to "regionalism," a geographic and social term also applied to 1930s art. In this work, those changeable boundaries are deliberately blurred, and the lower-

1 / Beulah Bettersworth, *Out of the Soil,* Columbus, Miss., 1940

2 / Joan Cunningham, cartoon for Poteau, Okla., 1940

3 / Warren Hunter, *South Texas Panorama,* Alice, Tex., 1939

artist's perception of who, specifically, was the lay audience and what she chose to paint for them that separate nonmidwestern regionalists from the midwesterners. And it is the artist's representation of that perception that explains why Beulah Bettersworth's cotton pickers were southern while those of Joan Cunningham and Warren Hunter were not.

In 1983 the Virginia Museum of Fine Arts undertook an ambitious and much-needed project, the exhibit Painting in the South, 1564–1980. In the 362-page catalog, however, the curator and the authors of the five period essays say little to define what is southern about southern art.[2] Perhaps their reluctance is excusable: much of the show consisted of work by nonsouthern artists that just happened to be done in or about the South. For example, portraits by northeastern artists John Singleton Copley, John Hesselius, and Charles Willson Peale were included, as were genre paintings by Eastman Johnson and Winslow Homer and George Catlin. Benton's and Edward Hopper's excursions into the South were represented, and the show included Josef Albers and Kenneth Noland because they each sojourned at North Carolina's Black Mountain College. With such an array, it is appropriate that the curator hesitates to generalize. Of course, only a brief section of that monumental catalog concerns itself with the period during the 1930s in which postulating regional characteristics in art was even acceptable. Before the war that would classify southerners as different from other Americans, southern art shared characteristics with other American art—it was representational, and most of it was portraiture. After the war, however, if one can judge from the southern paintings by southern artists selected for the exhibition, the art began to take on a distinctive regional flavor. Once the

---

case word alludes to the popular amalgamation of the concepts. In *Grant Wood: The Regionalist Vision* (New Haven, 1983), Wanda Corn uses Wood as a case study to demonstrate that "the regionalist vision" grows out of an artist's environment and background. Both works have been exceedingly useful in constructing this chapter.

2. In the exhibit catalog, *Painting in the South* (Richmond, 1983), xiii–xvii, Ella Prince Knox disclaims any effort to define southern art. A perusal of the separate sections, especially "Toward a New South: The Regionalist Approach, 1900–1950" by Rick Stewart, reveals that regional subject matter is occasionally identified and a regional treatment of landscape is hinted at, but no attempt is made to distinguish southern painting from other American painting.

southern social order had been thrown into chaos, southerners seemed to paint more and more a society in which classes and races were separated by lines in the picture, by position on the picture plane, or by size of figures. Otherwise, they do not even appear on the same canvas.

By the 1930s, the regionalist period, southern canvases seem to fall into two distinct categories. The first, which was never acceptable to the Section of Fine Arts, spoke of despair that a New South would ever be realized. In these works, hopeless figures appear lonely and isolated on a wide expanse of canvas, far from a threatening horizon. The land depicted is ravished; the colors are bleak; the figures, usually small, are alone or huddled in groups, their limbs close to their bodies, their faces without animation or hidden altogether. Robert Gwathmey's *Hoeing* typifies this category of southern painting.[3] In the left middle-ground, a white woman and man, bones protruding, sag on a watering trough next to an equally bony cow. Fallen fenceposts form an impotent cross at their feet. At the right, almost too small for our concern, a black child tends a younger sibling, both imploring us, the viewers, for help. But we cannot reach them; their legs are entwined in barbed wire from the fallen fence. Separated from the children by a fencepost and from the whites by a few growing stalks of corn, a large black man, hiding his face with his right arm and leaning dejectedly on his hoe, dominates the foreground and separates the picture's needy inhabitants from outside interference. The landscape is flat, open, unproductive, and unpromising. What should be the horizon is merely a line cutting the flat land off from the sky and promising no escape—unless it is to fall off.

The second category depicts a South independent, self-sufficient, and, though vulnerable to siege, fortified against it. In these works, there are no expanses of land, there is no horizon. The background is invariably circumscribed by buildings, forests, circles of people. The figures in the picture are protected from each other, from the viewer, and from the world beyond the South by some natural, artificial, or human barrier. The focus is often on the middle ground, and when it is not, an implied "fourth wall" concept still keeps viewers at a safe distance. Internal evidence in these paintings sug-

---

3. Gwathmey's *Hoeing* is illustrated in Knox, *Painting in the South*, 302.

gests a South not only protected from marauders but sufficient unto itself with small need for aid from outside.

For example, in John Steuart Curry's *Baptism in Kansas,* a young midwestern woman is being baptized in a watering trough amid a congregation of her peers. A white-clad group to the right awaits their turn for immersion. No artificial barriers separate those to be baptized from the others. No barrier separates viewers from the picture's inhabitants. We feel we are a part of the group of spectators in the foreground, their backs to us. The land, like the land in *Hoeing,* extends to a horizon, but the line is not sharp, and the land is verdant and productive. The scene is also open on all sides so that anyone can join the group. A house, a barn, and a windmill—all well kept, all cleanly drawn—assure us that Kansas is, if not prosperous, adequate to the task of feeding and sheltering its inhabitants. Above, the clouds open and two doves descend to bestow peace, we suppose, on the newly saved and their retinue.

The southern painting, *Negro Baptising* by John Kelly Fitzpatrick, also shows a baptism amid a comfortable and satisfied crowd, but outsiders are excluded. The crowd forms a barrier between the river in which the baptism takes place and any intruder from the rear and the right. And the crowd itself is protected by a dense background of trees. Those waiting to be baptized, who are identified by their white clothing, are separated from the crowd and from us by abutments on a bridge across the river. And the woman in the river with her pastor is entirely safe behind a barrier of water. Above this crowd, no heavens open; no doves descend. They are protected even from the sky by the bridge itself, from which more of their compatriots view the proceedings. Although *Negro Baptising* is an easel painting, its lack of a horizon and its refusal to admit the viewer are typical of post office murals in the South during the 1930s.

In America in the 1930s, art that reflected a region and represented an event was only marginally acceptable to the art establishment, which concentrated on ever more refined methods of abstracting content from painted form. An optimistic presentation of a region did have strong appeal for the populace and, thus, for the Section of Fine Arts. Art that was unintelligible to the people or that emphasized a region's trials was considered by neither the Section nor the populace to be appropriate. Section experiences in the

South also suggest that the works had to be by artists well versed in a region's culture. In her catalog of a nationally circulated Grant Wood exhibit, Wanda Corn writes: "It is impossible to understand Wood's art and his regionalism unless one places it in the context of midwestern history, most particularly the history of Cedar Rapids in the early part of the century. For Wood's regionalism was molded by the civic pride and booster spirit exhibited by his mentors and patrons, by their pride in the frontier origins of Cedar Rapids and its quick rise as a modern, prosperous city. Wood's regionalism was nurtured in a boomtown ambience."

This statement of Wood's midwestern regionalism can be paraphrased: It is impossible to understand southern art and regionalism unless one places it in the context of southern history, most particularly its nineteenth-century history of separation from the nation and its long defensive struggle to regain equal status with other American regions. For southern regionalism was molded by the shame, alienation, and fierce pride exhibited by southerners in the 1930s, by their shame as the region of slavery, sharecroppers, and the nation's most intense poverty; by their alienation from a greater community, which, though charmed by the culture they may once have had, were revolted by their present one and unwilling to acknowledge southern progress toward modern agriculture and industry, which seemed to forget that southern history extended two and a half centuries before the war that established that alienation, and which tried to solve southern problems from the outside; by their fierce pride in a history that contributed much to building the nation and a culture the Northeast had once sought to emulate.[4] Southern regionalism was nurtured in a defensive ambience.

Southern regionalism not only consists of the images created by painters in the South but also includes the painters' experience. Like Grant Wood, southern artists depended on their environment for their subject matter and how it was to be handled, as well as for clues about their audience. Let us consider not only the way such images as Bettersworth's cotton pickers are characteristically

4. Corn, *Grant Wood*, xiv. William R. Taylor's *Cavalier and Yankee: The Old South and American National Character* (Cambridge, Mass., 1979) documents a nineteenth-century infatuation among northeasterners with their perception of southern culture as the only New World manifestation of traditional European graces.

southern but also the distinctly regional characteristics of one southern artist, those of one nonsouthern artist who painted successfully in the South, and those of one southern town.

Looking at what makes one scene of cotton picking southern and another western will go far toward defining a conceptual South.[5] In Bettersworth's Columbus, Mississippi, mural, we find characteristics that endeared murals and muralists to southerners throughout the many regions of the abstraction we call the South and throughout the life of the Section of Fine Arts, from intense national depression well into the national prosperity and heartbreak of world war. The Columbus mural is, quite simply, lovely to look at. The colors, roses, blues, and pastel greens, are soothing, and no sharp, angular forms disrupt the flow. The painting is serene, pastoral. Its bucolic action is circumscribed by distant but reassuringly accessible churches, cotton gins, and luxuriously foliated trees—all made of good southern timber. The middle ground, the most demanding part of the picture, is occupied by a group of blacks picking cotton in an abundantly producing and endless field. And yet, even that boundless field does not offer unlimited possibilities. Not too distant, a curve—undoubtedly the result of contour plowing—assures viewers and pickers alike that they are protected from an unknown that seems to go on and on, that it is indeed a spherical world we inhabit and not one off of which we might fall.

The paintings by Wood, Benton, and Curry and the murals of the Midwest feature expanses of cultivated open land extending to the horizon and promising tillable soil even beyond it. Such bounty was not for the South, however. Time and again, before colonial farmers guessed that cotton was one of the most debilitating of all crops, southern soil had treacherously quit bearing, forcing planters to move westward in search of arable land until they were stopped by the very different culture of the West. Time and again, southern farmers in the rich Delta had been wiped out by uncontrolled Mississippi River floods. In other parts of the region, rampant soil erosion and frequent tornadoes had, time and again, destroyed hopes for prosperity for still another year.

5. Black-and-white photos of most of the completed murals and of many of the preliminary sketches and cartoons can be viewed in the National Archives, Still Photos Division, filed alphabetically by artist's name. Although boxes of pictures have classification numbers, Still Photos personnel prefer that they be requested by artist's name.

Bettersworth's mural reflects both the bounteous soil that southerners placed their faith in and its limitations. The productive land
does not extend beyond the horizon. It extends, rather, to the circle
of buildings and trees that minister to spiritual, habitational, and
commercial needs and at the same time may keep the enemy out,
whether that be natural forces or Yankee invaders. The boundaries
could reflect for southern viewers a conviction that though the
outside world could not be depended on for sustenance, a self-
reliant South need not depend on that world. Although American
society may never have been so free of class structure as we would
like to believe, the South has been honest in its recognition of social classes and its dependence on social barriers. The Columbus
cotton has been planted in careful rows, and each picker has a particular row from which she may not diverge but which protects her
from encroachment by other pickers. The black workers are separated from each other and from viewers as well by a white farmer
intently plowing with mules in the foreground. Except that he is
physically larger, perhaps because his position is in the foreground,
viewers might never suspect that the white plowman has greater
social status than do the black cotton pickers, only a different one.
Blacks and whites in Bettersworth's South work hard, but with a
"lento" rhythm; nothing is frantic, there is enough time that an
occasional breath and stretch of the back do not destroy the flow. In
this mural, the South appears to be orderly, enduring, hardworking,
self-contained, and safe from intrusion. Life is serious for its inhabitants, as it is for virtually all people in southern murals, and seriously they respond to it.

One who gives the Poteau, Oklahoma, mural but a quick glance
is likely to conclude that the action is a rodeo or a folk festival.
Only when we look closely at it do we perceive its true subject—
the harvesting and ginning of cotton. Everything in the foreground
and even in the middle ground suggests a festive occasion: the
jaunty attitudes of the picture's inhabitants, the skewed arrangement of the cotton bales, the number of idle people in the picture,
and, in the center front, the field hand with his back to us, resting
his elbow virtually on the lintel of the postmaster's door.

This western mural is occupied by twenty-six white men, only
six, possibly seven, of whom actually work. In the West, should the
cotton fail, there were oil and cattle to fall back on, and, at least in
1930s films, the West had a tradition of fun and song. Westerners,

according to the murals, work energetically and with unflagging attention to the activity at hand. But in Roy Rogers and Gene Autry films, they would stop to sing songs and joke with less able cowboys. The workers in Cunningham's mural are relegated to a distant middle-ground. Those who do not work dominate the demanding foreground, where they pass the time of day watching the cotton pickers or leaning against walls and posts contemplating the endless possibilities of an endless landscape.

These people demonstrate no need for self-sufficiency; they seem content to depend on other parts of the nation. Whereas Bettersworth's trees are lush and abundant, the wood for the fences and buildings in this picture must have been imported. The few visible trees are gnarled and twisted, and their foliage is spare. Most of the buildings that dominate the middle ground are adobe, a distinctly nonsouthern material made from western clay that formed wattles, if this picture is to be believed, with imported wood. And these westerners are so trusting that the lounging field hand in the foreground turns his back to us and seems to allow his arm to protrude into the post office lobby. The action in this picture suggests that work gets done despite the leisure most people enjoy. The juxtaposition of picking and ginning cotton suggests that the distinction between agrarian and industrial pursuits was not as great as it was in the South.

The Oklahoma land itself, however, provides the greatest contrast with truly southern scenes of cotton picking. The cotton fields here are ill defined and spread in all directions with no boundaries and no rows. They stretch into an infinite landscape. A series of barren mountains on the horizon provides no containment: passes are clearly visible, and the flat landscape leads to infinity—or to eternity. The message here is that the West in the 1930s, the dust bowl notwithstanding, had no need to ponder limitations, no need to feel insecure about onslaughts from the outside. Assured of a ready market for their cotton harvest (if they had one), Oklahomans could afford to bale their cotton less carefully than was done elsewhere in the cotton belt and to treat the bales with less respect. The bales are allowed to tumble recklessly in front of the gin.

Warren Hunter also featured cotton processing in his Alice, Texas, mural, and in his western picture the workers—cotton pickers, welders, a blacksmith, and a calf roper—work frantically. A

Mexican-American cotton picker fairly races across the frontal plane of the picture, threatening to knock the blacksmith off his feet. But the blacksmith himself works so rapidly that the horse will be shod and on its way well before the frantic picker reaches the spot. Here, pickers and weighers are Hispanic. They wear sombreros or flowing draperies on their heads; their skin is bronze; and their chiseled high cheekbones and sloe eyes contrast with the rugged, Teutonic features of the cowboy, the oil workers, and the entrepreneur who share the frame with them.

As in Bettersworth's Columbus mural, the cotton field in Alice is central and first demands the viewer's attention, but the field and most of the action are concentrated in a foreground vulnerable to intrusion. In this mural, as in the one by Cunningham in Poteau, the cotton field is ill defined, sluing into the oil field and the railroad bed. A wagon for hauling the lint to the gin stands where it could crush unpicked cotton. Premium long-staple cotton had been introduced in Texas, where it thrived. Thus, it could threaten the Deep South monopoly on that region's most enduring cash crop. *The Collapse of Cotton Tenancy* attributes much of the South's economic problem to the effective growth of long-staple cotton in the Southwest. *Cotton Goes to War*, a 1942 War Department documentary film, mentions only Texas when it assures cotton workers that what they do is vital to the war effort. Throughout the late 1930s, a syndicated Mississippi column attempted to counteract this emphasis on western cotton. It featured statistics on the percentage of cotton grown in Mississippi, and southern cotton producers cooperated in promoting Deep South cotton through a series of advertisements in such periodicals as *Life*.[6]

Texas had no need to convince citizens that its cotton was valuable or to seek a national market for a cotton surplus. Not only was Texas cotton in great demand, the state had other remunerative industries. As in Cunningham's mural for Poteau, the distinction between agriculture and industry is blurred. In the Texas middleground, we can see cattle bound for market being loaded into boxcars; in the background, rigs pump steadily while a welder with Mexican features completes the pipeline that will take the oil to

6. Charles S. Johnson *et al.*, *The Collapse of Cotton Tenancy: Summary of Field Studies & Statistical Surveys, 1933–1935* (Chapel Hill, 1935); columns appear in the Okolona *Messenger*, February 4, 1937, p. 1, and June 24, 1938, p. 1; ads to sell the cotton surplus appear in *Life* off and on throughout 1937 and 1938.

other parts of the country. Although the horizon in Alice is hidden by oil storage tanks, tank cars, and derricks, a train at the far right steams across the mural's background, reminding viewers that possibilities are endless, the horizon distant, and the means for pursuing one's dreams readily available.

In neither of these western pictures does one get a sense that the inhabitants are protected from any thing or any body. One might hesitate to enter the frantic action of the Alice, Texas, mural for fear of being trampled by cotton pickers and horses or run over by wagons. But we do not feel separated from the action. The scene in Poteau welcomes the viewer to a saunter through the cotton field with the rest of the observing crowd. In the Columbus mural, however, everyone is so intent on work, and the enormous foreground mules and their driver are so impervious to the outside world, that we know we are excluded.

Geographically, socially, historically, and economically, the American South is difficult to define. It is not now and it has never been so much a place as a concept. Scholars and journalists from North and South alike voice their inability to provide a clear idea of where and who the South is, but we all know what it is even when words fail us—and we don't all know the same thing. For some of us, the South is America's only enduring repository of the gracious life; for others, the seat of rampant racism and elitism. The South can be the point from which emanates the American drive to solve problems with violence, and the nation's most ignorant and slothful region. It is xenophobic; it is hospitable. It is columned mansions and blooming eighteenth-century gardens; it is unpainted hovels and erosion checked only by kudzu's alternative form of destructiveness. It is decadent aristocratic inbreeding; it is matriarchy, bastards, and peripatetic fathers. It is assiduously working toward a new, industrial image; it clings to the past and refuses to recognize the passage of time. Its strength is in its proud Americanism; it is the section that tried to form a new nation. The South never changes, but its defenders are Rebels. The catalog of contradictory images is endless, and most of us simultaneously harbor several of them.

And harbor several of them we must. "The South" is not a region; it is a plurality of regions. Not all so-called southern regions even supported the one cause that seemed to unite the South, the Civil War. Most mountain southerners stayed firmly with the Union.

Never was the South solidly Democratic, and when it was closest, the party ideal varied from place to place. Even at the height of the antebellum period, white nonslaveholders outnumbered slaveholders, and a few blacks and Indians themselves owned slaves. Cotton never defined the agricultural South any more than did tobacco or grain. And so on. All concepts of the South are to some extent correct, and few of them are apt for more than a sizable minority in any context.[7] And yet the term *South* is useful, and a few characteristics apply to most of the region identified as the South most of the time.

Little will be done here to set geographic, economic, or social boundaries for the South in the 1930s. But conceptual boundaries are fairly well defined in the mural projects for Amory, Mississippi; Summerville, Georgia; and Livingston, Texas. These boundaries encompass the traditional eleven secessionist states, Maryland, isolated parts of Texas, most of Kentucky, and southeast Missouri. Probably they include parts of Kansas, Iowa, and Nebraska as well. Wherever in this supposedly free nation, in which children are taught that possibilities are limitless, whole communities feel bounded, wherever in this nation of participatory democracy, people feel dictated to by the federal government, wherever people faced with externally created images that they believe to be inaccurate feel voiceless, there can be found what motivated southerners in the 1930s to respond as they did to mural projects for their post offices.

Because the Section of Fine Arts recognized that basic southern defensiveness but not subregional differences, it sometimes got into trouble with attempts to endow southern federal buildings with American murals appropriate to the region. It is when the concepts of an artist, a community, and the Section converged that the Section was most successful. Southerners know that their region is exceptional, inescapably different from the nation's other regions and one that needs special care from an insensitive government. At the same time, they know that the South's difference is merely geographic, that it shares equally in the nation's achievements as well as its setbacks and, thus, that it should not be treated

7. In "The South as Pernicious Abstraction," *Perspectives on the American South*, II (1984), 173, Jack Temple Kirby concedes "the South" to be a working—if perhaps overworked—concept.

to exceptional governing policies. When the federal government can respond to this paradox without tying itself in knots, it is likely to receive not only the support of the South but its gratitude as well.

Some parts of the South remained under military occupation until the mid-1870s. Even when most former Confederate states had returned to home rule, many white southerners felt as if a hostile federal government were imposing its will with total disregard for the region's distinctive contribution to the national culture. At the same time some also felt the need for federal regulation of a society out of control, they felt the military presence imposed foreign rule without giving aid. Although as early as the 1870s political control of most of the South returned to those who had governed before the Civil War, this period of Redemption was shortly followed by severe Jim Crow laws and the ascendancy in some southern states of demagogues unpalatable to the North and to many southerners as well.[8] After a period in which the non-South and the South celebrated a honeymoon of reunion wherein the non-South not only condoned southern policies but even at times emulated them, a resurgence of South-hatred seemingly spawned a new period of reprehensible southern behavior when lynchings increased and Jim Crow was vehemently enforced.[9] External condemnation, which seemed to reduce the South to racism and to ignore all else, was countered in 1930 by Twelve Southerners in the controversial manifesto, *I'll Take My Stand.*

In this collection of essays, Robert Penn Warren, Cleanth Brooks, Allen Tate, and others proudly proclaimed their love of the South and their belief that the region had much to offer an American culture on the brink of crumbling. They presented the South as a model of manners, gracious human interaction, and agrarian gentility from which the nation could learn. They believed that society would function better if its segments kept to the carefully delineated roles—represented by rows of cotton in Bettersworth's

8. C. Vann Woodward in *The Origins of the New South, 1877–1913* (Baton Rouge, 1971) provides a standard comprehensive study of Redemption by reactionary patriarchs who subsequently lost in many parts of the South to more populist—and more openly racist—governments.

9. In *The Emergence of the New South* (Baton Rouge, 1967), 143–83, George B. Tindall examines the "age of segregation" and briefly considers (pp. 143–44) national acceptance of Jim Crow during Woodrow Wilson's administration.

mural—prescribed for them. One was the federal government's function to serve the nation generally and the South specifically, gently and at its bidding. The South had no objection to reconstruction if it were courteous and if those affected were consulted.

A prime example of such gentle reconstruction was the government's effort to embellish federal buildings. When the system worked—when the Section moved politely into a community, paid homage to its social structure, observed its mores, placed a mural on a post office wall, and graciously departed—the federal government did well in the South. But to say that the system did not always work this way and that even this gentle reconstruction sometimes seemed harsh is to indulge in rather severe understatement.

When it did work, though, murals such as Bettersworth's, which not only employed local subject matter but reflected the concerns of the community, were installed. An appropriate work of art, however, was not the whole answer. The most successful southern artist was able to awaken the people in a southern small town to the possibilities of a national mural art precisely because he knew the South well enough to de-emphasize its regional differences and concentrate on its commonality with the broad American scene. Such an artist was John McCrady, and such a situation occurred in Amory, Mississippi. If Edward Bruce and Edward Rowan could have borrowed from the future when they sought approval for the mural project, they might have selected the Amory experience as the paradigmatic example of a government-sponsored art renaissance at work. And Amory was in the Deep South.

In March, 1936, when the Section of Fine Arts was beginning its work in small towns, E. J. Gilmore, assistant to the president of the Bank of Amory, wrote to Edward Rowan. Gilmore advised the Section, even before bids for the building were let, that Amory was eager to have a mural in its new post office lobby. The letter demonstrates that Gilmore was well informed about government art projects. That he was also well informed about and concurred with Section ideals was illustrated in his defense of Amory as a logical location: Amory was "typical of the moderate size cities of Northeast Mississippi. Its citizens are cultured and fairly well to do, but while appreciated, the actual act of mural painting is practically unknown." Here was a bona fide southerner inviting the federal government to reconstruct his community. He, like the Section, was interested in a popular mural movement and, like the Section, he was a trifle condescending toward the people for whom the mural was intended. Not only did Gilmore reflect the Section's zeal for an artistically aware populace, he suggested subjects for the mural that would endear him to Section officials: "Amory offers various intriguing themes or subjects for mural painting. It is located in the heart of the Red Chickasaw Indian Nation, the scene of the early struggles of d'Iberville Bienville. It is located on the historic Tombigbee River, immediately adjacent to the site of Cotton Gin Port, the famous northern terminus of pre-Civil War traffic on that river. Amory itself is vigorously modern, having been established only fifty years ago as the headquarters of the new railroad between Memphis and Birmingham which opened up this great territory."[10]

In its competition announcements and in letters to artists and community representatives, the Section specified that subjects should be drawn from three loosely defined areas: the local scene, local history, or post office history. They had early learned that, though these subjects were not controversy-proof, especially in the South, all others were definitely likely to cause grief.[11]

Gilmore seems not only to have anticipated the Section's thematic preferences, but, as a true southern son, he expressed the South's preference for early southern history. He, like his compatriots, wished to see the South's part in building the nation commemorated on its post office walls. And when he vigorously proclaimed his postbellum hometown's status as a "modern" town, he exhibited typical southern pride in any contributions toward the building of a New South. Amory, after all, had shared in opening "this great territory" to modern industry and technological achievement. And when he mentioned the Tombigbee River, he offered a topic that would link the area's pastoral past with its commercial future. At that time, congressional debates were under way that anticipated the development in the 1980s of the Tenn-Tom Waterway. Although Gilmore could hardly have known it, that waterway was to become Amory's hope for continued prosperity when it ceased in the late 1970s to be a junction of the Frisco Railroad.[12]

10. E. J. Gilmore to Edward Rowan, March 25, 1936, in Amory, Mississippi, file, Record Group 121, National Archives.
11. Karal Ann Marling, "A Note on New Deal Iconography: Futurology and the Historic Myth," *Prospects*, IV (1979), 423–27.
12. Barb Moreau, "The Big I—The Tennessee-Tombigbee Waterway," Amory *Advertiser*, Railroad Festival Edition, April 1, 1979, pp. 54–57, touts the Tenn-Tom project as do chamber of commerce brochures. Unfortunately, the waterway was ob-

In less than a week, Gilmore's letter had been answered. Impressed with Gilmore's astuteness and enthusiasm, Rowan effusively praised the bank president's assistant and Amory for their interest in a properly embellished post office. In the letter and in Gilmore's attitude, Rowan must have seen implications that justified the existence of the Section itself. News of the development of a national mural art had reached Amory, buried in the Mississippi hills, and it had been found good. People in the far reaches of America were hungry to know art, and people in the South could appreciate work that lauded the local scene. Rowan promised to take steps toward a mural for Amory when the time was ripe—that is, when the building was two-thirds complete. Gilmore, not a man to leave anything to chance, wrote again in early April, again promising full local cooperation to ensure that Amory's post office would indeed be decorated.

Apparently eager not to tamper with such profound local enthusiasm, the Section went right to work and, on May 6, sent a memorandum to the "Director of Procurement," that all-but-invisible Treasury official who had technical veto power over all Section fiscal matters, requesting a $560 appropriation for the Amory post office.[13] A curious sort of reckoning went into determining that amount. Given the architectural plans for the post office, the mural space was about forty-five square feet. Standard New Deal policy for all Treasury arts projects was to compensate artists at between $13 and $17 per square foot. Because the Amory post office itself was not large, the pool from which the money was drawn was likewise small. Thus the amount reserved for Amory was about $13 per square foot.

Included in the May 6 memorandum was the suggestion that "some local prominent citizen in that region, who is interested in art" be appointed to chair a committee that would sponsor a regional competition for the commission. The memo made clear, however, that a "final decision would be reached by the Director of

---

solete before it opened and is today used largely by wealthy northeastern sailors to move their craft home after Caribbean vacations.

13. Director of Procurement Admiral Christian J. Peoples is invisible to Section artists and to researchers because in Section correspondence he is identified by his title only and he communicates exclusively through form letters. Actually, to members of the Section, he was on occasion all too visible.

Procurement" and that approval even then was conditional—"providing sufficient funds are available after award of contract" for constructing the post office.[14] This proposal is unusual for a community the size of Amory. Small commissions were usually awarded to artists who had shown favorably in competitions for more remunerative projects. Such suggestions do, however, occur from time to time in Section records of projects for hamlets. But since the Treasury recognized that competition expenses were deducted from the original appropriation and competitions were impractical when the community and the appropriation were small, such suggestions were routinely ignored—as was the case with Amory.

For over a year, the Amory project rested in Section files. Finally, when the post office was presumably two-thirds built, in May, 1937, a new memo was sent to the director of procurement. The Section wished to appoint John McCrady to paint the mural for Amory on the basis of his performance in the Jackson, Mississippi, competition. When Secretary of the Treasury Henry Morgenthau, Jr., created the Section in 1934, the order listed five objectives, one of which was "to encourage competitions wherever practicable recognizing the fact, however, that certain artists in the country, because of their recognized talents are entitled to receive work without competition."[15] *Wherever practicable* meant admirable expediency in McCrady's case: ten days after his appointment was approved, he was invited to submit designs for the Amory post office.

The appointment letter—a form letter sent to each artist who received a commission—reveals much about the workings of the Section and its philosophy. McCrady was told that his designs would need the approval not only of Section officials as artistic authorities but of the director of procurement and the supervising architect as well; that he would have approximately one year to complete the mural; and that he would receive his fee (out of which he would pay expenses) in three installments, the last and the largest when the local postmaster had notified Washington the project was complete. Thus the Section was assured tight control over the mural, its content and its progress.

14. Edward Rowan to Director of Procurement, May 6, 1936, in Amory, Mississippi, file.

15. Francis Van O'Connor, *Federal Support for the Visual Arts: The New Deal and Now* (New York, 1968), 22.

Should McCrady visit Amory and the post office in preparation for his work—and he was advised to do so—he should call on the local postmaster. In a later revision the form letter suggested that the postmaster be contacted about suitable subject matter. But at this point, a courtesy visit was all that was asked. The letter also instructs McCrady to "use subject matter which embodies some idea appropriate to the building or to the particular locale of Amory."[16]

Fortunately for the Section, for Amory, and for the South, its mural-painting efforts coincided with, indeed were part of, efforts to communicate with local audiences through accessible art drawn from the local scene. Thus, the sanctioned subject matter appealed to many artists and critics, as well as to the people of communities such as Amory. In a seminal 1934 article, *Time* heralded the advent of that "Regionalist" art movement. A prominent voice of middle-class taste (as Gilmore's letter reveals, Amory was a middle-class town), the magazine reported that in the 1920s "painting became so deliberately unintelligible that it was no longer news when a picture was hung upside down."[17] Such painting, which *Time* called "outlandish," was hardly what the Section wanted and would hardly have been acceptable in small-town America. *Time* and its readers wanted paintings the bottom of which was unmistakable, and Amory, as Gilmore indicated, wanted art that reflected Amory.

John McCrady was not only a southern artist; having grown up in Corinth and Oxford, he was a north Mississippi artist. Although he had been selected on the basis of the Jackson competition, which he lost, he had a national reputation. That assured such culture-hungry towns as Amory, if not always the Section, that their artist was a fine artist. In 1936, McCrady's work was exhibited at Boyer Galleries in New York, and both *Art News* and *Art Digest* carried illustrations of his paintings. Then, in 1937, shortly after his appointment by the Section, Boyer Galleries featured his work in a one-man show, which was reviewed in the October issue of *Art Digest*. More important for Amory, perhaps, where few read the art journals, was that *Time* identified McCrady as "a star risen from the bayous" whose work would do for southern art what Faulkner's

16. Rowan to McGrady, May 18, 1937, in Amory, Mississippi, file.
17. "U.S. Scene," *Time*, December 24, 1934, p. 24.

was doing for southern literature. On the same day, *Life* featured his work in a five-page spread.[18]

Not only was McCrady a southern artist with national recognition; any Amory citizen could see on the pages of *Life* that his paintings reflected southern ways. At that stage in his career, McCrady was painting almost exclusively the southern black scene. The picture featured in *Life, Swing Low, Sweet Chariot,* is a white interpretation of the Negro spiritual that would be palatable to Yanks and Rebs alike. Through the open door of a humble but well-kept cabin, an "old darkie" dies surrounded by his loving family. Hounds bay in the yard, and a Model T is parked before the cabin door. But attention focuses on the sky, where an elegantly sweet chariot, piloted by a cherub and accompanied by a retinue of seraphim, swings low over the cabin roof. The foremost angel points through the roof to the prospective passenger while another fights off the devil, who is eager to get his hands on the soon-to-be-released soul. The angels are all black—this is after all a black tale. Modern whites would not take such a fantasy seriously. They would, however, accept the premises of this and McCrady's other works on similar themes: that blacks were clean, tidy, and humbly prosperous and that their religion was simple and unthreatening. The pictures reproduced in *Life* were "pretty"—their colors and composition neither created discomfort nor demanded much effort on the part of the viewers, and, like nineteenth-century genre paintings, they told a readily accessible story.

In October, 1937, McCrady accepted the Section commission and promised preliminary sketches. Usually, when southern murals enjoyed unqualified success, the artist spent some time in the community early in his search for a subject, sometimes even painting the mural in the town. McCrady did not visit Amory, but he became personally acquainted with the town and its people in other ways, and he took them seriously. The Amory postmaster was informed of McCrady's appointment, and when the artist submitted his first sketches, he reported:

I have selected a view of Amory, fifty years ago when it was first settled. This I did at the request of many letters that I received from people of

18. *Art News,* December 5, 1936, p. 15; *Art Digest,* July, 1937, p. 10; October, 1937, p. 15; *Time,* October 18, 1937; "'Swing Low Sweet Chariot' and Other Paintings by John McCrady," *Life,* October 18, 1937, pp. 38–42.

this little town who were interested. I have done my best to paint some-thing that the people of Amory will like. The buildings in this sketch are authentic. Later when the painting is done on a larger scale I expect to make the people familiar characters of the town. I have done my re-search from photographs and articles sent to me by different people in Amory, also much historical research was done in the museums here in New Orleans.

Last Fall, when your department wrote the Post Master of Amory that I had been selected to submit designs for the proposed mural,—letters, telegrams and telephone calls began to swamp down on me. I was amazed as well as pleased with the enthusiasm the whole town seemed to show in the fact that they were to receive a mural. Amory had just completed her Golden Jubilee celebration and they were anxious to have a mural of their city in its beginning. One person of that city has made three trips to New Orleans to bring material such as the photographs I am enclosing with the sketch.[19]

These paragraphs speak volumes about the type of community likely to appreciate Section murals. They also demonstrate why McCrady was an ideal exponent for a government's program of providing Amory people with art that was non-elitist and realistic in detail. Not only did McCrady paint a scene based on the town itself that was easily understandable. Pleasing his audience was his most important consideration—so much so that he was not above consulting them before he composed his design.

McCrady's South was not the severely flawed South of Faulkner's and Warren's fiction, nor was it the exploited and exploitive South of Erskine Caldwell and Margaret Bourke-White. His was the South of the twelve southern authors of *I'll Take My Stand* where agrar-ian traditions offered a way of life different from that of the rest of the country and in some ways superior to it and where the nation might learn something about gracious living in harmony with natural abundance.

In 1933, McCrady had won a scholarship to study for a year at the Art Students' League in New York. There he worked briefly with Thomas Hart Benton, who would eventually return to his na-tive Midwest. There, from Kenneth Hayes Miller, he learned the importance of basic design. There he also learned that he was a painter of the southern scene who would never be happy painting out of the South. Plagued by homesickness, he produced works

19. McCrady to Rowan, May 3, 1938, in Amory, Mississippi, file.

4 / John McCrady, design for Amory, Miss.

about the South in the concrete confines of New York.[20] And when the year was over, like other exponents of the regionalist movement after him, he returned to his homeland to paint what he knew and loved.

But it was not only McCrady's choice of regional subject and his decision to paint away from New York that made him an ideal Section artist. In 1946, when McCrady's national audience had accused him of racist painting and his fortunes were low, he wrote to a friend, "There is nothing wrong with an artist being commercial as long as he can keep his individuality. That, of course, is where the catch is."[21] His willingness to consider "selling" his art had likely served him well in his earlier dealings with the Section. He submitted and resubmitted versions of his mural to satisfy Section requirements and to receive installments on his stipend. Like many Section artists, he was asked to make changes that others might have found compromising. McCrady, however, apparently found nothing objectionable in Rowan's suggestions for adjustments in his original sketch (Figure 4):

> The subject matter was regarded as appropriate and interesting but it was felt that the figures of the three women in the foreground are rather unpleasant in your presentation. The flesh colors are unhappy as there is some question as to whether they are white as they should be in this design. I must ask you not to use the names of definite firms which may be in existence as there is a rule that no advertisement of any kind may

20. "Loneliness Stirred His Brush to Activity," *Art Digest,* October, 1937, p. 15.
21. Keith Marshall, *John McCrady, 1911–1968* (New Orleans, 1975), 16, 28. This exhibit catalog was prepared for the New Orleans Museum of Art.

be included in a Post Office. You may be able to omit these or treat the names in such a way that they are illegible. The foliage of the trees in the background is presented in an insensitive manner and this, of course, should be carefully studied so that it convincingly takes its place and form in the composition.[22]

Far from being indignant about the unhappy color of the women's faces or the insensitivity of his trees, McCrady, who might have objected that he was better qualified to judge the sensitivities of Amory people, quietly made the changes and submitted a cartoon of his proposed mural. After all, he needed the money, and what he had submitted had been only a preliminary sketch. McCrady was more fortunate than were many artists who painted for the Section. A design had to be approved before an artist could even apply for his first payment. McCrady's was approved, and he was trusted to make the suggested emendations. Since no travel funds were provided, an artist who wished to visit a site to search for material often had to wait for that approval to collect enough money to investigate the community properly.

Even when a muralist had spent some research time in an area, the Section, often assuming that it knew more about the community's preferences than the artist did, would reject sketch after sketch on its behalf. Before Doris Lee submitted designs for the Summerville, Georgia, Post Office, for example, she did visit Summerville at her own expense. As a matter of fact, she spent some months "sketching around in the South." When she submitted her design, she could report, like McCCrady, that she was "carrying on a correspondence with half the population in Summerville." The postmaster and the librarian, she said, "are particularly proud of their valley with its bluish background hills, their soil products, corn, cotton, and peaches. So in the sketch I show their reddish soil, Georgia peaches, corn & cotton."[23]

While Rowan was away on vacation the Section conditionally approved Lee's sketch (Figure 5), objecting only to the "somewhat theatrical" effect of the corn in the center of the panel and asking her to change that. A few weeks later, she wrote that the corn was in a less theatrical middle-ground and that "the mayor of Summer-

22. Rowan to McCrady, May 27, 1938, in Amory, Mississippi, file.
23. Doris Lee to Edward Rowan, November 22, 1938, March 23, February 1, 1939, all in Summerville, Georgia, file, RG 121, NA.

5 / Doris Lee, design for Summerville, Ga.

ville visited me here in the studio this week and he liked it [the design] a lot, said he thought it was beautiful."[24]

One can imagine Lee's chagrin, then, when Rowan saw the sketch and wrote:

> The only caution offered you is that all of the figures have the same stem-like necks and skinny arms and there is a danger that the people of Summerville will regard this as your personal characterization of them and will, no doubt, resent being presented as though they were half fed regardless of the poetry you have achieved by this mannerism. I am sure you are aware of how sensitive the people in the South are about such matters and it would be well for you to make the changes at this stage and have the mural happily received. . . .
>
> Will you kindly undertake the necessary revisions and submit a photograph of the half completed stage. It will be possible to forward you a voucher covering the payments due you as soon as your contract has been cleared.

Lee may have been chagrined but she probably was not surprised. She may even have intentionally tried to get her design through during Rowan's absence. This was not the first time she had fought the Section to maintain her style of humorous caricature. A few years earlier Rowan had forced her to revise her lovable and humorous designs into the vapid murals that now decorate the decomissioned Post Office Department building in Washington. That time, however, southern sensitivity had not been Rowan's excuse, and Section preference alone appears to be the basis for the objections.[25]

24. Inslee Hopper to Doris Lee, February 7, 1939, Lee to Rowan, n.d. [on or near March 15, 1939], both *ibid.*

25. Rowan to Lee, March 27, 1939, *ibid.*; Marling, *Wall-to-Wall America*, 59–62. In the long run, Lee's Georgia mural retains more of the naïve charm of her work than do those in Washington.

Lee lost that battle; perhaps she thought that by evading Rowan's critical eye, she would win the war. But that was not to be the case.

In contrast to McCrady, Lee had no contract until she had "undertake[n] the necessary revisions." And the revisions were for Rowan, not for the residents of Summerville, who, in the person of the mayor, had approved the design. Rowan was astute in recognizing that southern people were sensitive, but rather obtuse about what provoked that sensitivity. What riled southern folk was not improper representation of themselves, per se, but improper representation of themselves in areas in which they already felt misunderstood—racial attitudes, impoverished tenant farmers and sharecroppers, eroded soil, technological backwardness, and the stand taken several decades before. So there would likely be objections to mural designs that seemed to capitalize on those stereotypes. There were concomitant suspicions about federal largesse, especially when southerners did not ask for it and were not consulted about it.

Doris Lee's mural was in no danger of incurring southern wrath because she presented southerners as "half starved." Such anger was reserved for the likes of Margaret Bourke-White, whose photographs of the least prosperous southerners from the least flattering angles were published with Erskine Caldwell's socially conscious but inflammatory words in their mouths so that nonsoutherners could pass judgment.[26] *You Have Seen Their Faces* was widely acclaimed and nationally distributed, but one was not enough. The success of the first book brought about the production of the second. In *Say, Is This the U.S.A.?*, Bourke-White and Caldwell used the same format to present pictures of people and places all over the nation; unfortunately, those from the South again suggest only poverty and ignorance.

And the wrath was reserved for such artists as Stefan Hirsch, who painted the mural in Aiken, South Carolina. Not only had he not consulted the community about his proposed personification of Justice; he had flouted conventions by offering a difficult-to-read montage of vignettes. In his mural on a classical theme, he used angular twentieth-century forms to depict bony southern cattle, burning southern houses, thieving southern rascals, and, most

26. Margaret Bourke-White and Erskine Caldwell, *You Have Seen Their Faces* (New York, 1937).

alarming of all, an unorthodox figure of Justice. Although Rowan wrote Aikenites that Hirsch used his wife as his model, he actually employed one of his students, a woman with distinctly Latin features and a dark complexion. Even so, her face would have served had he not exaggerated those Latin features and darkened the face still further until it was so dark that wary southern newspaper editors assumed her to be mulatto. Then, he clothed her in what he intended to be the colors of the American flag; her red and blue skirt and blouse, however, suggest the gay clothing of a Mexican peasant outfitted for a fiesta. She did not in any way resemble the blond, white figure that middle-class southerners would associate with any abstract virtue—certainly not with the Justice they so often felt was denied them.

Doris Lee had made none of these mistakes. She had consulted the community and welcomed their comments. She had used their suggested themes, and though her rendition was modern, the subject matter, a prosperous southern farm, was also modern. More significant, in light of Rowan's criticism, she had not drawn her figures to look half-starved. True, they all had "the same stem-like necks and skinny arms," but they were not hungry. They were mildly amusing caricature that was not unflattering. A perusal of contemporary clothing advertisements reveals that thin arms and long necks were fashionable.[27] Lee's figures were not bony. Their smiling faces were fleshy, and they filled out their clothing. Not only that, but they stood in a field of flourishing corn flanked by a well-fed, frisky dog and a sleek horse—all slender, all childishly pleased with themselves and their lives. It was only in Rowan's own supersensitive mind that these farmers looked half-starved.

Lee's drawings were not judgmental; they demonstrated neither reformist zeal nor desire to profit at the South's expense. She, like

27. Images from 1930s southern newspaper advertisements were observed in a survey of the following: Abbeville (La.) *Progress*, 1938–39; Atlanta *Constitution*, October-December, 1935, and October-December, 1939; Atlanta *Journal*, October-December, 1939; Birmingham *News*, July-December, 1935; Memphis *Commercial Appeal*, August, 1939; Conyers (Ga.) *Times and Rockdale Record*, 1936–40; Louisville *Courier-Journal*, March, 1938; Meridian (Miss.) *Star*, 1939–40; Nashville *Banner*, 1938; New Orleans *Morning Tribune*, August-October, 1938; New Orleans *Times-Picayune*, March-April, 1938; Okolona (Miss.) *Messenger*, 1936–40; Owensboro (Ky.) *Daily Messenger*, 1938; Paducah (Ky.) *Sun-Democrat*, 1939; Petersburg (Va.) *Progress-Index*, October-December, 1937; Richmond *Planet*, 1937–39; Richmond *Times-Dispatch*, March, 1938; Tuskegee (Ala.) *News*, 1935–40; *Winston County Journal* (Louisville, Miss.), 1938.

McCrady, accepted the South as she saw it and left missionary activity to someone else. Southern anger was reserved for condescension—not caricature that represented their own view of things. Lee had sketched in and around Summerville; she had painted the residents' pride: their red earth, their peaches, and their corn; she had "corresponded with half the town"; and she had entertained their mayor in her New York studio. Rowan had done none of these things, and yet he could advise her on the sensitivity of southern people.

By this time, Lee was working on the second stage of her closely scrutinized work, at which point she should have gotten her second payment. Not only did the Section insist that a design be approved, all the while declaiming on the autonomy of the artist, before an artist could claim the first payment; before applying for the second one, the muralist had to submit a full-size cartoon of the work or a photograph of it when it was half-finished. And still later, a color sketch "suitable for framing" was to be submitted and approved—a stage at which there would be no payment.

When Doris Lee learned of Rowan's objections to her skinny-necked people, she had been ready to send the photograph of the half-finished mural, and still she had not yet been permitted to apply for the first payment. She revised the skinny arms and the stemlike necks, but Rowan still was not satisfied. This time, he hid behind the "Supervising Architect": "I immediately referred your . . . photograph to the Acting Supervising Architect and I regret to tell you that in our opinion you have not taken into consideration the criticisms previously offered relative to the strange necks which characterize both the white and the colored figures. . . . It will be necessary for you to revise the figures in accordance with my last communication before it will be possible to procure final approval on this work and authorization given you to install it." Dutifully, Lee made the required revisions: "I made the changes you suggested—but I'm rather afraid against my artistic integrity in this case." The result is a vapid picture of vapid people posing in front of an unlikely stand of corn (Figure 6). In the original design, a self-satisfied farmer and his wife, whose faces have a "Campbell's Kid" sort of charm, examine a healthy ear of their produce, make eye contact with each other, and chortle over the results of their work. In the final product, they stand woodenly in front of the corn, eyes vacant, minds probably equally so. In the original de-

6 / Doris Lee, *Georgia Countryside*, Summerville, Ga., 1939

sign, figures of a white child, a dog, a black musician, and a black female groom undulate with the landscape; in the mural, they are stiff and posed. In the original design, the all-important stand of corn was in the foreground, where, according to Lee's theory of mural design, all significant elements belong. In the installed picture, it is squeezed into the middle ground, and one improbable ear reaches toward the farmers.[28]

Even so, the mural was well received in Summerville, perhaps as much because Lee had done her homework there as for anything intrinsic in the mural. Even with the changes, the mural is southern. The Georgians are protected from a dangerous horizon by distant hills and from the post office patrons by a wary hunting dog. The white people are clean, tidy, and industrious without sweating over grueling labor. At the periphery of the action, the blacks, also clean and tidy, love fishing (their own pleasure) and banjo playing (giving pleasure to others). The land is bountiful, producing abundant cotton, corn, and peaches in the same season. Summervilleans did not object to this misrepresentation of fact, presumably because the truth was in the concept, not in the representation.

Although McCrady's mural for Amory was also caricature, he did not voice his differences with Section suggestions. And apparently exaggerated facial features on gossiping town women were more acceptable to the Section than were scrawny necks and arms on farmers. McCrady made the changes without comment, received his first payment, and proceeded with the full-size cartoon.

Not only was McCrady the ideal artist to work for the Section of

28. Rowan to Lee, April 21, 1939, Lee to Rowan, n.d. [late April or early May, 1939], February 2, 1939, all in Summerville, Georgia, file.

Fine Arts; Amory was the ideal town to receive its bounty. At a time when many people in the United States objected to the "waste" of government money on the decoration of public buildings while people starved, Amory had—or admitted to—no such concern. Of nearly two hundred pages of Amory lore published in two promotional "newspapers" on the occasion of the centennial celebration/railroad festival in 1979, only one sentence mentions the depression: "While sister communities fell victim to the boll weevil, the depression and other calamities, Amory thrived with its railroad jobs."[29]

Amory did not fare quite so well as this sentence implies. Perhaps it was the pervasive sense of shame felt by Americans unable to make sense of their lives and their country; perhaps it was southern reluctance to admit to the rest of a nation all too eager to step in with paternal remedies that the South was indeed suffering, but neither Gilmore nor prominent Amory citizens fifty years later admitted to the very real deprivation that did occur in Amory in the 1930s. Railroad jobs were not available to all people. One retired engineer who was laid off in the early 1930s recalls walking home with a loaf of bread for his five children and being besieged by hungry waifs who begged for a bite.[30] But the fact remains that whatever some Amory inhabitants suffered, the banks did not close; the railroad continued to hire people; not being a cotton community, Amory was little affected by the boll weevil, and the assistant to the Bank of Amory's president reported that its citizens were reasonably well-to-do.

The best way to describe a collective southern attitude (if such can ever be identified) toward Franklin Delano Roosevelt's New Deal is ambivalence. On the one hand, such enterprises as the TVA, the WPA, and the CCC were instances of a Yankee government's gentle reconstruction. All too often, though these projects brought jobs, new state parks, and cheap electricity, outside bureaucrats were sent to administer them, once again depriving the South of control of its own affairs. And even when the administrators were not Yankees, the money and the ideology were. Despite government efforts to keep TVA control in the region, some

29. Lucille Rogers, "Amory Was Mississippi's First Planned City," Amory *Advertiser*, Railroad Festival Edition, April 1, 1979, p. 21.
30. Interview with T. H. Beckham, April 10, 1980.

latter-day "carpetbaggers" did creep in, as Jonathan Daniels discovered. And on a 1938 visit to New Orleans, President Roosevelt once again embarrassed the South by pronouncing it the "nation's number one economic problem."[31]

On the other hand the South had eagerly sought northern capital since the days immediately following Reconstruction. In New Deal enterprises, the South, as beneficiary of nationwide programs, was treated as an equal part of the nation itself. The CCC and the WPA met a southern need for government jobs and capital that differed from that in the rest of the nation more in degree than in kind, and the TVA "chose" the South as the seat of a project that was to benefit the entire nation. Through providing the cheapest electricity in the nation, TVA also put southern residents, if not its industry, on a technological footing equal to that of the rest of the nation and in some ways superior.[32]

Amory, having suffered less than did many other southern communities and owing little of its relative prosperity to the New Deal, had no reason to resent the New Deal's gentle reconstruction and every reason to support it. The town could accept government gifts to the South because FDR had made clear his interest in Amory's votes. In 1934 the city of three thousand had been visited by President Roosevelt himself. True, he stopped only because his train had to refuel after a visit to nearby Tupelo in connection with the TVA, but he did stop, and he did speak, and many Amory residents got to shake his hand. Thus, Amory could feel that its new post office was a personal gift. A 1937 Amory *Advertiser* article reported, "It is a far cry from the dingy little postoffice [*sic*] in this grocery store with home-made fixtures and a Republican postmistress to our modern New Deal $40,000 Federal Postoffice building with a fox hunting Democrat for a postmaster."[33]

Amory was a receptive location for a Section mural for other reasons. Claiming to be Mississippi's first and only planned city in

31. Jonathan Daniels, *A Southerner Discovers the South* (New York, 1938). For examples of southern reaction to Roosevelt's statement, see New Orleans *Times-Picayune*, April 7, 1938, p. 12, and Nashville *Banner*, November 21, 1938, p. 4.

32. See for instance, "45 Percent Gain in Use of Electricity," Okolona *Messenger*, January 14, 1936, p. 1.

33. Bonnie Parham, "The Day the President Came to Amory," Amory *Advertiser*, Railroad Festival Edition, April 1, 1979, p. 51; Rogers, "Amory Was Mississippi's First Planned City," 20.

a decade when Americans were developing the concept of the planned community, Amory considered itself a pioneer. Amory's wide streets had anticipated heavy automobile traffic a half century before the New Deal designers of Greenbelt, Maryland, found it advisable to create pedestrian walkways inaccessible to motor vehicles.[34]

Founded in 1887, Amory did not have the antebellum traditions that may have made many southern towns resist government projects, and the town had always had a philosophy of openness to the new, the untried. Dependent on the railroad, Amory was a machine-age community whose lifeblood was commerce; the nearby towns of Okolona and Nettleton were agrarian. Although residents of Amory would have agreed that the South was a healthy part of the nation and had unique virtues of its own, they would have had small patience with the twelve writers of *I'll Take My Stand*, who deplored the coming of industrial technology to the South.[35] Amory had a rich history, which included no break with the national government; wide avenues; the railroad, which provided access to the world of bustling progress; and a new post office. Residents were proud of all these things. All they needed was an artist so the town could be a cultural center as well.

So John McCrady completed his mural, after he had made the changes suggested by Rowan, after he had examined the artifacts provided him by Amory people, after he had consulted three times with one Amory citizen. On August 31, 1939, McCrady came to Amory to install the mural. The people of the town had an artwork of which they could be proud, one that reflected with some accuracy Amory in the nineteenth century, but even more the town's concerns in 1939.

The mural, entitled *Amory, 1888*, depicts a panorama of town life soon after the city's founding (Figure 7). Like a medieval triptych, its tripartite structure depicts interrelated but not obviously connected scenes. As with a religious triptych of the Christian Middle Ages, the mural features icons that would assure its audience that the proper objects of faith and hope were immutable. Un-

34. See *The City* (American Documentary Films, 1939). Today, faced with contemporary residents' resistance to walking and their demand for parking close to home, Greenbelt has replaced some of the walkways with traditional streets and crossed others with thoroughfares.

35. Twelve Southerners, *I'll Take My Stand* (New York, 1930), xix.

7 / John McCrady, *Amory, 1888,* Amory, Miss., 1939
Photo by Richard H. Beckham

like medieval religious icons, however, the ones in this picture are
more likely to be read by the subconscious than the conscious.
Even so, they assure Amory citizens that in the city's youth, the
railroad, as was true in the 1930s, was the source of prosperity, but
only with the help of good southern men would all its manifesta-
tions be benevolent. They were reminded that times in 1888, already good, had gotten even better. The townspeople, who had,
after all, requested a scene from the town's early days, could look
back from the depression, whose hardships they denied, and imagine that if Amory had been that comfortably carefree once, it
would be again.

The picture proclaims Amory as a railroad community. It is set
out horizontally: the wooden sidewalk, the three groupings of
people in the foreground, the fishing pole carried by a whistling
youth, and the pigs ambling down Main Street are on horizontal
planes. The arrangement suggests the railroad's movement across
the landscape. All the lines in the picture—the clapboard and the
roofing materials, the roofs and porches themselves, the lumber in
the sidewalk, the traveler's suitcase, and the tilt of the horse-drawn
carriage—point toward one background point. Slightly to the right
of center is an 1888 locomotive, puffing clouds of clean smoke.
Clearly, all activity in Amory points toward the railroad. And yet
the people are protected from the more unpleasant effects of technology and from interfering outsiders by comfortably untechnolog-
ical frame buildings and abundant southern trees. The smoke from
the train, in an earlier version, black and palpable as the smoke and
tornadoes in Benton's paintings is now white and unthreatening.

In order to achieve his triptych structure, McCrady took liberties with the "authentic" buildings, much as Doris Lee did with the harvest of Georgia's produce. In an original 1890 photograph, Amory's wood buildings line the east side of Main Street in row-house style; those on the west side, behind which the railroad actually runs, are brick.[36] McCrady showed buildings, copied from actual nineteenth-century wood structures in Amory, as separate, independent entities lined up between the street and the railroad. The slightly skewed arrangement of the buildings, the hard outlines of the figures, the exaggerated disapproval on the faces of the gossiping women, and the raucous panic of the horse pulling the stuck carriage give the mural a playful animated-cartoon quality.[37] Amory citizens were thus assured that any difficulties encountered in the picture would be rectified in the next frame—or that any problems caused by the depression would be solved in the next decade.

McCrady followed Rowan's advice and made his white citizens clearly white. Only two of the nineteen human figures in the painting are black. Thus Amory residents know that the town will not be overpowered by its nonwhite population—that WPA jobs will, of course, go to whites. But McCrady does not ignore the mixed nature of the population. The two blacks are harmless, and they suffer no mistreatment from the white power structure. The black youth, muscular and healthy, whistles as he sets off on a fishing expedition—clearly for fun and not because he is hungry. There is some question about the other potential black. Amory citizens, asked to describe the picture when they are not looking at it, describe him as black, however. A somewhat unstable drunk, he trips over the pigs that roam the street, but he does not suffer. He has what he needs in a jug clutched in his right arm.

Despite earlier plans to do so, McCrady did not use actual faces of Amory citizens in his mural. The local newspaper reported that "surprisingly, Mr. McCrady has been able to recapture a suggestion of many of the features of early residents of Amory although no ac-

36. "Amory's Main Street as Seen in Earlier Days," photographs, Amory *Advertiser*, Railroad Festival Edition, April 1, 1979, p. 32.

37. Warren Susman, *Culture and Commitment, 1929–1945* (New York, 1973), 12–13, suggests that people of the 1930s, torn between two worlds, warmed to Walt Disney cartoons because they transformed nightmares into fairy tales and pleasant dreams.

8 / John McCrady, detail of Amory mural
Photo by Richard H. Beckham

tual portraiture was attempted."[38] Perhaps Rowan's concern about company names warned McCrady away from actual portraiture. Perhaps he was hurried because of his pending Guggenheim Fellowship. More likely, however, he perceived the need to give the mural a universal application. By merely suggesting features of typical Amory faces, McCrady preserved his animated-cartoon quality. The mice and dogs in Disney's productions look like no human we have ever seen before, and yet they look hauntingly like every human we have seen who faced a similar situation. McCrady did include one portrait, however. On the balcony of the center building, a minuscule John McCrady spreads his arms as if he tells a whopping fish story. Perhaps this is the artist's ironic comment on the picture he paints. Perhaps he has finally rebelled, however slightly, against government interference in his work (Figure 8).

In 1888 the Amory streets were mud, and horse-drawn vehicles frequently got stuck.[39] So it is in the picture, but the driver of the carriage is so muscular and so determined and his horse so spirited that we know he will be on his way shortly. Besides, the Amory viewers know that their streets are no longer mud, that progress has gotten Amory out of that difficulty. They have confidence that progress will take care of any difficulties they now experience.

A group of women gossip in the center (their distorted faces living proof that southern sensitivity did not extend to comical

38. "McCrady Hangs Mural Here," Amory *Advertiser*, August 31, 1939, p. 1, clipping, in Amory, Mississippi, file.
39. Rogers, "Amory Was Mississippi's First Planned City," 20.

caricature in works of art) possibly about the drunken man, but they are unconcerned about either the stuck carriage or the crisis to the left in the picture. Obviously cared-for women who have plenty of time to stand on the street exchanging comments, they seem oblivious to the pigs in the street—precisely, perhaps, because the pigs are there. Between the original sketch and the final mural, McCrady fattened up his pigs considerably. Pork is an important staple of the southern diet, and nobody in this picture is going hungry for lack of it. The sow has recently littered, thus guaranteeing a continuing supply of meat.

The most interesting group in the picture is the gathering of men in the right foreground. With firearms they confront a stranger just off the train. The traveler enters the picture from the post office lobby, to which he has his back. Somewhat aghast at his greeting, he drops his suitcase and stares at the shotguns aimed in his direction. Two of the five men hold handkerchiefs over their noses, and a sign behind them reads "Amory wants no yellow fever strangers. KEEP OUT!"

For many years in the nineteenth century, yellow fever periodically ravaged the South. The last great epidemic in 1878 spread through Mississippi and killed half the population in Holly Springs, about sixty miles west of Amory. Outbreaks continued through 1898, and small towns feared that travelers would bring the pestilence from Memphis.[40] The men in the mural are stopping the stranger before he enters their town and perhaps brings with him the dread disease—or any other plague strangers might bring with them into the South.

The message here for depression Amory is contained in the town's history. Amory never had a yellow-fever outbreak. Therefore, the men protecting the city must have been successful. The women and the child in the picture pay no heed to the stranger. They have no reason to question that the men can handle the job. In *The Grapes of Wrath* (1939), John Steinbeck shows one of the depression's great tragedies. Women's work—mothering, cooking, organizing the household—and women's identity remained un-

40. Federal Writers Project, *Mississippi: A Guide to the Magnolia State* (New York, 1938), 203; Gerald W. Capers, Jr., *The Biography of a River Town: Memphis: Its Heroic Age* (Chapel Hill, 1939), 211; William D. Miller, *Memphis During the Progressive Era* (Memphis, 1957), 68.

challenged, but men's position in the culture was threatened, often usurped. No such tragedy happened in John McCrady's Amory. In the mural, the men perform the male's age-old task, protecting the dwelling. And the women pay more attention to a local drunk than they do to a threat from outside.

The picture is a pleasant one for the Amory citizens, and it was received enthusiastically. McCrady and his wife, who stayed at the home of E. J. Gilmore when they visited Amory to install the mural, were given a reception that at least seventy prominent local citizens attended.[41] The local newspaper was so effusive in its support of Amory's own artist that it unwittingly printed several half-truths. It reported, for example, that McCrady's commission was "one of the few ever given without competition by a federal art project." And when the mural was mounted, the *Advertiser* reported that "Mississippi's celebrated artist" had been awarded "the Guggenheim for this year, the climax of his brilliant career." Although his first impulse was not to finish the Amory mural, he had "become so inspired by his determination to give the people of Amory a constant reminder of the progress they have made in the past fifty years, he requested that his fellowship be deferred until he could complete the mural for Amory."[42]

McCrady did become Amory's own artist. To this day, the only art besides the post office mural on public display are the portraits of E. J. Gilmore's parents painted by McCrady to grace the walls of Amory's only hospital, the Gilmore Memorial Sanitarium. And when the McCradys had a son, they named E. J. Gilmore his godfather.

John McCrady could not have been so enthusiastically received in Amory had he not known and conformed to the north Mississippi mores. He spoke, behaved, and painted as a native should. He showed the proper respect for Amory citizens by using their pictures and their suggestions in his mural, and he flattered them by postponing acceptance of his Guggenheim until he had finished their mural. His nephew, James Waring McCrady, knows what endeared his uncle to the South and to Amory: "It will be evident that [McCrady] was very much a product and a left over from the

41. Gilmore to Rowan, September 2, 1939, in Amory, Mississippi, file.

42. "John McCrady, Now Painting Postoffice Mural, Wins High Award," Amory *Advertiser*, March 30, 1939, p. 1, clipping, *ibid.*; "McCrady Hangs Mural Here."

1930's. I think that he might have made a bigger 'name' for himself if he had chosen to play the game in the Eastern art establishment. But he was much too devoted to his southland and to his family to do that. He was very philosophic, very humorous, loving and gentle; a very likable person. On the whole, he was not an innovative artist, but he thoroughly believed in what he was doing."[43]

What Doris Lee and John McCrady knew about the South they probably could not have verbalized and Edward Rowan could not have guessed. They knew that the South recognized its own problems, that for too long it had been condescended to, and they knew that southerners were most fierce in their contention that they could handle their own problems without help from Yankees or the federal government. Amory's train could bring pestilence as well as prosperity, and the Amory people could handle both.

Some insight into this fierce southern claim to self-sufficiency might be gained from looking briefly at another effort in the 1930s at gentle reconstruction. During that era, several antilynch bills were proposed in Congress, and all were defeated. Most Americans chose to blame only southern racism and perhaps southerners' predilection for taking the law into their own hands. One cannot deny that both racism and a tendency toward popular, often violent enforcement of the law are southern. But careful study of the nation's popular culture will show that both characteristics are, conceptually, at least, as much American as southern. What was southern about objections to federal antilynch laws and what was southern about objections to certain federal mural projects are similar. Although the elected southern representatives filibustered bill after bill until each one was discarded before a vote was taken, the metropolitan southern press often supported the antilynch bills and few southerners were ready to go on record as supporting lynching itself. But southerners would always oppose federal bills that would apply principally to situations in the South that Yankees could little understand. The editor of the Louisville, Mississippi, *Winston County Journal* wrote: "In commenting on the antilynching bill fight in the Senate, . . . popular commentator Paul Sullivan made a grave error in saying the 'fight was between Senators of the north who opposed lynching and southerners who fa-

43. James Waring McCrady to the author, April 7, 1980.

vored lynching of negroes.' Southerners do not favor lynching, but do oppose . . . northern Republicans and so-called Democrats who wish to lynch the states-rights part of the Constitution, as a means of courting favor of northern negroes." The editor of the Conyers, Georgia, *Times and Rockdale Record* cited another reason that southerners might oppose the bill: "Of course, we are not in favor of lynching, nobody is, in fact, nobody likes to see a person electrocuted, but when it comes home to you, such things appear as being the only thing to do and a poor recompense at that. . . . They say we have courts of justice to try such cases, but by the time a definite conclusion is reached the brute may have lived long enough to raise up a family of similar brutes."[44]

This country editor reflected the southerners' drive to solve their own problems and be free from meddling and often ineffective federal intervention. But even had he expressed it more clearly and acceptably, he would not have convinced nonsoutherners who consistently misinterpreted southern opposition to antilynch laws. That opposition was both attributed to and offered as further evidence of characteristics identified as southern. It is true, racism in the United States was, and perhaps still is, most obvious in the South. It is true the American South has always had the reputation for being ready with violent and repellent solutions to problems. It is true the South has a cult of pure white womanhood unequaled in other parts of the country. But to read opposition to antilynch bills only in terms of these South-specific characteristics is to miss at least a part of the point. Perhaps any other section of the country would be reluctant to support federal bills whose only application was to problems exclusive to that section.

It is true that the number of lynchings increased during the late 1920s and early 1930s. But by 1939, when the last New Deal antilynch bill was defeated, lynchings had decreased from twenty-nine in 1930 to three in 1938. Southerners might have seen evidence here that the South itself was taking care of the problem. And handling southern problems within in the South was a high southern priority. A 1939 Atlanta *Journal* editor expounds on the "far-reaching effects of the movement by which the South now seeks to cure its own ills" and quotes a University of Tennessee sociolo-

44. Editorial page of the *Winston County Journal* (Louisville, Miss.), January 2, 1938; Conyers (Ga.) *Times and Rockdale Record,* February 3, 1939, p. 2.

gist's strong words to support his thesis: "When the social history of the United States for the Twentieth Century is written, . . . nothing will be more outstanding in it than the interest of the nation in the problems of the South; the way in which the South has organized its own forces for the solution of its problems, and the actual development of the South."[45]

Southerners could well have concluded that nonsoutherners agreed that they had the wherewithal to cure their own ills. During the filibusters against antilynching bills, the favorable majority could not get the necessary two-thirds vote to invoke cloture. And in 1939, when the Section of Fine Arts was functioning at its peak, the Gallup pollsters revealed a startling national trend. At the very time when rural Georgians were writing editorials condemning antilynch legislation and a southern filibuster was keeping Congress from passing the bill, the poll showed that only 53 percent of voters favored the bill (the percentage in favor the year before was 72). Those who loved to level charges of racism and excessive violence at the South were no longer so sure that the federal government should take the South in hand.[46] Many had apparently been convinced by southern arguments that the bill was an encroachment on southern rights. Virtually everybody knew that in the best of all possible worlds lynching was not the way to deal with sexual miscreants, but white southerners in the Great Depression did not live in such a world and they knew from long experience that they alone had to take care of their own problems. The wheels of justice ground slowly, and, they felt, there was precious little justice meted out. The editor in Conyers wrote: "Senator Connally, Democrat of Texas, leader of the southern group opposed to the [compromise antilynching] bill, said he could not approve it because he viewed the compromise as an 'entering wedge' for later more stringent legislation, 'The compromise would carry no p[r]o-

45. Tindall, *The Emergence of the New South*, 551; George C. Rable, "The South and the Politics of Antilynching Legislation, 1920–1940," *Journal of Southern History*, LI (1985), 201–20, says that southerners' states' rights position, tinged with fear of outside interference in the race issue, was at the base of the argument; Atlanta, *Journal*, December 16, 1939, Sec. 1, p. 6.

46. Tindall, *The Emergence of the New South*, 551–52. Even Tindall, however, seems to miss the aspects of states' rights and slow justice that were part of the opposition to antilynch legislation. He mentions only the arguments for white supremacy and for the protection of southern womanhood.

vision for prosecution of dilatory state officials nor permit suits against the counties.'"[47]

Laws to abolish lynching should assure, first, that elected law officers did their jobs. Second, such laws should come from within the South, not from a federal government that had, southerners felt, all too often taken southern governance out of southern hands. Not all southerners opposed federal antilynching laws, but those who did, did so on grounds that most southerners could understand—and successful Section artists, at the subconscious level, at least, understood, too. When Doris Lee and John McCrady put blacks in their southern murals, they painted the southern blacks paternally cherished by southern people—and the rest of white America, as well—who would never require stern rebuke from the law and from whom white southerners would never need protection.

When Doris Lee reported the Summerville mayor's visit to her studio, she said that "he is still so busy fighting the war against Lincoln ('states should be left alone to do as they please') that I was overwhelmed in his liberality about the mural."[48] Lee misinterpreted the mayor's remark. He was not fighting Lincoln. He was concerned that Roosevelt and Congress sometimes did not seem to know that Reconstruction had ended and that the South had home rule. Although she misread the mayor on that point, she recognized his superiority over Rowan's as a critic of the mural in his city.

Lee and McCrady knew too that, for the South, the possibilities were not limitless. The land was badly depleted by irresponsible cotton and tobacco farming. But southerners could no longer move westward in search of fertile land because that trek took them out of the South. Their land was gradually being reclaimed in part because outsiders had decreed that certain cotton land was to lie fallow each year, but the struggle itself would be theirs. Lee reminded them that new crops, corn and peaches, not paternalistic outsiders, were their hope, but she did not neglect the crop that had sustained them, often inadequately, for over a century and a half. She gave the Summervilleans farmers who could sustain themselves along with a black farm hand or two. McCrady showed that Amory could take

47. Conyers (Ga.) *Times and Rockdale Record*, January 27, 1939, p. 1.
48. Lee to Rowan, March 27, 1939, in Summerville, Georgia, file.

care of Amory's problems even when the town's primary industry, the railroad, brought them. And both murals in their composition showed the South to be not only safe from intruders but as having no alternative to self-sufficiency.

When Alexandre Hogue agreed to decorate one wall of the new federal parcel post building in Houston, Texas, he added a post-script: "We abide by your decision," he wrote, "but why in god's name do you fellows think that every place west of the Mississippi wants a stage coach and Indians in their P.O?" Penciled in the margin by a Section official are the words "We don't." Maybe, literally, they didn't, but Postmaster James T. Coleman of Livingston, Texas, knew what Hogue meant. Apparently familiar with the murals to which Hogue referred and knowing that selected artist Theodore Van Soelen wrote from New Mexico to request *only* the dimensions of the mural wall, he wrote, "You failed to state in the letter the picture you were painting, if it is not the proper painting for this part of East Texas, then we don't care for it. . . . I have written the department our industry and it should be taken from that, and not some painting we will not appreciate. I would like very much to have an idea of the painting, and I will grant you I will assist you as you wish."[49]

The Section's ideas about what was South and what was West were as definite as Coleman's were. Since Section officials thought that Texas was West, they appointed an artist for Livingston who "drove Mules In Stagecoach Days of West Where Ranchers Laughed at Art As Livelihood."[50] The artist, convinced of his intimate knowledge of the West, designed a mural for Livingston based on no investigation whatever. Confident that his design was appropriate, he sent the Livingston postmaster a description. Irate, Coleman wrote Rowan:

> With reference to the mural painting for the post office. I will give you clearly the facts, and also the painting we expect, we are in the southern part of East Texas and a cow boy or wild west painting is something we don't want.

49. Alexandre Hogue to Edward Rowan, June 17, 1938, in Houston, Texas, file in RG 121, NA; James T. Coleman to Theodore Van Soelen, April 24, 1940, in Livingston, Texas, file.

50. Clipping from Cornwall, Connecticut, newspaper (where Van Soelen spent summers), n.d. [probably summer, 1939], Coleman to Rowan, May 7, 1940, both in Livingston, Texas, file.

August 7, 1939 I informed my good friend Mr. Purdom [Washington postal official who handled post office dealings with the Section] our industry in this section, and he in return stated our wishes would be granted as to the painting. We have the large pine tree forests, loblolly and long leaf (sawmilling) oil, farming, cotton corn and all the vegetables, especially tomatoes, we shiped several cars from this Co. last year.[51]

A good southerner, Coleman wanted no confusion about Livingston's relationship to the "western" part of Texas. Livingston was agrarian, self-sufficient, and wary of government plans to improve the town. And its industries—save only oil, which more recently reached the South—were southern: loblolly pines, sawmilling, cotton, and corn. What's more, the large stands of tall pines guaranteed a limited horizon, physically if not figuratively.

Aghast and bewildered at being rejected, Van Soelen wrote a panicky letter:

The enclosed letters [from Coleman] . . . speaks for itself (collective) [*sic*], and not in a soothing whisper either. . . . I just took for granted that everything was all right so long as the Department O.K.'d my sketch. . . . However, I put my feelings away in moth-balls and wrote the Postmaster a civil, tactful letter. . . . It calmed his fears a little I believe, but did no good so far as subject matter is concerned. Evidently, they want a tomato packing scene. I do not have a primadonna complex in such matters and up to now I have always had wholehearted cooperation.

How do you handle such situations?[52]

Rowan handled such situations when money was available by awarding recalcitrant post offices a second mural—when, that is, the postmaster was a good friend of Fourth Assistant Postmaster General Smith W. Purdom. Wary of receiving another barrage from Livingston, the Section quickly commissioned Van Soelen to do a second mural for a markedly unsuitable wall. The wall required a design that would accommodate grilles and a clock, but Van Soelen apparently gave little attention to the problem. Rather he designed the mural as if the wall were solid. The result is less than satisfactory from an artistic standpoint. The mural looks like landscape wallpaper with holes cut in it, but it pleased the residents of Liv-

---

51. Coleman to Rowan, May 7, 1940, *ibid.*
52. Van Soelen to Rowan, December 12, 1940, *ibid.*

9 / Theodore Van Soelen, *Landscape Mural*, Livingston, Tex., 1941

ingston—so much so that Coleman even complimented the first mural.[53]

The second mural has little cotton, no corn, and no tomatoes, and it is replete with oil wells (Figure 9). It does have a carefully circumscribed horizon of live oak and tall pines, presumably loblolly. And the empty landscape is protected from postal patrons by a standing pine and an alert wild turkey perched on a logged pine stump. A cabin stands in the cotton, and a road, which might have led to distant and dangerous places, appears to circle back upon itself.

It is little wonder that when the federal government set itself up as a propagator of popular culture, the Livingston postmaster insisted a bit belligerently that his community get a mural it could live with. As a southerner, he had no desire to be allied with a romanticized West. He believed that the Section of Fine Arts was a place wherein the South could have voice in how the government ministered to his region. He was surely going to use that voice. Once he had been heard, he could appreciate the earlier piece, which, though it was not Livingston, was as fine piece of art as Livingston had seen.

In his penultimate letter to the Section of Fine Arts, E. J. Gilmore, who had also been heard by his government, reported:

The people of Amory are as a whole extremely well pleased with the mural. The majority think it is "pretty" or "beautiful," but you under-

53. Van Soelen to Rowan, n.d. [summer, 1941], *ibid.*

stand of course that there can be no higher praise. The ones with advanced appreciation are immediately conscious of the excellence of Mr. McCrady's workmanship, his splendid color sense, and the startling fashion in which he has recaptured the spirit of the early Amory and its people. I do sincerely believe that this one mural will do more to advance the appreciation of art in this section, to inspire a greater interest in modern art, than anything you people could have done for us.

"We do thank you."[54]

The Section was so pleased with these comments that a typed copy of them was placed, out of the usual order, at the front of its Amory file. There is little doubt that other copies were used, as was Section custom with particularly complimentary community responses, as propaganda for their ongoing crusade to become a permanent government agency. But the meaning of the words seems to have escaped Rowan and his colleagues. Had Rowan looked carefully back over the Amory file, he could have found clues that would save him much heartache and bureaucratic difficulty with other southern commissions, but he did not. He absorbed the compliment and commended both McCrady's work and Gilmore's public spirit, but he learned nothing from the experience.

54. Gilmore to Rowan, September 2, 1939, in Amory, Mississippi, file. Quotation marks in the original.

II / PORTRAIT OF THE ARTIST: WHO PAINTED
THE SOUTH AND HOW THEY GOT TO

In the old days, commencement at Kentucky's Berea College used to be more than an academic celebration for the college community. The festival, akin to husking bees, log-rollings, and the county fair, drew citizens of Berea and country folk from miles around. As many as three days before the ceremony, people came on foot, in carriages and wagons, on horseback and muleback "to meet friends, to drink moonshine, to trade horses, pistols, watches, barlow knives"—anything that could be traded—to shoot their enemies, to court their ladies, and to while away the evening dancing to fiddles, guitars, and dulcimers. Whole families camped on the spacious college grounds, where lawful entrepreneurs set up lemonade stands and candy booths in the quadrangle while the other kind sold white lightning in obscure corners.[1]

It was this scene from some indefinable mythical time near the turn of the century that Berea artist Frank Long immortalized on the Berea Post Office wall. The work on the mural became something of a year-long festival for Berea, the town and the college, and a resounding success for the Section of Fine Arts. In January, 1939, an emissary from the Section had toured a significant portion of the South. When asked, she lectured on the Section mission, commenting on the aesthetic merits of Section artworks and assessing community response to murals and the government that provided them. In a mild-mannered understatement, she reported that "the townspeople appreciate it when the artist comes to the town and tries to learn something about the background and the life other than what he or she can get out of a book or just a walk around the town."[2] The ideal situation was Berea's: the commissioned artist

1. Owen Rickard, "Mural Painting at Post Office," Berea *Citizen*, July 20, 1940, clipping, in Berea, Kentucky, file, Record Group 121, National Archives.

2. Helen Appleton Read, "January Report of Work Done in Connection with a Grant from the Carnegie Corporation to Study Art in Federal Buildings," February 16, 1939, Record Group 121, Preliminary Inventory Entry 129 [Folder: Field Reports], p. 4, National Archives. Citations to National Archives Record Group 121,

knew all about the town because he practiced his trade on its Main Street. Had this official observer reported more forcefully or had the Section paid more attention to signals received from communities, it surely would have had fewer problems in the South. The Section may not, however, have been able to ensure that southern post offices were uniformly decorated by what the Section considered excellent art.

Although the South did undergo something of an art renaissance, southern artists were virtually unknown outside the South. Perhaps *nascence* would be more accurate, since the South had been struggling for over two centuries to give birth to southern art by southern artists. To be sure, paintings of southerners and southern subjects had been a part of American art since well before the Revolution, but southern artists had been a rarity. In the eighteenth and nineteenth centuries, southerners who could afford portraits had, as a rule, been painted by nonsoutherners traveling in the South.

In colonial times, southern portraits were a significant portion of America's artistic output because money and culture were largely concentrated in the southern colonies. New England Puritans did have portraits made, but as pristine records of their religion. Coastal southern planters, on the other hand, who aspired to a New World aristocracy and who had no intention of breaking with European traditions, commissioned elaborate portraits to advertise their wealth and social status. Colonial artists Robert Feke, John Hesselius, and even Charles Willson Peale, among others, traveled south to accept such lucrative commissions. Other so-called southern art of the colonial period was done by such expatriate American artists as Benjamin West and John Singleton Copley in their London studios.[3] Well-heeled southerners could afford to make the crossing to have their portraits painted by those recognized as the best American artists. And those who did not could still have their portraits made by prominent European artists. It was not uncommon for would-be southern aristocrats to send cursory descriptions of favored subjects to artists in Europe with instructions to paint portraits.

"Records of the Public Buildings Service," not found in Entry 133 will hereafter include specific entry number, a box number and/or a folder title when appropriate.

3. See Carolyn J. Weekley, "The Early Years—1564–1790," in *Painting in the South* (Richmond, 1983), 1–36.

Although fairly productive artists' colonies developed in early nineteenth-century Baltimore, Charleston, and, surprisingly, Kentucky, southern art during the Federal period—at least that which was worthy of scrutiny by the art establishment—still consisted largely of portraits by northern artists such as John Trumbull and Rembrandt Peale who traveled south to paint aspiring aristocrats.[4] The trend for non-southern men to paint the South while southern women painted china continued as nineteenth-century artists moved toward landscape and genre painting. Although the South did produce its own accomplished genre painters—Richard Norris Brooke and James Adams Elder, for example—most notable southern painting was done by seasonal visitors who were avoiding northern winters and taking advantage of all the exotic subjects. The southern genre painting that gets attention even from scholars of southern art was by Yankees such as Winslow Homer and Eastman Johnson who were fascinated by the chance to paint blacks, not many of whom lived in the North. French artists who stopped in New Orleans and traveled from there to paint the rural South were legion. English and German painters also crossed the ocean to paint the American South. And the American North contributed a few landscapists who moved south to paint the subtropical abundance: both Martin Johnson Heade and William Morris Hunt moved to Florida. Very few nineteenth-century canvases by native southern painters, however, have survived, if indeed many were done. Thus, southern artists who joined southern writers in the southern Renaissance had practically a virgin field in which to develop their medium.[5]

And develop it they did. By 1939, when Frank Long won the competition to paint the Berea, Kentucky, mural, quite a few southern artists were making names for themselves, at least in the South. Although "the [southern] art of the period never rose to the heights of literature," the one serious examination of southern art history does demonstrate that it "made an important and lasting contribution to regional and national culture."[6] Lamar Dodd, John Kelly

4. Linda Crocker Simmons, "The Emerging Nation, 1790–1830," *ibid.*, 43–70.
5. See Jessie J. Poesch, "Growth and Development of the Old South," *ibid.*, 73–99.
6. Rick Stewart, "Toward a New South: The Regionalist Approach, 1900–1950," *ibid.*, 105.

Fitzpatrick, Anne Goldthwaite, John McCrady, and others were doing with southern material what Thomas Hart Benton, John Steuart Curry, and Grant Wood were doing with that of the Midwest, but with less fanfare.

As a matter of fact, even while regional southern artists were creating a visual arts renaissance, literary artists were still writing of a paucity of opportunity for the development of painting in the South. At least two artists, frustrated by their failure to gain recognition in the South, became authors. They were probably inspired as much by a desire to be a part of the more successful southern Renaissance in letters as by a chance to tell the story of their disappointment in the visual arts. Harry Lee's positively reviewed but little-read *Fox in the Cloak* chronicles the efforts and repeated failures of Neil Glass as he struggles to build a career in art. During the depression in Atlanta, he moves through an array of obstacles that represent how little opportunity there was for an artist in the South. First, after a long struggle to find any art teacher at all, he watches an excellent one die from starvation—spiritual as well as physical. Glass allies himself with a series of organizations ostensibly devoted to promoting and developing artistic talent in Atlanta but whose only real concern was the status that might be gained through association with culture. One by one, several of his talented friends either succumb to practical needs and turn to trade or give up on the South and retreat to New York, where art is appreciated. He tries to support himself by painting murals for an untrained boss who presumes to know more about mural design than the painter does. Glass's one desire is to stay in Atlanta and paint its black residents. But he finally joins the legions who move north to escape the stifling atmosphere and to earn a living at their trade.[7]

In a book reviewed as notable only because of the paintings its author did as illustrations, Frederick Wight includes as cocktail-party conversation frequent allusions to the scarcity of painters in the region. Probably set in Georgia, *South* is the story of a northern artist who comes south to paint blacks and poor whites but who associates only with aristocrats. And they are delighted that he has come. The attitude of Wight's South toward fine arts is aptly summed up by one socialite and potential patron: "We've been rich

7. Harry Lee, *Fox in the Cloak* (New York, 1938).

in writers and musicians . . . but poor in painters."[8] The artists
were in the South, but the South was not aware of it.

And neither was the Section. Although artists were painting in
the South more than they ever had, the Section had trouble locating them because nationally known nonsouthern artists, such as
Benton and the painters from the Woodstock colony, still traveled
in the South to paint its exotic people and landscape. The problem
was exacerbated by the tendency of the few southern artists whose
national reputation brought them to the Section's attention to refuse graciously to enter competitions. Lamar Dodd, for example,
found creating a respectable art department at the University of
Georgia and simultaneously building his own reputation as a southern regionalist more important than designing murals he had no
guarantee that he could execute. He explained that he was interested in Section work and pleased that government-sponsored art
projects offered opportunities for southern art to develop. He served
on competition juries, and he encouraged his students and protégés
to compete. But he was fully employed and far too busy with his
own work to compete for the chance to do someone else's.[9]

Frank Long, however, had no such compunction. Unlike artists
employed by universities, he was trying to earn his living as a
painter; unlike artists with wide reputations, he needed the
money.[10] He needed it so much that he continued to enter Section
competitions and accept commissions long after his zeal for mural
painting had burned low, but the only mural he ever painted farther
south than his native Kentucky was in the West—Oklahoma. This
artist, with a southern sensibility, had chosen not to join his colleagues in New York so he could live and paint in Berea, Kentucky.
His commitment to painting in his region would probably have
made him very successful as a painter of southern murals. But the
Section seems not to have considered him a southern artist. His ap-
pointments were in Kentucky (Louisville, Morehead, and Berea),
Indiana, Oklahoma, and Maryland—not the areas for which the
Section had trouble finding artists.

8. Frederick Wight, *South* (New York, 1935), 48.
9. Lamar Dodd to Edward Rowan, January 22, 1940, in "General Records of
the Section," Entry 122, and records of the Harrisonburg, Virginia, competition,
wherein Dodd served as committee member in Harrisonburg, Virginia, file, Entry
133, RG 121, NA.
10. Frank Long to the author, October 24, 1983.

Why Frank Long was sent to Indiana and not to Tennessee, to Oklahoma and not to Louisiana might be suggested in the organization of the Public Works of Art Project, or PWAP, whose director was Edward Bruce, later chief of the Section. Founded in 1933 as the first New Deal effort to provide relief work for unemployed artists, PWAP was organized to ensure that artists in all areas of the country would have equal opportunity to earn a living working for the government.[11] So that the New York art establishment would not benefit disproportionately, the nation was divided into sixteen regions, each with its own chair and budget. One region included mid-Atlantic states (Virginia and Maryland); another, Deep South states (Alabama, Georgia, and Mississippi). Kentucky was yoked with Missouri and Indiana in a sort of midwestern region. The Section, which grew out of PWAP and inherited some of its administrators, apparently did not free itself from the regional concept. Although Long began early painting Section murals and had a total of six commissions, most as a result of honorable mention in southern competitions, he was never asked to paint in the Deep South, where the Section had trouble locating suitable artists. This kind of myopia contributed much to Section difficulties in finding artists for the South.

Then, of course, the Section was committed to what it supposed was an objective selection of artists. The program certainly cannot be faulted for consciously or intentionally selecting artists by other criteria. In fact, had the Section been less "objective," it might have been more successful in its southern public relations. And had it placed less stress on the fairness of the anonymous competition system, it might have more easily appointed artists appropriate to the South. As it was, many southern competitions were not far from disastrous. The Berea competition, however, worked as a competition should work, probably because Berea was a small town (1,827 souls) and the proffered fee for the work was small ($740).

Section practice was to appoint a respected local citizen knowledgeable about art to chair the competition committee. But when the community was no larger than Berea, options were limited.

11. Richard D. McKinzie, *The New Deal for Artists* (Princeton, 1973), 5–32, discusses PWAP history at length and questions PWAP's effectiveness as a haven for all American artists.

Fortunately, Berea was a college town, and one with little town-gown tension—Berea owed its very existence to the college—thus the appointment of art department head Mary Ela was fortuitous. Berea College was founded in 1855 to contribute "to the spiritual and material welfare of the mountain region of the South, affording to young people of character and promise a thorough Christian education, elementary, industrial, secondary, normal and collegiate, with opportunities for manual labor as an assistant in self-support." In today's language, that meant that students were required to earn at least a part of their expenses through manual labor (low-income students could earn most of theirs); that students were trained in such trades as teaching and crafts, skills that they, in turn, could pass on to other mountain folk to prepare them to be Berea students. It was hoped that Berea graduates would stay in Appalachia to help bring prosperity and a high standard of living to those underprivileged and under-Americanized mountain people. Berea College was originally interracial and hoped to Americanize Kentucky blacks as well. A 1904 Kentucky statute prohibiting integrated schooling took care of that, however, and a new all-black college was provided far away in Louisville.[12] Today, and certainly, one supposes, in 1939, hardly a black face can be seen on campus or in the mountain town.

This revolutionary institution was built in the Kentucky wilderness, and the town grew up around it—first to supply what the college needed and later to sell Berea crafts to tourists. In 1939 the college was almost equal in size to the town, and the two functioned in a mutually beneficial way. It was in that spirit that Mary Ela accepted the Section's appointment to the competition committee on two conditions: that she be permitted to exhibit the entries at the college gallery for community viewers before they were judged, and that the next college exhibit be a one-man show of the winning artist's work. Rowan agreed to the first condition, once he was assured that only committee members educated in art would actually participate in selecting the winner. About the second condition he was enthusiastic.[13]

12. Federal Writers Project, *Kentucky: A Guide to the Bluegrass State* (New York, 1939), 269; "Berea College: An Historic Monument to Equality," *Berea Magazine*, April, 1983, p. 16.

13. Mary Ela to Forbes Watson, February 15, 1939, in Berea, Kentucky, file.

Such a plan would not have worked in many college towns, as
Anne Goldthwaite discovered when she painted a mural for Tuskegee, Alabama. In 1936, when she was appointed to do the mural,
the Tuskegee Institute was a matter of pride in its hometown. The
local newspaper reported on the black institution as it would have
any college in that area. (Later, as competition for WPA funds increased and as the antilynch-bill controversy brought undesirable
publicity to the South, that would change.) Goldthwaite, having
grown up in Alabama, was aware of the pride Tuskegee took in its
unique institution and in the fact that George Washington Carver
resided, researched, and taught there. Thus, she thought that the
mural should feature the institute. When she visited Tuskegee,
however, she discovered that "the Tuskegee Institute for Negroes
has a post-office of its own and this new one is for the town. . . . To
make the Negro the theme of the decoration would be out of
place—not at all tactful, though the town and the Institute are on
excellent terms."[14]

In most college towns, in or out of the South, to feature the college in the mural or to have involved the college too much in the
competition would have been "not at all tactful," but Berea was
different. Ela distributed announcements of the competition, and
by September, 1939, all the entries were in—eleven of them. The
small stipend virtually guaranteed that few artists of repute would
submit designs. From the Section perspective, a limited field was
not good. Bruce, Rowan, and their colleagues counted on competitions to provide competent losers who would form a sort of talent
bank from which could be appointed artists for lesser commissions. George Biddle, one of the angels behind all the government
art projects, observed that the anonymous competition system had
"one great, outstanding, obvious merit, for which [Edward] Bruce
has the thanks of American artists. It continually holds open the
door for fresh talent and younger, unknown painters. It prohibits

14. Anne Goldthwaite to Rowan, June 29, 1936, in Tuskegee, Alabama, file,
RG 121, NA. The Tuskegee *News* from 1935 through 1940 reveals a marked change
in attitude toward the institute. Early numbers featured front-page stories on the
college, reported changes in faculty, theater productions, sports events, etc., and the
local high school received similar coverage. By late 1938 and 1939, one would be
hard put to know that there was an institution of higher education in Tuskegee,
though Carver continued to get occasional recognition.

one small group . . . from getting all the gravy. On the whole it is the best contribution of the Section."[15]

In any case, eleven designs were adequate to the needs of Berea, and since the town had its moderately successful resident artists, the number would ensure that at least one design would be worthy of the commission. The designs were displayed in the college gallery, and Bereans flocked to see them. Committee members were there to hear comments, and they provided notebooks in which visitors could write their responses.

By October 9, Mary Ela could announce the committee's selections. The unanimous first choice was entry 7. Not only had the artist submitted a design suitable for the community and demonstrated technical expertise; he had demonstrated his familiarity with the problems of mural design by making a scale model of the post office lobby that showed how the mural would work with the architecture. Most New Deal post offices had a vestibule—to protect postal workers and the mail from drafts—that jutted about five feet into the lobby at the center front. However practical, the vestibules seemed out of place and certainly interfered with the view of the traditional mural space over the postmaster's door at one end of the lobby. These glass and wood protrusions looked like architectural afterthoughts, unnecessary additions to a well-proportioned room. Frequently, when Section artists designed murals for those lobbies, they considered the vestibules appendages that, like the human appendix, were too ridiculous to be permanent and potentially subject to surgical removal. Thus, instead of taking this limitation into consideration, artists often painted traditional designs with large figures and a central focal point that, for proper appreciation, needed to be viewed from many feet across the lobby. Then, once the mural was installed, the artists would complain about the obstruction. The person who submitted entry 7, however, had designed around the vestibule. Mary Ela stated, in her report on the competition: "In relation to the area which it is to enrich, this composition with its small figures suffers less from the jutting vestibule and the lack of distance from which to view it than does a composition like #VIII (the sketch with the mountain backdrop, the small contrast houses and the very large foreground

15. George Biddle, *An American Artist's Story* (Boston, 1939), 276–77.

figures). The little model, which the author of the commencement scene submitted with this sketch, demonstrates vividly the problem of scale which is created by that jutting vestibule, and the lack of space and distance from which the mural can be viewed."[16]

After seeing all the entries, the Section concurred in the committee selection. That design was, of course, by Frank Long, who had already wanted to paint this mural for over three years. In January, 1936, he had written to the Section:

> According to an AP article labelled from Washington and appearing in the Louisville Courier-Journal sometime ago, I am to do a mural panel in the new post office to be built in Berea soon. I have an idea that this report was due to confusion arising over my doing the Louisville job here. I just wanted to say that such a project, however small, if it could be arranged would be most agreeable to me and that in order to place some of my work in this, my place of residence, I should be glad to do the job for any consideration whatsoever.[17]

Long was accustomed to greater stipends, but he was so eager to do this particular mural that he had gone out of his way to ensure that his entry in the Berea competition would be the best.

The unanimous choice in Berea probably resulted from the relatively low number of entries and from the fact that nine entrants had not painted a mural before. Such agreement between the Section and the committee was frequently not the case. When the stipend was larger, artists from a wider area submitted designs, and the Section was more particular about selecting a winner. A southern competition that demonstrates all the hazards of the system was held for the Jackson, Mississippi, Post Office and Court House.

The Jackson competition was fraught with unpredictable complications from the beginning. Shortly after the committee was formed, one member died suddenly. Then, just as entries were to be judged, its chair, Walter F. Henderson, also died. Undaunted, the Section and the remaining members formed a new committee with the widow of the original chair, Lucille Henderson, as its head. Then the real problems began.

The committee made its selection and submitted the results to

16. Mary Ela to Rowan, October 9, 1939, in Berea, Kentucky, file.
17. Long to the Section, quoted in Mr. Dows to Mr. Hopper, Memorandum, January 27, 1936, *ibid.*

the Section, which rejected the committee's first, second, and third choices and announced its intention to appoint the unanimous fourth choice, entry 21, to do the job. One can imagine that after all the unrecompensed work a committee put into announcing a competition, keeping track of the entries, conferring, and selecting, this decision would be difficult to take. The Jackson committee, which had also experienced other frustrations, was more than disturbed. After sending an irate telegram, committee chair Henderson expressed the committee's feeling in a letter:

> Upon receipt of your letter . . . , I called a meeting of my committee, to discuss your decision in regard to the mural. . . . You have, no doubt, received our telegram which was sent as a result of this meeting.
>
> The committee as a whole and I personally cannot understand why you so wholly disregarded our comments in regard to our choice in this matter. The design which you selected was put in as a fourth choice, and because I personally knew who did the work, and remembered our conversation when I was in Washington in regard to this particular artist. It is not liked here and we as a committee cannot accept your decision as it now stands.

Theoretically, the number 21 in question was by none other than Frank Long, but now the plot thickens. The committee and the Section were likely not looking at the same design. The committee said of entry 21 that "we all like it but feel that the subject depicting such violent strife and action is neither sufficiently restful nor appropriate for the place in the courtroom." And in her letter, Lucille Henderson reported seeing an almost identical design somewhere else when she was traveling around to look at murals. The design attributed to Long is indeed full of violence and strife, but it is not in fact his. Recalling his work for the Section and the many competitions he entered, Long writes:

> I never conceived an historical design for any of the competitions I entered, having a basic prejudice against such subject matter both in painting and in literature. My philosophical and aesthetic reasons are beside the point, which is simply that a mistake was made somewhere if such a design was attributed to me. . . . I cannot see the details of my conception [for the Jackson Post Office and Court House] but remember it made an effort to represent the federal judicial system. . . . The design was broken into arbitrary areas of different scale with a large, ghost-like figure of a judge brooding in the background over several smaller-scale

10 / Jackson, Miss., competition, entry 21, falsely attributed to Frank Long, 1937

scenes illustrating law enforcement and perhaps the beneficent effects of judicial decisions on various sections of the public.[18]

The design is raucous: Spanish explorers and Indians are locked in deadly combat, their swords and spears meeting just over the judge's bench (Figure 10). The figures are stylized and not very convincing. Charging horses and helmeted conquistadors are frozen in positions from which, were they live, they would collapse onto nonexistent turf. They rest, in part, on tiny men who move miniature cannon and raise minuscule crosses. Indians with chiseled faces charge in a cluster at the precariously mounted Spaniards. Some draw their bowstrings while standing on one foot, the other leg raised in a position that would challenge a prima ballerina. Below them are more tiny individuals, the grieving Indians who are noncombatants. The design is appropriate to the space, but otherwise it is not very much like the "realistic" pictures the Section usually favored. But one similar design was approved. The mural by Charles R. Hardman for the Miami Beach Post Office (Figure 11) features a raging battle between Spaniards and Indians. Overdeveloped horses rear, but this time in fright. The difference is that these legendary figures, however exaggerated their physiques, are believable human beings. They writhe; they suffer; they make war on one another. The costumes, subject, and composition are similar, but

18. Mrs. Walter F. Henderson to Rowan, October 7, 1935, in Jackson, Mississippi, file, RG 121, NA; Frank W. Long to the author, December 3, 1983.

11 / Charles R. Hardman, *Episodes from the History of Florida,* Miami Beach, 1941

the Indians in Miami stand on both feet and the conquistadors cling to rearing horses. It's a Renaissance painting, not a medieval one.

When letters of resignation began to arrive from Jackson committee members, Edward Rowan graciously asked their reconsideration. From Lucille Henderson's suggestions and his own ideas, Rowan hatched a plan for a "recompetition." Only the creators of the designs most favored by the committee and by the Section would be invited to enter. Five new designs were submitted, and the results were less than satisfactory. The Jackson committee dutifully chose one with which it was pleased and offered a second choice. But the Section response was that "the members of the Section have very carefully studied these over an extended period and in the opinion of this group there is not one design which is regarded as an adequate decoration for this important space. The competition will, therefore, be announced as terminated with no award offered."[19] In fact, the designs so disappointed the Section that it returned them to the committee without keeping the usual photographic record of them.

Three months later, Mrs. Henderson replied, "I was so overwhelmed by the decision of your department that I have not been able to acknowledge your letter. I know that I must gracefully accept the 'powers that be,' and since you have informed all of the contestants, there is no recourse to 'recapitulation,' as it were." She added that she and the other committee members would never-

19. Rowan to J. G. Chastain, Jr., October 9, 1935, Rowan to Mrs. Henderson, May 22, 1936, both in Jackson, Mississippi, file.

theless continue to work with the Section on whatever efforts might be made to fill the allotted space. Male members of the committee were not so conciliatory. Emmett J. Hull, who said he had Lucille Henderson's approval, angrily protested the decision against the committee's first choice in the recompetition, indicating that the artist thus rejected had been the Section's second choice in the original competition. And he had some important remarks on artist Walter I. Anderson's behalf—anonymity having long since been abandoned:

> [Anderson] is a Mississippi artist and I think, every thing being equal, a Mississippi artist should have preference. A point is involved here which I would like to stress. The southern states are apt to bemoan the fact that the young artists and others of exceptional talent and ability leave the South and locate in the large cities in the East, yet very little has been done to encourage the worthwhile people to remain in the South. They are prone to use local people for the lesser commissions and bring in the outsiders to do the worthwhile things—things which would mean the making of a reputation for an artist. . . . It is not right and we think it should be corrected just as rapidly as we produce creative artists equipped to do work of a recognized standard of excellence, which certainly applies to Mr. Anderson.[20]

Point well taken. Frank Long was not from Mississippi, but he was southern and his appointment might have encouraged southern artists. The appointment of Walter I. Anderson would have been even more encouraging to Mississippians, but his original design was criticized by the Section for being too stylized, for being more appropriate to textiles than a mural—criticism that might have been directed at the entry attributed to Frank Long. And the Section's explanation that the discrepancy in scale among the figures made the committee's second choice, by southerner Lumen Winter, unsuitable could certainly have been directed at entry 21 in the first competition. But the appointment in July, 1936, of Russian-born artist Simka Simkhovitch, a resident of Connecticut, did nothing to lead the people of Jackson or artists who might wish to remain and work in the South to believe that the Section was really looking for regional talent (Figure 63).

Nor did it convince Jackson that the government gave Missis-

20. Lucille N. Henderson to Rowan, June 13, 1936, Emmett J. Hull to Rowan, April 11, 1936, both *ibid.*

sippi's wishes much consideration in its gentle reconstruction of the South. Disappointed on his own behalf and on behalf of all those who were rejected after being asked to submit designs in the recompetition, Frank Long wrote that he agreed that none of those entries was strong and moving, but "I do consider the logical ones to create something that is are those who have already grappled with the problem." He reminded Rowan of a situation described in a recent Section *Bulletin*: "You speak of meeting with a group of competitors in Chicago, who had submitted sketches in several competitions for Illinois Post Offices, over which your fellow members of the Section were 'all but in despair.' You offered these artists suggestions which they accepted and presumably found valuable in recreating their first conceptions. Why cannot the same help be extended to us artists in the present situation?"[21]

Why indeed. It was a continuing problem that southern competitions attracted comparatively few entries. And the Section could not figure out why. Was it because there were few artists in the South? That's only one possibility. Another is that southern artists looked at the Jackson competition, an early one, and decided not to bother. Entering a competition was no mean task. A prospective entrant had to examine the space, preferably by visiting the building, but at least had to send for copies of the blueprints; he had to investigate the area for appropriate subject matter; he had to create a convincing design in reduced proportions; he had to supply not only the miniature of the large design but often full-scale studies of figures. Then, in the case of Jackson, the "winners" had to do it all again. And finally everything was thrown out in favor of a Russian-born artist from Connecticut. No wonder knowledgeable southern artists avoided competitions.

This fiasco happened so early in Section efforts to decorate the South that the Section might have learned something about dealing with local committees. It did not. But the Section did learn something about the malleability of Lucille Henderson. After her indignation at having her work so ungraciously superseded, she made good on her promise to support the Section's efforts. She even expressed apparently sincere delight at Simkhovitch's appointment, which was based on the Justice Department Competition in

21. Frank Long to Rowan, June 9, 1936, *ibid.*

Washington.[22] Thus, a year later, when it was time to appoint a jury to administer a competition for the Vicksburg, Mississippi, Post Office and Court House, Jacksonian Lucille Henderson was asked to be its chair. Vicksburg might give the Section some trouble over selecting a winning entry, but Mrs. Henderson would not.

The Vicksburg competition was announced to aspiring artists of Arkansas, Kentucky, Louisiana, Mississippi, and Tennessee. To the committee's credit, there were sixty-five entries, from which the jury dutifully selected and ranked five designs and submitted them to the Section—which, in turn, replaying the Jackson scenario, rejected the committee's first, second, and third choices and selected its fourth. Despite his reverence for the competition system, George Biddle did have something to say about its limitations:

> A competition rarely insures the choice of the best submitted entry. Why? Because the selection is made by a jury. The selection therefore is probably never the best. It may be very bad. Often the juries for political reasons are third-rate juries. The Section knows it and of course the artists know it. Second, even if the award of the jury were an intelligent one, it would only demonstrate that the artist selected was clever enough to win a competition. Rivera and Orozco could never win a competition because they have not the specific—and quite unessential—faculty of polishing up convincing sketches.[23]

Thus, a cartoonist with some talent might win a third-rate jury's endorsement and be judged by the Section as unable to decorate a wall. The Section said of Vicksburg's first choice that it was more cartoon than mural design. The runner-up was considered too affected, and the third choice was "in our [Section] estimation much better but not particularly comprehensive in subject matter or pertinent to Vicksburg." Not pertinent to Vicksburg is what the Section wrote from its Washington office as it appointed the committee's fourth choice. The design the Section thought appropriate to Vicksburg was by H. Amiard Oberteuffer from Memphis, quite a different Mississippi River city. And the committee members could tell the difference in their river cities. One committee member wrote: "There is no doubt that this design would make a very beautiful mural as it is, without any changes. [But the subject matter] in

22. Mrs. Henderson to Rowan, July 13, 1936, *ibid.*
23. Biddle, *An American Artist's Story,* 277.

my opinion is not Vicksburg. True it is symbolic but Vicksburg as represented in the background could never be recognized as such. It could be any river place but never Vicksburg."[24]

A river city is not a river city is not a river city. Mrs. Henderson was conciliatory as usual: "The mural will be altogether lovely just as sketched, I think, but the people of Vicksburg have some suggestions to make. . . . Of course, the fact that most of the scene would appear to be on the Louisiana side of the river does not please them." Understated but clear. Once that minor detail was taken care of, there was another matter: "Everyone who has seen the photo of the final production to be installed has commented on the excessive number of negroes in the picture, especially in the foreground. They are in the predominance. If it is not too late to change the color of some of those folk it would help a lot. After all, though there may be more of the negro race in our vicinity the whites *do* rule."

Lest we forget. If the ruling class is to spend $2,900 decorating a Mississippi courtroom, it should be amply represented. Mrs. Henderson goes on to assure Rowan that Mississippi, despite the low ranking given its education system, did have more colleges per capita white population than did any other state in the Union. "I have had the opportunity to investigate this and I am convinced that because there is more leisure down here among the white people (because the negroes do the hard work) to study and travel and read and cultivate their minds that there is more real culture and refinement than many people in the north are wont to believe. Just because they do not do things as rapidly these folk are not slovenly in their mental habits."[25]

The cause of this outburst is not quite clear, but Mrs. Henderson, like people throughout the South, was fearful that local artistic judgments were being devalued because of the general low opinion of the South. Certainly Judge Harris Dickson, whose courtroom would be the site of the mural, was sure that Washington bureaucrats had no respect for the Vicksburg committee. When Mrs. Henderson had tried to convince him that the nearly completed mural should be installed as soon as possible, he "left in a 'huff' at the

24. Rowan to Mrs. Henderson, June 14, 1938, Mrs. Leon S. Lippincott to Mrs. Henderson, June 17, 1938, both in Vicksburg, Mississippi, file, RG 121, NA.
25. Mrs. Henderson to Rowan, June 21, 1938, June 19, 1939, both *ibid.*

12 / H. Amiard Oberteuffer, *Vicksburg: Its Character and Industries,* Vicksburg, 1939

department saying that the local committee didn't amount to anything anyway in so far as the attention the 'powers that be' in Washington paid them."[26] And he may have been right. Oberteuffer did lighten some faces and move Vicksburg into Mississippi, but she never pleased local historians with her inaccurate rendition of the city skyline. However, the mural was put in place (Figure 12).

Although the Vicksburg competition drew many entries, many were incompetent, others were inappropriate, and still others showed ignorance of what the government would and would not pay for. The creator of Vicksburg entry 41, for example, entranced by the equal number of blacks and whites that had made Mississippi what it was in 1937, divided his canvas right down the middle. At the bottom lie two dead men, a Confederate soldier under the weight of his rifle and a black field worker under the weight of

26. Mrs. Henderson to Rowan, June 19, 1939, *ibid.*

his hoe. Planted on their graves is a field of cotton inhabited by a white in a lab coat who looks through a microscope at a boll and by a ragged black who is picking—both in the same bent position. And standing over them are a third white man and a third black one, their backs to us, offering globs of cotton to some god or other that cannot be seen.[27]

Another design for Vicksburg has an almost intelligible view of cotton-laden steamers landing on the right, but a stream of blacks trail cotton sacks on their road to Heaven. A third design, competent and well drafted, by an artist who did indeed later decorate southern post offices, features kinky-haired blacks having a hoe-down on the levee. No whites, no steamships, no representation of the ruling class.

Glaringly unsuitable designs did account for many of the rejected entries in southern competitions, but these were not chosen by the competition committees either. As Lucille Henderson observed, those people were not slovenly in their mental habits. It is possible, however, that southern competitions drew such a small proportion of suitable entries because competent and established artists did not find entering those competitions worth their time and effort.

Frank Long supported himself and his ailing mother with his art, and he continued to try. Long's entry in the Vicksburg competition, depicting early settlers arriving at Vicksburg when it was still a western settlement, did not place—perhaps because it was a little subject for a big wall; perhaps because Vicksburg was prouder of its lengthy heritage as a metropolitan river port than of its humble origins. Long could be proud, however, because his Berea protégé was among the five finalists. When, in the early 1930s, Long ran out of money to study in France and mural commissions in Chicago, where he had continued his studies at the Art Institute, he retreated to his family in Lexington, Kentucky. His father, an artist, was finishing wall decorations for a new movie theater. Long was helping with the painting when Bert Mullins, expert Berea cabinet-maker who had always dreamed of a career in art, applied to the elder Long, a well-known Kentucky portrait painter, for instruction.

27. Copies of Vicksburg competition entries can be found in the National Archives, Still Photos Division, Record Group 121, Entry 150. Within that entry, they are arranged alphabetically by city.

The father deferred to his son, who was less established and more talented, and so began a long and profitable association, but there were problems. The two found much in common and soon became friends as well as colleagues. When Long received a commission to paint a series of tall murals for the University of Kentucky library, he had difficulty finding a suitable studio in Lexington. Mullins, on the other hand, had to travel some sixty miles—no mean trip, with 1930s automobiles on 1930s highways—for his instruction. And then Mullins came up with the perfect solution—a loft with ten-foot ceilings and skylights over a bank on Main Street in Berea. Long moved bag, baggage, paint, and palette and began work.[28]

Mullins was an apt pupil. He learned enough in a short time to do some portraits and some church murals, the latter a mainstay of the southern muralists. Usually a variation on a River Jordan theme, these works decorated baptistries in Southern Baptist churches. Julien Binford and John McCrady, both southern regionalists, both successful Section painters, got through lean times painting such murals. Mullins was casting his lot with the best. During his apprenticeship, Mullins entered the Vicksburg competition, wherein he was second runner-up. As a result, he was appointed to paint murals for Morganfield and Campbellsville, Kentucky, where he was popular as much for his mild and self-deprecating manner as for anything he painted.

Southern communities did not much like arrogant artists, and neither did the Section. Frank Hartley Anderson of Birmingham is a case in point. From the time he and his wife Mary submitted their first joint entry in a southern mural competition (Jackson, 1935), he failed to show the submissiveness appropriate for a southern artist seeking government work. When Anderson received the form letter announcing that all entries had been rejected, he shot it right back with a handwritten note at the bottom: "Will you answer these questions—Was our entry sent to you in Washington? If not—how can you know whether to reject it or not?"[29] He received a polite and firm reply that left no question that the Section had rejected his sketch and all the others. But he kept trying.

Some time later, after several other unsuccessful competition de-

28. Frank W. Long to the author, October 24, 1983.
29. Rowan to Frank Hartley Anderson, January 16, 1936, in Jackson, Mississippi, file.

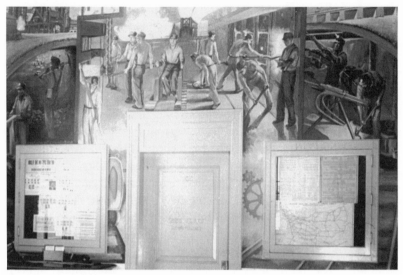

13 / Frank and Mary Anderson, *Spirit of Steel*, Fairfield, Ala., 1938

signs, he and Mary were commissioned on the basis of their entry in the Miami competition to paint a mural for the Fairfield, Alabama, Post Office. This they did, with great local success. Fairfield was a suburb of Birmingham, and the Andersons had the advantage of being local artists selected by a beneficent government to decorate a local building. The postmaster loved their mural of brawny steelworkers (Figure 13): "The way [the subject] was treated, and the wonderful color that was developed from this subject is a tribute to the good taste, and artistic talents, and abilities of the artists." The Birmingham *News-Age Herald* devoted a whole page of its rotogravure section to it. And the Birmingham *News* wrote several shorter articles about it, one of which states that many people, pleased with the addition to their post office, wished to know who had sponsored it.[30]

Rowan, however, did not like the mural or, one suspects, Frank Anderson. From the first letter he wrote accepting the commission and promising that he and Mary would get right to work, Anderson was presumptuous about his moderate success. He kept writing

30. Wm. H. Gandy, Postmaster, to Rowan, June 14, 1938, clippings from Birmingham *News-Age Herald*, June 19, 1938, Birmingham *News*, n.d. and June 27, 1938, all in Fairfield, Alabama, file, RG 121, NA.

letters in which he enclosed articles about his prowess as a southern printmaker and his status as officer of the obscure Southern Printmakers Union. In each epistle, he presented more reasons why he should receive more commissions: Surely his entries in the Jackson and San Antonio competitions were competent enough to merit another assignment; he must be the most qualified artist to decorate the wall in nearby Cornelia, Georgia, where he had grown up; if the Birmingham papers thought highly enough of the mural to devote whole pages of the rotogravure to it, it must be good enough to merit further opportunities; and, finally, how can artists support themselves on one mural at a time? With each letter requesting more commissions, Anderson gets a little more belligerent; with each reply, Rowan gets more determined: It is not Section practice to assign a second mural while one is in progress; the figures are not "convincingly realized"; the draftsmanship is not good. All along, we suspect that Rowan is bothered less by Anderson's draftsmanship than by his arrogant insistence. For the next three years, the Andersons continued to enter competitions—and to write letters. And then, finally, Anderson wrote to Rowan: "At any rate, with your reception of the Fairfield mural, I was through. There was absolutely no prospect in Birmingham, nothing to look forward to, so I turned the house (our total savings) over to H.O.L.C. and left Birmingham, for good."[31]

Admittedly, the Fairfield mural is not great art, but neither is it bad. The questionably drafted but wholly recognizable steelworkers perform their tasks believably. The piece is balanced, and though it assumes that viewers can see through the vestibule, it is appropriately designed for the architectural space. The picture is busy but not cluttered. The color, which to Anderson's disappointment Rowan never saw, ranges through bronzes, oranges, and browns, which harmonize with the post office decor and add dimension to the place. This mural is certainly not as ill conceived as was New York artist Harold Egan's design for Okolona, Mississippi, for instance. Nor was Frank Anderson any more arrogant than Egan was. But Egan got a second chance—in the South, at that.

Visitors to Okolona in 1939 (but not for long thereafter) could see a symbolic and somewhat abstract mural that purported to repre-

---

31. Frank Hartley Anderson (on Southern Printmakers stationery) to Rowan, March 10, 1941, *ibid.*

14 / Harold Egan, *The Richness of the Soil*, Okolona, Miss., 1938

sent the abundance of Mississippi soil (Figure 14). The central figure is an angular reclining woman draped across the postmaster's door. Her robes suggest a Greek goddess, and in one enormous arm, she holds a sheaf of unidentifiable flowers. Her hair, stylized to resemble the artificial wavelets of the river, drops beneath her arm and across her midriff. She dips her free hand in some kind of muck in the foreground. Behind her and shading her feet is what, according to its scale, could only be a bonsai tree, a balance to her head at the mural's other end. She is flanked by baskets of cotton at her feet and freestanding ears of corn around which peers a timid cow at her head. The river flows around her raised knee, behind the tree, and down into the post office lobby. This mural bears no relationship to Okolona and was very likely unintelligible to the residents. Rowan tried to convince Egan of its inappropriateness when he submitted his first design, but to no avail.

The original sketch, in which the woman indecorously exposed her navel and an embarrassing expanse of thigh, elicited Rowan's suggestion that Egan redesign along more realistic lines in order to please the people of Okolona (Figure 15). Egan, who had never set foot south of the Mason-Dixon Line and who researched his subject, if at all, in the encyclopedia, replied that he thought Rowan had underestimated the "good people of Mississippi." They might say they did not like "modern art" simply because they had not been exposed to it. Once they had seen Egan's design on their post office wall, he was convinced, all of Okolona would clamor for more modern art. Besides, Egan had another reason for wishing to

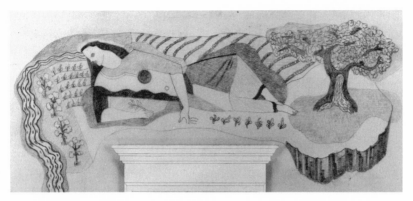

15 / Harold Egan, design for Okolona, Miss.

stick with his "modern" design: "It will convince some of my fellow painters that the Section of Fine Arts has recognized the fact that there is such a thing as modern art in America. . . . I cannot understand why uninteresting historical and documentary murals designed by these 'covered wagon' and 'storm over Kansas' painters are allowed to decorate Post Offices which are themselves definite statements of modern architecture."[32]

Rowan acquiesced. A town of two thousand inhabitants whose only attribute worth mentioning in the WPA guide to Mississippi was that the Yankees burned it twice, Okolona was not important enough for an extended argument with the artist. However, Egan would have to cover the navel and arrange the leg in a more decorous position. Actually, Egan probably need not have bothered. The original sketch is so "modern"—Cubist, really—that an untrained viewer looking at the circle in the center of the mural would not be certain whether he was seeing a navel, a misplaced breast, or a second unidentifiable circular form to echo the black blob where the woman's left breast should be. Egan condescended to make the required changes:

I notice that you have objections to certain parts of my mural, namely the position of the legs and the navel. I am sorry to hear that these objections are based on the idea that they might be offensive to the dignity of the State of Mississippi, rather than being offensive to the plastic con-

32. Harold Egan to Rowan, December 2, 1938, in Okolona, Mississippi, file, RG 121, NA.

tent of the design. However, subject matter has always been of little importance in my designs and since I have no desire to trespass on the sacred grounds of dignity, I shall remove the navel and put the legs in order. But please understand that, Okolona or no Okolona, there are certain limitations beyond which I cannot conscientiously go.[33]

After designing without consulting Okolona and redesigning to correspond to Section ideas of decorum, Egan made his first trip south to paint the mural directly on the wall. He reported that he was studiously ignored by the local folk. Just another irritation out of the North. The Yankees had failed to reconstruct Okolonans; Egan certainly would not. They would give neither Egan nor Washington the satisfaction of overt opposition to the inevitable. They had survived the Civil War, yellow-fever epidemics, and depression poverty. They would surely outlast the indignity on their post office wall.

Although Okolona's New Deal post office is still in service, no trace of the mural can be found. And almost no one remembers it. Postal workers who have served the area for twenty years or more are convinced that no such painting ever existed. But Tom Woodfin, assistant postmaster for forty-two years, said, "There is a mural there. Painted over it. Postmaster didn't like it." When was it painted over? Only a couple of years after it was installed. "But you could see the outline of it through the paint until about ten or fifteen years ago." And what was it like? "There was a cow in it—and some corn—and some cotton. There was a river." When the eighty-one-year-old gentleman was asked if the mural did not also feature a woman, he hesitated before confirming that it did.[34] Egan's symbolic figure was not the type of woman that one mentioned in front of ladies.

Despite his cold reception in Okolona in 1938, a considerably subdued Harold Egan was invited three years later to submit designs for Wake Forest, North Carolina. One suspects that Egan had spent some time in unrecorded conversation with Rowan in the intervening years: when he submitted his sketch, Rowan wrote, "I am sure that this will carry more meaning for the public for whom

33. Egan to Rowan, December 2, 1938, *ibid.*
34. Interviews with unidentified postal worker and Tom Woodfin, August 20, 1981.

16 / Harold Egan, *Richness of the Soil II*, Wake Forest, N.C., 1941

the mural is designed."[35] It probably did, but it is essentially the same mural. The title is the same—*Richness of the Soil II*. Here, however, two gigantic stylized farmers, sporting recognizable overalls and straw hats, have replaced the soil goddess (Figure 16). Her wavy hair has become the river symbol, a series of wavy lines across the center of the painting. The problems of scale remain, and there is some difficulty with the landscape. In the center background is another, more realistic waterway—the ocean, perhaps, with a liner steaming across it. But the ship apparently sails from a landlocked factory and straight toward a landlocked barn. One farmer carpets the ground with tobacco leaves, and full-blown magnolia blossoms grow directly out of the soil.

Egan himself was well pleased with this work and its reception. He reported that the postmaster and postal patrons were enthusiastic about his work. Perhaps he was right; perhaps he mistook traditional southern politeness for approval. When he had finished the mural, Egan chose to wait in Wake Forest until his work had been approved in Washington in case he needed to make emendations, and Section policy was not to issue final approval until the postmaster had written that the mural had been satisfactorily installed. After waiting for two months, Egan had not heard from the Section because the Section had not heard from the postmaster. Finally a Section worker wrote to vacationing Ed Rowan and enclosed a photograph supplied by Egan himself that proved beyond a doubt

35. Rowan to Egan, November 29, 1940, in Wake Forest, North Carolina, file, RG 121, NA.

that the work was finished, including the information that "he is waiting in North Carolina for your approval. . . . [I] thought it would not be well to let him just wait, and wait, and wait. If the work is approved will you wire him that he may now leave and go home?" No final approval of the mural got into Section files, and the only communication the Section ever received from Wake Forest is from one disgruntled citizen who "has yet to find anyone who admires [the mural], in my opinion it is terrible."[36]

That is not to say that Yankee artists were doomed to failure in small southern towns. When an artist took his commission and the community seriously, when he set out to reconstruct neither the South nor the Section, and when he could afford to travel to the town and stay long enough to get to know the people and something of the community before he painted his mural, his chances were excellent. Aldis B. Browne made the trip from Connecticut to Oneonta, Alabama, under strenuous and vociferous protest. Couldn't he, he wanted to know, have a commission in an area with which he was familiar? As a New Yorker, how was he to deal with a rural setting—much less southerners? But, rather than lose the opportunity to paint for the Section altogether, he accepted the commission and went to work on a design. He "blocked in" the farm and drew wooden people; he would wait until he got to Alabama to fill in realistic details. Then he moved to Oneonta, where he set up a most gratifying working relationship with postmaster William Wilson and the Oneonta people that would have been the envy of many a Section artist all over the country.

Despite his initial reluctance, Browne did not, like Egan, go to the South merely to show the ignorant folk what real art was like. He went to get to know those folk. And he made quite a hit. Not only was he asked to speak at local civic functions; he was hired to paint a baptistry mural as well. By the time he prepared the post office wall for the mural, he could report that he was "really nuts about Oneonta, and . . . glad to be able to say the people of the town and the farmers of the surrounding countryside almost without exception seem to very much like the up and coming mural though they understand it not." In fact, he had such a good relationship

36. Egan to Rowan, n.d. [mid-1941], two requests for approval so that he can go home; Hazel to Edward Rowan, n.d. [mid-1941], [?] to Honorable W. E. Reynolds [relayed to Rowan], March 11, 1942, all *ibid.*

with local citizens that he felt free to paint a joke directly on the wall: "I have a large audience most of the day. . . . The subject of greatest debate, Blount County being bone dry, is whether or not it is corn whiskey in the jug I have drawn on the wall." His audience seems to have been constant. One can guess that the show in the post office broke up otherwise fairly monotonous day-to-day activities. And they were especially fortunate to have an artist willing to stop his work to answer their "millions of questions" and to listen to their criticism. His only problem seems to have been in finding models for his figures. Most of the people, he reported, found that form of picking up extra cash "almost immoral."[37]

Browne overcame the objections to modeling, and he painted a mural scene sure to warm a rural southern heart. His chose a farming montage for his foreground theme, but he included recognizable local landmarks—a traditional covered bridge, for instance, and the Baptist and Methodist churches as well as the new post office—in the background to represent the town and to close off the horizon to unwelcome ousiders. He drew a typical farmhouse instead of taking the suggestions of the local elite: "The house represents, as nearly as I could make it a mean between the best and the worst. It could have been shown as a great deal sorrier looking and been most truthful or it could, as the local Civitan Club . . . wished, [have been] a model of the best taste as Oneonta sees it. However that I did not do and everyone still seems entirely satisfied." Browne could not, however, resist including a bit of didacticism, but even that endeared him to the local power structure. In the mural he contrasts an uneroded, terraced field with a neglected field, "as most are, cut and worn by water." The local extension agents were so pleased that, even before the mural was completed, they brought certain guilty local farmers to the post office to show them "what a little time and scientific effort can accomplish."[38] The mural focuses on a group of black and white men and women involved in a prosperous farming venture with cotton, livestock, and chickens. The whites work less strenuously than the blacks do, but everybody is productive, and everybody is comfortably well off.

37. Aldis Browne to Cecil Jones, Chief, Section of Fine Arts, January 29, 1939, in Oneonta, Alabama, file, RG 121, NA.
38. Browne to Jones, February 1, 1939, Browne to Rowan, March 15, 1939, both *ibid.*

The picture was one the locals would probably have liked even if they had not known and grown to love the artist. But their relationship with Browne made their mural that much more precious. Browne reported that the people had taken a great interest in the whole process and "generally I believe most here rather like the mural and all of them, excepting for a crank or two are pleased that the Section has sent a painter to *their* Post Office." The finer praise, however, came from Postmaster William W. Wilson, who wrote the Section a lengthy, positive critique of the mural and then said: "May I at this time say to you that Mr. Browne is certainly a gentleman in the fullest extent. He has made scores of friends here in Oneonta. . . . His work and his personality is a credit to your Section and so long as we have men of his character in our service we will have the whole hearted approval of the public."[39]

One wonders why Aldis Browne was not appointed to do other southern murals "on the basis of competent work done for the Section," as were many far less successful Section artists. Instead, like Egan, he had difficulty getting paid. He had moved to Oneonta to paint the mural and he had stayed to become a friend of the people, but he never intended to become a permanent resident. He supported himself with church jobs while he was there, but he needed his mural money to move back home. He would probably have loved to leave in a blaze of glory just after successfully completing the job. Instead, he was still living on Oneonta credit and trying to plow through Section bureaucracy in order to get his *first payment* weeks later.[40] Finally, two and one-half months after the mural was finished, he received that first payment, paid his Oneonta debts, and slunk out of town. So far as the records show, he was never again asked to paint in the South—even as a reward for his patience.

Mild-mannered Bert Mullins was just what the Section needed, and he seems to have been better appreciated. After two years' study with Frank Long, he entered the Petersburg, Virginia, competition and was judged qualified to decorate a small-town Kentucky post office. Assigned to Campbellsville, he considered the thematic suggestions offered by the postmaster—the Confederate monument, the Revolutionary War Battle of Green River Hill, a

---

39. Browne to Rowan, March 15, 1939, William W. Wilson, Postmaster, to Rowan, March 31, 1939, both *ibid.*
40. Browne to Rowan, April 13, 1939, *ibid.*

brick dwelling once occupied by General John Hunt Morgan—and rejected them all in favor of a topic such as his mentor would have chosen. He painted a scene of Kentucky farming, with some industry in the background. All the while, the people of Campbellsville, grateful to be important enough to merit a mural, wistfully complained that they really wanted a historical subject. But when Mullins came to install his mural, the postmaster and the townsfolk were so impressed with his manners and self-deprecation that they waxed enthusiastic over the mural they got. The local paper was especially impressed, calling the mural "extraordinary" and allowing as how "it is very unusual to find a mural painting of this quality on the walls of a post office in a town no larger than Campbellsville and the people of this city . . . are proud that they have been thusly honored." They still wanted a historical painting, however. And Mullins himself wrote the Section: "I have enjoyed this work with the Section of Painting and Sculpture. I am very grateful to you for your kind advice and criticisms, they have taught me much."[41]

Only an artist new to the profession could have been so perfectly behaved and so grateful for Section interference in his conception, and only a town unaware of its own potential power could have been so grateful for what they did not want. And the Section rewarded them. Mullins was appointed to paint a second mural for the other end of the lobby, this time with a historical theme. Mullins, like Long, might have been a help farther south, but, despite his good showing in the Vicksburg competition, the only other murals he was asked to do were in Kentucky.

In the meantime, Long and Berea continued their happy arrangement. After exhibition of the competition entries at the college the committee selected Long's design of the mythic commencement exercises. It was not the local favorite, but it was one they liked, and when they learned it was by a local artist, they were satisfied. Long had, after all, chosen Berea as his base of operations. He had, as a matter of fact, intended to join other up-and-coming artists in New York. It was "the rigors of the depression and the salvaging program of the government that reoriented my thinking," he re-

41. "Mural Painting on Wall of Post Office Here Is Extraordinary," Campbellsville *News-Journal*, August 18, 1938, clipping, Bert Mullins to Rowan, August 6, 1938, both in Campbellsville, Kentucky, file, RG 121, NA.

17 / Frank Long, cartoon for Berea, Ky., 1940

ports. He agreed with the Section desire to promote "regionalism" in the arts and abhorred the cultural erosion of large areas of the country occasioned by the migration of artists to New York. And he enjoyed his status as a prominent Kentucky artist and as Berea's own son. Regarding his experience at Berea and echoing the Section observer who inspected the South in 1939, he wrote: "It would, of course, have been desirable if in every instance an artist who was a member of the community could have been selected to do the work."[42] And he took full advantage of the ideal situation when he had it.

One weekend, Long invited Bereans to an open house to view the full-scale cartoon (Figure 17). He reports that many came and offered comments that were "encouraging and sometimes helpful." Mary Ela, committee chair and sponsor of the project, describes the event:

> I wish that you could have looked into Frank Long's studio last week end, and have seen the citizens of Berea viewing the cartoon for the Post Office mural. He invited them in on Saturday and Sunday, and they came in such crowds that it was as much as one's life was worth to see the crowds at "old time commencement" without a pretty emphatic foreground of contemporary Bereans. Mr. Long was generous in his explanation of procedures, and patient in his reception of criticisms. One of the most amusing and profitable of the criticisms was that there are not enough babies in the cartoon to really re-capture the festival of other days. Mr. Long is reported to have said that that can be easily reme-

42. Frank Long to the author, November, 1984, October 24, 1983.

died, and I do think that we need to demand a contract for a certain number . . . of babies.

Actually, it seems that Long added no babies. The design of the final rendering is virtually the same as the cartoon submitted to the Section for criticism—but it is, at least, replete with ambulatory children. Long felt that his duty was to listen to Section criticisms of his designs rather than to local response to content, and the Section was satisfied with older children—babies would add nothing to the design. As a matter of fact, Berea was the only community he consulted at all, and Bereans were satisfied to have been listened to. The figures in the cartoon were, in Rowan's words, "wooden," and the trees appeared more like architectural features—straight, stiff, and arbitrary—than natural parts of a landscape. That is because, in his cartoons, Long paid more attention to design and less to representation. He may have been voicing a common problem of mural painters forced to account for every step of their composition process when he said, "I find that I lose a great deal of spontaneity and looseness of execution by a repetition of draftsmanship."[43]

What the people of Berea saw when they visited Long's studio and when they visited the post office in later years was a montage of festive people celebrating a community tradition. For his design, Long used a rectangular arrangement of five interlocking triangles, three set squarely on the bottom of the mural space so that the vignettes therein would be in the foreground, and the other two inverted so as to spread into the middle distance. Thus a viewer can stand close to the painting, at any point across the right end of the lobby, and see a complete vignette within the larger design that is very difficult to view because of the omnipresent vestibule. People, horses, dogs, buggies, and refreshment stands fill the foreground and the middle ground, and in the completed mural, true to southern tradition, they are protected from a mysterious and ominous horizon by a row of red-brick college buildings. What delights viewers, however, is not the design—that is obscured in the finished mural—but the vignettes themselves.

People in the mural engage in all the activities traditionally a part of commencement in the old days. At the far right, a young

43. Mary Ela to Rowan, February 19, 1940, Long to Rowan, April 29, 1940, both in Berea, Kentucky, file.

swain (according to Long, a portrait of folksong collector John Jacob Niles) plays the dulcimer for his lady fair. Behind him two old friends greet each other, and farther back, a group of horse traders try to calm a frightened horse while they examine its teeth. At the far left, a young woman brings lemonade to a seated man who is barefoot and holding his shoes. He is either too footsore from dancing the night before or, in true Kentucky mountain tradition, too unaccustomed to wearing shoes to keep them on for long. At the woman's feet is a full picnic basket, which the young man has undoubtedly bid on and bought at auction. An unnoticed redbone hound sniffs at the feast. A matronly woman feeds her willing husband candy, and children suck peppermint sticks, stare at the activities around them, and make halting overtures to each other in every spare piece of canvas. An ox-drawn wagonload of new arrivals, seated in commandeered dining room chairs, plows through the crowd to find a place to park. A wood lemonade stand does a thriving business, people picnic, politicians speak, women scold their men, and one fancies that a few moonshiners can be seen in the corners selling their wares. The picture has never ceased to entertain Bereans and visitors to the city, and in a frame on the wall hangs the original newspaper account of the government's largesse to Berea.

Unfortunately, though he continued to be in demand as a Section artist, Frank Long was never again as successful with his mural designs as he was in Berea. Even when he painted the mural in his adopted town, he was beginning to suffer from a sort of mural "burnout." He had never considered himself a mural painter; he preferred easel painting. Even so, the first few murals he did were a challenge and thus a delight. After doing a series of murals for the Louisville Post Office and Court House, two panels for the University of Kentucky library, and numerous murals for private concerns, though, he was beginning to tire of the restrictions of the mural form. When Rowan wrote in response to the Berea cartoon that he was pleased with the design but saw elements in sketches for the Louisville project that were superior to any of Long's later work, Long responded:

I must sadly admit that in some respects, at least, my more recent mural designs lack a vitality I feel in some of the older ones. This is a rather devastating conclusion at which to arrive. Whatever the reason for it, in spite of any extenuation, the fault lies somewhere within myself. . . . I am afraid that some of the diminution of intensity has been caused by my capitulation to circumstances in the form of an increased financial urgency. . . . I am sure I have entered several competitions during the later period which would not have interested me in the least before. . . . Under these circumstances my enthusiasm was forced and lacked conviction.

Even though he did not win another competition, he was good enough or pleasing enough to the Section to continue to receive consolation-prize commissions even when his heart was not in his design. Nearly fifty years later, Long is able to analyze his malaise and to shed light on the problems of other repeatedly commissioned Section artists:

I never considered myself primarily a mural painter, although I spent a good (or bad) ten years at it. I was far more interested in easel painting in which there is complete freedom to create the artist's interpretations of his visual-emotional world. Although there were hardly any conditions or restrictions imposed by the Section of Fine Arts, those inherent in the art form itself were never really congenial with my particular talents. . . . Very accurate and fully developed sketches showing the artist's exact intentions must normally be presented for approval by any prospective patron. When approved, they must be followed exactly in the finished work, for which a "cartoon" to exact size must be prepared to transfer the outlines of the design to the wall or canvas.

All these indirect procedures tend to become a dulling process to the spontaneity and enthusiasm of many artists. . . . I found this very restraining in mural work, no matter who the patron might be. There is also the requirement that the painting must harmonize with the interior as well as the use of the building; as well as with the community and its setting; as well as with the preconceived ideas of those who officially judge the work. My dissatisfaction with these conditions is evidenced by the fact that my first murals were my best and that artistic quality steadily diminished from that point.

My having continued for so long with something that did not command my fullest artistic interest is due, I'm afraid, to sheer economic necessity. . . . When I entered the army, I actually felt relieved at the break with what was becoming an irksome career. . . . I feel sure that many others who participated in this program felt as I did about the situation.[44]

44. Long to Rowan, April 29, 1940, *ibid.*; Long to the author, October 24, 1983.

Something of the same problem must have confronted Nikolai Cikovsky when he painted a very unpopular mural sequence for the post office in the Baltimore suburb of Towson, Maryland. In 1937, Cikovsky had done a successful mural, based on specific local history, for nearby Silver Springs. By 1939, when he contracted to do the murals for Towson, he had done several other murals and was widely recognized as an easel painter. But recognition does not always mean wealth, and he probably needed the $1,400 the Section offered him. Cikovsky certainly did not evince much interest in the Towson work. He painted a facile and derivative sequence on the history of transportation, which had nothing to do with Towson. When the Section suggested he redesign on more original lines, Cikovsky refused. His interest was directed elsewhere: shortly after the Towson job was finished, he was selected by *Life* and the Cranbrook Art Academy as one of the sixty leading American artists.[45] The Towson residents, however, were not interested in that. As Lucille Henderson could have predicted, they were well versed in art, and they were outraged at the insult done them. Had the Section chosen a more local, less competent, and less experienced artist who would have taken the Towson mural seriously, the lengthy conflict between Washington and Towson could perhaps have been avoided—and the Towson Post Office would have had a better mural.

The general population might wish that most murals could have been conceived, executed, and completed in the ambience that Frank Long had in Berea. It is not at all clear, however, that the Section encouraged that sort of situation. For all Rowan's protests that he wanted Harold Egan to design for Okolona, that he was endorsing the selected design most appropriate to Vicksburg, that he wished to encourage regional artists to paint what they knew, the evidence suggests that artists in the South were not encouraged as they might have been and that the Section all too often ignored the actual preferences of southerners. Too frequently, it seems, a Yankee artist was chosen because he was more convenient or because the Section held out for an excellent painter when a good artist would

45. Rowan to Ernest Green, Postmaster, February 24, 1940, in Towson, Maryland, file, RG 121, NA. In Towson, the once-hated mural sequence is highly prized as a historic artifact (visit to Towson Post Office, June 10, 1984). In *Wall-to-Wall America* (Minneapolis, 1982), 148–55, Karal Ann Marling extensively examines the Towson controversy before, during, and after the mural was installed.

have better fulfilled the commission. That it was difficult to find regional artists to paint murals in the South cannot be denied, but the Section was too ready to take the easy or the familiar way out.

By the early 1940s, when the Section was going out of business, the South had produced a respectable amount of recognized talent. Julien Binford in Virginia, Lamar Dodd in Georgia, Marie Hull in Mississippi, H. Amiard Oberteuffer and her equally talented husband in Memphis, Hobson Pittman (who left North Carolina in search of a career but continued to paint the South), and Charles Shannon in Alabama are but a few. And they kept coming. But by then, it was too late. A war was coming, Edward Bruce was dying, and few in Washington were interested in an American mural movement. Scores of Section artists joined Frank Long in the camouflage division of the army if they could qualify, in the infantry if they could not. The nascence was over, southern art was born, and it was now up to southerners to see that America continued to have an art in the South.

III / TOBACCO ROAD: CULTIVATION, CONDESCENSION, AND CONTOUR PLOWING

The *Progressive Farmer* was, as it labeled itself, "the South's lead-ing farm and home magazine." Read by practically every southern farmer who could afford a subscription, it brought messages of hope and prosperity for the agricultural South. It was the farmers' wishbook carrying ads for tractors, refrigerators, and fertilizers that would both replenish southern soils and increase yields. Its articles endorsed diversified farming, crop rotation, contour plowing, judi-cious fertilization, and "two-armed farming"—all practices de-signed to rescue southern soil ravaged by exclusive tobacco and cotton farming and to save the southern farmer from himself. "Two-armed farming," the special 1939 promotion, was the prac-tice of investing in, in addition to soil crops, a livestock profit ven-ture. Thus, if soil crops failed in a given year, the two-armed farmer would have another source of revenue, and the land devoted to grazing could recover in the meantime.[1]

Farming was a family enterprise, and the magazine, published in four editions, one for each of four southern subregions, was a fam-ily institution. Each issue included three sections: "Farm and Gen-eral Features," "Home Department," and "Young Southerners." Al-though the family was carefully delineated into subgroups, no one was left out. According to *Progressive Farmer* editorial policy, southern farmers were a modern, progressive, self-sufficient lot en-tirely capable of caring for their own interests. And though the magazine assumed most of its readers to be landowners, it did not forget the tenants who, the magazine assumed with characteristic optimism, would soon become landowners anyway. "Anywhere in the South today / worthy tenants are helped by the FSA" was the gleeful refrain to an article about proffered Farm Security Admin-

---

1. Clarence Poe, "A Sound Platform for Two-Armed Farming in the Southeast," *Progressive Farmer* (September, 1939), 50. Although the question of raising live-stock for profit in the South is considered in articles in each 1939 issue, this article by the president of the Progressive Farmer-Ruralist Company is the most indicative of the magazine's editorial viewpoint and of the promotion.

istration aid for tenants to buy their own land—as long as they were worthy—"with the share of the crop they have been paying as rent." A month later, the magazine reported that response to the article "proved that our tenant farmers in our territory are just about as eager for progress as landowning farmers."[2] The *Progressive Farmer* was not, like so many southern publications, defensive. It just assumed southern farmers to be capable and southern farming to be salvageable—a note of confidence in a land of doubt.

Unfortunately, southern ruralists did not often find such encouragement, and when the *Progressive Farmer* let them down even subtly, they had subtle ways of showing their disapproval. Among the blessings the magazine offered southern farmers was the full-color picture on the cover. Often these illustrations were made especially for the *Progressive Farmer*, but occasionally a classic painting, such as Eastman Johnson's *The Young Lincoln* (a very popular cover), was reproduced. A very unpopular cover was *Fall Plowing* in September, 1939. To keep in touch with its readers, the journal frequently surveyed its readers about articles, about policy, and about the cover pictures. According to one poll conducted at the 1939 North Carolina State Fair in November, the least-liked cover picture in the last twelve months was *Fall Plowing*.[3] The magazine did not address possible reasons that certain covers were loved or rejected, but the similarity of *Fall Plowing* to the mural design proposed for Conyers, Georgia, offers some clues.

The September, 1939, cover features a farmer taking a break from his fall plowing. He stands in the left foreground lustily swilling something—probably iced tea, since he's southern—from a thermos. His two healthy, grinning sons wait with their collie in the lower right corner. His horses and the plow wait on the plowed earth, the rows running across the rise on which they stand. In back of this group, the land stretches to a waterway of some sort. And beyond that body of water are rolling hills alternately wooded and cultivated. Every field has been plowed straight, sometimes, it seems, directly uphill. Still farther in the background the hills merge into gently sloping aqua mountains that in turn merge with the paler aqua horizon. Like the *Progressive Farmer* cover, artist

2. "Anywhere in the South Today Worthy Tenants Helped by the FSA," *Progressive Farmer* (May, 1939), 12; "Anywhere in the South Today Worthy Tenants Helped by the FSA," *ibid.* (June 1939), 3.

3. "Our Most Popular Covers," *Progressive Farmer* (December, 1939), 48.

18 / Elizabeth Terrell, design for Conyers, Ga.

Elizabeth Terrell's proposed design for Conyers, Georgia, featured a farmer doing his fall plowing (Figure 18), with horses straight across the contour of the land. In the cover illustration and in the Conyers design, the land extends unchecked to the horizon, and in both, dogs are unusual breeds on southern farms.

In 1939, Conyers residents were delighted to learn that a federal mural was to be placed in their town, and Postmaster Hal Austin hastened to write the Treasury Department of his delight.[4] That was before they saw the publicity photo of the proposed mural. When residents saw the design for Terrell's *The Ploughman*, which had actually been submitted for the Seneca, Kansas, competition, they were outraged. One Sally Fanny Gleaton wrote the postmaster general and her congressman exactly what was wrong with the picture:

> I am writing at once to you and to Mr. Ramspeck, my Congressman, to protest. First of all I resent untrue history rammed down the throats of children and unsuspecting adults. And secondly the spending of public moneys (taxpayers money) in the depicting of untruths.
>
> I doubt if there is a pair of percherons being plowed in Georgia outside our Agricultural College. And I know there are none nor have there ever been any in the Fifth District. Another thing of which we are rather proud in this section as Mr. Ramspeck should know, is our having origi-

4. Hal D. Austin to Treasury Department, June 26, 1939, in Conyers, Georgia, file, Record Group 121, Entry 133, "Case Files Concerning Embellishments of Federal Buildings," National Archives. Information on present-day Conyers was supplied by local booster Glenn Hodges, who took nearly a day from work at his hardware store in August, 1981, to show me historic Conyers.

nated the idea of terracing of fields with the contour of the land. This print of the mural has a big pair of percherons being plowed straight up hill with all furrows running up and down hill. I am sure a one mule plow running with a terrace would more truly show history as is and has been in these parts for generations.

Will you please see that this untrue mural is swapped with some other Post Office where it might be applicable.[5]

Sally Gleaton knew that this design had not been meant for Conyers, or she at least suspected that the Section assigned a mural drawn for one place to an altogether different location. And she wanted this one placed where it would be more appropriate. Even so, her feelings were salved when Ed Rowan wrote her that Terrell had been selected on the "fine quality of her painting" and was being asked to "redesign completely, using subject matter appropriate to the locale." As a result, Gleaton began to provide the artist with examples of "true history." Actually, Terrell never received a request to "redesign completely." She was under the impression that her design had won and that her design would be used in Conyers. When Terrell began to receive "tons" of photographs and penny postcards from Gleaton, she wrote an anguished letter to Rowan in which, apparently unaware of his promise that she would redesign, she stated,

I have tried to make Miss Gleaton feel that she is an active participant in this work with me, but now I am worried that Miss Gleaton may take this idea much too seriously. I am handling her as tactfully as I can and also am accepting a number of suggestions from her. The suggestions are the inclusion of Stone Mountain which is apparently a landmark in that part of the country, mules instead of horses drawing the plough, and a suggestion of contour plowing. Aside from these additions is it all right for me to proceed with my sketch as I had originally planned?

Who is Sally Fanny Gleaton? Does your office know whether she has any authority in the Conyers Post Office? And may I ask whether the Post Master's approval is essential?[6]

5. Sally Fanny Gleaton to Hon. James Farley, October 23, 1939, in Conyers, Georgia, file. Gleaton's allusion to "history" in the present is not unusual in Section annals. See Karal Ann Marling, *Wall-to-Wall America* (Minneapolis, 1982), 95ff., for the Section interpretation of "present history."

6. Edward Rowan to Sally Gleaton, November 9, 1939, Elizabeth Terrell to Rowan, January 22, 1940, both in Conyers, Georgia, file.

Rowan replied that he had "carefully studied" her letter, and "it is the feeling of this office that if you can include . . . some section of Stone Mountain and mules instead of horses . . . , you will have met the local requirements." In addition, Rowan professed to know no more of Sally Gleaton than Terrell did and stressed that the postmaster had "no authority in relation to the aesthetics of a design." He did reiterate that the postmaster was a good source of information regarding theme because "we find that in decorating Post Offices for the public that the public is more receptive of the art if the subject matter is regarded as appropriate to the place."[7] Of course, Conyers' objections to the design were on the basis of theme and not on aesthetics—and rightly so. The subject matter was appropriate to Seneca, Kansas, not to Conyers, Georgia.

Gleaton did articulate what Conyers would find objectionable in Terrell's design. What Conyers residents saw in the publicity photograph was not unlike what North Carolina farmers saw on the cover of the September, 1939, *Progressive Farmer*—a single farmer plowing, not with progressive tractors or with the more traditional mules but with horses. Whether or not Gleaton's impassioned plea that Georgia farmers did not plow with percherons sprang from awareness of the symbolic association of percherons with Marxism, she did know her southern draft animals. Horses were used only at the state agricultural college, where experimental farming was standard. Both the cover farmer and Terrell's appeared to be plowing across the contour of the landscape rather than terracing their fields in harmony with it. And neither design offered adequate protection from the unknown and the perilous horizon. In *Fall Plowing*, the mountain slopes are gentle, passes clearly visible, and they actually merge with, lead to, the horizon. In the original design for *The Ploughman*, nothing separates the vulnerable farmer from the great beyond. The field just stretches to infinity.

To echo Elizabeth Terrell, who is Sally Fanny Gleaton, anyway? She may have been a local schoolteacher. She may have been one of those self-proclaimed local historians who abounded in the South during the 1930s. Or she may have been an avid reader of the *Progressive Farmer*. Nobody knows for sure, and few people care. The mural project in Conyers certainly led to no heated controversy. A few strokes of Terrell's paintbrush calmed their heat, but Sally

7. Rowan to Terrell, January 27, 1940, *ibid.*

Fanny Gleaton is important. Her plea for "accurate history" reflects the feelings of people who owed their livelihoods to agriculture throughout the South, and her desire for a landscape that looked like home to Georgians, like the South to southerners, was felt throughout the region. The South had had enough of "untrue history."

The people of Conyers narrowly missed losing their mural or at least having to hide it. When the new post office was built a few years ago and the old one converted into the Soil Conservation Agency, Conyers citizens wanted to continue displaying their memorial to early soil conservation. Sally Gleaton had been justifiably proud of stories that the idea of terracing the soil had developed in the Conyers vicinity, and Conyers people were justifiably eager that others should know those legends. So the mural was moved to the town's century-old jail, now a community museum. It was one of those jails such as William Faulkner describes in *Intruder in the Dust* and *Requiem for a Nun*: the jailer lived on the first floor and the cells were on the second. Despite twelve-inch-thick exterior walls and a structure capable of supporting the iron cells above, the interior walls, the only suitable place for a five-by-twelve-foot framed canvas, could not support the mural. Fortunately, the realization that the mural would have to be moved a second time came just as the town fathers, eager to preserve anything of potential historic interest in Conyers, devised a plan to make a community center out of the defunct railroad station. And so the mural was placed in the lobby of the railroad station cum theater and reception hall just over the ticket window and behind a ceiling fan. The view is no more obstructed than it was by the vestibule in the original location.

Despite their conviction that the mural was a WPA project, as a plaque in the railroad station lobby proclaims, Conyers residents today are proud of their mural (Figure 19). The mural depicts a ploughman, in straw hat, red plaid shirt with rolled-up sleeves and carefully authenticated suspenders, plowing with two mules in what appears to be an overgrown hayfield. Between the farmer and the viewer in the right foreground, apparently sniffing at a rabbit hole, is the farmer's beagle. Although the breed was usually owned by fox-hunting aristocrats, it is no stranger than the collie in the *Progressive Farmer* picture, a dog more likely to be seen on thoroughbred horse farms. In true southern mural style, the back-

19 / Elizabeth Terrell, *The Ploughman*, Conyers, Ga., 1940

ground is circumscribed by buildings, timber, and what appears to be a huge rock. To the left is a barn flanked by a rail fence and one of stone. To the right a dirt road leads to two unpainted farmhouses. Near the center, all access and egress are blocked by the rock, actually the suggestion of a famed Georgia landmark. The largest granite formation on the North American continent, Stone Mountain has been the site of many a historic event, from Indian palavers to Ku Klux Klan conclaves (only when "fissures in public morality have allowed this disorder in the body civil"), and in 1939 it had narrowly missed being the site for Georgia's answer to Mount Rushmore.[8]

Gutzon Borglum of Mount Rushmore fame had attempted a colossal Confederate monument on the face of Stone Mountain during the 1920s, but funding problems caused him to abandon the plan.[9] A crumbling but still impressive tourist stop was what the memorial remained when Terrell represented it as a rock in 1940. Terrell had met southerners' expectations that idyllic scenes be protected by man-made and natural barriers; she had included local landmarks; and perhaps she had suggested contour plowing. But in front of the circumscribed background, the mural looks hauntingly like several that Joe Jones did for Kansas and Missouri.

8. Federal Writers Project, *Georgia: A Guide to Its Towns and Countryside* (1939; rev. ed., Atlanta, 1952), 307.

9. A complete, if somewhat biased, narrative of the Stone Mountain story can be pieced together from Federal Writers Project, *Georgia*, 306–10; and Robert J. Casey and Mary Borglum, *Give the Man Room: The Story of Gutzon Borglum* (Indianapolis, 1952), 171–213. The monument has been "finished" by other stonecutters and is an important tourist attraction.

Conyers people today swear that the rock is an exact representation of Stone Mountain, that the barn is typical, and that the plowing is an accurate rendering of the way it was done in Georgia fifty years ago. Although the typical barn in the Conyers area is of quite a different style, a dilapidated barn or two similar to the one in the mural can be found, but the suggestion of contour plowing is in the eye of the beholder. Gleaton's impression that the original farmer was plowing straight uphill had been due more to problems with perspective than to anything that was actually in the picture; he had been plowing straight across a Kansas plain, but he appeared to be plowing straight up the picture's plane rather than straight west. Likewise, contour plowing in the finished picture arises more from optimistic Conyers viewers than from anything the artist put into it. But by November, Postmaster Hal Austin could report the successful installation of the mural and local satisfaction with it.

One suspects, however, that Sally Gleaton's outrage probably had more to do with the image of the South in contemporary popular culture than with specific questions of what type of draft animal drew plows in Georgia. As the voice of the beleaguered southern farmer, she, like those who voted on their favorite 1939 *Progressive Farmer* cover, probably felt that fellow southerners had experienced enough of "untrue history."

Terrell was engaged to paint a mural for Conyers only seven years after Erskine Caldwell's *Tobacco Road* hit the nation with all its foofaraw about the southern conditions "revealed" therein. In 1939 the play based on the book still ran on Broadway and the touring company still played to thunderous applause throughout the nation—except, that is, in the South, where most people despised both works. Nevertheless, the week before the road show was to open, the Nashville *Banner* in a front-page story recounted the play's success in glowing terms—"only one other stage play in the history of the theater exceeding it in popularity"—and quoted reviewers who praised the "truth" of the drama. The day after the troupe performed in Nashville, the *Banner* changed its tune. Again on the front page, the proclamation this time was that *Tobacco Road* was a "new low in theatrical presentations."[10]

10. "'Tobacco Road' Soon Starts Sixth Year," Nashville *Banner,* November 25, 1938, p. 1; James J. Metcalfe, "'Tobacco Road' Seen New Low in Theatrical Presentations," *ibid.,* December 2, 1938, p. 1.

One can imagine the consternation of Nashvillians—or Atlantans or Memphians—when the "truth" and "honesty" for which the play had been praised meant a white southern farm family who could not farm, a family more interested in stealing turnips from the son-in-law than in the slow and painful death of the grandmother, who had been hit by an automobile, more interested in mating an oversexed, harelipped daughter than in the potential unfaithfulness of that same son-in-law to the other daughter. The audience also saw sex performed onstage while a sixteen-year-old character guffaws at the sight and an Augusta car salesman chortles over his ability to make fools of the already foolish.

Not only were the novel and the play set in Georgia; the South had been betrayed by one of its own. Caldwell's hometown of Wrens and the vicinity in which he set his novel were not far east of Conyers. And Caldwell's minister father was a regular contributor to the Augusta *Chronicle,* for which Caldwell himself occasionally wrote. Some of their articles claimed that the people of Caldwell's fiction were typical of Georgia. That claim might have been less offensive if the Caldwells had kept their opinions in the South. But besides *Tobacco Road, God's Little Acre,* another novel about decadent and incompetent southern farmers, had drawn nationwide attention, and Caldwell also did "documentaries." In 1935 he wrote a series of articles for the New York *Post* about how inept southern farmers were and how poorly southern tenants were treated.[11]

Like the messages in Caldwell's fiction, what he wrote for the New York *Post* carried southern problems to potentially judgmental nonsoutherners, and his articles had the added respectability of journalism. Whatever claims Caldwell and his reviewers made that *Tobacco Road* was essential truth, it was, after all, fiction. Reports published in newspapers had an aura of accuracy that only the southern press seemed willing to question. Sally Gleaton might have read the Augusta *Chronicle* reports that farmers such as Caldwell described were exceedingly rare, but she knew that Elizabeth Terrell and government agencies probably had not. She knew that

11. New York *Post* articles by Erskine Caldwell in 1935 that drew unfavorable attention to southern agriculture appeared on April 17 (pp. 1, 26), April 18 (pp. 1, 19), April 19 (p. 19), April 20 (p. 4). The effect was compounded by an anonymous editorial at the end of the series. Entitled "Hell on Earth," it spoke about the life of tenants and sharecroppers in the South (April 22, 1935, p. 10). All the articles are in Scott MacDonald (ed.), *Critical Essays on Erskine Caldwell* (Boston, 1981), 223ff.

when in 1935 the *Chronicle* set out to see if family situations such as Caldwell described for the Lesters actually existed in Georgia's Jefferson and Burke counties, it did find poverty and depravity among the "poor whites." Newspaper investigators did find inadequate housing, children begotten by incest, ignorance, amorality, and abysmal apathy. But the families in this group numbered only about a dozen. Their investigation kept leading them back to the same substandard dwellings, the same suffering people.[12]

The *Chronicle* writers concluded that lives such as Caldwell depicted were few but that only one person living in such conditions was too many. They contended that there would always be poor farmers. The dozen or so they had uncovered, however, were not living in old-fashioned poverty. These weak beings could not help themselves, no matter what opportunities the government and benevolent landlords gave them. There may have been truth in Caldwell's representation, but for the editors of the *Chronicle*, that was not a widespread southern truth. Their only finding that reached the national press, however, was that such people existed. The *New Republic*, for example, congratulated the *Chronicle* on its courage in publishing the story but failed to make the point that such depravity had been found to be the exception rather than the rule.[13]

In his New York *Post* series, Caldwell told of southern man's inhumanity to southern man. In *Tobacco Road* and in *God's Little Acre*, Caldwell depicted white human beings and white human families on the verge of decomposition, farmers who only dreamed of farming. Dying of pellagra and starvation, Caldwell's rural characters emerge, not as tragic, not even as pathetic, but as absurd, farcical. They are victims only of their own ignorance and apathy, though Caldwell claims to indict a pervasive system. Even while *Tobacco Road*'s Jeeter Lester dreams of planting cotton, smelling the newly turned fields, and living the agrarian myth, his primary concerns—how to steal those turnips from his son-in-law and thereby from the mouth of his own daughter and how to marry off

12. This series of articles in 1935 in the Augusta *Chronicle* appeared on March 10 (pp. 1, 19), March 11 (pp. 1, 4), March 12 (pp. 1, 4), March 13 (pp. 1, 3), March 14 (pp. 1, 3, 4), March 24 (p. 16). All are in MacDonald (ed.), *Critical Essays on Erskine Caldwell*, 117–31, 135, 138.

13. "Editorial Commentary," *New Republic*, March 27, 1935, pp. 172–73, also in MacDonald (ed.), *Critical Essays on Erskine Caldwell*, 139–40.

his other two children so that he need not support them—move the reader either to raucous laughter or to disgust. Southerners trying hard to tell the nation their "true" story and trying even harder to salvage a failing economic system and use improved farming methods found that the only southern "truth" in which the nation was interested was Caldwell's version.

There was irony even in the title of *Tobacco Road*. The book was not about tobacco. One writer remarked in the *Saturday Evening Post* that tobacco was the only wholly southern industry in which the agricultural product did not leave the South for manufacture and ultimate profit.[14] That may have been an exaggeration, but cigarettes at least did remain in the South from the planting of the tobacco until they were ready for the retailer. And tobacco farming under the New Deal did not suffer as cotton did. Could a book with the title *Tobacco Road* not have been about this southern success story? But Caldwell's Tobacco Road got its name from unwise tobacco farming that depleted the soil long before Jeeter Lester got hold of it. The book is about one more farmer, oblivious to the advice of the *Progressive Farmer*, hoping to eke out a living with the southern perennial, cotton—without even last year's seed cotton to plant.

When someone did try to tell a tobacco story, he often did not find it compelling enough to investigate properly. One southern crop with which southern states had done well, one industry that was southern from raw materials to the finished product, one crop that continued to bring profit into the South was tobacco. Perhaps it was excessive pride in a job well done; perhaps it was self-consciousness because the comparative prosperity of tobacco planters did little to help their tenants. Despite the support of the *Progressive Farmer*, small tobacco farmers were perhaps still suspicious of recently instigated Department of Agriculture quotas, an effort to save southern soil and prevent market gluts. Perhaps it was the import duties that penalized tobacco on the British market and Turkey's entry into the tobacco market.[15] Whatever it was, people in

14. Garet Garrett, "The Problem South," *Saturday Evening Post,* October 8, 1938, p. 91.

15. Anthony J. Badger, *Prosperity Road: The New Deal, Tobacco and North Carolina* (Chapel Hill, 1980), shows that tobacco growing was even more labor intensive than was cotton and had long been tenant dominated. He also demonstrates the influence Clarence Poe and the *Progressive Farmer* had in the South. See How-

tobacco country were more concerned than were those in other agricultural regions that their crop be precisely represented. What the Section never realized about most mural subjects was that usually people were tolerant of a bit of artistic license in the presentation if the way people lived and worked was sensitively and optimistically represented. Rowan used a great deal of energy ensuring that mules were harnessed precisely, that draftsmanship was excellent, that animals had the requisite number of legs, that cotton rows were the correct width. Most of the time, he missed the point of people's objections. But when the subject was tobacco, most communities were as concerned with precise representation as he was.

Tobacco processing varied in southern agricultural regions, but the Section and Section artists seemed unaware of that. For Franklin, Kentucky, artist Carl Hall, selected on the basis of the Birmingham, Michigan, competition, painted an acceptable representation of the processing of flue-cured tobacco and a barn suitable for curing burley tobacco. The trouble was that the crop in Franklin was "one-sucker" tobacco, which is cured neither by smoke as is the flue-cured nor in barns as is the burley, but in the field on the stalk before it is harvested. Hall had done his research in the Detroit Public Library on generic "tobacco," not any particular type. He learned from a booklet distributed by the Liggett & Myers Tobacco Company that "the harvesting of the tobacco crop is the result of a common family effort, and a really fine tobacco crop means everybody has contributed his full share." Hall announced his intention to paint a family harvest scene.[16] He did indeed include a number of people who could be members of the same family, but there is not a female among them (Figure 20).

It was not the makeup of that family, however, that caused Franklin's postmaster Henry S. Bogan not to allow the installation of the mural; it was the fact that the scene belonged in North Carolina. Hall made his first trip to tobacco country to install his laboriously conceived and carefully executed mural, and Franklin re-

---

ard W. Odum, *Southern Regions of the United States* (Chapel Hill, 1936), for a widely read and even more widely respected contemporary view of the southern tobacco industry. In Odum's view, tobacco was "becoming" tenant dominated (p. 61).

16. Carl Hall to Rowan, August 25, 1941, in Franklin, Kentucky, file, RG 121, NA.

20 / Carl Hall, cartoon for Franklin, Ky., 1941

fused to have it. The local paper expressed Franklin residents' feelings:

> A beneficent government conferred upon Franklin and Simpson County a federal building that gives tone alike to town and county, and in the entire population not an inhabitant could be found who is not both mindful and grateful. It is the policy of the postal department to provide a mural to be used in decorating the wall of such buildings and not infrequently, the scene depicts a local industry.
>
> Postmaster Henry Bogan has received and has declined to accept a mural, which, unfortunately, is a typical North Carolina scene. . . . If it is the government's intention to depict a tobacco growing scene, since Simpson County is the home of the finest quality one sucker tobacco grown in all the world . . . , the mural would be a distinct misplacement; wholly out of its element, and impossible for it ever to become acclimated . . . against the wall of the local post office.

Rowan was unmoved either by the newspaper article or by Bogan's complaints relayed from several non-Section officials; nor was he convinced that the mural was unsuitable by a letter from Fourth Assistant Postmaster General Walter F. Myers, quoting Bogan and seeking Rowan's "advice." The same Rowan who had cautioned Elizabeth Terrell to make sure that the hitch on the mules was authentic advised Myers that since he had authorized the Franklin mural's installation, it was his job to see that it got on the wall, welcome or not. Miffed because the complaints had been addressed to the Post Office Department and not to the Section, Rowan thought that the Kentucky postmaster's presumptuous action had "caused the artist unnecessary expense which the latter can little afford and this office no small embarrassment."[17] The embarrassment such a mural might cause the community was to Rowan unimportant.

After haggling with the postmaster to take the mural, then instructing Hall to make a new sketch, which the postmaster promptly rejected, the Section reluctantly decided to search for a new home for the orphaned artwork. In 1942 the war meant that the Section was under pressure to complete its work expeditiously. There was no time for Hall to keep trying to design an acceptable mural of western Kentucky tobacco. The Manning, South Carolina, postmaster replied to Rowan's offer of the mural, saying that they would welcome the decoration except for one small detail: because of the war emergency, the post office was never built. A new post office was going up in Florence, South Carolina. Of course, the space was too large and the colors of the mural had nothing to do with those of the building, but couldn't Hall add a solid-color border and rectify both problems? The building was far from finished, however, and that plan also had to be tabled. Stuck in early 1943 with a fast-expiring agency for decorating public buildings and an unplaceable mural, Rowan finally made arrangements to settle with Carl Hall—his full fee, *less* forty-five dollars (the likely charge had the mural been installed). What happened to Hall's work is a mystery.

Hall's research, however, had been meticulous compared with that done for the Mullins, South Carolina, project. Mullins was the South Carolina town selected for the Forty-eight States Competition, and thus only those with South Carolina connections could compete. Lee Gatch of New Jersey, before he even began designs, wrote the secretary of the Mullins Chamber of Commerce, asking for thematic suggestions. The man responded that tobacco would be nice, and he offered to answer any further questions. Gatch was grateful, but "not wishing to burden [him] too much with the matter, I tried to do what I could by my own efforts. Unfortunately I was completely misinformed by a librarian I depended on for the right information."[18] Perhaps, had Gatch been as considerate of the

17. "Misplaced Mural," unidentified clipping, Rowan to Walter Myers, May 20, 1942, both *ibid.*
18. Lee Gatch to Mr. S. R. Pidgeon, November 11, 1939, open letter published in the Mullins *Enterprise* shortly thereafter. Undated clipping in Mullins, South Carolina, file RG 121, NA.

21 / Lee Gatch, design for Mullins, S.C.

librarian and done his own research, his laughable interpretation of South Carolina tobacco growing would not have materialized.

But he didn't. He learned from a librarian that tobacco was grown under canvas. To an extent, that is correct. In the early weeks after planting, a cheesecloth-like material called tobacco canvas is stretched over the tobacco beds a few inches from the ground. It protects the young plants from late frosts and too much sun until they are about two inches high, when they are transplanted, and tobacco, like most crops, must be tended in the presence of the elements.[19] What Gatch drew, however, was a picture of farmers tilling, harvesting, sorting, and preparing tobacco for drying under a cheesecloth canopy supported, like a circus tent, on poles (Figure 21). Draft animals, people, wood floors, curing sheds, and endless rows of tobacco plants are protected by this canvas. Given that image, Mullins citizens began looking for other mistakes. And once you seek, of course, you find.

Like many muralists, Gatch attempted to show several phases of his subject in the same painting, though they would occur at different seasons and in different locations. Usually, viewers respected this artistic license because they found so much more in the picture to look at. But once the artist made a profound mistake, every other potential error would be taken seriously. Thus Mullins citizens criticized the design for having wood floors in a tobacco patch, for plowing at harvest time, for sorting before curing, for driving narrow-gauge carts into the tobacco, and, most shocking of all, for

19. Badger, *Prosperity Road*, 4–5, describes raising flue-cured tobacco.

juxtaposing a mulatto woman with a male "negro of the gullah type" and a mulatto child.[20]

Gatch was asked to redesign, since the defects had been found early in the process, but he did little besides remove the Big Top and make his black workers very black. He concluded from further research, which included hiring a Mullins photographer to take pictures of the process, that despite what the people of Mullins told him, he had made few other errors. He must not have examined the photos closely, however. Even so, his final product would probably have been tolerated as a work of art and not of fact—despite the plow in the field of mature tobacco, the manufactured tables, and the child sitting on what appears to be a pile of valuable tobacco—had it not been for the history of the design. As it was, Mullins residents would not be pleased with that design, no matter what. Gatch correctly concluded that "their first prejudice created by the mistakes of my first sketch could not be changed in any case regardless of the concessions I made in the redesigning of the mural."[21] If he had redesigned, instead of trying to make changes in a detested picture, Mullins could well have been flattered. But Gatch took only some of their suggestions, and his design looks little different from the published first draft.

The mural went up in Mullins; the citizens, the postmaster, and the local paper were disappointed. Since Mullins and Franklin, Kentucky, were only a few in a series of bad experiences with tobacco murals, Rowan decided to check up on the growing of tobacco. Never guessing that the issue might be Section relationships with southern communities rather than actual inaccuracies in the murals, Rowan in mid-1941 asked Charles Gage, head of the Department of Agriculture tobacco division, to comment on the accuracy of photographs of tobacco murals. Of the murals as a group, Gage said what Rowan wanted to hear: "Inasmuch as these murals appear in public buildings in tobacco-producing areas, they are naturally viewed by many tobacco growers who, I assume, would attach a higher value to realism than to symbolism. With that in mind, my comments will be directed to those features of the painting

---

20. Anonymous letter to Mullins *Enterprise*, dated October 26, 1939, undated clipping, in Mullins, South Carolina, file.
21. Lee Gatch to Rowan, August 18, 1940, *ibid.*

which seem to be lacking in authenticity with respect to the areas in which they appear." Gage thus placed the blame for any problems with the murals just where Rowan wanted it: the artist's research and not public relations practices. In July, 1941, about twenty artists received letters from Rowan with Gage's comments on jobs they had long ago finished and were helpless to do anything about if they had wanted to.[22] Although Gage was polite, his responses were universally critical. The artists' renderings did not reflect the botanical accuracy a specialist in the science of tobacco would like to see. But the one for Mullins received perhaps the most devastating criticism. Gage, expert in all the various ways tobacco was grown in the United States, a professional who could instantly spot Maryland procedures in Virginia, one-sucker procedures in a burley region, air drying in a flue-cured region, could not identify what was going on in Gatch's montage: "The group at the right in which tobacco is being prepared for hanging in the curing barn seems to be very good. The other operations are not understood and do not suggest phases of tobacco handling with which I am familiar."[23]

Inaccurate representations of tobacco-growing procedures may have been one of the Section's recurring nightmares. But the South slept fitfully in the face of more pressing problems. Southerners were getting bad press. Farm Security Administration photographers were swarming over the South, taking pictures of "Southern Conditions." And they did not photograph the "Master Farmers" featured each month in the *Progressive Farmer*. In 1936, James Agee and Walker Evans had actually lived for two months with a subsistence-level tenant family in Hale County, Alabama, in order to report for a northern audience both the squalid conditions and the inherent dignity of their lives. Dorothea Lange had taken exploitive pictures of the most unsavory aspects of southern life in her expeditions to document suffering and hardship all over the nation. Farm Security Administration efforts to help tenants buy their own land were too little and too late; only those whose lives had already offered hope could take advantage of FSA loans. Most

22. Rowan quoted Gage's statement in letters to each artist who painted a tobacco mural before mid-1941. See, for example, Rowan to Gordon Samstag, in Reidsville, North Carolina, file, RG 121, NA; and Rowan to Gatch, in Mullins, South Carolina, file.

23. Rowan to Gatch, August 29, 1941, in Mullins, South Carolina, file.

southerners knew of at least some of these situations, which were freely reported in southern newspapers and became stories in *Time* and *Life* magazines, in newsreels, and in social protest movies.[24] Then Erskine Caldwell and Margaret Bourke-White's *You Have Seen Their Faces* burst upon the scene with even more publicity than any of the other so-called documentary efforts received.

Caldwell's fiction may have been damaging. His reportage may have been worse. But the ostensibly documentary photographs gave the text a ring of truth that no mere words could match. Thus, when Caldwell added a "photo-documentary" book to his repertoire of works that exaggerated the "plight" of the South and brought ignominy to it, he committed what was for southerners the unforgivable sin. In 1937, Caldwell and his wife-to-be, *Life* photographer Margaret Bourke-White, published their widely praised and exceedingly popular *You Have Seen Their Faces*. Hailed as revolutionary in its approach and praised by all and sundry for its "truth," this book, which seemed to prove with real photographs that *Tobacco Road* was an accurate rendering of southerners and southern conditions, was difficult for southerners to accept. They were impelled to concede the excellence of the photography. And they were impelled to admit that they were moved by the pictures, which sometimes, at least, depicted heroic acceptance of horrid conditions. But they could not accept the implications of those pictures that emphasized cruel planters and apathetic farmers, and they could not accept Caldwell's charge that the book represented the South.[25]

Caldwell's text began, "The South has always been shoved around like a country cousin." Most southerners would probably have agreed. But he continued: "It buys mill-ends and wears hand-me-downs. It sits at second table and is fed short-rations. It is the place

24. William Stott, *Documentary Expression and Thirties America* (New York, 1973), 211. Stott demonstrates that documentary expression is an art form, in that it represents the "artist's" interpretation of things as they are. He also reveals that much documentary photography in the 1930s was unabashedly commercial and cites particularly *You Have Seen Their Faces* as exploiting the photographic subjects. Even so, he distinguishes between what to him is Caldwell's basic respect for his subjects and Bourke-White's more insidious exploitation of them (pp. 218–24).

25. See, for example, Donald Davidson, "Erskine Caldwell's Picture Book," *Southern Review*, IV (1938–39), 15–25; and W. T. Couch, "Landlord and Tenant," *Virginia Quarterly Review*, XIV (Spring, 1938), 309–12. The essays are in MacDonald (ed.), *Critical Essays on Erskine Caldwell*, 59–67 and 55–59.

where the ordinary will do, where the makeshift is good enough. It is the dogtown on the other side of the railroad tracks that smells so badly every time the wind changes."[26] If reactions to murals are any indication, southerners were offended by the suggestion that the plight of the sharecropper and the millhand defined the South. In the book, this sort of commentary was accompanied by pictures, which left no place in the national mind for southerners whose lives were comfortable and progressive farmers who had rescued their land. The pictures in *You Have Seen Their Faces* were calculated to elicit pity and head-shaking over the sheer animal nature of southern life. Southerners are shown alternately swollen or shriveled by disease. They enjoy the sunshine inside a house that lost one wall in the last flood—with no apparent concern for the morrow when it might rain again. They sit on dirty, oily mattresses, the ticking worn through and the filler escaping. They do not farm productive soil, reclaim eroded land through contour plowing, or rotate their crops. And they seem to be unaware of their predicament.

Lest the images somehow fail to convey southern depravity, there are the legends which nearly lie to the reader. Under each picture is a statement in dialect and enclosed in quotation marks, apparently the words of the person photographed. Only on the back of the title page does a reader learn that "the legends under the pictures are intended to express the authors' own conceptions of the sentiments of the individuals portrayed; they do not pretend to reproduce the actual sentiments of the people." In the meantime, readers see a mother holding a well-fed but dirty child, her own jaws distended by snuff, squinting into the camera and saying, "Snuff is an almighty help when your teeth ache." And they see a man standing in his cabin door, saying in true Jeeter Lester fashion, "My son and his wife sleep in the bed, and I was alright on the floor until the high water floated my mattress away." A woman sitting in the doorway of a screenless, windowless, paintless shack comments on the rusted chassis of a Model T: "I remember when that automobile was a mighty pretty thing to ride around in," again evoking images and language from *Tobacco Road*.[27]

26. Margaret Bourke-White and Erskine Caldwell, *You Have Seen Their Faces* (New York, 1937), 25.

27. Plates in *You Have Seen Their Faces* are not numbered and are, therefore, difficult to cite. Each is labeled with a fictional southern town name in a real south-

But the pictures showing the exploited southern farmer as unaware that he was exploited were the most objectionable. For example, one toothless farmer smiles and says, "I get paid very well. A dollar a day when I'm working." If the photo-documentary was the exploitive medium of the 1930s, using emotional appeal to sell books to northern liberals, the collected letters of the down-and-out is its counterpart in the 1980s. Faithfully preserving every misspelling, every syntactic infelicity, and every punctuation error, Robert McElvaine's *Down and Out in the Great Depression* nevertheless offers devastating evidence that the words were indeed Caldwell's sentiments and not those of the people in the photographs. One Macon, Georgia, worker writes in 1935: "Mr president dear sir Just a few lines to let you here from me They have cut us down to 17 1/2 cent an hrs and I cant make any thing at that rate. They pay us every 2 weeks and then some time we dont have enought food to last." In the same year another writes to Harry Hopkins: "Please send some one here to see how We Poor Men ar faring. Just Hardly can get a living i get curst at on the Job and fired if I say any thing and the City Manager Dont treat us right. He say 1 Dollar a Day is a Nuf to Pay any Man."[28] The people who wrote these letters may not have been educated in the niceties of English composition, but, unlike the subjects in Bourke-White and Caldwell's book, they do know they're being had. Unlike Jeeter Lester, they know that the conditions in which they live are unacceptable and that there must be recourse.

Southerners tried to rebut the offensive picture-book, to suggest that Caldwell had his facts and concepts wrong, or at least had misrepresented the proportions, but only in southern publications. In the *Southern Review*, Donald Davidson, the most conservative author in *I'll Take My Stand*, acknowledged the artistic excellence of *You Have Seen Their Faces* and the need many southern farmers had for better working and living conditions, but tried to refute Caldwell's claim that 10 million southern souls lived so abjectly.

---

ern state to suggest where the photo might have been shot. The three captions quoted are "McDaniel, Georgia," fifth plate after 145; "Nettleton, Arkansas," tenth plate after 82; and "Rose Bud, Arkansas," fifth plate after 169.

28. "McDaniel, Georgia," in Bourke-White and Caldwell, *You Have Seen Their Faces*, fourth plate after 145; Robert S. McElvaine, *Down and Out in the Great Depression: Letters from the Forgotten Man* (Chapel Hill, 1983), 128, 135.

Probably counting only heads of household, he cited census figures to show only 716,356 sharecroppers in the South. The number of people in tenancy was nearer 3.5 million, but both Caldwell and Davidson failed to make some important distinctions. Sharecroppers were tenants, but other tenants paid their rent in cash rather than a share of the crop.[29] A few tenants were indeed in as much need as Caldwell portrayed them, but he represented the most impoverished few as typical and then emphasized their degeneracy. The South would have to wait until 1941 for the publication of Agee and Evans' *Let Us Now Praise Famous Men* to reveal the self-respect and the intelligent struggle of a goodly portion of Caldwell's 10 million.

Although farm laborers appear often in the murals, subsistence farmers were rarely depicted, and very rarely did a mural painter actually own up to painting sharecroppers. Those who were painted were well supplied, well clothed, strong, healthy, and successfully farming. Renderings of poor farmers using potentially outdated farming methods were not inflammatory so long as the assumption was, as it was in the *Progressive Farmer*, that they had the wherewithal to better themselves. Harwood Steiger's mural for Fort Payne, Alabama, depicts a twentieth-century farmer using nineteenth-century equipment (Figure 22). In the foreground, farmers on the left pick abundantly growing cotton and at the right they process sugarcane. In the center, at the focal point, sits the traditional farmhouse. The house has the familiar silhouette of a dogtrot, with the peak running from side to side and an extension of the roof shading the porch. A window, however, closes off the place where the dogtrot usually runs the length of the building and traps every breeze for the comfort of the residents.[30]

Everything in the picture is "realistic." Steiger's farmers have a successful harvest, but they are not affluent. The long skirts and sunbonnets on the women are a bit outdated. The cistern in the

29. Davidson, "Erskine Caldwell's Picture Book," in MacDonald (ed.), *Critical Essays on Erskine Caldwell*, 59; Charles S. Johnson *et al.*, *The Collapse of Cotton Tenancy: Summary of Field Studies & Statistical Surveys, 1933–1935* (Chapel Hill, 1935), 4, cites actual figures from computations by Rupert Vance. There were 1,790,783 tenant families in the cotton belt (1,091,944 white; 698,839 black). The total number of human beings involved in the system ran to approximately .5 million whites and slightly over 3 million blacks.

30. See William Ferris, "The Dogtrot: A Mythic Image in Southern Culture," *Southern Quarterly*, XXV (Fall, 1986), 72–85.

22 / Harwood Steiger, *Harvest at Fort Payne*, Fort Payne, Ala., 1938

front yard and the mule-drawn wagon show that they do not yet have indoor plumbing or gasoline-driven farm machinery. In the upper left corner, the area usually reserved in southern murals for contrasts with the foreground activity, another farmhouse sits on what might have once been a rise. Now this island of level ground falls away in eroded gullies where farm laborers nevertheless try to work. Stretching above the foreground farm, however, is the indication that these farmers are "worthy" and will therefore improve their lot. Electric poles and electric lines near the farm and extending up the road signal that the Rural Electrification Administration (REA) has entered the area and that soon lines will be connected to these farmers' houses.

Southerners knew that sharecropping was a problem and that southern farmers should get a better return for their labor. But they knew that progress had been made, and as long as a Section artist shared their hopes, they were not riled by pictures that showed farming as it was. But the rare mural design that suggested that there was no hope, that the plight of the southern farmer was irremediable or, worse still, laughable—that he had not the sense to work himself into the twentieth century—provoked outrage. It is no wonder, then, that when the citizens of Paris, Arkansas, saw Joseph P. Vorst's design (Figure 23), they raised an outcry.

What they saw was a fanciful rendering of a rickety, unpainted, tin-roofed shack, a clump of sunflowers towering over it. In front of the shack in the foreground, a farmer plows a scrawny piece of land with a hand plow while two mules loiter in the next field. Paris was fortunate in its artist, however, and in his proximity. He "met with a committee of leading citizens, including the Postmaster, Editor and Banker," all of whom emphasized that it was not his art they objected to but the subject—precisely what Rowan told Elizabeth Terrell they had a right to speak on. Vorst reported that "their contention was that Arkansas had been the butt of 'backward' quips

23 / Joseph P. Vorst, design for Paris, Ark., winner in Forty-eight States Competition, 1939

long enough and now, the 'truth' should out—that Arkansas is a modern and progressive state."[31]

It is easy to see why Paris residents might have regarded the design as another in a series of jokes at Arkansas' expense. The sunflowers are bigger than the house. A birdhouse totters dangerously on a pole that towers above both the house and the sunflowers. A farmer plows straight toward the road—and by hand while two mules loll in the field. Not only did the design show Arkansas using nineteenth-century farming methods. As a picture and not as a design, it was ridiculous.

Vorst listened to the leading citizens of Paris and they to him, and by the end of the meeting "they were all very happy over the results of the gathering and we parted very good friends." And Vorst did not then whine to Rowan about the need to make minor changes to please them. He was delighted: "Experiences like these make me love this country of ours more and more. Where else in the world could one find the earnestness, the serious interest shown by one and all in every move of the government, local, state, and Federal, even to the choice of a subject for the village Post Office. Everyone has a voice and uses it! May we never lose our democracy."[32]

And when he returned to St. Louis, he did not try to modify his original design to appease Paris; he redesigned completely. The figures in the new design are still rangy and double-jointed. Beyond

31. Joseph P. Vorst to Edward Rowan, December 15, 1939, in Paris, Arkansas, file, RG 121, NA.
32. Vorst to Rowan, December 15, 1939, *ibid.*

24 / Joseph P. Vorst, *Rural Arkansas*, Paris, Ark., 1940

that, however, it is altogether different (Figure 24). To the left is a "modern stockbreeding farm with foreman, hired men and a prize bull." And that bull would win a prize at any state fair—it is as broad as any two of the hired men and its face and short horns speak of strength and determination. In the center is an active modern cotton gin, and though the cotton wagon now unloading is pulled by mules, Arkansas farmers also use horses. Two farmers ride them, and a foal indicates the promise of more riding stock. A coal mine, modern and in good repair, and the requisite cotton field with black women picking cotton are visible in the background. At the right, "two weight recorders are reclining and a sack of cotton is being weighed."[33] The recorders are black men and are therefore expected to recline. The rest of the picture's inhabitants, save only the paunchy foreman, are hard at work and nobody appears foolish. When the mural was installed, the postmaster eschewed the standard moderately pleased letter of approval in favor of an exuberant statement that the mural has "gloriously met with the approval of all the citizens of the city."[34]

Had it been only Caldwell who called negative attention to farmers in the South, Sally Gleaton and the civic leaders of Paris, Arkansas, for example, might not have felt so beleaguered by misrepresentation and condescension. But others had written fiction about southern farmers who could not prosper. John Steinbeck's

33. Quotations are from the description Vorst provided the Section, in Entry 136, "Biographical Data File Concerning Artists," Box 2, RG 121, NA.
34. W. F. Elsker to Edward Rowan, June 27, 1940, in Paris, Arkansas, file.

Grapes of Wrath depicted the dignity of displaced Oklahoma farmers. But the Deep South had no such champion. Instead, William Faulkner achieved notoriety in his own region for his indictment of a South composed of decadent aristocrats, heroic blacks, and ignorant dirt farmers. Although Faulkner's writings present universal themes, they are set in an unattractive South. Faulkner does at times seem, like Caldwell, to mock the extremes to which civilization might be perverted at the lowest economic levels. And his work, like Caldwell's fiction, was roundly condemned in the South, not as literature but as social exegesis. Although in plot and character, for example, *As I Lay Dying* and *Tobacco Road* are very similar, the differences between the two books are greater than the similarities are. The head of Faulkner's farm family tenuously owns his own land and his children farm it. At least in part, this book does celebrate the resiliency of a family rather than its dissolution—the survivability of agrarian stock—while *Tobacco Road* emphasizes its helplessness and depravity. More than that, characters in Faulkner's book wrestle with important questions: the nature of God, the implications of life, the nature of morality.

Faulkner, however, was read only by the elite and the erudite—his prose was cumbersome and difficult to follow, and his tales were not neatly tied up at the end. Harry Harrison Kroll, son of a Tennessee sharecropper, wrote novels of repressed but not beaten sharecroppers. His books were entirely accessible—he used the language of the people to spin a romantic yarn that ordinary people might enjoy reading. Unlike Caldwell, Kroll depicted the sharecropper as a human being with the desires and the intellect of people who at least eat regularly. Unlike Faulkner, he did not attribute profundity to the sharecroppers, only recognition of his plight and his potential power.

In Kroll's *Cabin in the Cotton*, Danny, son of a white "peckerwood," has attracted the planter's favorable attention. Danny is convinced that his employment in the plantation commissary and his selection from among his peers to get a high school education are steps toward a new life. His ambivalence about which stratum of southern society is his—there are only two in Kroll's South—is signified by the two women in his life: the planter's daughter, for whom Danny is but a puppet she can dress and mold for her amusement; and a sharecropper's daughter, who is wholesome and loves him for what he is. Danny does learn some things in the local school, but his real education comes from his fellow tenants who have found the landowner's secret account book, which reveals how numbers were skewed so that each tenant owes almost exactly what he earned in any given year. The book ends with Danny allying himself with his own kind in a hopeful effort to unionize farm workers and end the planter's hold on their very souls.

Despite its romanticism and simplification of the problem, the book *The Cabin in the Cotton* made a stronger statement than did the movie based on it (Warners, 1932). Whereas readers made no mistake about the evil of the sharecropping system and knew precisely where their allegiance belonged, moviegoers learned that the South consisted of two equally misguided classes of equally well meaning people. Not only is the suggestive name of Kroll's planter changed from Lord to Norwood; in the movie, the two sides are reconciled after each has the opportunity to understand the other. And the producers want it clear that they are out to alienate no one. A legend at the beginning of the movie reads,

> In many parts of the South today, there exists an endless dispute between the rich landowners, known as planters and the poor cotton pickers known as tenants or "peckerwoods." The planters supply the tenants with the simple requirements of every day life and in return, the tenants work the land year in and year out.
>
> A hundred volumes could be written on the rights and wrongs of both parties, but it is not the object of the producers of "The Cabin in the Cotton" to take sides. We are only concerned with an effort to picturize these conditions.[35]

Once that point is made, the movie follows the book's plot fairly carefully until the final scene. Danny, now called, for some inexplicable reason, Marvin, manages to straddle the fence between labor and management until the movie is over. Whereas in the book,

35. The quotation appears on the screen at the beginning of the movie. Edward D. C. Campbell, Jr., in *The Celluloid South: Hollywood and the Southern Myth* (Knoxville, 1981), 80–81, only mentions the movie *The Cabin in the Cotton* and, in fact, says more about the book (two sentences) than he does about the movie. Much of the popular culture treated in this chapter is also examined by Jack Temple Kirby, in *Media-Made Dixie: The South in the American Imagination* (Baton Rouge, 1978). His emphasis, however, is on how popular culture created a South for non-southerners rather than on how southerners responded to that fictional creation. Even so, what he says is so insightful that I find it difficult to be original here. He only mentions the book *The Cabin in the Cotton*, however, though his plot summary of the movie is more detailed than the one here (pp. 46–47).

after Danny had spoken out in court against the planters, he left to join the tenants' union, in the movie's melodramatic courtroom scene, Marvin brought about rapprochement between the two sides. Audiences left the theaters convinced that if everyone would just talk it over, everything would be all right. Even so, once again, southern audiences had seen themselves depicted as uninformed, illiterate, and exceptional.

Both the movie and the book, by their simple omission of blacks, managed to perpetuate the myth that white southern farmers were the real sufferers in the system. Nearly half the subsistence farmers in the South during the 1930s were black, and the percentage of blacks held in bondage to the land was much greater than that of whites. In keeping with the greater status of whites nationally, most fictional and many documentary studies depicted only whites. The consumers of popular culture were, after all, largely white. It was still a nation that could not muster a majority in Congress to pass an antilynch bill; it was still a nation in which Jim Crow was enforced in many areas—the armed forces, for instance, and the Civilian Conservation Corps and professional baseball, the AFL and the CIO.[36] And where Jim Crow did not prevail, the black population was often so small as not to constitute a threat. A racist people who could be roused to indignation seeing whites suffer at the hands of other whites were often inured to injustices dealt blacks. That was the way of the world. While most Americans failed to notice that whites and blacks joined in 1934 to organize the Southern Tenant Farmers' Union and many who did found it scandalous, virtually all Americans were shocked to learn that whites lived in the pitiable conditions Caldwell described.

The emphasis on the plight of the white southern farmer was a two-edged sword for southerners. Where blacks were a cherished if

36. Leslie H. Fishel, Jr., "The Negro in the New Deal Era," and W. E. B. Du Bois, "Race Relations in the United States, 1917–1947," both in Bernard Sternsher (ed.), *The Negro in Depression and War: Prelude to Revolution 1930–1945* (Chicago, 1969), 7–50, 7–28, 29–50. They emphasize the gains toward equality made by blacks during the era, though Jim Crow remained widespread. John A. Salmond, "The Civilian Conservation Corps and the Negro," in the same collection, speaks generally of discrimination in the southern CCC but speaks of widespread segregation throughout the nation except in New England (pp. 78–93). And in the same volume, Herbert R. Northrup, "Organized Labor and Negro Workers," makes no geographic distinctions in his consideration of discrimination in labor unions (pp. 127–49).

inferior and exploited part of southern culture, "poor whites" were all but ignored by the southern media. The Augusta *Chronicle* investigation into Caldwell's allegations is a case in point. Once the *Chronicle* determined that a few residents of Georgia did indeed live as Caldwell depicted them, it offered a solution: isolation and sterilization. The ordinary poor, the paper concluded, misinterpreting the biblical quotation, they would always have with them; they were, therefore, not worthy of special action.[37] The Jeeter Lester types were another matter. They were beneath notice; to notice them would be a tacit admission that all blacks were not inherently inferior to all whites. On the other hand, those who had given in to the cycle of poverty, because of their status as whites, were dangerous. It was the white sharecropper in whom Hollywood was most interested, though there were oblique acknowledgments that sharecroppers of both races underwent similar hardships. In the movie *The Cabin in the Cotton*, all the sharecroppers who had speaking parts were white, as were all who participated in the sabotage against the planters and most who attended union meetings. It was even a white who was lynched by the degenerate aristocrats for killing one of their number. In the obligatory cotton-picking scenes, however, only blacks bent over the rows. And both the most pitiable and the most heroic pictures in *You Have Seen Their Faces* were of whites.

It was not only the rural South that Hollywood indicted as ignorant, biased, and untenable in a democracy. *They Won't Forget* (Warners, 1937), loosely based on the Leo Frank case in Atlanta, made the protagonist a Yankee instead of a Jew and depicted a South unsafe for outsiders. The movie was not a box office success—its conclusion was ambivalent—but it was undoubtedly seen by enough people to justify for southerners their xenophobia. Misconstruing that xenophobia, not as fear that visiting Yankees would return north with stories of southern degeneracy, but as complete inability to accept outsiders, the movie implies that northerners in the South cannot hope to be treated fairly. In the absence of any logical suspect in the murder of a young local woman and on the dubious testimony of a black janitor merely that the northerner had been in the vicinity, the Yankee, suggestively named Hale, is convicted of the crime. Viewers of the movie never learn whether

37. The Augusta *Chronicle* editorial appeared on March 17, 1935, p. 4.

Hale is guilty. But they do learn that a fair trial in the South is an impossibility for an encroacher from the North. The actual evidence is not considered in court; the outsider is convicted because he is an outsider.

If *They Won't Forget* did not spread its message to large numbers of moviegoers, another film indicting the southern legal system did. The box office success *I Am a Fugitive from a Chain Gang* (Warners, 1932) was ostensibly an exposé of southern work farms. The movie depicted chain gangs as Thomas Hart Benton would later describe them in his autobiographical travelogue:

> All over the South men dressed like clowns, black men and white men, are to be found strung out along the roads with picks and shovels. Tight-lipped men guard them with sawed-off shot guns. Much has been written of the evil of southern chain gangs and of the abuse of power by officials in charge of them. A great deal of it is true. . . . No doubt there is much to say in defense of the southern penal system if it is frequently and openly investigated, and kept out of the hands of profiteering individuals. . . .
>
> Coming abruptly on a chain gang around some bend in the road, you get a sort of sinking feeling in the chest. It is as if you yourself were under sentence and about to be put in line without hope of appeal or escape. The guards with their guns have a menacing air. They look dangerous and merciless.[38]

But the chain gangs in the movie were not "frequently and openly investigated." If reform-minded southerners were inspired to see reform by the cruel way convicts were treated in the first half of the film, they certainly must have become defensive when they saw the last half. The protagonist, wrongfully convicted of a crime, suffers inhuman treatment on a chain gang. The khaki-clad guard meting out pain and humiliation to black and white prisoners clad in striped uniforms was not yet a stock figure in movies about the work-farm South. Here his appearance and his treatment of the prisoners were revelatory and shocking. The movie might have accomplished some good, except the protagonist's particular experience suggested a need not only for prison reform but for reform—reconstruction, perhaps—of the whole South.

Once all his efforts to get justice through proper channels fail,

38. Thomas Hart Benton, *An Artist in America* (1937; 4th rev. ed.; rpr. Columbia, Mo., 1983), 184–85.

the prisoner/protagonist manages to escape north, where, through his industry and intelligence, he becomes a wealthy and influential engineer. Just as the last of his dreams is to come true with his marriage to Miss Right, the woman he rejected years earlier exposes his true identity. Rather than go through extensive and costly extradition battles, the hero agrees to go back and serve a minimal sentence. The governor and others in high places promise that he will be quickly released to resume his career. Both business and fiancée promise to wait as he descends into the southern hell. It is not long, however, until the hero realizes that neither the governor nor any state official intends to abide by the bargain. Still this admirable man plays it by the book. For years he fights for an appeal, which is never granted. Finally, used beyond endurance and devoid of hope that justice will ever be done, he escapes again. This time, he is too recognizable to surface as a law-abiding citizen—those diabolical southerners would surely track him down, and would probably use vicious dogs. He is thus sentenced to remain forever nothing more than "a fugitive from a chain gang."

As if irresponsible sensationalism about the South were not enough to cause southerners to beware of Yanks bearing gifts, even ambitious efforts to probe the region depicted a South filled with "ignernt" if well-meaning country folk and repressed farmers. Jean Renoir's critically acclaimed *The Southerner* and *Swamp Water* (Twentieth Century-Fox, 1939 and 1941) make no accusations. The sharecropper in *The Southerner* is more exploited by the land itself than he is by unfeeling, greedy human beings. Even so, he is uninformed, his farming methods are primitive, and his family is poorly clad. Despite his zest for life and his determination to overcome all setbacks, he does not represent southerners who own their land, work in small businesses, or hold lower-echelon professional positions. And despite the denouement of *Swamp Water*, in which almost everybody turns out to be virtuous once they understand the situation, much of the movie depicts southerners wronging the good people in their midst while being unable to see the evil they embrace.[39]

39. The impression that Renoir was one more outsider depicting southerners as ignorant and primitive could only have been augmented by the publicity. Benton, whose drawings in *An Artist in America* depicted a dilapidated South ravished by flood, child labor, and erosion, painted the promotional posters.

Popular books and movies had much to do with local outrage, but the press had even more. Garet Garrett reported in a 1938 *Saturday Evening Post* article "The Problem South": "In the spirit of discovery, newspapers and magazines send men to explore, observe and report on [the South's] manners, customs and social systems, as if it were a foreign country. In another spirit, Washington sends forth men trained in the new social zeal to study the evils of Southern farm tenancy and share cropping and to say how they may be abolished; private organizations send missionaries to work with the victims. They see it all for the first time, with Northern eyes, and it is terrible. The share cropper, dramatized at his worst in the newsreels, becomes a national shudder." The irony is that this article was itself offensive to southerners. Responding in part to the president's pronouncement that the South was the "nation's number one economic problem," Garrett wrote a paean to the South, or the myth of the South. His recommendations for how the South might cease to depend on northern capital and thus keep profits in the South were certainly well intentioned. When he wrote that "work as an end in itself, like thrift for its own sake, is a maxim no Southerner can comprehend," he merely stated, with admiration, what was to him a truism. Southerners may have recognized some truth in the words, but they would find it unflattering in a nation in which the Protestant work ethic deified its practitioners. When Garrett suggested a way to use southern natural resources to keep southern capital in the South, southern newspapers responded not with gleeful superiority that his suggestion was already in practice, but with outrage. Had Garrett written with any firsthand knowledge of the South, they wrote, he would not have suggested a remedy already in progress.[40] The spirit in which the South was pronounced deficient was irrelevant; the fact that it was so labeled was all-important.

The president was undoubtedly as well intentioned as Garrett was when he made his "number one economic problem" pronouncement. He said it only to stress the need for the government to do something about economic conditions in the South. But to southern newspapers, the South had been found wanting once again. The

40. Garrett, "The Problem South," 23, 91. See "The South Problem," Louisville *Courier-Journal*, quoted in Nashville *Banner*, November 17, 1938, p. 4. The *Banner* had earlier published an exposé of Garrett's "blunders."

New Orleans *Times-Picayune* referred to the president's "blistering address." The Nashville *Banner* was especially unhappy with the fact that "100,000 copies of the critical [president's National Emergency Council] report [had] recently been distributed to the high schools in three Southern States, in addition to the national circulation which has been given to the council's findings." Perhaps with some justification, the newspapers deplored the pronouncement. The *Banner* was just as upset over what was omitted from the report as what was included. According to its research, the South's economic growth in percentages since 1880, despite contemporary economic problems, had outstripped the rest of the nation, and the paper cites figures. Southern schoolchildren, it seemed, should not read material about their region that emphasized "error and obstacles" unless they also read about what the South had done for itself.[41]

As if that were not enough, a spokesman for the Farm Security Administration described rural housing in the Southeast as "the poorest in the nation." Then, on a visit in the South to inspect TVA work in combating disease, Surgeon General Thomas Parran, Jr., pronounced the South the nation's "No. 1 health problem." For the edification of the nation, he called attention to the hookworm and pellagra, to the malaria, typhoid, and tuberculosis, and to the small per capita number of physicians. Again southern newspapers rushed to the defense, citing the improvement in southern health over a half century before.[42] The pronouncements got national coverage, however, while the replies were limited to southern newspapers. Once more, the South saw the nation to be more interested in its failures than in its successes. The inadequacies of the South were trumpeted on all sides. Sometimes, southerners felt, they were actually misrepresented; at other times, it was merely a matter of saying too little or emphasizing the negative at the expense of the positive or seeing only the least able minority. But however the

41. "Farming South's Way Out," New Orleans *Times-Picayune*, April 7, 1938, p. 12; Nashville *Banner*, November 21, 1938, p. 4. Perhaps the *Banner* got its figures from the South's leading contemporary social scientist, Howard Odum, who had used the same figures and a great many more for the same purpose in *Southern Regions of the United States*, 105–35.

42. "Farming South's Way Out"; Frank McNaughton, "Parran Labels South No. 1 Health Problem," and W. P. Hoffman, "Dr. Haggard Takes Issue On Health Problem in South," both in Nashville *Banner*, November 15, 1938, p. 1.

25 / Frank Long, design for Morehead, Ky.

word was spread, southern newspapers hastened to defend their constituency against what was perceived as misrepresentation.

Even with all the information floating about, the Section continued to misunderstand what was causing the ruckus. Rowan would choose the least offensive detail to expunge in order to avoid upsetting southerners. When Berea's Frank Long designed a mural for Morehead, Kentucky, his sketch represented his intimate acquaintance with Kentucky mountain people. Entitled *Rural Free Delivery*, the design features a mountain family sitting on a cabin porch while the rather large and imposing matriarch reads aloud a recently delivered letter and the horse-drawn mail wagon recedes into the left background (Figure 25). The log cabin forms a backdrop, cutting off any view of the horizon and offering a haven for any who need it. The supports for the porch, incompletely trimmed saplings, perform several functions. The patriarch steadies himself with one truncated branch, and another is a convenient hook for the lantern. Other items for outdoor use—the washtub and a bucket—hang on pegs driven into the wall. The parents are joined by their two sons, the family hound, and the cat. Ma sits on a ladder-back chair in front of the open door as if to guard the one family member who does not join the group on the porch.

The porch was *the* gathering place for southern families, black and white, prosperous and poor, before air conditioning. It was the sitting room during the eight or so months of every year when the house was sultry and stifling. It was where Faulkner placed the Bundren family of *As I Lay Dying* when they considered whether they had time to sell another load of lumber before they were called to the mother's deathbed, and it was where guests and family alike gathered before the funeral. Caldwell's Lesters were truly deprived. Lacking a porch, they had to gather on the grassless lawn. Southerners sat on porches to exchange anecdotes, which were more often than not familiar repetitions of family history embroidered by each teller and just as amusing on the thirtieth telling as the first or second. Zora Neale Hurston gathered southern black folklore on southern porches for *Mules and Men* (1935), and in her novel *Their Eyes Were Watching God* (1937), she contributed a poignant picture of porch culture that speaks of the whole southern social tradition: "When the people sat around on the porch and passed around the pictures of their thoughts for the others to look at and see, it was nice. The fact that the thought pictures were always crayon enlargements of life made it even nicer to listen to."[43]

The porch swing was the traditional retreat of courting couples, but not in Long's family gathering. Ma guards the entrance to make certain her one treasure stays out of harm's way. A side window, however, is just the right height to allow the fair young damsel, imprisoned in the cabin, to get on with her courting, but too high for easy access. A young man leans on a hoe outside admiring the view. The mountaineer's daughter is curvaceous, her hair is carefully coiffed, her mouth is a Cupid's bow, and her downcast eyes are just demure enough for the young man to know she is not about to climb out of that window. The contrast between her comeliness and Ma's obesity, whose feet swell over the edges of her shoes, is quite shocking.

At least Rowan thought so when he accepted the design on condition that those two figures be altered. The mother's size, he suggested, might lead sensitive southerners to think they were being made fun of, and a young woman living in those conditions was unlikely to be so attractive. Long agreed to "make the old lady a little more prepossessing, and the young one perhaps a little less so," but he could not resist editorializing.

> Regarding criticism of the two females in my sketch, I can only say I wish you people could come down to these parts and see for yourself the types of womenfolks we have. Generally the old ones have developed into living caricatures of what we might image when we think of old

---

43. Zora Neale Hurston, *Their Eyes Were Watching God* (1937; rpr. Urbana, 1978), 81.

26 / Frank Long, *Rural Free Delivery*, Morehead, Ky., 1939

ladies, and the young ones, even on the farms, are pretty interesting to look at as regards pulchritude. Dress them in the latest styles, hide their hands and feet, seat them in a graceful pose and I would defy anyone to distinguish them, at a distance of twelve feet, from something you might expect to have come off Park Avenue.

The secret of the difference here between youth and age is probably the hellish existence most of these mountain farmwives endure. It puts lumps where once were curves. If they happen to get fat, as did this old girl, the cause is glandular; not luxuriant living. It was this contrast I had in mind when I so gaily made the sketch.[44]

Once Long modified the women, the mural was satisfactory to the Section and to Morehead (Figure 26). The family was healthy, happy, and, perhaps most important, literate. A gathering on the porch was a familiar and comfortable image for southerners, and this one provides a marked contrast to the two porch photographs in *You Have Seen Their Faces*. In one picture, two drained old women sit alone on the ubiquitous ladder-back chairs in worn-out shoes and holey stockings. Lonely they are—no letter, no young folks to occupy them. They gaze longingly at a landscape beyond the camera that offers them nothing. In Bourke-White's other porch photo, the family, like Caldwell's Lesters, is too poor to have a porch, and everyone crowds onto the cabin doorstep. The barefoot grandmother has a huge tumor distending her face, the grandfather has the shadow of his useless hoe across his lap, and a child rubs

44. Frank Long to Rowan, August 15, 1938, in Morehead, Kentucky, file, RG 121, NA.

what may be a tear from his eye. Nothing of the outside world for any one of them to focus on.[45]

Even the pleasant depiction of *Tobacco Road* conditions was relatively rare in the murals. More often, artists, under the impression that they should paint *Tobacco Road* in *Tobacco Road* country, would try to avoid it. Asked to paint the mural for Osceola, Arkansas, Orville Carroll wrote, "It seems that farming is the only industry in the country around Osceola. . . . The farming is not so good, the farms I saw were great flat belts of plowed ground with the tenants' 'houses' spotted about a quarter of a mile apart. These shacks are in a miserable condition. Papered with newspaper, propped up to keep them from falling over, unpainted and really dirty. The farming as I saw it was ugly." Much to his relief, and likely to the Section's as well, Carroll had an alternative—steamers on the nearby Mississippi River. When Lucile Blanch eschewed the obvious mining theme and undertook to paint the largely unnoticed beauty surrounding Appalachia, Virginia, she had a more difficult time of it. Appalachia was one of those marginal mining towns in the eastern mountains where the relationship of the miners to the mine was the same as that of the sharecroppers to the crop. They lived always behind, owing more to the company store than they earned. Right after she was appointed to paint the mural, Blanch visited Appalachia, where she early concluded that "paint-[ing] miners for these people" would not do: "They are completely aware of their miserable condition and the town is without pride and hope. The visual aspect of the town settled along the stream between mountains is extremely beautiful and they cannot see that this is so knowing the wretchedness of its detail."[46]

Although tenant farming accumulated the lion's share of bad press for the South, outsiders did not neglect conditions in the mining and textile industries. Starting in the 1920s, violent and bloody efforts to unionize southern industries had called attention to the exploitation of southern labor. And still in 1939 the United Mine Workers were making only slight inroads. Miners tended to

45. "Lansdale, Arkansas," "Sweetfern, Arkansas," both in Bourke-White and Caldwell, *You Have Seen Their Faces,* third plate after 169, sixth plate after 149.

46. Orville Carroll to Rowan, August 10, 1938, in Osceola, Arkansas, file, RG 121, NA; Lucile Blanch to Rowan, June 21, 1939, in Appalachia, Virginia, file, RG 121, NA.

be grateful just for the fact that they had jobs, and happenings in Kentucky's Harlan County in 1938 had taught them that to join any but the "company unions" could just as easily cost them their jobs as bring about better working conditions.[47]

Knowing these things, Lucile Blanch submitted her sketches with which she hoped "to bring to their consciousness the beauty they may possess." For Blanch, artist in residence at Converse College in Spartanburg, South Carolina, painting a mural was not a job to support herself; neither was it a chance to build her reputation. And though she owed her job in part to the recommendation of the Section of Fine Arts and was cooperative with Washington in every respect, she was less concerned with their aesthetic judgment than with painting something meaningful for the people she served. "I do hope," she wrote, "that they will . . . see that there is at least this beauty in their lives. Psychologically they need it as they see no hope either for themselves or the town."[48]

The picture on the post office wall is Appalachia seen through a wide-angle lens (Figure 27). The viewer stands about halfway up one of the mountains between which the city nestles. The distance is great enough that grit and dinginess are invisible, but short enough that windows in buildings and wrought-iron fences around yards are clear. The stream winds through center and under the railroad bridge. The railroad tracks follow the stream until they cross the bridge and disappear. To the left is the residential section, which is crowned by two imposing brick houses. To the right is the business district with several multistoried buildings. Everywhere are pathways and trees, but it is winter so that foliage does not block the view of familiar structures. Clearly visible electric poles and the smokestacks of distant factories announce that Appalachia is progressive. Enclosed by mountains and forests, the town could be a prison for those unlucky enough to live there, but in this view it is more haven than hell.

Blanch's efforts to show the townspeople the beauty amid which they lived were lost on the postmaster, and her dedication to her task was apparently lost on Rowan. She completed the mural and

47. George B. Tindall, *The Emergence of the New South* (Baton Rouge, 1967), 505–39, summarizes the unionization of the South during the 1930s and early 1940s. He concludes that though unions were part of the South after the 1930s, their numbers were too small and too few workers benefited from the ones that existed.

48. Blanch to Rowan, June 21, 1939, in Appalachia, Virginia, file.

27 / Lucile Blanch, *Appalachia*, Appalachia, Va., 1940

shipped it to Appalachia with directions and money for installation. In short order, Rowan received two communications. The postmaster wrote that the mural was "pretty," but "I could not understand why the artist did not select some place in this neighborhood." The second communiqué was actually from the postmaster too, but it was filtered through the office of Fourth Assistant Postmaster General Smith W. Purdom, with whom relations had always been coolly cordial. It contained the admonition to Rowan that "your further advice will therefore be appreciated." The postmaster complained that the dimensions of the mural were one foot greater than the space both horizontally and vertically. Blanch hastened to take the blame for the size mistake, and Rowan hastened to let her have it. The postmaster had, she reported, reluctantly measured the area for her, and she had trusted to memory for the dimensions.[49]

Just returned from a month's vacation in Mexico, Rowan was not delighted to be faced with an ill-fitting mural, an inappropriate subject, and a veiled suggestion from Purdom that the Section was incompetent—all related to the same project. "I was a little shocked," he wrote, "that your dimensions of the mural were arrived at from memory rather than from notes that you might have made on your visit." That was, after all, why the Section recommended that artists visit the buildings. On the topic of thematic suitability, he wrote, "It is distressing to have him complain about

49. Appalachia, Virginia, Postmaster to Rowan, March 31, 1940, Smith W. Purdom to Rowan, February 26, 1940, both *ibid.*

the subject matter as we were under the impression from your letters that you had selected material following your visit to Appalachia." He counseled Blanch to go immediately and personally supervise the installation "and the necessary cutting of the canvas." Very little, he told her, would be lost by that arrangement— except, of course, some teaching days and her expenses. Having more than a passing interest in the mural, Blanch went to Appalachia, where she put on "slacks and a polo shirt and joined [the workmen] on the ladder." She found that the mural was the correct size after all. Further, everybody in town except the postmaster recognized the location:

> The old boy [the postmaster] never could figure out the thing, I'm sure. The audience which gathered to watch the installation were busy identifying places all over the canvas. I took the view from a bit higher than most of them ever get to see the town and consequently some of the things they are familiar with are hidden behind tops of trees and embankments. . . . They accepted my explanation of the nonappearance of [those things]. The Postmaster refused to come out and watch any of the proceedings so he missed all of those discussions. As a white collar worker he probably felt that the people there were scum and he also probably resented the disruption of his quiet routine.

Her only disappointment was that the two large brick houses she had placed at the focal point belonged, she learned, to the judge and the former senator. Blanch as an artist of the people would hardly have chosen to feature those buildings. She confided to Rowan that Appalachia's postmaster was "very stupid," whereupon Rowan acknowledged the man's intransigence and the logic of the artistic license Blanch had taken with her view of the town.[50] Rowan did not apologize for scolding her unjustly, or for not recognizing that her previous satisfactory work for the Section might have indicated that the fault for the confusion lay elsewhere.

Blanch was dedicated to raising public awareness of what was good in their lives, not to changing them, but when a known reformer undertook to paint the benighted South, fireworks were sure to result. And when the reformer was unwittingly assigned to a post office whose postmaster knew nothing of art and yet cared passionately about the decoration in his lobby, it was even worse.

50. Rowan to Blanch, May 1, March 18, 1940, Blanch to Rowan, May 4, 1940, all *ibid.*

New York artist Philip Evergood in the 1930s was identified with the school of social realism; that is, much of his work during the period expressed his belief that social values needed to be changed.[51] In his paintings of social injustice, Evergood painted figures that southerners would likely find unrealistic. Although Evergood's figures appeared in a variety of proportions, in his more poignant social commentary they were foreshortened, their eyes were exaggerated, and their arms and legs were disproportionate to their torsos.

When Evergood was appointed on the basis of a competent entry in a Texas competition to decorate the Jackson, Georgia, Post Office, he modified his social realism somewhat. He did not show cotton workers overtly misused by planters and foremen, but his figures retained the characteristics that people in small southern towns hungry for beautiful pictures would find offensive. As a matter of fact, admirers of Evergood's art would also probably find them offensive. Although the figures, with their sloe eyes and their breasts, biceps, buttocks, and backs based on circles, do resemble other Evergood figures, they are unnaturally static, anchored in their positions, showing none of the vitality Evergood usually gave the characters in his work. The design, a semicircle, is simplistic. Further, much of Evergood's work was narrative, but the action here is boring.[52]

Early on, nearly a year before the artist began work on the mural and three before it was installed, Jackson Postmaster Victor Carmichael wrote the Section, asking to be advised of the mural subject before the final design was approved. Hearing nothing for two months, Carmichael wrote Evergood, requesting that a photograph of the proposed work be submitted to him so that he could check on the "truthfulness of the design." Whereupon Rowan informed the artist that the Section would send a photo when Evergood sub-

51. Evergood was selected by David Shapiro in *Social Realism: Art as Weapon* (New York, 1973) as one of five artists who represent "the best in social realism" (p. 145).
52. For similarly drawn but vital figures, see Evergood's *Street Corner, The Pink Dismissal Slip,* and workers and dancers in *The Story of Richmond Hill.* Black-and-white prints of the Jackson, Georgia, mural appear in Oliver Larkin, *Evergood: 20 Years* (New York, 1946), and J. I. H. Baur, *Philip Evergood* (New York, 1964). Both authors comment that this mural is not as successful as Evergood's other work, and Baur suggests that the extended struggle to meet both Section requirements and those thought to be southern may have damped Evergood's spontaneity.

28 / Philip Evergood, *Cotton—From Field to Mill*, Jackson, Ga., 1940

mitted "one he could stand behind."[53] Over the next few months the artist did considerable research on cotton in Georgia—what else?—and he dutifully wrote Carmichael several times for information that would help him design an appropriate mural. From these requests he got only counterrequests for photos of the design.

Meanwhile, Rowan approved Evergood's fourth effort, a design never seen by Carmichael or Jackson residents, with two admonitions. "Care should be used to avoid carrying the tones of the negroes too low in value as this is a sensitive point," and a colonial mansion should be added to the background so viewers would not think that all southerners were cotton workers.[54] Rowan did not make good on his agreement to send a photograph, and, as Rowan had instructed, Evergood did not send one either. Despite some New South features, *Cotton—From Field to Mill* (Figure 28) was not a good one for the South.

In a single panel are cotton fields, a gin, and a cotton mill. Literal-minded Georgians did not much care for Evergood's panorama of the process without regard to its verities. Cotton is weighed in front of the mill, but that takes place in the field; it seems that cotton is loaded onto wagons as much in front of the gin as in the field. The scale of the mill, the gin, and the train is unbelievable, for the train practically dwarfs them both. And there is no protection from the horizon or the North. The mountains and abundant

53. Postmaster Victor Carmichael to Treasury Department Procurement Division, November 11, 1937, Carmichael to Philip Evergood, January 19, 1938, Rowan to Evergood, February 4, 1938, all in Jackson, Georgia, file, RG 121, NA.
54. Rowan to Evergood, August 10, 1939, *ibid.*

trees in the picture are inconsequential compared with the boundless space in front of and behind them.

But the most offensive part of the mural is undoubtedly the
renderings of the figures. Evergood seems to have included the
whole ill-fed, ill-housed, and ill-clothed third of the nation. People
are everywhere, and all of them are lumpy. It is hard to believe that
the same Rowan who insisted that Frank Long put his mountain
mother on a diet and that Doris Lee truncate the necks of her Summerville, Georgia, farmers allowed Evergood to get by with these
misshapen people. Even worse, they all wear translucent clothes.
These lumpy people being peasants well removed from the teensy
mansion on a distant hill might have been acceptable in Georgia,
except for the grossest error of them all. Whites and blacks, males
and females work together doing *precisely the same thing*—as
they might do in real life but not in the ideal South that should
appear on post office walls. The social order has been turned upside
down. At the New York Public Library, Evergood apparently found
the agricultural facts but not the social ones. As a social realist, he
painted what happened along Tobacco Road and, at the same time,
a vision of what the South could be if workers united. He did paint
one suit-and-tie-clad foreman supervising the weighing in the right
foreground. This man is smaller than the muscular black workers
surrounding him, and he is almost hidden by the scales. Clearly
only a sense of obligation to the middle class caused him to be included at all, just as only obligation to Rowan caused the inclusion
of the distant mansion.

When a photo of the completed mural was submitted to Rowan
before installation, he insisted on one last change. In the center
front, just above Postmaster Carmichael's door, was a woman with
her child. She was lumpier than any of them, and her translucent
dress concealed nothing. The baby was skinny and, for some reason
known only to Evergood, had an imbecilic expression on its face.
Maybe the artist was making a statement about the negative effect
of cotton tenancy on the newborn. Whatever her purpose, Rowan
knew that this woman and her child would have to go. In an understatement designed to salve Evergood's feelings, he wrote:

> Obviously, the work has grown considerably by the further study that
> you have given it and with one exception it is now ready for installation.
> The people of the South place great stress on dignity and it is our feel-

29 / Philip Evergood, detail from Jackson mural
Photo by Richard H. Beckham

ing that they are not going to accept the mother and child as you have presented them in the foreground. She frankly looks a little too much like a tramp that is accompanying the workers and for this reason I suggest that you introduce instead of [the] two figures plant growth of shrubbery eliminating mother and child.

Shrubbery was substituted (Figure 29), and Evergood wisely sent his mural to be installed by a New York professional rather than face Jackson himself. Asked to report on the work, Victor Carmichael wrote: "So far as this office is able to determine the mural has been properly installed. Comments have been unfavorable and critical."[55] When Washington received many complaints from other Jacksonians, Rowan chose to blame it all on Evergood. He chastised the artist for not supplying the postmaster a copy of the design, though it was never a policy of the Section to let postmasters pass on designs. Rowan must have known of Evergood's reputation as a social realist; if not, he should have recognized the style of the mural as one with which rural Georgia could never be at peace. But he

55. Rowan to Evergood, July 29, 1940, Carmichael to Rowan, October 28, 1940, both *ibid.*

did not. As with Lucile Blanch's mural for Appalachia, he assumed that if the mural was not appreciated locally, the fault could be with no one but the artist.

Southerners could say all sorts of things about the South for the South that outsiders could not say for nonsoutherners. When a reformer was actually of the South, he could acknowledge the South's limitations. Samuel Lee Chestnut, professor of agriculture education at Alabama Polytechnic Institute (Auburn University), wrote a "social science" textbook called *The Rural South: Background— Problems—Outlook*, which was looked on with such favor, at least in Alabama, that it was adopted as required reading for all Alabama school systems. Despite some condescending assumptions about how blacks had to earn equality through emulating white ways of life and white values, which might have been echoed in any 1937 American textbook, the book looks fairly at the South's problems especially on farms and in mills. Chestnut clothes his hard truths in genteel language, but the hard truths are there: "Surely, few in this passing generation have realized that their children would live to see Uncle Sam reach the maximum of his waistband and begin walking with a cane. Whether or not we continue to grow numerically, the matter of most importance to the rising generation is where in the nation the better life will be found. Will it be in an urbanized or a rural community? Should the nation have more or fewer persons living on that land?"[56]

He concluded that fewer should live on the land, an impossibility in the South in 1937. And he concluded that living on the land could be good only with half as many doing it and only if the South drastically changed its systems of farming, of tenancy, of discrimination. According to Chestnut, the "factors" that make the southern situation untenable are:

1. Our high rate of tenancy, with the consequent impoverishment of the soil and the people.

2. Our adherence to the one-crop system, with its added tendency to the same result.

3. Our comparatively low and unequally distributed farm income.

56. Samuel Lee Chestnut, *The Rural South: Background—Problems—Outlook* (Montgomery, Ala., 1937), 68. See G. M. Beech, "'The Rural South' Adopted As Text in Alabama Schools," Tuskegee *News*, March 7, 1940, p. 6.

4. Finally, as a natural result of the three facts just mentioned, the prevalence of a class system.[57]

Samuel Lee Chestnut could utter those truths about the South, in the South, and for southern consumption. And like the *Progressive Farmer* and the county extension agents, local residents who had studied at such places as Alabama Polytechnic, he could preach long and hard about improved methods of farming and ways to salvage the soil. Even an outsider, when he had actually adopted a career in the South, when his desire for reform came from love of his adopted land rather than from radical visions, had a chance. Hollis Holbrook, commissioned to paint the mural for Haleyville, Alabama, could preach in his mural—as long as his voice was soft and he spoke as a gentleman. Shortly after his appointment, Holbrook visited Haleyville:

> After viewing the country and seeing it laid bare to deep gashes caused by erosion and thinking about the future of those who would follow this generation and have nothing, no soil to work and knowing that it takes generations to bring back the soil, I cannot but feel that a kindly interpretation of soil conservation might be helpful to those people. I would not, naturally, try to teach a lesson to those people by saying, this is wrong and this is right. . . . I will try to show the benefits of land terracing and the benefits of the top soil in contrast with the old worn out methods of burning the grass and of pulling up the roots of trees, etc.[58]

Fortunately for Holbrook and for Haleyville, the Civilian Conservation Corps was already at work reforesting the land and the extension agents were already teaching farmers how to reclaim their soil. All that remained was for Holbrook to paint what he saw, altering the proportions a bit. In his mural (Figure 30), the example of the way the land was destroyed is relegated to about a sixth of the canvas and to the far distance. The rest is dominated by terraced fields, reforested land, and general plenty. In the foreground are two life-sized men, one a portrait of Mr. Wilson, the local forest ranger, planting a pine seedling, which would hold the soil and retard erosion. The other figure, from imagination, is a "CCC boy" looking back on the outdated and destructive methods represented in the upper-left-hand corner.

57. Chestnut, *The Rural South*, 75.
58. Hollis Holbrook to Rowan, March 29, 1940, in Haleyville, Alabama, file, RG 121, NA.

30 / Hollis Holbrook, *Reforestation,* Haleyville, Ala., 1940

If we follow his gaze, we see distant farmers engaging in just the type of land clearing with which Jeeter Lester destroyed his land and himself. In the penultimate scene of *Tobacco Road,* Jeeter's hunger for the agricultural life prompts him to set fire to his worthless fields in the time-honored method of clearing southern land for planting. Innately lazy, he goes to bed while they burn. The result is that his hovel, his wife, and himself are burned with the fields. Readers might think that Jeeter's death by the very means that had destroyed his spirit and his land would pave the way for new generations to create new life. But Caldwell did not allow that much optimism. In the closing scene, Jeeter's son, who has not inherited even Jeeter's archetypal love of the land, visits the ruins of the home and the fields. But this sixteen-year-old boy grieves only for the new Ford he destroyed through carelessness and ignorance the day before.

The message in Holbrook's mural is just the opposite. The CCC worker represents the generation that will save the land so that future generations can cherish it. In the mural, the future is a reality. Most of the land has been reclaimed, and only an ignorant few cling to the old destructive methods. Residents are protected from any threat from the outside by layers of cultivated hills extending into the distance, and in the middle ground, the windbreaks planted by conservationists have grown to useful height, but conservationists plant still more. Just inside the mural, facing the viewers in the post office, the gentle, paternal face of Mr. Wilson implores them to join him in planting pine trees to preserve the land on which they depend for their livelihood.

Holbrook saved the final touches on his mural—making the egg tempera blue of the sky exactly match the post office wall, matching other details to the pink marble wainscoting—until his second trip to Haleyville, this time for installation. There he used "three dozen brown Haleyville eggs" to mix his paint and there he listened, elated, to people's comments:

> I have never felt so well rewarded as I have for this task. The people of Haleyville have lauded my efforts with exhaustive praise. Honestly they are starving for some good art works. . . . [One says,] "Doc, that sure is the prettiest sign paintin' I've ever seen." Another says, "By God, that sure is the prettiest thing I've ever seen!—another—"Ain't that the prettiest doggone thing you've ever seen." Somewhat the same but there have been hundreds of the same thing. I've heard that a picture isn't so good when it is liked by all but right now I want to say "Who cares?"[59]

At the urging of the local newspaper, Holbrook wrote his own story of the painting. His style is made vaguely comical because he avoids the first-person pronoun when expressing his own views. But because of that artificiality, his own experience becomes more general, a message for anyone who would paint for the inhabitants of Tobacco Road:

> To do a first rate job on a mural an artist must know his subject and get first hand information from his community. This is always an expensive way of doing work. Not only were photos taken of Winston County in this case but many sketches and paintings were made of the people and landscape of the community. These were formulated into a plan . . . that would be enjoyable to look at. Every detail in the mural had to have a study made for it. . . . These drawings included hands, boots, shirts, pants and faces. . . .
>
> The painter thoroughly enjoyed his work in Haleyville because the people were enthusiastic about the work and because they were the most sincerely cordial and likable people he had ever met.[60]

The important lesson, the one that might have taught the Section something, from the experiences of Evergood and Holbrook is that to build good will among southerners, an artist had to keep his audience in mind. He could not, like Evergood, lecture them from

59. Holbrook to Rowan, September 4, 1940, *ibid.*
60. "Mural Completed At Post Office," September 26, 1940, clipping, *ibid.*

outside about the possibilities if only southern workers would band together; and he could not expect rural southerners to appreciate unlovely figures that purported to portray them. He could, like Chestnut and Holbrook, deliver a warning about the necessity of preserving the land for posterity, but only if it seemed to spring from the South and only if it was couched in believable, hopeful terms. The CCC and the FSA were doing something about the situation even if it would take several generations to reap the benefits. Evergood's happily cooperating workers of all colors and sexes were not there in spirit anyway, and few in the South during the 1930s could see that as a possibility. Evergood did, however, put Rowan's colonial mansion in the upper-left-hand corner—so distant and so tiny it could hardly be seen. The days of such mansions were over; if the South were to revive, it would happen through the efforts of yeoman farmers and working-class southerners such as those whose sons joined the CCC.

When the people of Clemson, South Carolina, learned that they might receive a mural for their new post office, one Ben Robertson wrote the Section about a possible subject.

Please could we have some murals for the new Post Office here? The setting here is almost endless as a source of theme. . . . Clemson College is located here—one of the landgrant institutions, the state agricultural and mechanical college . . . ; there are 2,000 students, all studying farming, engineering, textile design and engineering architecture, etc.

The college is located on the old plantation estate, Fort Hill, of John C. Calhoun, and the Calhoun home is here; the Calhouns are buried here—some of them, but not John C.; he is buried in Charleston, among the aristocrats where like Herbert Hoover he belongs. Calhoun was an upcountry man, a member of the small farm people, and he sold the upcountry out to become the spokesman of Charleston and the great plantations. . . . The Pinckneys and Pickenses and Calhouns and Ravenels all had great plantations in this valley and all of them are washed away with the exception of the Calhoun estate and that has not washed away because the state has taken it over—the federal government had taken over the old plantations as ruined land.[61]

61. Ben Robertson to Edward Bruce, November 8, 1939, in Clemson, South Carolina, file, RG 121, NA. Robertson's northwest corner of South Carolina is profusely peopled with Robertsons—there could have been two Ben Robertsons with a gift for folksy politics. It seems entirely possible, however, that the author of this letter and the author of *Red Hills and Cotton: An Upcountry Memory* (New York, 1942) are the same.

The day of the upcountry man had come to Clemson. At the Calhoun estate young men and women—not the ones who went to the state university to learn dancing, politics, and sports boosterism and came home with gentlemen's C's—studied to be farmers and engineers who would plant piney woods, terrace their fields, and build a New South. The Pinckneys, the Pickenses, and the Ravenels had their day and left the land ruined. The Lesters had died along with unscientific methods of preparing the soil. The yeoman farmer was to inherit the South at last. And to proclaim the new agriculture, the Clemson mural commemorated Clemson College. Nine of the college's founders stand on the lawn of the old Calhoun plantation, defending the land from any old-fashioned farmer who might try to retake the ground and debilitate it with unsound farming methods.

The murals that celebrated the progressive farmer went on post office walls, as happened in Clemson, with little ado and no controversy. That also was true of Natalie Henry's mural for Springdale, Arkansas. "Springdale's new post office building this morning had its long awaited mural," reported the Springdale paper. "No elaborate celebration marked its installation last night, as it would have received in metropolitan cities. It was simply hung on the building's interior east wall above the postmaster's door." Neither was the mural itself elaborate; it was satisfying. And we do not celebrate satisfaction; we sit back on the porch and enjoy it. On her first visit, Natalie Henry observed that Springdale was more "prosperous and alert than most Arkansas towns."[62] And so she had abundant material to choose from. She finally elected to paint something of almost everything that characterized the town. Strawberries, vineyards, wheat fields, the poultry business—all are represented in the mural.

But what probably satisfied Springdale most were the people she put in the mural. They are busy, but they are not drudges. Their backs are straight, their faces solemn as if their minds are peacefully occupied. The group is arranged in a frieze across the fore-

62. "Local Post Office One of Nation's Few Having Mural," clipping, n.d., Natalie Henry to Rowan, October 15, 1940, both in Springdale, Arkansas, file, RG 121, NA. The color sketch of the Springdale mural is featured on the dust jacket of Marlene Park and Gerald E. Markowitz, *Democratic Vistas: Post Offices and Public Art in the New Deal* (Philadelphia, 1984), and the mural is illustrated inside in black and white (p. 117).

ground, each person in comfortable modern dress because each can afford to order from Sears-Roebuck. There are no dowdy flour sacks such as the "people" in murals so often wear. A suited man appraises another man's fat white hens. Another proudly shows his strawberries to the extension agent. A child climbs a tree while his sister feeds a friendly rooster. But the most satisfied and satisfying of all the picture's inhabitants is the slightly rotund farmer in the center who is about to take a good drink of Arkansas well water from the community dipper. The fields stretch far into the background, but finally they run into the Ozark foothills and the requisite protection from invading outsiders. The Arkansas children have far to roam; they are not so restricted as are the mountaineers on Frank Long's Morehead, Kentucky, porch. But they do not have the horizon. That would be too dangerous.

Henry painted a prosperous agricultural scene and a believable agrarian dream, but she painted the traditional rural South. When Robert Cleaver Purdy painted a dairy farm for New Albany, Mississippi, he painted a truly new South, a languid, spacious, green idyll (Figure 31). And his vision was so successful that he did not need to circumscribe the scene with architectural and natural barriers to invasion.

In the 1930s, cotton growers in northeastern Mississippi, with the kindly help of county agents, were learning to practice two-armed farming. Dairy farming never quite took in the area, but in 1938 it seemed to be working. The Carnation milk company established two plants in the region, bringing enough prosperity that the Baptists in nearby Okolona named their new church the Carna-

31 / Robert Cleaver Purdy, *Milking Time*, New Albany, Miss., 1939

tion Baptist Church. And it worked well enough to provide Purdy with his subject. On the New Albany Post Office hangs a picture of a southern dairy farm (restored in 1980).[63] New Albany is no longer a dairy community, but it is a thriving town. Its textile industries, though not agricultural, are southern, and thus the promise of the mural has been fulfilled in unexpected ways.

The South was struggling in the 1930s to build an economy both compatible with the rest of the country and uniquely southern. And in many ways, it was succeeding. Statistics showed that despite a woeful economic and educational lag behind the rest of the country, because the lag had been even greater in years past, its growth had outstripped that of the nation as a whole. Sally Gleaton did not need to be reminded that southern land had been ruined by farmers who did not plow with the contour of the land, and the South did not need Erskine Caldwell's reminders that it had failed. As Lucile Blanch recognized when she designed the Appalachia mural, southerners were all too aware of the shortcomings of their lives and their land. They needed the Section to show them the beauty surrounding them.

63. Information on New Albany's excursion into dairy farming is gleaned from interviews and conversations with long-term residents in August, 1981.

IV / OF MELONS AND MEN: THE DIVISION OF LABOR BETWEEN THE RACES AND THE SEXES

Until recently, the post office in St. Martinville, Louisiana, was a converted antebellum mansion. Despite the necessity of partitioning the ancient parlor with marble wainscoting and brass grilles, some of the gracious appurtenances of the original dwelling were retained. The building, remodeled in 1939, presented unusually challenging problems for the muralist who would decorate its lobby. New York artist Minetta Good was deemed the best Section artist to design wall paintings for the four, molding-encircled areas that had surrounded the original chandeliers. These she embellished with circular arrangements of pelicans, magnolias, azaleas, and crawfish. But Good would have to design the largest and most important of her St. Martinville decorations to hang over the ornate mantelpiece in the post office lobby. For that space, she was asked to paint a picture of the town's most famous resident, and one of whom no actual pictures existed—Evangeline.

The St. Martinville Evangeline is not the Evangeline of whom Henry Wadsworth Longfellow sang in his New England poem. The post office "portrait" depicts the Evangeline whose story was told in the 1930s in Cajun country and is still told there today. The historical figure upon whose life both stories are based was among those Acadians who, over two centuries ago, were suddenly and ruthlessly exiled from their Nova Scotia homes. Southern Louisiana Creole aristocrats, hearing of the plight of their fellow French-speaking immigrants, offered them refuge and small tracts of land in the area around St. Martinville where the Creoles had settled some time before. The Cajuns, as they call themselves today, having adopted the once-despised nickname, had been forced to evacuate overnight. In the confusion, Evangeline was separated from her fiancé, Gabriel, the one love of her life. When she arrived in Louisiana, Gabriel was not there, but Evangeline was confident that one day he would arrive on the same waterway—the Bayou Teche—that regularly brought new boatloads of refugee Acadians.

In Longfellow's poem, Evangeline set out to search for Gabriel in every port where Cajuns landed or settled. Not so in the legend told along the Bayou Teche. In her unquestioning faith, the South Louisiana Evangeline spent the daylight hours of every day under an oak tree by the river waiting for Gabriel. One day, after her long vigil, he arrived. Ecstatically, the lovers rushed into each other's arms—but then Gabriel remembered. Having despaired of finding Evangeline, or unable to distinguish one waiter from another, he had taken a wife. Evangeline, as the story goes, swooned on the spot and fell into a decline that was to end only in death. And this Evangeline remains a South Louisiana heroine to this day.[1]

Straining to find some elements of heroism in Evangeline's story, one concludes that feminine heroism among the Cajuns devolves from patient expectation. Evangeline in Minetta Good's picture is well designed to wait (Figure 32). She sits in traditional Acadian costume, carefully authenticated by the artist in collaboration with the St. Martinville postmaster and other residents who provided photographs and descriptions, beneath a live oak from which cascades Spanish moss.[2] Patience emanates from the lady's unfocused eyes and placid features, tastefully rouged. She dare not exert herself, for fear of mussing or smudging her carefully ironed white apron and her starched white cap. Her smooth, idle hands, having not the strength to lift the book she holds, are ill equipped for any work other than patient waiting or the suggestion of her defensive wish to preserve her body as incubator for future generations. Her long fingers and longer fingernails, laid protectively on her breast, are well tended, and her hair is elegantly coiffed in the latest 1939 hairstyle. At her throat, this penniless refugee wears a

1. This story is reconstructed from August, 1983, interviews with residents of St. Martinville and New Iberia, Louisiana; brochures directing tourists to the live oak beneath which Evangeline waited—the Evangeline Oak—and to her grave by the ancient Catholic church; and a plaque by the tree itself. Neither the Evangeline "portrait" nor the circular designs can be viewed at this time. When a new post office was built for St. Martinville, the city bought the mansion to restore. According to a St. Martinville postal worker, when the murals were removed, one of them was damaged. The United States Postal Service punished the St. Martinville office by recalling the murals to Washington. Nobody has yet been located there, however, who knows the whereabouts of the murals.

2. Howard J. Durand, St. Martinville Postmaster, to Hon. Robert L. Mouton, Congressman, August 1, 1939, Minetta Good to Edward Rowan, February 12, 1940, Mouton to Rowan, May 1, 1940, all in St. Martinville, Louisiana, file, Entry 133, Record Group 121, National Archives.

32 / Minetta Good, *Evangeline,* St. Martinville, La., 1940

golden cross, put there at the request of the congressman from the region who wrote the Section to request it.[3] Flanked by water hyacinths and other flora native to the area, she sits by the bayou, which flows into the distance. No agitation in Evangeline's visage disturbs the tranquillity of her natural setting. In the background is a precise representation of the Catholic church whose contemporary function was to solace her and on whose grounds she would eventually be buried. This woman has known no struggle, and at this point in her faithful vigil, she knows no anguish. Her work is to wait and to remain worthy of her lover.

One is tempted to defend Evangeline as an exception, to suggest that her story is almost as tragic as it is sentimental and to justify it in terms of the many visitors who come to the very live oak under which she waited, the very gravestone beneath which she still waits. But once we examine the images of white women prevalent in the South and in the nation, we conclude that Evangeline is not an exception, that she is the prototype for virtually all representations of southern white women.

It is interesting, however, that neither Evangeline nor other southern white women during the depression are depicted in the act of working. Probably at no time in United States history has the idea of work been examined so thoroughly and by so large a part of the population as it was during the Great Depression. In that era, the very lack of work for up to 30 percent of the people who needed it focused attention on its nature, on its effect on the laborer, and on who was entitled to do it for pay. Most of the population agreed that what paid employment there was should be reserved for heads of household, usually male, and those, also usually male, who would prepare themselves to be heads of household. Women who had to support themselves or who were unfortunate enough to be themselves heads of household were grudgingly entitled to work in the marketplace when work was available, but with less pay and less status. Work, even that for which there was no remuneration, was considered a meritorious endeavor in and of itself, and the act of doing it was thought to be ennobling even for women—except in fictional images of southern white women.

Two exceedingly popular and trend-setting movies of the late 1930s illustrate the predominant thinking on work and the sexes.

3. Rowan to Good, January 3, 1941, *ibid.*

Walt Disney's first feature-length cartoon, *Snow White*, is permeated with the idea that work is not only virtuous but fun. The dwarfs not only worked furiously for their living, they loved it. As they went off to dig for jewels—no salt mines for them—in the morning, delighted that they could work, they sang lustily, "Heigh ho, heigh, ho / It's off to work we go." Once they put their picks to the rock, their pleasure in honest labor was even more zealous as they sang "Dig, dig, dig, dig / We mine the whole day through / Dig, dig, dig, dig / It's what we love to do." And when they returned in the evening, they still sang of the joys of toil.

Snow White was a princess, however, and should never have needed to work. Unfortunately, her experiences were not worthy of a princess and she was forced to care for herself. Exiled from the castle, barely in possession of her life, lost in a hostile forest, and hungry, Snow White—like Evangeline, a refugee—stumbled upon the house of the Seven Dwarfs, where she took refuge. In the traditional Grimm fairy tale, the little house was "as neat and as clean as could be." The dwarfs had kept it that way themselves, but faced with a woman in need of shelter, they suggested that if she would "look after [the] household, cook, make the beds, wash, sew and knit, and keep everything neat and clean," she could stay with them.[4] The American version of the tale as told in the 1930s is quite different. The male household Disney's heroine finds is both messy and dirty—scandalously so. And Snow White, grateful that she has found shelter, undertakes to surprise its inhabitants with a tidy home. She is helped by enterprising forest denizens as eager to work as she. And she is delighted to work. It is from this cartoon epic that Americans learned, as Snow White led the chorus of domestic laborers, the song "Whistle While You Work." When the dwarfs return, suspicious at the change in their lair, it is Snow White who asks to work for her keep. Audiences agree that her offer is noble.

A quite different relationship between the white woman and work is seen in an equally popular cinematic epic of 1939. In the movie *Gone With the Wind*, as well as in Margaret Mitchell's 1936

4. Lore Segal and Randall Jarrell, "Snow White and the Seven Dwarfs," *The Juniper Tree and Other Tales from Grimm* (New York, 1973), 262. Similar translations appear in Arthur Rackham (illustrator), *Grimm's Fairy Tales: Twenty Stories* (New York, 1973); and Iona Opie and Peter Opie, *The Classic Fairy Tales* (London, 1974). In both the tale appears under its original title, "Snow Drop."

novel, work is degrading and socially unacceptable for white women. Scarlett O'Hara's whole family and her beloved plantation Tara would have ended in absolute ruin had she not worked in the fields and engaged in business ventures. And yet the audience is led to feel that by outshining her ineffectual second husband in the business world, Scarlett has committed the unforgivable sin. And when her farmsmanship demonstrates Ashley Wilkes's uselessness in the New South, the audience knows something irretrievable has been lost. The movie's leading lady is the traditional "plucky little woman"—an admirable role when played by Katharine Hepburn, but unacceptable for the southern lady.

Scarlett's spoiled and selfish younger sister, who is unwilling to mar a carefully manicured fingernail or risk sunburn working in the fields to save Tara, becomes almost a sympathetic figure when Scarlett indulges in unwomanly activity in order to feed them all. Had Scarlett not stolen this feminine child's fiancé and made a success of his business, he would hardly have made enough to shelter himself and his wife—much less the O'Hara family. But Scarlett is condemned by the movie's characters and the theater audience as well. One suspects that most audiences secretly admire Scarlett, and her loss of Rhett Butler is very nearly heartbreaking. Scarlett is sympathetic when she is helpless and weeping. But when she recovers and announces her decision to go to Tara, because "after all, tomorrow is another day," audiences are convinced that she has learned nothing from her failure as a southern lady— that she will go on doing what is necessary to care for herself and her family, and that she will once again involve herself in ventures and attitudes appropriate only for men.

The ideal of southern womanhood in this movie is, like Evangeline, a waiter. Melanie Wilkes waits patiently and confidently through the war for her husband's return; she waits through the siege of Atlanta for Scarlett to deliver her child and rescue her; and she waits through the rest of her life for Scarlett to realize that Melanie really is her soul mate. Her only exertion comes when it is necessary to remove a dead Yankee from the foyer—the home is, after all, woman's sphere. But Melanie is too frail, too much a lady to work in the fields. Her duty is to keep up morale by setting an example of patient and optimistic waiting for the southern men to return.

Gone With the Wind was no exception. In southern fiction during the period, work for white women, when it is not immoral, is tragic. Early in Carson McCullers' 1940 novel, *The Heart Is a Lonely Hunter*, readers are grieved because Mick, the female protagonist, must babysit for her little brother instead of playing the piano. Mick's shallow, rich friend takes lessons but does not appreciate her own advantages. And when Mick must finally take a full-time job at Woolworth's to help support her family, a sense of tragedy is the reader's only emotion. Katherine Anne Porter's short stories "The Source" (1930) and "The Old Order" (1934) create a southern grandmother grown callous from having to support those dependent on her, despite the fact that she has done it well. And in *Light in August*, the ability of Faulkner's earth mother, Lena Grove, to move men and married women to do for her so that she need not lift a finger is her key to the admiration of her audience.

Southern fiction is not the only place that we see images of where women and men properly belong in the southern work force. That St. Martinville's Evangeline, with her unfocused eyes, useless hands, and apparent lack of purpose, constituted a type for the period and the region can be demonstrated in the images of men and women used by department stores to sell clothes. Advertisements are a reliable barometer of public taste, particularly if the same images appear year after year. Sellers of clothing want people to be convinced that if they buy those clothes, they will resemble the drawings. Advertisers spend much tax-deductible money finding out what people want to look like. On the pages of any southern newspaper during the 1930s, one can see ladies and gentlemen as southerners would like to see themselves. And what one sees is Evangeline of the 1930s. Women in the ads gaze listlessly into space. If they are in the same frame with other women, they do not make eye contact; they are unaware of each other. The exception to the unfocused-eye rule is the woman who flirts with an imagined male reader. Occasionally, a woman selling formal gowns or seductive lingerie will look directly, albeit out of the corner of her eye, at the reader who, she hopes, will buy the item for the female he wishes would look at him that way.

The women in the ads, flirtatious or vacant, have useless hands or no hands at all. As often as not, the hands are cut off by the edge of the ad. A southern woman does not need hands anyway. And when hands do appear in the ads, they listlessly grasp tiny bags or lie relaxed on breasts, protection from potential marauders but not from the serious suitor. These women may have arm muscles, but they are never flexed, because limp arms mean light work. The women in ads typically pose in ways that separate them from the reader and from each other—backing away, shielding themselves with their otherwise useless hands. However, the men who advertise clothing are purposeful and aggressive. Invariably they walk directly toward their audience, eyes focused, or they raptly converse with each other. Sometimes their hands are, like the women's, invisible, but even when masculine hands rest in pockets, the muscles are flexed ready for action.

Two ads from the Nashville *Banner* in 1938 well illustrate this division of sex roles. In the Sloan Co.'s advertisement of its Christmas fashions, there are five women. Two of them model "Peak-of-the-Week Frocks that charm" (Figure 33). These two ladies, hats on, apparently at some social function, stand in front of the same chair. But they might as well be on opposite sides of the same mountain. One rests her right hand on the back of the chair—she hasn't the strength to stand alone—and gazes off to her right, in the direction of the other woman, but through her or over her. Her other hand disappears behind her back. Her legs drift into obscurity at the calf. They do not vanish behind a picture outline; they just fade away. Her companion, with the same vanishing legs, wears her hat tilted so that her eyes are invisible, but that's acceptable because her gaze can only drop off the edge of the page.

The other three ladies in the ad sell lounging pajamas, a new fashion in the late 1930s. These women lounge on 180 degrees of nothing. Five of their six feet are cut off by the line separating them from their fully dressed counterparts. Two of these women's arms are amputated just far enough from the shoulder that the prospective buyer can see the detail of the garment sleeve. Each uses her left hand provocatively to control some curl just out of sight behind her head. And one lounger lets a listless hand lie on the nothing beside her. Two of these women do look at readers—in that position they are, after all, issuing invitations—but their eyes are mere black blobs, no expression, no awareness.[5]

5. Nashville *Banner*, November 15, 1938, Sec. 1, p. 22.

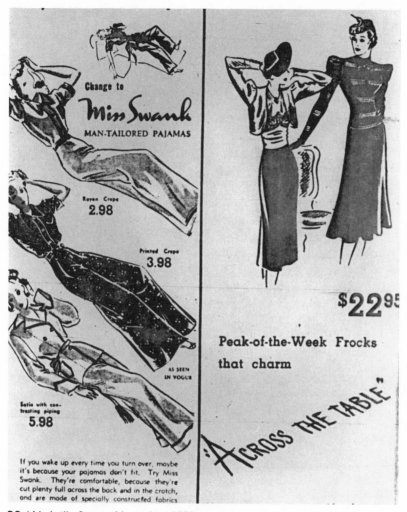

Change to

Miss Swank

MAN-TAILORED PAJAMAS

Rayon Crepe
2.98

Printed Crepe
3.98

Satin with con-
trasting piping
5.98

AS SEEN
IN VOGUE

If you wake up every time you turn over, maybe
it's because your pajamas don't fit. Try Miss
Swank. They're comfortable, because they're
cut plenty full across the back and in the crotch,
and are made of specially constructed fabrics

$22⁹⁵

Peak-of-the-Week Frocks
that charm

Across the Table

33 / Nashville *Banner*, November, 1938

Castner-Knott Co.'s ad for a clearance of men's suits and topcoats
("National Brand Lines Excepted") is quite different (Figure 34).
Here three successful middle-management men walk directly out
of the picture. Although they look at their public it is evident that
they are aware of each other because they walk in step and their
arms swing in rhythm. They wear smiles, their eyes are focused,
and their half-fisted hands are visible at the ends of determined,

CASTNER-KNOTT CO.

By all odds the greatest collection of Suits and Topcoats we've been able to sell at this price in years—

EVERY SUIT IN OUR STOCK INCLUDED IN THIS CLEARANCE *(National Brand Lines Excepted)*

TOPCOATS

muscular arms.[6] One might argue that such images appeared in advertisements throughout the United States, that useless hands and unfocused eyes are always signs of females who live as females were intended to live. And the argument bears scrutiny. The skeptic is correct: such images in ads and in post office murals are not uniquely southern. But in nonsouthern newspapers, women advertising clothes usually have a full complement of limbs, and most of the time they look at their audience or at a definite point within the ad. In the same month when women lay on space and leaned on chairs in Nashville, a couple of vacant females did advertise fur coats in the Boston *Evening Transcript* and the St. Paul, Minnesota, *Pioneer Press*, but they were not missing limbs and they stood on their own two feet. Outside the fur trade, women with usable limbs walked toward the reader, they smiled, and they used their hands.

A St. Paul ad for Brucewood Coats presents a woman whose legs do fade away, but she faces the audience, makes eye contact, and smiles (Figure 35). She uses one of her hands to adjust her hat, almost as if she were tipping it. The other is in her pocket, but her arm muscles are flexed. She can pull this arm out the moment it is needed. In the Boston paper several days later, two women advertise "Hand Made Silk Slips" without issuing invitations (Figure 36). The taller of the two stands facing the audience, on her own casually crossed legs, leaning on nothing. Her companion does look away from the audience and she does adjust her hair, but all four arms and hands are visible and their muscles are toned. No limp limbs, no fragmented bodies, no careful avoidance of the audience.[7]

These advertising types exist on a continuum apparently ranging from South to North. Although during the 1930s ads can be found in Yankee newspapers featuring women with vacant eyes, useless arms, and truncated legs, they are comparatively rare. And once in a while a southern clothing model makes eye contact with the audience and stands on her own. It is the distribution that makes the difference. In the Louisville *Courier-Journal*, for example, fewer

6. *Ibid.*, November 30, 1938, Sec. 1, p. 27.
7. These observations are supported by surveys of the Boston *Evening Transcript*, November, 1938, and the St. Paul *Pioneer Press*, November, 1938. Specific examples from St. Paul *Pioneer Press*, November 3, Sec. 1, p. 2, and Boston *Evening Transcript*, November 16, Sec. 1, p. 3.

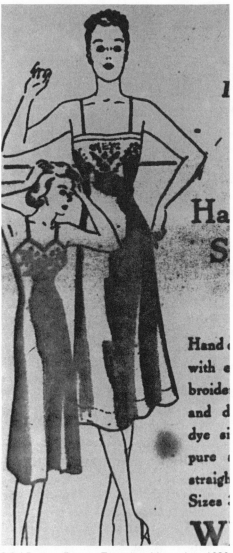

BRUCEWOOD
DESIGNED
IN STOCKHOLM

MAURICE L
ROTHSCHILD

BRUCEWOOD COAT

with gay Scandinavian
backs designed in
Stockholm

$19⁹⁵

Waist deep quilted Earl-Glo scientifically
insulated and edged with gay
Scandinavian designs

Here are more of these history making coats
—coats that captured not only the flashing
colors of the fjords but the hearts of St. Paul
women as well. You'll love the fleeces,
tweeds and dressy boucle weaves—sturdy
and rugged as the Norsemen themselves and
styled in the smartest box swaggers as well
as fitted models. You won't believe they're
only $19.95. It seems a miracle, but it's true.

Sizes for all—11 to 17—12 to 20—38 to 44

2ND FLOOR

Maurice L Rothschild

35 / St. Paul *Pioneer Press,*
November, 1938

Ha
S

Hand
with e
broide
and d
dye si
pure
straigh
Sizes

W

36 / Boston *Evening Transcript,* November, 1938

"waiters" are found than in Nashville and Atlanta, but more than in Boston and St. Paul. Even though clothing ads depicting vacant-eyed women with useless limbs could be found in newspapers throughout the nation, even though murals with waiting females could be found in the Midwest, the popular culture and the literature pointed to the waiting woman as a southern ideal. While Evangeline and Melanie Wilkes had to wait, could do aught but wait, would be, like Scarlett O'Hara, ruined if they lifted fingers in their own behalf, Disney's Snow White and other American women should seek to look and act southern, but, if the need to labor actively was thrust upon them, they could do so with honor and, at least, they had hands to do it.

Newspaper ads do much to reveal why white men and women appear as they do in the murals. Popular images of blacks, southern or otherwise, were much more difficult to find. Few pictures of black Americans were published in southern newspapers, and those that were featured the likes of Aunt Jemima selling pancakes. Black males did not appear in ads. Even in black newspapers where ads featuring white women modeling clothing were occasionally darkened to suggest that blacks could wear the clothes too if they had money, only women appeared in ads. Usually, they were fair skinned, and most ads were for some cosmetic that would straighten black hair or lighten complexions. Of course, only large cities had black newspapers at all. In small towns, where most of the murals were placed, newspaper readers could see only Aunt Jemima. The images of black men in most newspapers were verbal ones in headlines such as "Negro Arrested in Slaying of Local Man." The contrast between a "negro" male and a man was clear.

Images of blacks did appear in southern white literature of the period, and they bear out the impression one gains from the murals and the ads. Faulkner's most admired figure is Dilsey, Mammy to the Compson family in *The Sound and the Fury*. Dilsey is, perhaps, the only wholly strong and virtuous creation in all of Faulkner's Yoknapatawpha canon. And she works. She is cook, housekeeper, and nanny. She brings up her own children and those of the Compsons according to an ethic any honest Yankee laborer would admire. Her most important function, however, is to hold the family together despite the father's absence and a matriarch whose devotion to waiting and helplessness would make Melanie Wilkes and

Evangeline appear energetic. Similar black female mainstays of white families are major characters in Carson McCullers' *Member of the Wedding* and Katherine Anne Porter's "The Old Order" and "The Last Leaf." And, of course, there's Scarlett's Mammy.

The black male is virtually as invisible in the movies, the literature, and the murals as he is in the ads. True, David O. Selznick's Tara does have a ubiquitous black male retainer, but he is faithful, a bit foolish, and almost useless. In *Sartoris*, Faulkner has created virtually the same type to chauffeur old Colonel Sartoris around in an archaic horse and buggy. These were the days when Stepin Fetchit was a fixture in movies set in the South. Other black males just disappear into the woodwork holding a silver salver of mint juleps or troweling the azaleas.

Subconsciously at least, the Section seems to have aimed to present America as it should be, as Americans wished to believe it was. Designs about soil erosion were routinely rejected for southern murals.[8] So were pictures of overweight women and mine disasters. These might remind people of human frailty or of the hardships and disappointments inevitable in the South. Even so, when the Section set out to decorate new federal buildings with art that was both excellent and meaningful to the people, it created an impossible task. Fewer than half of the southern murals purported to represent the communities in which they were placed seemed to have meaning for the post office patrons. If the murals were not hated, they were ignored, but none was rejected because of the way it depicted the division of labor between women and men, between black and white.

Often murals seem to have been ignored by the public for whom they were made. And ignoring implies a form of consent. The people and the postmaster objected, sometimes fiercely, when a mural was not appropriate to an area. The congressman who represented St. Martinville and the postmaster objected to an inappropriately old Evangeline in inaccurate clothes. But very few ever objected to the division of labor between the sexes and the races as it was depicted in any mural. And when an objection was voiced— for example, to white women shown picking cotton in the Gastonia, North Carolina, mural—designs were changed before they were installed. Since no objections were ever raised to idle women,

8. See Karal Ann Marling, *Wall-to-Wall America* (Minneapolis, 1982), 81–127.

unfocused female eyes, white men charting courses while their wives sat listlessly, idle black men in cotton fields or black women in positions of strength and occasionally of authority, the implication is that no fault was ever found with these representations. When certain themes were repeated time after time with virtually no variation, and they never brought protest, one can assume that these aspects of the murals were invisible because they were seen as correct, as southerners wished the division of labor to be.

The duty of a white woman in a mural was not only to wait; she must do so, if not with Evangeline's patience, certainly with no anguish. Minetta Good's first sketch of Evangeline was rejected (Figure 37). In it, Evangeline sat beneath the same oak; she clutched the same book; she pressed a similarly manicured hand to her breast. But her face and head were quite different. Dull, lifeless hair is pulled into a severe chignon. Her eyes look searchingly up the bayou, and in them are traces of doubt, even fear. Her complexion is feverish and drawn. She has known the indignity of forced evacuation, of homeless travels, and of the travail of a new home without the hope that would make her whole. The letter rejecting this sketch asked only that Evangeline be made younger—a girl of nineteen. In the meantime, Good had received the photographs supplied her by St. Martinville residents. She had learned what was expected of southern women, and she modified her heroine into a fully acceptable portrait. The southern woman could wait, but she could not suffer.

She could wait in Acadian costume under a live oak in St. Martinville or in modern dress by a fence in Eunice. The design for the Eunice, Louisiana, mural features a shapely young woman, arm resting on a fence beyond which a plowed field stretches to a distant vanishing point (Figure 38). Although this vista is not the usual southern landscape, in which trees or buildings are reassuringly close, the woman is protected from the vastness by the fence beside which she waits. And she need not clutch her hand to her breast, because she is separated from the post office lobby by an apparently empty house, a deserted barn, and an abandoned plowshare. Dark open doors to the house and the barn suggest an emptiness in need of filling. In the final version (Figure 39), a cat sips cream on the porch and a dog slumbers in the endless sun. Healthy white chickens dot the lawn. But still the woman waits. She has the land, the buildings, the livestock, and the equipment for a pro-

37 / Minetta Good, design for St. Martinville, La.

38 / Laura B. Lewis, design for Eunice, La.

39 / Laura B. Lewis, color sketch for Eunice, La., which closely resembles the completed mural, *Louisiana Farm*, 1941

ductive farm, but she looks forsaken. One can surmise that the empty house and barn will be filled, the plowshare used, only when this Evangeline's Gabriel arrives.

Laura B. Lewis, who painted this mural, won the contract on the basis of her entry in a Texas competition. She was warned in her appointment letter that "since your successful design dealt with specific subject matter related to a town in Texas it would be necessary, due to the fact that the jury chose your work for a Louisiana building, for you to investigate suitable subject matter in connection with Eunice, Louisiana." Her first new design was similar to the final one (Figure 39). When Rowan saw its open spaces, he was doubtful. He approved it only when he was assured that she had indeed conferred with the Eunice postmaster and knew the actual landscape. Even then he added a provision: "It is our feeling that you . . . [should introduce] some further elements to relieve the starkness of the barren house. Are there no plantings around the house in the way of one or two shrubs? Are there no chickens? . . . The sheer design is not enough to carry the forsaken quality which is all but overstated."⁹

Lewis, a New Orleans artist, did not think her design stark at all. She found it "grand to find in lush Louisiana a country that had the sweep and space of those great open fields—and wide skies."¹⁰ But she added a few sunflowers, some tall grass, and some dirt clods. And she gave the young woman the company of some pets and productive chickens. The result is similar to the changes in Minetta Good's Evangeline design: the woman is still forsaken, but she no longer appears hopeless. The plowed rows stretching to the horizon promise other worlds, but she cannot reach them for the fence. Nor would she want to, unless she was ready to brave Scarlett O'Hara's fate.

The women in the St. Martinville and Eunice, Louisiana, Post Offices, Mick in *The Heart Is a Lonely Hunter*, Lena Grove in *Light in August*, and Katherine Anne Porter's resourceful grandmother were all unattached. Southern women who had had children and had men to care for them no longer needed to emanate hope. Hope for them, one assumes, had already been fulfilled. Still, the most difficult work they could perform was to hold or watch over children. Several southern murals depict early settlers in progress toward or arriving at the site of their homestead. In most, the white men bring women with them—they must if they are to carry on the line—but the women are merely accessories.

When the first settlers arrived by boat at what would be Tuscumbia, Alabama, according to artist Jack McMillen (Figure 40), the father, the three male children, and the dog participate actively in the labor: they pole or row the boat, they confer with each other about where to land, or if, like the smallest boy and the dog, they cannot work, they look eagerly at the Indians who welcome them. Only the mother, clutching a swaddled baby to her bosom, refuses to look at the Indians, perhaps because she wants no part in taking their land and destroying their way of life. But it is equally

9. Edward Rowan to Laura B. Lewis, January 19, May 28, 1940, both in Eunice, Louisiana, file, RG 121, NA.
10. Lewis to Rowan, June 10, 1940, *ibid.*

40 / Jack McMillen, *Chief Tuscumbia Greets the Dickson Family,* Tuscumbia, Ala.,
1939

41 / Daniel Rhodes, color sketch for Clayton, Mo., 1941

likely that she averts her glance because even to look at the work
to be done to build their homestead would taint her southern
womanhood.

The offspring of the family who will settle Clayton, Missouri,
are all male but they are grown (Figure 41). Three versions of this
mural were done. In each, the family pauses in its westward trek so
that a wagon wheel can be mended. In each, the three males either
work on the wheel or examine maps to chart the rest of their journey. And in each, the female member of the party sits listlessly,
waiting for work to be done, for Gabriel to deliver her to her new
home. The biggest change in the three versions is that the artist
cannot seem to decide whether to lean her against a post of an im-

probable building, put her on a crate far enough from the action that she cannot interfere, or seat her on the wagon tongue. But he never doubts what to do with her hands. They are not manicured and they do not protect her breast. She is beyond all that. Instead, they atrophy in her lap. Her hands and her face are entirely without animation. They exist merely to provide some formal balance to the picture.

Van Buren, Arkansas, was settled by a younger family, according to artist E. Martin Hennings (Figure 42). The white men and women he created for *The Chosen Site* have no doubts about their function in the new land. Youthful father and son stand to the right in front of a yoke of oxen, symbols of work, and, like their counterparts in 1930s clothing ads, they look directly at the audience, their muscles flexed, their feet ready to move forward. And in case their poses do not entirely define their function, each has a rifle to help with the destructive work of taming the land. The wife and the daughter, occupying the left side of the picture, pose in front of the covered wagon, the dwelling in which they find their place. The mother, still of childbearing age, adopts an almost vampish stance, one arm akimbo, torso thrust forward, eyes vacant, ready to do her part in populating the new land. Too young to have learned her duty to be either seductive or apathetic, the daughter waits, excited—her eyes sparkling. But the fact that she is seated suggests that she will not spring to work the land that will be her home.

To display their childbearing ability seems to have been acceptable for historical women in the murals, but contemporary women

42 / E. Martin Hennings, *The Chosen Site*, Van Buren, Ark., 1940

43 / Louis Raynaud, design for Bay St. Louis, Miss.

had to be careful that decorum was maintained. Louis Raynaud's first design for his Bay St. Louis, Mississippi, mural, *Life on the Coast,* looked for all the world like a travel poster (Figure 43). He assumed that unattached American women could advertise their availability and that married ones could enjoy a swim with their youngsters. In the drawing, a small fishing boat is in unconvincing juxtaposition to a scene of recreational swimming. In the center just beyond the foreground, two virile white men land a load of recently caught fish. To the right, three equally virile Indians—in costumes out of history—prepare the fish for market. At the left, a bathing-suit-clad mother stands with her toddler son in the water. In front of the white men sits a young woman with downcast eyes. She holds a fishing net and a spindle as if she would mend the net, but her flaccid hands and arms seem incapable of even that effort. Next to her stands an attractive young woman—because of her height and her placement in the mural, its most prominent figure. Her left hand is behind her head, in the standard pin-up pose, and the split in her skirt reaches to the thigh. Perhaps the most unconventional aspect of this mural is that she makes eye contact with the audience. None of the men in the picture are more than marginally clothed, but it is the half-dressed women who distressed Rowan. The same Section that had approved the Van Buren, Arkansas, mural, with the mother's less than demure stance, rushed to protect the reputations of these women:

> In studying the cartoon I wish to say that parts of it are very handsome but the figures of the two white women should be treated less like fig-

ures in an advertisement. It is suggested that you put a complete skirt on the central figure and if possible give her some function in the decoration besides that of merely posing. The seated woman with the net is a much more satisfactory arrangement. The woman in the bathing suit is also objectionable from the poster standpoint. Could you not reduce her in scale and have her standing on the shore on the left watching the child as he plays with his boat in the water? I believe that in the end you yourself would prefer such an arrangement.

Kindly let me know of your decision in this matter.[11]

Of course, Raynaud's decision was to comply with Section suggestions, since he wanted his first payment. Rowan had been clear: he wanted modest women who would not overshadow the working males, and he wanted no travel posters. In the final mural, all the women are demurely clad and each has an appropriate function (Figure 44). The mother has receded into the background where she no longer competes with the men for attention. She stands fully clothed on the shore. Although she would have difficulty aiding her son if he were to encounter danger in the water, she looks as a southern mother should look. She is passive and self-effacing. The woman with the spindle still holds it limply. Now, however, she has the dubious help of the other woman, from whose passive hand dangles a portion of the net. The men still work purposefully.

When they were not clutching fishnets, tiny purses, or children to their breasts, women in the South, as they had been in art for centuries, were inextricably bound with food, fertility, and fecundity. Rowan knew well what he was doing when he advised adding chickens to the Eunice, Louisiana, mural. In the 1930s, the association of women with chickens was both traditional and contemporary. Raising chickens had always been women's province on the farm, and the most popular artists in the 1930s often featured the two creatures in symbolic proximity. John Steuart Curry juxtaposed them in much the same way in his murals *Homesteaders* and *Kansas Pastoral,* and Grant Wood used chickens with and *as* women in *Appraisal, Adolescence,* and *Farmers Wife with Chickens.*[12] But the association has a special meaning for southern

11. Rowan to Louis Raynaud, December 2, 1937, in Bay St. Louis, Mississippi, file, RG 121, NA.

12. See Sue Kendall, "Rethinking Regionalism: John Steuart Curry and the Kansas Murals" (Ph.D. dissertation, University of Minnesota, 1983), 236–67; Wanda Corn, *Grant Wood: The Regionalist Vision* (New Haven, 1983), Plate 10 (p. 81), Plate 30 (p. 125), and Plate 18 (p. 95).

44 / Louis Raynaud, *Life on the Coast,* Bay St. Louis, Miss., 1938
Photo by Richard H. Beckham

45 / Carson Davenport, design for Chatham, Va.

women. Chickens lay eggs—they provide food—but if they work at it, they do so in private and because they cannot help themselves. In the South, young ladies used to be told, "If you must scrub your own floors, by all means do it, but never, ever, let anyone see you do it." Like the chickens, southern women labor, if they must, in private and then sit on a nest or under a live oak, waiting for something to happen.

Corn was often an acceptable accompaniment to the chickens, as long as the women did not actually work with it. For Chatham, Virginia, Carson Davenport designed a nearly perfect farmscape (Figure 45). To the right, black men in the middle ground work with cotton as they should in a southern mural if they are to work at all. In the right foreground, capable, muscular white men tend tobacco plants. At the left, white men till the soil with the help of the all-important southern mules. And in the center foreground, a woman flanked by chickens appears in front of a stand of corn, indicating both that Chatham has abandoned the one-crop system in favor of more lucrative diversification and that the woman knows her place among food crops. There are, however, salient flaws in the presentation of the woman. According to the Section, she is too large in scale. And the second flaw, which Rowan never mentions, but which Davenport, a Virginia artist, figured out for himself, is that energetically, almost gaily, she picks the corn.

In his second sketch, Davenport followed minor suggestions from the Section about the male figures and made some changes of his own. Both the cotton and the blacks were gone, and the central female figure now merely holds a basket of corn. But there are still problems: this southern woman appears to be walking out of the mural toward an audience of whom she has no fear, and her face is no less than aggressive. Not only that, she is even larger than she was in the first design. Davenport justifies that departure from "realistic" scale, saying that "the figure of the farm woman was intentionally drawn larger to give prominence to her and power to the center of the design. . . . I think it is perfectly decorative."[13]

Rowan did not like it: "It is noted that you still feel that the panel would be better if the central figure were larger than the others. I regret that this office does not concur in this instance and I trust that you are making the necessary revision." Decoration was irrelevant if figures were out of scale, especially when it meant that a farm woman towered above farm men. Davenport made the necessary revision—he was offered no option—and the result is Evangeline with corn. In the installed mural, a stoic woman in scale with the men who surround her stands placidly amid fat white hens and a basket of fruit (Figure 46). Even if her unfocused eyes were purposeful, she would have a hard time doing anything because one arm is laden with juicy ears of corn—themselves out of scale—and from the other hangs a basket filled with more corn. Apparently, the final rendition was all that Chatham, Virginia, could want. The Chatham postmaster wrote that "we think it is a

13. Carson Davenport to Rowan, May 9, 1938, in Chatham, Virginia, file, RG 121, NA.

46 / Carson Davenport, *Harvest Season in Southern Virginia*, Chatham, Va., 1938

47 / Chester J. Tingler, *Cantaloupe Industry*, Sylvester, Ga., 1939
Photo by Richard H. Beckham

beautiful piece of work and all the citizens of our town are proud of it."[14]

Just as often as she waits with corn or chickens, Evangeline waits with fruit. Sometimes she sits, madonna-like, holding melons while multitudes of men both white and black produce them. On the Sylvester, Georgia, Post Office wall, a comely young woman wears contemporary clothing whose cut and pale color suggest Greek drapery. She sits atop a large pile of cantaloupe, holding a luscious half melon in her lap (Figure 47). Sharing her position at the apex of a pyramid formed by the melons and the men grouped

14. Rowan to Davenport, June 6, 1938, J. J. Patterson to Rowan, July 23, 1938, *ibid.*

about her stands a grandfatherly gentleman, submitting the other half for her inspection. This melon goddess is surrounded by men of both races bent on preparing a worthy harvest. They calculate the number of melons and their value, haul full crates to the pile and fill others with fruit, and, in the background, coax recalcitrant mules to pull wagons filled with still more fruit.

The black men in this picture are of particular interest. One tired man leans between his hoe and a tree, wiping his face with a red bandanna; three tiny figures trudge out of the background, carrying pails and sacks. Another black at the lower left balances a white man on the right who is moving a crate of melons. The difference is that the white man's back is straight, his face purposeful but placid as he empties a heavy load of melons, but the burden the white man shoulders with equanimity requires back-breaking effort from the black.

The most interesting grouping of blacks, however, is a series of three men, each with a crate of melons on his shoulder. This group is almost Egyptian in its stylization and simplicity, quite in contrast to the painstaking representational quality of the rest of the picture. The three men, in identical positions, overlap each other. Although the right arm of only the front bearer is visible, the positions of the others indicate that each holds the crate the same way. Every indication is that Florida artist Chester J. Tingler felt that he was presenting a particularly sympathetic view of the travails of blacks in the South. Rowan said, "I particularly wish to congratulate you on the charm of the presentation of the three negroes left of the tree carrying baskets of melons. The implications are unusually beautiful and poignant in this area." Tingler replied, "I am particularly happy that you felt what I tried to express in the three negroes left of the tree."[15]

Despite Tingler's efforts, the NAACP has attempted to have this mural removed because of its demeaning presentation of blacks.[16]

15. Rowan to Chester J. Tingler, October 18, 1938, and Tingler to Rowan, October 28, 1938, both in Sylvester, Georgia, file, RG 121, NA.

16. Interview with Jack Mowrie, August 16, 1982. The Sylvester postmaster told of pending NAACP legal action. Mowrie thought that his meeting with one local black leader and one white leader, wherein he defended the mural as a historic document, was sufficient to defer further action indefinitely. Mowrie gave no names and dates, preferring to keep the incident as quiet as possible. He did, however, say that similar protests had occurred in other Georgia communities, and he thought that the resulting efforts in Sylvester and those other Georgia communities had brought

48 / Ward Lockwood, *Harvest of the Rio Grande Valley*, Edinburg, Tex., 1940

The black workers are depicted as less capable than the white, and the special stylization reserved for the grouping to the left of the tree (in contrast with the overall realism) makes a distinction between men and black males that newspaper headlines in the 1930s also made. Their features are exaggerated but not in the style of American popular art. They have the high cheekbones and sloe eyes attributed to North Africans rather than Stepin Fetchit's thick lips, toothy grin, and pop eyes. When one examines the conventions that inform mural depictions of white and black women, white men and Indians, however, the black males in this picture do not do so badly. Most of them work—hard, at that—and the stylized bodies and faces of the group have a certain dignity that workers or purposeless white women in other murals often lack.

Tingler's melon goddess sits atop melons; other white women were not so distinct from the fruit with which they were associated. For Edinburg, Texas, Ward Lockwood painted another woman with melons (Figure 48). Around her are veritable mountains of grapefruit, tomatoes, oranges, gourds, and, of course, melons piled in pyramids. Strategically placed bunches of gladioli break the monotony, and bananas cascade from the ceiling. The plenty extends as far as the eye can see. In the center, balanced between baskets and boxes of melons and gourds, the woman sits, two melons on her lap and a third clutched to her breast in such a way that it is difficult to tell her right breast from her left melon. The associa-

---

about a new awareness of the murals and a statewide move to preserve them as documents.

49 / Marguerite Zorach, *Autumn*, Ripley, Tenn., 1940

tion between the fruit of the land and the fruit of the bosom has a tradition in art of many centuries' duration, perhaps most graphically in the serene bare-breasted women in Paul Gauguin's paintings of Polynesians with fruit. Lockwood was certainly aware of the tradition, and his juxtaposition of this Texas woman with her wares was undoubtedly an intentional allusion to it. But one is not certain that all artists were aware they were making such associations.

Marguerite Zorach's Ripley, Tennessee, mural depicts a contemporary hunting and gathering society (Figure 49). In a multicolored forest—this mural is called *Autumn*—two men in plaid shirts and high-top shoes carry weapons intended for unwary birds and rodents while their needle-nosed coon dogs sniff for potential prey. A third man gathers nuts from the ground, and a fourth has just caught a snake that might frighten his lady fair. And what does she do? She *waits*, apron extended, for nuts to fall out of a tree. But she is productive. Any who doubt it need only look where her breasts should be to see instead melons covered by her dress.

The southern confusion between women's anatomy and fruit did not stop with the muralists. It was pervasive. In July, 1938, a Farm Security Adminstration photographer captured "Miss Rachel Tinsley with some of the peaches grown on the John Tinsley farm 12 miles NW of Spartanburg, South Carolina" (Figure 50). In this photograph are five bushel baskets of peaches, each labeled "Palmetto Queen," and literally emanating from the one in the center

50 / [?] Welch, "Miss Rachel Tinsley with Peaches"
Farm Security Administration photograph no. SC-D3-166, courtesy Library of Congress

front is Miss Rachel Tinsley, a Palmetto Queen peach can for a crown. Miss Tinsley looks very like a young girl from the shoulders up, but from there down she is a bushel basket of peaches. Since the Farm Security Adminstration sent photographers into the South to make documentary photographs of conditions as they were, one must assume that girls did indeed have basket-of-peaches bodies.[17]

And if girls could have melon breasts or a bushel-basket body, it is not too hard to imagine Evangeline actually merging with her oak. Agnes Tait describes her Laurinburg, North Carolina, design (Figure 51):

17. Farm Security Administration photographs are housed in the Photograph Division of the Library of Congress, where they are filed by region and by subject. Each photo has a negative number, photographer, approximate date, and a descriptive title. Hereafter, such photos will be identified by title and date (when not mentioned in the text) and negative number.

51 / Agnes Tait, cartoon for Laurinburg, N.C., 1939

I carried away an impression of agricultural opulence which the local melon crops there seemed to typify. Then too the characteristic and most decorative chinaberry tree with its massive umbrella like shape presented a nice contrast to those flat coastal plains. With the workers, white and colored, and the idle children in the shade of the foreground tree, I could develop some nice color and detail. While in the pale background . . . I would show cotton fields and melon fields, perhaps even a distant peach orchard with perhaps a cow or mule and a few tiny workers. The clouds in a summer sky would carry throughout the melon shape.[18]

By the time the mural was completed, all the workers were black men and women, and the idle children, too, were black (Figure 52). The only white in the picture is at the apex of a triangle similar to the one in the Sylvester, Georgia, and Edinburg, Texas, murals. And this woman is mentioned in neither Tait's own description nor the one that appeared in the Laurinburg *Exchange*:

As a work of art it has merit and depicts in interesting manner a pastoral, or rustic scene, in which such products as melons, cantaloupes and cotton are mixed with slight regard for time or season. There is also the typical chinaberry tree, the darkies working in the fields, and the irreconcilable picture of cantaloupes, melons and cotton being harvested at the same time. Perhaps the most impractical feature is that of a hefty colored man leisurely pushing an open wheelbarrow loaded with

18. Agnes Tait to Rowan, November 13, 1940, in Laurinburg, North Carolina, file, RG 121, NA.

52 / Agnes Tait, *Fruits of the Land,* Laurinburg, N.C., 1941

big striped watermelons. Nobody ever saw anything like that here in actual life and nobody who knows melons would undertake to move them
in an open wheelbarrow.

But aside from such apparent incongruities, the picture is pleasing,
the colors are harmonious and there is serenity and plentitude in the
total effect.[19]

Apparently the image of the picture's only white figure, a woman,
fading into the chinaberry tree is not incongruous in the reporter's
experience. Today's feminist scholars would have much to say
about it, especially since the artist is herself female. But for the establishment in the 1930s, only one interpretation is possible. The
white woman waits, as she always does, and has no part in the action. This mysterious white woman, in the mural's dead center, is
surrounded by the idle children only one of whom pays her any attention. The female child offers the lady what appears to be a piece
of fruit. But the lady herself merely melds into the tree, her face
barely visible between the thickly bearing branches.

The black women in the Laurinburg mural, and in virtually all
others wherein black and white females appear together, offer
marked contrast to the passive white women and the incapable
black men. They are invariably accorded the dignity of manual labor and even, in a few cases, positions in which they evince authority. Here the hardest-working and, according to the Laurinburg

19. "Mural Painting At Post Office," Laurinburg *Exchange,* May 22, 1941, p. 1,
clipping, *ibid.*

Exchange, not incongruous laborers are the two black women load-ing cantaloupes into crates in the left foreground. These women work, but they in no wise suffer. They are well-clad, sturdy women quite up to the work they are assigned.

Another mural showing agricultural abundance is the one in Haynesville, Louisiana. Apart from being a handsome design, this mural suggests much about the relative positions of black and white males and females in the southern labor force. For the Clai-borne Parish town, "noted for its oil refineries, lumber mills, oil and gas wells, timber, farming—cotton, corn and oats," Connecti-cut artist Joseph Pistey, Jr., like most northern artists commis-sioned to paint southern murals, chose to feature cotton.[20] It is true that the grouping of white men at the right is supposed to represent the lumber industry, that corn is featured at the extreme left, and that a few tiny oil wells appear in the left background, but the cen-tral grouping "works" with cotton (Figure 53).

The white lumbermen have just felled a huge pine tree. Muscles aripple, they lift its trunk. What they plan to do with it is unclear, since it disappears at the right end of the design, but their ability to work, their attention to the job at hand, and the effort they put into their labor are quite apparent from their focused eyes, their taut legs and arms, and the intensity with which they ignore any pos-sible audience. The grouping at the extreme left is more varied. Here a white youth struggles to carry a sheaf of corn stalks—a min-iature of the hardworking men at the right. His father kneels to shuck ears of corn, and his mother does just what one would expect her to do. She waits. Chicken at her feet, she stands, glassy-eyed and flaccid-armed, holding a basket of corn. According to Pistey, this is "a sharecropper family doing their farm chores."[21] In the mythology, then, a woman's place in a sharecropper family is no different from her place in any other segment of southern society.

Between these two all-white vignettes, the cotton grouping con-sists of four black men, two black women, and one white male who, Pistey writes, depict the weighing of cotton. One black male drives a cotton wagon out of the middle ground toward the right;

20. Maria Ealand, Administrative Assistant to the Section of Painting and Sculp-ture, to Joseph Pistey, Jr., September 1, 1938, in Haynesville, Louisiana, file, RG 121, NA.
21. Pistey to Rowan, September 24, 1938, *ibid.*

53 / Joseph Pistey, Jr., *Agriculture and Industry of Claiborne Parish, Louisiana*, Haynesville, La., 1939

he is balanced by a black female picking cotton, but her effort is small, since she only plucks the top boll. Near the center, the white man, in the position of authority, holds the scales, but even he can be instructed by a powerful black female worker. Absolutely central to the painting, muscles flexed, she moves ominously toward the weigher, her eyes intent on what he does. Perhaps she suspects that he plans to give her short weight. She points a determined finger at the sack, as if directing the white to take care how he measures her labor. One is reminded of Scarlett's Mammy in *Gone With the Wind*, the only person with any control over Scarlett's willful behavior and a slave whose strength of character gives her the freedom to advise even the plantation master. Two black males, sturdy and sinewy but perhaps not competent, carry baskets of cotton presumably to be weighed. A third, no less physically imposing than his fellows, his basket overturned, appears to spill his cotton right into the postmaster's office. One suspects that Pistey had a design function in mind for this man and his cotton. They fill what might otherwise have been a dead spot at the mural's focal point, just above the postmaster's door. But the message is clear—a "darkie" might just as easily ruin a valuable product as take care of it.

Black males in the murals often did harvest and haul cotton and melons competently and steadily. Almost as often, however, they lay or sat around and did little to earn their keep. For the Leland, Mississippi, mural, Louisiana artist Stuart R. Purser painted *Ginnin' Cotton*, a panoramic view of a huge ginning operation in

54 / Stuart R. Purser, *Ginnin' Cotton*, Leland, Miss., 1940

which appear no fewer than seven wagons laden to overflowing with cotton (Figure 54). Each wagon is drawn by two mules, and on top of each load loll one or two black men. In the center, surrounded by the wagons, which themselves are circumscribed by buildings, two white males seem to be examining the quality of some cotton piled on a table. Not involved in muscular labor, they wear suits and ties; their positions at the center of the action label them as figures of authority. These are the men who make it possible for the others to rest on the loads. The other live figures in the picture are eight mules, all waiting to be made use of, and the black males on top of the loads. One black man does actually guide a vacuum pipe into place above a wagon, and three tiny men in the background appear to await their turn at a cotton scale. The other active figure is an exuberant youth who stands on his load to wave energetically. While Purser's interpretation of the need for black workers to wait, idle, for their turn to unload was accurate, scenes that featured unmoving black men were too frequent in southern murals to be entirely coincidental. And they did please the folk. Postmaster William A. Armstrong reported himself very pleased with the mural, and he heard "mostly favorable comments from the local citizenry."[22]

Although few murals show as many obviously idle black men in the work place as the one at Leland does, Negroid males usually work only in cotton fields. A few Mississippians, at least, were vocal in their distrust of the black male's ability to be useful in other

22. William A. Armstrong to Rowan, August 20, 1940, in Leland, Mississippi, file, RG 121, NA.

55 / Julien Binford, *Forest Loggers*, Forest, Miss., 1941

forms of labor, and they were especially disappointed if blacks were industrious without white supervision. Julien Binford designed a mural about lumbering for Forest, Mississippi—named, not for General Nathan Bedford Forrest, as many suppose, but in honor of the lush woodlands surrounding the town. The mural features two mules and four black lumber workers struggling to move the heavy trunks of two tall trees in the midst of a dense forest (Figure 55). Concerning the reception of the mural, Binford wrote:

> It is now installed in Forest where I went to mount it on Monday. Most of the people I met expressed great interest in the picture. The only adverse criticisms it received came from the postmistress who, although she liked the forest scene, expressed her disappointment that there should be negroes in the painting.
>
> The officials of the lumber company were naturally delighted with the subject matter but said that "those niggers wouldn't be working that hard unless they were being watched by a white foreman." I expected such talk as this and it makes me doubly glad that I chose this subject. Everyone else whom I met seemed to comment on the painting favorably, the general opinion being that it is "a good lookin' painted muriel" and "certainly looks like around here."[23]

23. Julien Binford to Rowan, April 30, 1941, in Forest, Mississippi, file, RG 121, NA. Today the Mississippi town spells its name Forest; in the 1930s, apparently Forest and Forrest were used. Both spellings appear in the correspondence and in articles about the mural. I have chosen to use the modern spelling as given, for example, in the Rand McNally Road Atlas (1983).

The lumber officials would probably have been delighted with the mural Joe Jones of St. Louis originally planned for Magnolia, Arkansas. In the background were a well-maintained sharecropper's cabin, a flourishing cornfield, and a spreading oak. In the foreground sat a group of black children, male, gorging on watermelon. At least four watermelons can be discerned in the mediocre photograph among five happy lads, and the father of one of them comes walking into the picture carrying a fifth. Their hounds wait for the orts. Rowan lost no time rejecting this sketch in his usual oblique manner, and he took no chances that he would get another similar design: "In view of the splendid landscapes which you did in your series . . . dealing with the story of wheat, it is suggested that you develop a design chiefly landscape in character." Jones complied, but it was several months before he learned, after his new design was approved, just why the Section disapproved of the first: "because we knew you could create a much superior design and one in which negroes on a picnic would not have quite the importance you gave them."[24]

The Forest, Mississippi, lumber officials and even the people of Magnolia might have been satisfied with a picture of Negroes on a picnic, but is Binford's condescending attitude justified? Perhaps he takes too seriously his own southern background as a son of Virginia, the Cradle of Democracy. Other evidence suggests that, though Binford undoubtedly described accurately the comments he heard, he probably took the joshing comments of his favorable audience too seriously and was, perhaps, too willing to believe in their ignorance. Before the mural was installed, it was exhibited in a Charlotte, North Carolina, museum. The Charlotte *Observer* had only the highest praise for the work, and for the artist:

> With consummate skill the artist has constructed a forest scene to be enjoyed and remembered for its fidelity to subject matter. The flesh, bone and sinew of men and animals engaged in peaceful labor are masterful interpretations. . . .
>
> It is artists with the sincerity of purpose of a Julien Binford . . . who are enlivening the artistic sensibilities of the South. It is such men of vision and accomplishment who are best able to convince the Southern

24. Rowan to Joe Jones, June 3, 1938, in Magnolia, Arkansas, file, RG 121, NA.

artist that theirs is a rich field of subject matter and again it is they who are doing so much to justify public confidence in their ability.[25]

A better gauge of southern sensibility than a city newspaper, perhaps, is the *Progressive Farmer*. If the Forest postmistress and the lumber officials represented southern sentiment, *Progressive Farmer* editors would likely not have planned to feature the mural:

> I think about as fine a mural as I have seen designed for any Southern building is the one by Julien Binford shown herewith. I suggest that we run it four columns wide sometime with a feature forestry article and the following legend:
>
> A FOREST SCENE FOR FORREST
>
> This exceptionally fine Southern rural scene is from a mural appropriately designed for the Forrest, Miss., Post Office. The artist, Julien Binford, himself is a country-dweller, living in Powhattan County, Va.[26]

Those editors knew, and they knew that Binford knew, that most southern farmers would not find the image of hardworking black lumber workers offensive. Whatever the opinion of black men as lumber workers, they were certainly permitted to pick cotton with impunity. When Boston artist Caroline Rohland designed the Bunkie, Louisiana, mural, she wrote that she wanted to paint "the darky" picking cotton and that "it would not seem that the southerners could be offended if I [included] a glorified white overseer." She would, she continued, be glad to change the plan if the Section thought there could be any objection. Even after the Section correctly assured her that darkies in cotton fields even without white overseers were acceptable, she replied that she considered omitting the white power figure a bit dangerous and included him as a precautionary measure. In expressing an intense desire to paint blacks at work in the cotton fields, Rohland, like many other artists of southern murals, demonstrated that she saw with the same eyes as did the popular culture in the 1930s. For instance, when Selznick prepared to film *Gone With the Wind*, he wanted the first scenes to illustrate what would be lost when the North waged war on the South. He wanted a scene of darkies hoeing cotton. Blacks singing

25. Marion Wright, "Art and Artists," Charlotte *Observer*, April 6, 1941, clipping, in Forest, Mississippi, file.

26. Clarence Poe, Raleigh office of the *Progressive Farmer*, to Alexander Nunn, Birmingham office of the *Progressive Farmer*, December 6, 1940, copy, *ibid.*

in the cotton fields, after all, meant that God was in his Heaven and all was right in the South. It took months of debate to convince Selznick that such a shot would be incongruous in April, the setting of the first scene. He finally compromised with a brief scene of blacks tending young plants.[27]

Whites in the cotton fields, on the other hand, were not at all reassuring unless they adhered to rigid rules. The labor of hoeing and picking cotton was menial, seasonal, and very low-paying. For whites to do it suggested that they, like blacks, were desperate for work, that images of "poor whites" might be accurate. Whites, both men and women, did hoe and pick cotton, but not in the murals. The South is replete with federal murals featuring the cotton industry—about one-fourth of the total—and most of those depict field workers. In only two are whites shown actually doing the hand labor. White male overseers abound, white males drive mule wagons and plows, but seldom do they touch the cotton itself. White women occasionally bring water or mail to their husbands, but seldom do white women actually handle a cotton sack or touch a cotton boll.

Farm Security Administration photographs record white and black women working together in the cotton fields. The foreground of one photograph by Dorothea Lange looks very like Beulah Bettersworth's murals for Indianola and Columbus, Mississippi, except for one salient difference. Bettersworth's female cotton pickers are comfortably surrounded by southern buildings and natural barriers that shelter them from nonsouthern interference in their way of life and suggest southern self-sufficiency. The FSA photo (Figure 56), on the other hand, was intended to record "conditions." It features a boundless cotton field offering no shelter and in no way circumscribed. The workers, though dressed similarly to Bettersworth's, posed similarly to hers, and standing in a field that closely resembles the painted ones, look lonely and hopeless. Much scholarly work has been done to show that the scenes in the documentary photographs of the depression era were edited to present hopelessness, as the scenes in the murals were for images of comfort

27. Caroline Rohland to Rowan, August 27, 1938, Forbes Watson to Rohland, August 1, 1938, Rohland to Rowan, September 29, 1938, all in Bunkie, Louisiana, file, RG 121, NA; Edward D. C. Campbell, Jr., *The Celluloid South: Hollywood and the Southern Myth* (Knoxville, 1981), 19.

56 / Dorothea Lange, "Cotton Hoers Leaving the Field for Lunch, the Farmer's Daughter and White and Negro Laborers, Georgia, July 1937"
Farm Security Administration photograph no. LC-USW 3-17698-C, courtesy Library of Congress

and security.[28] Lange's field hands may be on their way to eat, but the viewer sees nowhere for them to go—not even a tree offers them shade in which to eat lunches they brought with them.

That would not happen in the murals. Hopelessness was not permitted. When Bettersworth's cotton pickers stop to rest and gaze at the distance, it is with hope and confidence that shelter and rest are just over there, as is, perhaps, a better life. But all of Bettersworth's women were black. When Francis Speight wished to paint whites and blacks at work together in the fields, the Gastonia, North Carolina, postmaster rushed to the whites' defense. Although Speight had visited Gastonia and sketched the two races picking in the same field, the postmaster objected to the depiction of white women picking cotton. Speight deferred to his request; in the mural only blacks pick cotton.[29]

28. Dorothea Lange, "Cotton hoers leaving the field for lunch, the farmer's daughter and white and Negro laborers, Georgia, July 1937," LC-USW 3-17698-C. William Stott, *Documentary Expression and Thirties America* (New York, 1973), 224–31, thoroughly treats this type of editing, particularly as practiced by Lange.
29. Francis Speight to Rowan, January 28, 1938, in Gastonia, North Carolina, file, RG 121, NA.

57 / Carl Nyquist, *Picking Cotton,* Bolivar, Tenn., 1941

58 / Arthur Covey, *Corn, Cotton, and Tobacco Culture,* Anderson, S.C., 1940

The Gastonia postmaster had put ideas into Rowan's head. When Carl Nyquist submitted his design for Bolivar, Tennessee, in which a group of whites harvest the cotton, he was warned to "check the locale to see if white workers are employed in the cotton fields." He did, and they were. So he finished his mural of white share-croppers picking cotton and installed it in Bolivar (Figure 57). For Anderson, South Carolina, Arthur Covey also painted whites work-ing in the cotton field, but with a difference (Figure 58). He stated his purpose in his first letter describing his design: "It is of the dig-nity of common labor that I hope to sing always rather than an actual reproduction or illustration of picking cotton. Hence my liberty in showing growing tobacco & corn with ripe cotton."[30]

He may have taken that liberty, but the corn and tobacco do little more than form a frame for the mural. The dominant scene in the center is one of dignified common labor in the cotton field. The description he provided the Anderson newspaper does much to explain why in this case whites could work, unquestioned, amid the cotton: "My characters are American citizens descended from several generations in the South who stuck to their lands in the reconstruction days and fought their own economic problems. They are not sharecroppers, nor have they ever been on relief. They are intelligent planters who plant their crops realistically. I have shown no children working in the field because they have been sent to school. These are people who believe in the New South."[31]

Both the mural and the Yankee artist were well received in Anderson. And it is no wonder. He said he was intrigued to paint for a community farther south than he had ever been.[32] And not only did he paint of the dignity of common labor; he emphasized the ways South Carolina was like the rest of the country. He knew exactly how to depict the division of labor between family members. Despite the "cotton-picking vacation" in September that was a standard event in many rural southern school calendars, these people's children were at school. There is no child labor in Covey's South Carolina. And the woman is as incompetent as he and Joseph Pistey of the Haynesville mural imagined white sharecropper women to be.

In the mural's center foreground, one virile man empties a laden basket into the wagon. Another lifts a second basket from the ground. He is in the same position on the picture's plane as the black who spills the cotton out of the picture in the Haynesville mural, but he, being white, manages to keep his basket upright. Just to the right of the wagon and in scale with the men is the farm

30. Rowan to Carl Nyquist, February 24, 1941, in Bolivar, Tennessee, file, Arthur Covey to Rowan, December 12, 1939, in Anderson, South Carolina, file, both in RG 121, NA.

31. "Mural Painting Is Installed at Local Post Office Today," Anderson *Daily News*, May 13, 1940, clipping, in Anderson, South Carolina, file.

32. Covey to Rowan, September 27, 1938, *ibid.*

woman, looking vaguely toward the left. Her cotton sack trails at her feet, its contents spilling into the path of the turkeys, which are here substituted for chickens. In a distant middle-ground can be seen a group of cotton pickers both male and female—the ones presumably who had not "stuck to their lands in the reconstruction days and fought their own economic problems" and thus, now, must pick for those who did.

In Bolivar, Tennessee, where white sharecroppers picking cotton do dominate mural space, a similar division of labor reigns. Among the straight rows of abundantly producing cotton are five male pickers, two adult females, and one young girl who has no function but to fill a potentially dead space at the picture's right. Three of the men and the lad work assiduously. The fifth stands up, his full sack on his shoulders, to return for another sack. One woman does pick cotton—the only white female in the South who actually does so—but her sunbonnet hides her face. The second adult female is quite a different matter. At least this woman does not spill what she has apparently picked, but she gazes vacantly off into empty space, sack trailing beside her, her flaccid hand at her side. The few women in southern cotton fields look no different from those in the clothing ads or those who would settle new territories, and they function no differently from Melanie Wilkes and Evangeline. Tennessee sharecroppers may not send their children to school during cotton-picking vacation, but they see to it that their daughters learn to be Evangeline. The young girl, about eleven or twelve, stands with no sack, her hand resting on a cotton boll. She is neatly dressed, her hair is combed, and she alone of the women in the fields, white or black, wears no protection from the sun.

The catalog of murals depicting the work roles of the races and the sexes need not end here. Many more southern murals show the proper roles of people in the fields and in the family. White men in the South always work, though often with their brains rather than their brawn; black men sometimes work, are sometimes incompetent; black women always work—and do so with dignity; white women never work and seldom do anything else. But when Francis Speight painted the Gastonia, North Carolina, mural, his failure to depict productive women may have had as much to do with Gastonia's special problems as with those traditional roles. Since Gastonia was an important cotton mill center, Speight and the postmaster agreed that the cotton industry should be featured in the

59 / Francis Speight, design for Gastonia, N.C.

mural. And Speight's first design was based on a novel premise. He knew that in 1929, Gastonia had taken the epithet "The South's City of Spindles," and spindles suggest spinsters to operate them. His idea was to illustrate something of the history of the industry by painting "a picture of ladies on a porch or under an arbor spinning and carding cotton as it was done about the time of the revolution." Thus, he would demonstrate the early importance of spinsters to the textile industry—a time a century and a half earlier when unmarried daughters were valuable to their families as wage earners (Figure 59).[33]

The idea was not even considered by the Section, and Gastonia would not accept it. No reasons were given. Everybody thought that other designs would be better. One can, however, speculate on the reasons. It may not have been politic in Gastonia to emphasize the importance of white women to the cotton industry, and since Gastonia's particular trials had received unfavorable national publicity, the Section probably knew it. Gastonia's Loray mill had been the object of a violent and tragic union action in 1929.

The Loray strike was one of many against the southern textile industry in the late 1920s and early 1930s the leadership of which was largely women and which grew from a groundswell of indignation among women and men unable to keep their families fed or, often, even alive. Beyond the traditional union demands for better pay and shorter hours, certain demands had special appeal for those who had to work long hours by day and manage a family and household at night, or work long hours by night and leave ailing children

33. Speight to Rowan, November 30, 1936, in Gastonia, North Carolina, file; Louise A. Tilly and Joan W. Scott, *Women, Work, and Family* (New York, 1978), 111–12. Although Tilly and Scott concentrate on late eighteenth- and nineteenth-century France and England, they did enough research to ascertain that similar conditions existed in the United States.

at home in the care of "older" brothers and sisters, often ten or eleven years old. They demanded abolition of the piecework and stretch-out policies that forced people into ever greater "productivity" for the same or less pay and denied them the brief rest periods they had managed under the wage system; they demanded better housing (screens and bathtubs), clean restroom facilities at the factory, cheaper electricity; and, most shocking of all, they demanded equal pay for women and children. And no wonder—a large percentage of the strikers were females and their children. At the Loray mill, even if married men could have earned enough to support families, husbands would not be hired unless their wives would also work, and they would be laid off if pregnancy forced their wives to quit.[34]

As with most union activity, music was important in keeping up morale. The nine-month-long Loray action had spawned its own collection of "balleteers" of whom the favorites were the child Odell Corley (eleven years old) and the women Daisy McDonald and Ella May Wiggins.[35] Ella May's ballads and her strength and determination to fight for a better life for her children made her a leader at the rallies and in the tent city to which strikers, evicted from company housing, fled for shelter. She knew the family hardships caused by intolerable working conditions. A twenty-nine-year-old widow, she once had nine children. Of them, four had died of whooping cough in the care of their eleven-year-old sister while their mother was forced to work the night shift in an effort to afford medical attention for them. Ella May's "ballets," popular with male and female strikers alike, kept spirits up when all else looked hopeless. Her best-loved song, "The Mill Mother's Lament," illustrates the woman-centered nature of Gastonia's troubles:

> We leave our homes in the morning,
> We kiss our children goodbye,
> While we slave for the bosses,
> Our children scream and cry.

34. A detailed account of the 1929 Gastonia strike, clearly showing the woman-centered nature of the protest and the fact of female leadership, is in Philip S. Foner, *Women and the American Labor Movement: From World War II to the Present* (New York, 1980), 230–39.

35. See Steve Wiley, "Songs of the Gastonia Textile Strike of 1929: Models of and for Southern Working-Class Women's Militancy," *North Carolina Folklore Journal,* XXX (Fall-Winter, 1982), 87–98, for the best account.

And when we draw our money,
Our grocery bills to pay,
Not a cent to pay for clothing,
Not a cent to lay away.

And on that very evening
Our little son will say,
"I need some shoes, dear mother,
And so does sister May."

How it grieves the heart of the mother,
You, everyone must know,
But we cannot buy for our children,
Our wages are too low.

Now listen to me, workers,
Both you women and you men,
Let us win for them the victory,
I'm sure it will be no sin.[36]

"The Mill Mother's Lament" was sung at Ella May's funeral. On September 14, 1929, a truck carrying a group of unionists calling for a new walkout in Gastonia—the movement had continued to gain support from workers who began as scabs—was forcibly stopped on the road. Ten automobiles surrounded the truck. Shots were fired at the unarmed strikers. Several were wounded, but the only fatality was Ella May Wiggins. Her death brought much-needed publicity to conditions in Gastonia's cotton mills, but it also effectively ended the strike some nine months after organizers first entered North Carolina on New Year's Day. The blot of the strike action, the inhuman working conditions and the atrocities suffered by strikers, would not have been erased by 1936. When the WPA published the *North Carolina Guide*, Gastonia was classified as a textile center, but there is no mention of "The South's City of Spindles."[37]

Perhaps the association of trouble and heartbreak in Gastonia with women in the cotton industry dictated that the traditional association of white females with textiles be muted in the mural. *Millhands and Preachers*, Liston Pope's classic 1942 study of the

36. Quoted in Foner, *Women and the American Labor Movement*, 237, and analyzed in Wiley, "Songs of the Gastonia Textile Strike," 91–92.

37. Federal Writers Project, *North Carolina: A Guide to the Old North State* (1939; rpr. Chapel Hill, 1954), 386.

Gastonia strike, mentions stretch-out and low wages, but it does not concentrate on conditions that brought about the strike. Rather, it examines the interactions between the Communist organizers, at the time widely blamed for the workers' uprising, and the religious leaders to whom Gastonians turned for leadership. Until the last chapter, readers of Pope's book are hard put to find the internal causes of the strike, and they must be detectives to observe that the leaders were female. The death of Ella May Wiggins is mentioned, and those who carefully examine the notes can piece together that she wrote popular strike songs and helped organize the action.[38] Pope's oversights certainly were not malicious; he had other purposes, and feminist scholarship was forty years in the future. But his omissions do illustrate contemporary lack of concern with the problems of white women at work and with their potential as an active force in the South. In any case, Speight's design of productive spinsters was abandoned, and the Gastonia mural depicts a cotton mill, its door open so that the workers inside can be seen, and a cotton field (Figure 60). The mill workers are white men, and the cotton pickers of both sexes are black. Gastonians who visited the post office would not be reminded that Evangeline might leave her oak and participate actively to protest conditions unacceptable to women.

The 1929 strike and the shorter ones that followed may have suggested that people in Gastonia were not prosperous, that married women had to work alongside their husbands to earn enough to feed their families. Rowan and Speight, however, had ways of putting such suppositions to rest. *The North Carolina Guide* describes Gastonia as comprising several mill communities "composed of identical though solidly constructed houses." These dwellings would not assure Gastonians that they were American individualists. Instead, Rowan knew what the mural needed to offset the

---

38. In *Millhands and Preachers* (New Haven, 1942), Liston Pope enlists a formidable array of facts and sources to show the role of religion in southern economic affairs, using the Loray strike as his case study. Ella May Wiggins is spoken of three times. When Pope speaks of increasing resentment toward working conditions, the note tells us the mother he quoted was Ella May Wiggins (260n67). His example of how textile workers found opportunities in strike work to develop hidden talents is Ella May Wiggins (261n70). When he mentions poets and balladeers, one of them is Ella May Wiggins (261n71). Ella May's death and the subsequent trial get two pages (pp. 293–94).

60 / Francis Speight, *Cotton Field and Spinning Mill*, Gastonia, N.C., 1938

idea that all Gastonians were underpaid mill and farm laborers. "It might be well," he wrote Speight, "to include in the middle of the landscape one representative great house so that the region does not have the appearance of a poor settlement."[39] Speight added such a house in the distant background, and he added another reassuring touch. Lest viewers think ill-paid mill girls were hidden in the depths of the open mill, he painted a vacant-eyed woman walking serenely and with no apparent purpose along the road. She is not bound to spend the daylight hours breathing cotton dust to support her family; she has the freedom to explore the countryside while white men and black laborers work. Thus, in the mural at least, Gastonia had been gently reconstructed into the image of the South that would make Americans comfortable.

It would be unfair to insist that all southern murals depicted happy and prosperous blacks and idle, vacant women. Two do not: Louis Raynaud's mural for Abbeville, Louisiana, and Ethel Magafan's for Wynne, Arkansas. *The Harvest* in Abbeville shows men and women harvesting cotton, sugarcane, and muskrat hides (Figure 61). White men gather cotton and tend the cane. A white couple prepares hides for drying. Two male children do what children have always done when they were not pressed into premature labor to support mill families or sit for younger siblings—they hang around. A man prepares to cut a clump of cane, and one white woman waits, holding a bucket of water for the workers. But in the position right above the postmaster's door, a young white woman bends to gather an armful of felled cane, one of the hardest tasks in

39. Federal Writers Project, *The North Carolina Guide*, 386; Rowan to Speight, January 11, 1938, in Gastonia, North Carolina, file.

61 / Louis Raynaud, *The Harvest,* Abbeville, La., 1939

the cane field. There are no blacks in the picture. The scene is what one would imagine is usual among southern rural laborers who earn their living on their own land. Whole families are involved in the labor, and women and men work together at whatever needs to be done to ensure a successful harvest.

In *Caste and Class in a Southern Town* (1937), Yale psychologist John Dollard wrote of "lower class Negroes," primarily tenants and sharecroppers, who benefited from their dependent status. As he presents it, using primarily evidence provided by "middle class Negroes," these people replaced some of what they lacked economically with freedom from sexual and social restraints. According to this line of reasoning, the freedom from responsibility for the future offsets in some way the lack of opportunity to "get ahead"; the freedom to live from day to day offsets in some way the lack of material comforts.[40] Some southern black writers of the period appeared to agree. In *Their Eyes Were Watching God,* Zora Neale Hurston's protagonist spends years emulating white values (though they were never called "white"—she writes of a black culture in which whites are incidental) and finally finds peace in a day-to-day existence as a worker in the Florida Everglades. Most blacks writing in the 1920s, 1930s, and 1940s—James Baldwin, Richard Wright, Langston Hughes—write of anger at the white race and of blacks' efforts to carve out their own working lives against insurmountable odds. Perhaps, however, the most eloquent brief statement and certainly the most relevant to murals created by and for middle-

40. John Dollard, *Caste and Class in a Southern Town* (Garden City, N.Y., 1937), 390–433.

62 / Ethel Magafan, *Cotton Pickers,* Wynne, Ark., 1940
Photo by Richard H. Beckham

and working-class whites is in Maya Angelou's *I Know Why the
Caged Bird Sings.* As a child in Arkansas during the 1930s, she
watched her friends coming home day after eleven-hour day, backs
aching, spirits broken, from picking cotton, with less than the
price of a nourishing meal to show for a day's work: "The sounds of
the new morning had been replaced with grumbles about cheating
houses, weighted scales, snakes, skimpy cotton and dusty rows. In
later years I was to confront the stereotyped picture of gay song-
singing cotton pickers with such inordinate rage that I was told
even then by fellow Blacks that my paranoia was embarrassing. But
I had seen the fingers cut by mean little cotton bolls, and I had wit-
nessed the backs and shoulders and arms and legs resisting any further demands."[41]

If Angelou had visited the Wynne, Arkansas, Post Office, perhaps
her rage would have been less (Figure 62). The scene is of black men
and women coming home from a day's labor in the fields, but these
people do not look happy with their lot. A young couple enters the
frame from the left, their backs bent, their faces resigned, the
woman dragging her long white sack. Three blacks still pick cotton
in the background, their sack not heavy enough to bother weighing
yet. The cotton in this mural is, if not skimpy, certainly not the
unbelievably productive stuff of most murals.

An elderly woman stands immobile, peering into a distance that
does not offer a better life. Her anguished and wrinkled features reveal that she has lived too long to hope for anything else, and still
she works as she did when she was a girl. Another couple near the

41. Maya Angelou, *I Know Why the Caged Bird Sings* (Toronto, 1970), 7.

right waits for their cotton to be weighed, trepidation on their faces—the scales could be inaccurate. And a white overseer, his hand shading his eyes, watches to make sure that none of these workers get more than is coming to them. Unlike the field workers in 1930s movies, these darkies did not sing as they returned from the fields. They had no energy left. The one bright note in the painting is a child greeting her dog. With the resilience of childhood, she has forgotten the heat and the drudgery of the day, and no one has told her about the possibility of weighted scales. Because she is a child, she can dream that her life will be different. This mural, like the one in Sylvester, Georgia, has been the subject of NAACP protest. Here too awareness increased, and the mural was saved as historical document.[42] But in Wynne's mural, there seems to be more genuine empathy with the subjects, less reason for protest.

Wynne and Abbeville, however, are exceptions. When Simka Simkhovitch painted a mural called *Pursuits of Life in Mississippi* for the Jackson Court House, he demonstrated his knowledge of the work-role mythology (Figure 63). As a backdrop, protecting Mississippians from outsiders to the north and possibly symbolizing enlightenment is an antebellum, Georgian colonial building— possibly the Lyceum, the administration building at the state university. Its shape and proportion duplicate those of the marble coping behind the judge's bench over which the mural hangs. The building divides the mural into two parts, the right for white men, the left for women and blacks. In the grouping to the right are farmers in overalls, laborers with rolled-up shirtsleeves, men of letters, and a judge wearing his robes and clutching his book of law. To the left are black male and female cotton pickers, none of their faces visible—one man holds a cotton basket in front of his face, those picking have on straw hats. The one white man is there to weigh the cotton. The only black whose expression we can see is a merry banjo player, singing happily for the court.

In the center, just above the judge's seat, is a suit-clad white man whose occupation is a mystery, but whose function is entirely clear. He is surrounded by waiting females. A young mother on his right clutches her baby and stares into space. Next to her stands

42. Interview with Jimmie James, county historian, Wynne, Ark., August 20, 1982.

63 / Simka Simkhovitch, *Pursuits of Life in Mississippi*, Jackson, Miss., 1938

Evangeline of the coming generation—a blond-haired girl staring just as vacantly in another direction. And clutching his left hand is an old, old woman who waits for him to tell her what to do, but she does not dare to look into the eyes of one so superior. In the 1960s, a protest by whites resulted in the draping of the mural.[43]

The ideal position for white men and women in the South during the 1930s was much as it had always been, but depression conditions that threatened its reality made the ideal that much more sacred. The man was to be the breadwinner, the decision maker. The white woman may have had as many options as did other American women, but she was subtly trained to exercise those options with a difference, a deference. Perhaps because the concept of southern womanhood is so well known, the only scholarly studies point out how inaccurate it is. Anne Firor Scott's *The Southern Lady*, for example, does not refute the ideal, the image, but she does demonstrate that literate women at least have never been wholly comfortable with those images and ideals. She accurately concludes that the shape of women's lives had changed by the 1930s. Even then, she has to admit, however, that only the strong and the energetic woman could avail herself of the new freedom.[44] Evangeline may

43. Patti Carr Black, Director, Mississippi State Historical Museum, to the author, November 29, 1982.

44. Anne Firor Scott, *The Southern Lady: From Pedestal to Politics* (Chicago, 1970), 230.

have had a place in the 1930s power structure, but she, like the chickens, still hid any discomfort or dissatisfaction she might have felt with her role.

Black males had literally and figuratively a harder row to hoe. They had to support themselves in a society that needed to believe in their inferiority. Not to do so would be to acknowledge that blacks had a right to compete for jobs that white people needed. Section artists, possibly unwittingly, reinforced the assumption that meaningful labor belonged to the powerful while black males could have what was left over. Even so, the myth of the black female retainer, the woman of such strength that she could, with little actual power and less remuneration, maintain her own dignity and a white family's structure, remained so strong that artists used it repeatedly. The relationship of blacks to work, however, was just part of the story of minorities in the South. Large numbers of blacks continued to call the South their home, as the other minority race that had helped build the region did not. Both the blacks and the Indians in pursuits other than work provided subjects for murals throughout the South.

V / THE RED AND THE BLACK: IMAGES OF MINORITY RACES IN THE SOUTH OF THE 1930s

For the Vicksburg, Mississippi, competition, Robert C. Purdy submitted an attractive design of a group of blacks sporting on the levee. The backdrop is a river steamer, smoke billowing from its twin stacks. Hanging from an invisible crane, a bale of cotton, presumably being loaded onto the steamer, looms precariously above the blacks. In the center, just under the ominous cotton bale, a black man and woman raucously dance. Surrounding them, black men, women, and children sit on whatever presents itself—a cotton bale, pilings, the wooden planks of the pier—laughing and clapping to the music. One man plays a banjo, another a harmonica. A few whites hard at work are squeezed between the rollicking group and the ship. The light behind the black smoke of the steamer proclaims the time to be midday. Although the situation is pleasant and the attitudes joyful, the implication is that the blacks have nothing more important to do with their time than to dance and sing while whites do the strenuous manual labor.

To the credit of the Vicksburg committee, the design was not even considered for the Vicksburg Post Office and Court House. Neither was the entry by Olivia Brown Morrison. This one was also a levee scene, backed by a river packet, and here cotton was also being loaded, but this time a group of hardworking blacks load it. Even so, two blacks find time to dance to the tunes their compatriot picks on his banjo as he lounges on a convenient cotton bale.

Stuart Purser's entry for the Newton, Mississippi, competition— a small-town post office rather than moderate-sized city court-house—was not considered appropriate by a local committee to grace a federal building. Here a street of ostentatiously electrified cotton gins and warehouses extends into the distance. A row of towering electrical poles runs beside the dirt street, and the lines extend to each of the buildings. All along the street, white and black—mostly black—workers can be seen hard at the task of pre-

paring the cotton for market. But in the foreground are two less industrious groups. At the lower left, a white man weights someone's
cotton sack while a group of children who might best be described
as "pickaninnies" observe. It is not clear whether these grinning
children with braids springing from every surface on their heads
are themselves waiting for a turn to have their day's pick weighed
or whether they just watch. And at the lower right an overweight
bandanna-clad woman holds an infant, its hair already in pigtails,
while a grown man and two other "pickaninnies" look on.

In each of these cases, the designs are well laid out and the individual artist had received other mural commissions. But the designs did not merit the consolation prize. None of the artists were
awarded less prestigious commissions on the basis of a competent
design submitted in a competition. The sketches in each case had
been rejected because of subject matter.

On the wall of the St. Joseph, Missouri, Post Office, however, a
group of minstrels stage a show that outclasses the rejected sketches
for stereotyping (Figure 64). With the requisite river steamer in the
left background and a tree on the right that resembles nothing so
much as an illustration of the Tree of Life, male darkies dance,
sing, and strum for all they're worth. Swinging hands, hats, and
feet, three men do a jig. Resting on a plank stretched between two
empty crates, two more strum banjos while a third, perched on an
unidentifiable wood structure, plays soulfully on his harmonica.
Another man, barefoot, stretches full length behind them, and a

64 / Gustaf Dalstrom, *Negro River Music*, St. Joseph, Mo., 1941

last figure sitting on the plank claps his hands and stomps his foot to the music. The ground is cluttered with paper, and a keg, contents unknown, stands suggestively to one side. The whole arrangement of the mural—performers in a semicircle facing the post office audience, some elevated behind the others, banjo player in the center—suggests a minstrel show. And the ebony complexions of the musicians contrasted with the brilliant whites of their eyes and teeth call to mind blackface makeup more than the varied skin colors of American blacks.

The St. Joseph mural is one of twelve panels painted by Swedish-born artist Gustaf Dalstrom for the major northwestern Missouri post office. The series celebrates the city's history. Among the murals are the artist's representations of the Pony Express, for which the eastern terminus was St. Joseph; river traffic; early rail travel and commerce; the Lewis and Clark expedition; the home of the city's founder, Joseph Robidoux; the horseless carriage; Indians having a canoe race; settlers crossing "a river"; and blacks dancing on the riverfront. The races that contributed to the history of Missouri and St. Joseph are carefully segregated in separate panels with one exception. In the panel featuring a river steamer, three white men supervise while eight blacks do the heavy lifting. In the rest save two, white people work or carry on commerce. In the remaining two, the minority races play. In Dalstrom's vision, they had played no part in making St. Joseph the state's third-largest city and its third most prosperous.

A river figures in four of the twelve murals: the Indians' boat race, the river packet picture, the settlers crossing in a flatboat, and the one entitled *Negro River Music*. What river Dalstrom had in mind, however, is debatable. St. Joseph is located near the northwest corner of the state on the Missouri River. The Indians racing the canoes wear headdresses and carry spears that might have been used by the Plains Indians, thus suggesting that the river is, as it should be, the Missouri. Their breechcloths, however, could just as easily have belonged to members of the Five Civilized Tribes of the Southeast. The settlers are clearly crowded into a flatboat, but the river packet scene, wherein blacks load the ship, is more typical of a port on the Mississippi. Although steamers did stop at St. Joseph, sometimes as many as twenty a day, the Missouri River has never been legendary for that type of commerce. And for *Negro River Mu-*

sic, Dalstrom could only have been reproducing a sentimental scene associated with Mississippi River levees and the American South.[1]

The southernness of Missouri itself could be questioned. The home of Dred Scott and the site of John Brown's violent effort to rescue slaves, it is, perhaps more than any other, a border state. Kentucky and Maryland, for instance, were divided between North and South during the Civil War, but that is irrelevant to their modern and historical popular identities as southern. But Missouri is another story. Legal problems there, more than in any other state, are used in the endless efforts to explain the Civil War. In agricultural and cultural terms, most of Missouri belongs in the Midwest, and bits of it can even be identified as western. The Bootheel, the cotton- growing, sharecropped southeastern tip of the state, is definitely southern. St. Louis, home of W. C. Handy and the "St. Louis Blues," is usually associated with the South; often its Mississippi River port is identified as the beginning of the South. The Gateway to the West, the monument to St. Louis's desire for a tourist attraction, which overlooks the river at St. Louis, may indeed lead to the West, but it is a gateway from the South. But St. Joseph? How could Dalstrom have painted *Negro River Music* for that city? And how could the Section of Fine Arts have approved such a picture for that city? And how could St. Joseph citizens have accepted the design for that picture when they saw it months before it would be painted on the wall?

Those are the questions St. Joseph blacks asked in 1941. Maybe the answer lies all the way back in the city's Civil War history. One patriotic nineteenth-century writer was a little embarrassed that Missouri was divided, but proud nevertheless that even those who fought for the Confederacy "did their duty" during wartime. He re-

---

1. Federal Writers Project, *Missouri: A Guide to the "Show Me" State* (New York, 1941). In this guide, the Missouri River is mentioned as a navigable waterway, as a boundary, etc. Of fifteen pictures in the portfolio entitled "The Missouri and the Mississippi" (following p. 62), only one is of the Missouri, and it is a distant landscape suggesting nothing of human culture. In the index under "Negro music," Missouri is credited as the home of many pioneers of jazz, and the Mississippi River is indeed associated with some of that development, but mostly "Negro music" is considered a St. Louis tradition. In *Missouri: A Geography* (Boulder, 1980), Milton D. Rafferty treats the Missouri River as a means of finding geographical locations and as a means of transportation.

ported that Missouri provided a goodly number of troops for both sides, but only 28,000 for the South—far fewer than for the North. Of those, however, 2,000 came from St. Joseph, and when the war began, 2,000 slaves lived in the city. It was the site of skirmishes between Kansas abolitionists and Missouri slave sympathizers. And when the transcontinental railroad was planned, logically it should have followed the route of the Pony Express and other main traveled roads and come through St. Joseph. Local legend has it that Confederate sympathy in St. Joseph persuaded the government to route the road through Omaha instead. According to one recollection, the Union government decided on an alternate route because, in 1861, demonstrating Confederate sympathizers in St. Joseph had torn down the Union flag. An even more colorful tale, however, has it that when he was still a general, U. S. Grant had visited St. Joseph, scouting a location for the railroad. There he was asked to speak, and while he was speaking, a single drunken southern sympathizer heckled him mercilessly. Enraged, the general—soon to be president—recommended that the railroad be routed through Omaha.[2]

Perhaps Dalstrom accurately read the sentiments of St. Joseph's whites, but neither he nor they took into account St. Joseph's blacks. As soon as the designs for the murals were published, a local black leader notified Postmaster Theo F. Quinn that blacks would have a mass protest meeting the following day. Quinn suggested that he meet with the "leader" and "discuss the matter calmly." Then, "if it were not possible to arrive at a definite conclusion," there would still be time enough to hold a mass meeting. Apparently, the black community held its meeting anyway, and a barrage of telegrams protesting the "Negro River Mural" went to the Section, to Fourth Assistant Postmaster General Walter F. Myers, and to the president. Although many of the telegrams and letters were individually worded and written, they all expressed the sentiments of the one suggested at the rally and duplicated by many of the protesters: "Negro citizens of St. Joseph strongly resent mural 'Negroes dancing on the levee' being painted on walls of Post Office here starting Monday. No historical value no levee ever

2. Nathan H. Parker, *The Missouri Handbook Embracing a Full Description of the State of Missouri* (St. Louis, 1865), 22; Rafferty, *Missouri: A Geography*, 183; Federal Writers Project, *Missouri: A Guide*, 287; Ada Clarie Darby, *"Show Me" Missouri* (Kansas City, Mo., 1938), 130.

in vicinity shows race to disadvantage. Urge you intercede and stop picture."[3]

Quinn, however, talked with some of the protest leaders—not necessarily representative of the community as a whole. Although he failed to convince them, they agreed to cooperate: "[The day after the meeting] I met with a committee consisting of seven Negro men and one woman, and listened attentively and courteously to their protests and the reasons for them. Mr. Dalstrom and Mr. Barent Springstead, Assistant Postmaster, also attended this meeting. After they were through we endeavored to make them understand that there was no thought or intent on the part of anyone concerned to hold the Negro up in an undesirable light; rather, we insisted to them that this picture was a depiction of Negro life in one of its finest phases."[4]

Of course, to Quinn *et al.* the design was a depiction of "Negro life in one of its finest phases." Minstrels dancing and singing on a nonexistent levee did not hold mass meetings, and they did not organize telegram and letter-writing campaigns to Washington. Blacks' objections to the mural are probably similar to the instincts that told sensitive Deep South competition committees to reject such representations of blacks. The intelligentsia of Mississippi and Alabama, from whose ranks the committees were selected, cherished the dream that blacks would, through diligence and hard work, earn the right at some future time to be first-class citizens. Samuel Lee Chestnut, author of the required Alabama textbook, expressed the prevalent white attitude: "Time will temper the attitude of the white man; it will prove to the negro that citizenship and merit are to be won by honest effort, self-improvement, and loyalty. It will heal the wounds and scars of war. The process may seem slow; but, with patience and good will on the part of both, time will bring it to pass."[5]

Needless to say, no one was predicting when that would happen. But while southern intellectual leaders waited they would not suggest on federal building walls that such evolution was possible. In

3. Theo F. Quinn to Rowan, March 21, 1941, Dr. W. A. Simms to THE PRESIDENT, February 28, 1941, both in St. Joseph, Missouri, file, Entry 133, Record Group 121, National Archives.

4. Quinn to Rowan, March 21, 1941, *ibid.*

5. Samuel Lee Chestnut, *The Rural South: Background—Problems—Outlook* (Montgomery, Ala., 1937), 72 and *passim.*

the meantime, representatives of St. Joseph's black community had more immediate concerns. Quinn had only relayed to Rowan the objections as he understood them himself, and the telegrams had condensed blacks' anger and anguish. It remained for the local newspaper, one of whose reporters was invited by the black delegation to attend the meeting with postal authorities, to repeat the objections for the general public and the Section. Black representatives charged that the single design among the twelve to feature blacks "depicts the negro as wanting nothing more than a place to dance and a banjo to pick." And the Reverend F. E. Nunley of the Colored Methodist Church objected to the depiction of his race as "lazy people with no other thoughts but singing, dancing and clowning" because in reality they were trying to be "good hard-working citizens." His compatriots were not ashamed of poverty, but they did want credit for their attempts to "rise above our humble beginning in this country."[6]

Reverend Nunley was forthright but quite gentle. Dalstrom attempted to counter those arguments with careful explanations that Stephen Foster was inspired by such music to write "his many negro ballads that have become so dear to the American public." Dalstrom was correct. Those ballads by a white writer, often written for use in minstrel shows featuring white actors with black faces, had indeed become dear to a *white* American public. But the black delegation was having none of it. When the female member of the delegation spoke, the extent of black resentment became clear: "We don't like to be portrayed as a race by the figures in this picture any more than you white people would like to have the rest of the world judge your race by the characters in 'Tobacco Road.' . . . You consider those people as trash and we negroes feel we have a right to be portrayed as good citizens of this country, where we are trying to do our work, where we are paying our taxes and where we are attempting to add something to its cultural development."[7]

Although Postmaster Quinn proceeded to argue the justice of the depiction and the white affection for the black race represented therein, Dalstrom finally got the message. The artist agreed to write Washington for permission to redesign the mural along lines

6. "Protest Against Postoffice Murals Voiced by Negroes," St. Joseph *News-Press*, March 3, 1941, clipping, in St. Joseph, Missouri, file.
7. *Ibid.*

acceptable to the black population. And then he asked them for suggestions.

Unfortunately, two events just at that point convinced Quinn, the Section, and the artist that the blacks were without credibility. The first is that the suggestions made by the black delegation, when they were finally asked for their opinions, were not subjects the Section preferred, and a picture based on them would have been inconsistent with the rest of the mural sequence. Having little experience with 1930s mural tradition and limited time to make suggestions, the blacks suggested representations of Booker T. Washington and George Washington Carver. Since all the other panels featured nameless people who contributed to Missouri and St. Joseph history, a panel of famous non-Missouri leaders would indeed have been out of place. Given the artistic imagination that created a harvest supper on the lawn of the founder's home and a canoe race among Indians, however, one suspects that Dalstrom could have created a scene that would have represented blacks' efforts and his theme of northwestern Missouri history.

The other, more damaging event was Quinn's meeting with "another element of Negroes in town [who] did not feel that the picture was derogatory, and showed us pictures of murals in other parts of the country which had for their subjects the same theme." It would be as interesting to know where these murals were found as it would be to know who in St. Joseph employed the members of this second delegation. Although they talked with Quinn, they did not manage to contact the Section, the government, or the newspaper, and only he seemed aware of their opinions. He said they commented that pictures with similar themes had won prizes at the "Chicago Negro Worlds Fair of 1940." The reference seems to be to the American Negro Exposition in 1939. Investigation into the few extant references to that exposition reveals that murals were indeed painted for this event, but a list of major prize-winning murals shows nothing that could be compared to Dalstrom's mural for St. Joseph.[8] Perhaps murals celebrating the American Negro's

8. "Tuskegee Institute Clippings File," Microfilm, reel 246, Art and Music, 1933–40 (copy of series in Wilson Library, University of Minnesota), indicates black artist William Edouard Scott painted murals for the exposition. Prizes were awarded to black artists Frederic Flemister for *Man With a Brush*, Eldzier Carter for *Sense of Loneliness*, Marvin Smith for *Landscape, Greenswood Lake*, Edward L. Loper for *Behind the Tracks*, William Carter for *Peonies and Old Porcelain*, and Lois Mailou

contributions to American music did receive prizes, but records of those murals seem to be lost.

No doubt the distinction between such prize-winning representations of black music at the American Negro Exposition and Dalstrom's interpretation of it escaped Quinn and the "other element of Negroes in town" as well. But that would not have escaped the articulate and educated blacks who were in the delegation that first met with the postmaster and organized the protest. As citizens of Missouri, they were probably familiar with the state's own artist, Thomas Hart Benton, and his work in the South. Although Benton claimed to love the South and its people, black and white, his canvases that purported to record the lives of ordinary southerners would not endear him to blacks or whites. Benton's representations of blacks were considered by Stuart Davis, fellow artist and archrival in the raging abstract-versus-representational-art controversy, to be "gross caricatures": "The only thing they directly represent is a third-rate vaudeville character cliché with the humor omitted. Had they a little more wit, they would automatically take their place in the body of propaganda which is constantly being utilized to disfranchise the Negro politically, socially and economically."[9]

Davis did not exaggerate. *Cotton Pickers, Georgia, 1928–29*, for example, is almost a three-foot square of skinny, misshapen darkies dragging their laden sacks, not through carefully planted rows of cotton, but in skewed directions through a field blanketed with cotton snow. In the background are a rickety cotton wagon, a black worker drowsing on the seat, and an equally rickety cabin—not a fit home for any worker, black or white. But the pickers themselves seem to have no respect for the crop they harvest, tramping in any direction through it. They are clearly underfed, and their twiglike arms are long enough to reach their knees. The center foreground is dominated by what must be the white foreman. Sitting hunched in the midst of the cotton, pipe hanging from his mouth, arms idly folded, he has as his only function to see that none of the darkies escape to go play the banjo and dance on a levee somewhere.

Jones for *Still Life With Green Apples*. Although no reproductions are available, the titles alone suggest that none of these were musical gatherings.

9. Stuart Davis, "The New York American Scene in Art (1935)," quoted in Diane Kelder (ed.), *Stuart Davis* (New York, 1958), 152.

But *Cotton Pickers* is not too bad compared with Benton's monumental (96 by 156 inches) *Arts of the South*. The southern segment of his mural sequence at the New School for Social Research, this mural proclaims the arts of the South as gambling, fiddling, speaking in tongues, and exhorting. The whites in the painting are bad enough, but they are relegated to an inconspicuous corner. Above the other figures but slightly in the background, partially blocking a sign that reads "Get Next to God," stands a white minister. The glass and pitcher on his lectern could indicate that he is not a preacher but the emotive southern politician. Flinging his arms in the air, he could threaten his listeners with hellfire and damnation, or with another reconstruction if he is not elected. Two white males look up fearfully from their guitar and fiddle. The two white women in the picture writhe and clutch at parts of their bodies (one her mouth, the other her groin) as if seized by the spirit. Another man imperviously rolls a cigarette.

Blacks, however, dominate the scene. In the center at the focal point for the mural, a virile young black lifts his voice in song, opens his mouth to pray, or folds his hands in prayer. He may be doing all three. Other blacks, unshod, listen pensively, join him in his song, or shout amen. A black woman at the lower edge of the composition feeds her child from her own meager bowl. Blacks in the left middle-ground enjoy a furtive crap game. All the figures have the same outrageous bodies—apelike arms and elongated torsos. But the blacks are further distorted with the enormous thick lips and broad, flat noses of caricature and huge feet. In front of the whole scene, falling out of the picture, is a junk heap—beer bottles, empty bean tins, and worn-out tires—that seems to indicate that the arts of the South are but a pile of rubbish.

On his trip through the South in the early 1930s, Benton camped for eight days on a Louisiana levee so that he could sketch the last remaining cotton-hauling river packet, the *Tennessee Belle*, when it stopped to pick up a load of cotton. In his account of the event, he describes muscular blacks laboring one to a bale to move the cotton onto the ship. Because they were "naturally well co-ordinated [and] handled their weight skillfully . . . no bales got away to roll in the water." Benton clearly admired the workers' skill and efficiency, but when he sketched them, he drew a different picture. One of his lithographs shows two men struggling with each bale and several unoccupied blacks lolling on the levee apparently exhausted from just watching such work.[10] Benton's intention may have been no less innocuous than was Dalstrom's or Quinn's, but to southern blacks working to better their economic and social circumstances and to instill a sense of confidence in their compatriots, his work offered no more inspiration than did Dalstrom's interpretation of blacks' contribution to American music. At least, Benton had traveled to the Deep South to find material; Dalstrom claimed to have found his right there in progressive St. Joseph.

Unfortunately, Dalstrom's interpretation of blacks and music was not original. Blacks had been painted as dancers and players of banjos ever since the mid-nineteenth century, when William Sidney Mount painted *The Banjo Player* and *The Power of Music* and Eastman Johnson unveiled his oft-reproduced *My Old Kentucky Home.* It is possible that prize-winning artworks at the American Negro Exposition celebrated the black origins of such American musical forms as jazz and blues. But those were *black* interpretations of *black* music. What Dalstrom recalled were white purveyors of the myth, such as Stephen Foster and Daniel Emmett (the first recorded black impersonator), who perpetuated the image of gentle, childlike black folk who would be lost off the plantation without Ole Massa's kindly ministrations. The St. Joseph blacks who had read *Tobacco Road* were not ready to accept still another artwork that proclaimed black music as the play of a helpless people marking time until their pie-in-the-sky reward.

The distinction between the music celebrated at the American Negro Exposition and that portrayed in Dalstrom's design was no more apparent to Postmaster Quinn than it was to Dalstrom. Once he found a few blacks who had bought the myth, he concluded that no changes should be made in the mural: "I am therefore very much of the opinion that Mr. Dalstrom should proceed with the picture as originally proposed and feel that when it is completed, not only will it have its particular place in the entire group, but we should have no fear of any undesirable reaction on the part of the colored population in this community."[11]

Quinn was probably justified in his confidence. Once again, American blacks had trusted that the American government was indeed for all the people, and once again they had found that, even

10. Thomas Hart Benton, *An Artist in America* (1937; 4th rev. ed.; rpr. Columbia, Mo., 1983), 140, illustration facing p. 145.

11. Quinn to Rowan, March 21, 1941, in St. Joseph, Missouri, file.

when no slight was intended, nothing would be done about the offense. Indeed, in Newton and Vicksburg, Mississippi, local committees and not the Section had rejected designs that suggested the minstrel stereotype. There, as in St. Joseph, the Section was satisfied not to be bothered with the sentiments of real people, and Rowan was only too happy to pass over the event of blacks speaking on their own behalf. In answer to inquiries from the Post Office Department about the conflict in St. Joseph, Rowan wrote: "You may recall that while the work was in progress a number of telegrams and petitions were received in your office, as well as in this office, protesting the subject matter of one of the murals. Investigation at the time indicated that these protests were unfounded and were probably started by a small group wishing to excite certain colored organizations in the city."[12] Unfounded? Hardly. But the idea of inside agitators was a comfortable one for the white power structure and it justified the presence of widely read, knowledgeable, and articulate protestors. Blacks who were that widely read and could express themselves that well were obviously exceptions. Had they been typical, blacks would no longer have to try to earn citizenship; they would be ready for it.

The blacks of St. Joseph openly protested a less-than-flattering depiction of themselves. Of the other southern minority race, there were probably neither enough remaining nor enough organization among them to lodge a protest. That is not to say that all Indians had left the South by the 1930s. Some hardy souls had hung on for a century after they were legally expelled from their homeland. The 1970 census counted 76,656 cultural Indians in the Southeast, or nearly 10 percent of the Indians in the United States.[13] Their numbers were probably smaller in the 1930s, but at that time, whites with missionary zeal and the federal government were setting up schools for the Indians, whose existence few bother to acknowledge. The children and adults who would attend these schools in Mississippi and Alabama were able to do so only because their ancestors had hidden in tiny communities when they remained or

12. Rowan to Walter Myers, December 8, 1941, *ibid.*

13. Charles Hudson, *The Southeastern Indians* (Knoxville, 1976), 477. Hudson's anthropological examination of the southeastern Indians includes some history but, like so many other texts, says little about what became of those who remained after removal. Not until his last chapter does he consider the Indians' situation in the 1970s.

they had separated and either assimilated through marriage into white or black families or lived lonely lives. In the 1830s the surviving members of the southeastern Indian tribes—those who had not died from the white man's diseases, had not been killed in the white man's wars, had not died fighting the white man who would drive them from their land and their civilization—had been forcibly removed from the Southeast to the newly created Indian Territory. By the second quarter of the twentieth century, Indians had become so invisible in the Southeast that most of the Federal Writers Project guides to the states treated the race as having merely archaeological interest.[14]

Southern novelists of the 1930s, slightly more aware that Indians had remained part of the culture for at least a while after removal, acknowledged their existence in historical fiction. In *So Red the Rose*, Stark Young's antebellum southern family had an Indian retainer. Not a slave, nor yet precisely free, since he was dependent on this white family, Dock provided the family with game and rode into town daily for the mail. "Not the stale Indian of the tales, but a Choctaw who had stayed behind with the . . . family when his tribe was robbed and sent West," Dock earned six dollars a month and his keep for the services he rendered.[15] Unlike the slaves, he would be asked rather than ordered to retrieve the mail, saddle horses, and deliver messages. And unlike the slaves, he was neither accorded pity nor considered unable to care for himself by the characters in the book. Even so, Dock's presence is felt throughout this novel of failing southern aristocracy, and occasionally he provides choruslike commentary on the action, as literary members of ban-

14. Federal Writers Project, *Kentucky: A Guide to the Bluegrass State* (New York, 1939), for example, speaks of Indians only in its section entitled "Archeology and Indians," and it stops in the early eighteenth century. *Alabama: A Guide to the Deep South* (New York, 1941) concludes its respectable section on Indian history with the statement, "Descendants of the Indians who once occupied Alabama now live in Oklahoma" (p. 39), with no acknowledgment of those who remained. In *Louisiana: A Guide to the State* (New York, 1945), the state's association with Indians virtually ends in 1721, when the Natchez threatened to massacre New Orleans (p. 40). *Mississippi: A Guide to the Magnolia State* (New York, 1938), 59, contains the statement that Indians were removed to Oklahoma, where they thrive— despite Hudson's finding that over four thousand Choctaw still live in Mississippi and that Indians who went through removal suffered hardship and deprivation (*The Southeastern Indians*, 489). This is common through most of the southern states.

15. Stark Young, *So Red the Rose* (New York, 1934), 43.

ished social groups are wont to do—especially those to whom taciturnity and wisdom are attributed.

William Faulkner created tragicomic plantation owners and reluctant slave traders Issetibbeha, Ikkemotubbe, and Moketubbe as clearly white on the outside (they convert a wrecked river steamer into a "steamboat gothic" plantation house) and red on the inside (they hang the French brass bed from the ceiling, roast a dog on an open fire and bury each chief's body slave with his master).[16] And he created the moving Sam Fathers, mentor of Isaac McCaslin in *The Bear*, a noble savage whose Chickasaw heritage gave him the respect for the land and wildlife that white recreational hunters lacked. It was Margaret Mitchell's Indian character, however, who perhaps provides the best analogy with the post office mural Indians in the South. Scarlett O'Hara's most efficient, most intelligent, and most dignified servant and, during hard times, her most effective field hand was Dilcey, a female half-breed slave. Mitchell repeatedly made it clear that Dilcey's Indian blood was responsible for her superior character traits.

Had there been enough Indians in the South to hold mass meetings to protest their depiction in murals, they would probably have had less reason for so doing than did blacks. Indians in the murals with few exceptions were, like Scarlett's servant and Sam Fathers, noble and worthy of respect. They welcomed the people who would steal their land, they signed treaty after treaty that would be broken, and they fought hopeless battles—all that was to the good. So had southerners trusted those who would turn on them and take from them their right to govern themselves. So had they fought bravely in hopeless battles and nobly faced defeat in their own homeland. The Indians had been conquered by southerners who would themselves be bested in war; it spoke well of southerners' ability to wage war if those they had defeated were brave and strong and noble. And unlike the blacks, tribal people no longer posed a threat.

The Indians had been defeated, and as a defeated people—or group of peoples, since one reason for their defeat was the inability of the various Indian nations to organize into a single fighting force—they could be admired after the fact. The Indians had ex-

16. William Faulkner, "Red Leaves," *The Portable Faulkner*, ed. Malcolm Cowley (New York, 1967), 57–84. The story is also told with fewer tragic implications for the blacks and more for the Indians, foreshadowing William Sutpen's doomed dynasty in *Absalom, Absalom!*.

hibited one trait that American white people perenially revere. They *fought*, first with their own weapons, later with with the white man's. Blacks, isolated from their native land, despite being kept dependent on their white masters for their very food, did revolt from time to time. But organization had been even harder for them than it was for the Indians. Besides having been moved from their native soil and thus having no base of operations, early slaves had to struggle with the same tribal differences in language and tradition that the Indians did. The Indians were visited on their own turf; they had their own national organizations within tribes and they had the means for their own subsistence. As a matter of fact, white planters had to give up their early efforts to enslave the Indians because it was too easy for them to escape and go back home.[17]

The Indians were, from the beginning, a worthy foe. In many ways, of course, their civilization was entirely foreign to the first whites to colonize the Southeast, but they were not so different as is often thought. The southeastern Indians built cities, they owned and cultivated land, and they were shrewd traders. These were all traits Europeans could understand. They and their ancestors had for centuries taken land, traded goods, subjugated societies. They had for centuries acknowledged the intrinsic worth of those they had defeated with difficulty, and they had no respect for the easily conquered. So it was in the murals. Indians, even when they were depicted as waging war on whites, raping, scalping, and ravaging, were presented as noble beings. Unlike blacks, tribal Americans had no time to dance jigs or lounge around on cotton bales.

The mural for Smithfield, Virginia, depicts the similarity of Indian interests and those of the white invaders. For that mural, William A. Cheever immortalized the "first business deal in Isle of Wight County." It seems that on a 1607 expedition, Captain John Smith went to the mouth of the James River to trade with the Warroscoyak Indians for produce. Although Smithfield residents fondly remember the event as the county's first business proposition, the Warroscoyak must have been familiar with trade, just not with whites. Smith reports no hesitation on their part when he ap-

---

17. Hudson, *The Southeastern Indians*, 437–38 and *passim*, briefly discusses the difficulty of keeping Indian slaves. Because they were not helpless in their own land, they were shipped during the seventeenth and early eighteenth centuries to the West Indies and other places where they would be as helpless as blacks were in the Southeast. This practice was soon abandoned as impractical.

proached them with the scheme. Rather, the whites were invited to the Indian settlement, where they struck a deal for no fewer than thirty bushels of corn.[18] And it is clear from the history of Cheever's design that people who understood capitalism were entitled to a certain amount of dignity when they appeared on post office walls.

According to Section practice, after his design was approved, Cheever submitted a full-sized cartoon. The Section called for further revision. In the cartoon, larger and more detailed than the design, the Indians do look like the "sauvages" they were often labeled in Smith's day. They are foreshortened, their foreheads are high, their arms long, and they squat more like apes in a zoo than like a noble race of primitive man. One red man squints quizzically into a mirror; another runs beads through his fingers. Cheever redid his cartoon, and in the second rendition, though positions and composition remain largely unchanged, the Indians look more like the Hollywood version of noble savages than men in an earlier stage of evolution. Some of them still squat as they examine the loot from Smith's trading party. But their eyes are clearly defined and intelligent. The man with the mirror no longer squats dumbfounded at his own image; now he performs research. No longer do the Indians with the beads play with toys; now one nearly naked businessman hands a string of beads to another for his appraisal. These Indians are taller than those in the first cartoon, and their arms and legs are strong and sinewy. Their cheekbones are high, their foreheads are appropriate to the worthy foe or the business associate of modern man.

But Indians were worthy tradesmen only so long as the white got the best of the deal, and so long as they were doomed to disappear from white society altogether. The mural that reveals the ideal concept of the southern Indian is the one in Pascagoula, Mississippi. Memorializing a tiny and long-extinct tribe, the mural also calls attention to the town's leading tourist attraction. It seems that at one point in the city, the Pascagoula River emits a humming sound at twilight every evening. In the 1930s the sound had yet to be satisfactorily explained by scientists. One suspects that any such explanation would have been rejected in favor of the alluring legend associated with "The Singing River." Likewise, no

18. Charles E. Davis to Edward Bruce, November 9, 1940, and unidentified clipping, both in Smithfield, Virginia, file, RG 121, NA.

conclusive anthropological explanation for the sudden disappearance of the Pascagoula has yet been advanced. But they did disappear, and the legend does explain both their absence and the mysterious singing of the river. The Pascagoula, a slight and beautiful people, were involved in a long and losing war with the ferocious Biloxi, because a Biloxi prince insisted upon marrying a Pascagoula princess. As most southeastern Indian tribes were matrilineal, and as the gentle Pascagoula were more willing to accept a member of the enemy tribe than were the Biloxi, the young couple made their home with the bride's people. The Biloxi went to war to win back their favorite son, and in a truly noble gesture, the Pascagoula refused to relinquish him and break the heart of their princess. As the war progressed it became clear that the gentle tribe would lose and the survivors would be enslaved. Being noble savages, indeed, the tribe chose death to defeat. One warm Gulf coast evening they gathered at the river to end their lives and their travail. With the women and children leading, the elders behind, and the braves last, they joined hands and walked singing into the river to their deaths. But they did not disappear without a trace. In commemoration of their brave act, they can be heard to sing in the river to this day.[19]

At the request of the post office custodian, Arthur V. Smith, and without visiting the location, Pittsburgh artist Lorin Thompson painted the Pascagoula entering the river (Figure 65). The design is pleasant, and it is a good wall decoration. True to legend, Thompson's Pascagoula are a beautiful people, delicate and lyrical. And the subject matter is moving without being sentimental—a particular struggle for Thompson, who did not wish to be maudlin. In the center of the mural, a narrow stream with high clay banks winds away from the viewer. In the river and on both banks, Indians, many of them clad in blue to blend with the sky, the foliage, and the distant mountains, bid farewell to each other and move into the river. One mother and child take their leave of the father who must wait and come with the braves. An older brother hands a dog to his younger sibling already in the water. It seems that the dogs were as noble as their owners; another canine has already entered the river of its own volition. The people are clad in typical pre-European southeastern Indian dress: breechcloth for the men, knee-length skirt for the women, cloaks to keep the older people

19. Federal Writers Project, *Mississippi*, 287–88.

65 / Lorin Thompson, *Legend of the Singing River*, Pascagoula, Miss., 1939

warm. All carefully stand so that no nudity will offend the post office patron. And, lest the viewer become emotionally involved with any single individual, all the faces are merely suggested. The colors and the arrangement of the figures with hair and wraps often blowing gently behind are as horizontal and serene as a seascape on a quiet day.

Although the mural is well designed and pleasant to look upon, and many Pascagoulans were immediately fond of it, not everyone found it satisfactory. First there was the "appalling technical omission of Spanish moss on any of the trees." Then, the artist persisted in identifying the Biloxi as the Natchez. And no one could walk to his death in the shallow New England stream Thompson drew. As Thompson saw when he visited Mississippi to install the mural, the real Singing River is wide, deep, and sandy. The banks are such that people could actually walk into it holding hands rather than be lifted or jump down into waist-deep water as they would have to in the mural stream. Thompson reported that "there was a healthy controversy regarding the mural," but he could not change anything:

> From local comment, I judge that the color and the mood of the painting are greatly appreciated by almost everyone but public opinion . . . has it that I have failed to reproduce faithfully the Pascagoula River and its banks. . . . True I have no Spanish moss on the trees and many Pascagoula trees have. But more have not. I wanted no vertical Spanish moss in my design. I still don't want it. I bow to the horrible fact that I have a mud bank on the river shore whereas Pascagoula is a sandy country and has no such mud bank, but I can do nothing about that as any such attempt would alter the entire design.

. . . I have been both twitted and complimented, and have left Pascagoula with the feeling that in spite of such technical errors of locale, the mural is considered by most to enhance the Post Office and has created genuine interest and appreciation among the townspeople.[20]

One can hardly fault Thompson for not making those changes and thus betraying his design. But had he done his homework, he might have found the gentle sand slopes and the wide river even more conducive to the horizontal flow of this design, and without the verticals of the inaccurate banks, a bit of Spanish moss might have been acceptable. However, the Pascagoula mural was better received than many, and it has gained in popularity through the years. When a new post office was built a few years ago, the picture was moved from its original mooring to a new home above a new postmaster's door. The sterile new lobby—no marble, no brass, no wood—was painted in muted aquas and off-whites to blend with the mural. The Pascagoula mural and the legend it portrays provide a fitting allegory for the expulsion of all the southeastern Indians. The mournful journey of the Pascagoula into the river suggests the equally mournful journey of most of the Cherokee, Choctaw, Creek, and Chickasaw over the Trail of Tears to the newly created Indian Territory in the 1830s, a century before Thompson painted his mural.

When the Section approved the Pascagoula mural, it had one suggestion: Thompson was cautioned not to "overemphasize the nudes in the further progress of the work as you realize that certain citizens might find such treatment objectionable."[21] Although such admonitions were standard when the subjects were white, the issue usually did not arise when Indians were to be portrayed. Artists seem to have been particularly fond of using southeastern Indian subjects because their traditional costume offered an opportunity to paint the uncovered human body.

The uncovered human body was repeatedly shown to be unacceptable when the subjects were white. When Ethel Edwards submitted her cartoon for Lake Providence, Louisiana, a scene of young white women and men picnicking and fishing, it was re-

20. Arthur W. Smith to Rowan, November 8, 1939, Lorin Thompson to Rowan, September 28, 1939, both in Pascagoula, Mississippi, file, RG 121, NA.

21. Rowan to Thompson, March 30, 1939, *ibid.* See Karal Ann Marling, *Wall-to-Wall America* (Minneapolis, 1982), 242–92, for an extensive consideration of the problem of nudity in Section murals.

66 / Ethel Edwards, design for Lake Providence, La.

67 / William Dean Fausett, *The British Come to See August,* Augusta, Ga., 1939

jected primarily because of a single figure (Figure 66). One woman sits reading under a cypress tree. Hair upswept and wearing shorts, she leans on one hand and holds a book in the other. So far so good. But it is her legs and trunk that are unacceptable. One knee rests on the ground; the other is bent so that the complete length of each shapely leg is visible in a posture that the Section found indecent. Southern ladies did not sit that way, and in the mural world, they wore neither shorts nor bathing suits—even on picnics. Edwards redesigned, and in the final mural the woman, now decidedly a lady, reclines on one elbow, her knees together and her feet tucked under her skirt. She wears a dress and a demure pageboy, and to make sure that everything is properly covered, her friend sits between her and the viewer so that even her feet can no longer be seen.

No such revision was required of William Dean Fausett's mural of the first English visit to the site of Augusta, Georgia (Figure 67).

This picture, replete with the Spanish moss omitted from Thompson's Pascagoula mural and never seen in the latitude of Augusta, shows the Englishmen as distant figures just landing beside a river. The Indians who, according to the local newspaper account of the subject, meet the English dominate the foreground. The English, of course, are fully clothed. But the Indians, male and female, are clad only in loincloths. Muscular, regal, and virtually nude, they eye the intruders, and their eyes are wary. They do not know who these strangers are, but they seem to sense danger in the intrusion. That is, all of them except the female. She alone faces postal patrons, and her startled demeanor suggests that they, rather than the eighteenth-century explorers, are the real threat. From the waist down, her pose is much like that of Ethel Edwards' Louisiana white woman. Her legs are spread, and though the corner of a blanket covers her most private parts, her position is quite undignified. Aside from the blanket, she wears only several necklaces that cascade between voluptuous breasts. Yet nobody seems aware of her—not the braves who so warily watch the English, not the Section, and not, it seems, the clientele of the Augusta art club where the mural was exhibited before being installed in the post office.

One can only assume that she was allowed to go about in this state of dishabille because she was an early-eighteenth-century Indian who was long dead. And no one can guess why she was in the woods alone with four armed braves. She alone of the southern mural Indians is not presented as dignified and noble. It is true that one other southern Indian woman was allowed to parade her nudity before postal patrons, but she was dignified, even heroic. On the wall of the Richmond, Virginia, Parcel Post Building, Pocahontas saves Captain John Smith's life by throwing her body between him and his would-be slayers (Figure 68). In contrast to the blanket thrown over the Indian woman in Augusta, the few stitches that Pocahontas is allowed to wear appear to be clothing. Her garment is probably more authentic than it first appears. Women of at least one southeastern tribe—but not one in tidewater Virginia, where no Spanish moss has ever grown—fashioned garments from Spanish moss that hung in tendrils from their waists.[22]

In even greater contrast to the unfortunate Indian woman in Augusta is Pocahontas' position. With a long and slender leg forming

22. Hudson, *The Southeastern Indians*, 264.

68 / Paul Cadmus, *Pocahontas Saving the Life of Captain John Smith and Early Governors of Virginia*, Richmond Parcel Post, 1939

a single arc that continues through the extension of a long and slender arm, the Virginia lady is both graceful and in control of the situation. Never to be caught unaware, she it is who stays the tomahawks of Smith's would-be assassins. And since she is identified, viewers have the comfort of knowing that she eventually made a good marriage (into the English aristocracy).

Female nudity even among Indian subjects was relatively rare on post office walls. Not so male. Although the actual breechcloths worn by tribal men of the Southeast covered both front and back, and although the leggings donned in cold weather were worn with breechcloths, artists who painted southern murals preferred to omit any covering for Indian men's backsides.[23] The most prominent feature in the Pocahontas mural is neither the Indian princess nor the English captain. It is, rather, the posterior of the Indian brave in the center foreground who aims his tomahawk at Smith's vulnerable belly. Arms, back, waist, and buttocks from one continuous mass of rippling sinew. Only his legs are covered, and the fringed leggings would befit a Plains Indian. But the Section objected neither to exposed female Indian breasts nor to exposed male Indian backsides. What Rowan did strive to have changed in this picture was the protective garment on another tomahawk-wielding Indian who faced the audience.

23. Hudson, *ibid.*, 261, describes a breechcloth as a piece of leather about five feet long worn through the crotch and looped over a belt so that it fell down before and behind.

Artist Paul Cadmus was well known to the Section as a playful artist who would break rules in order to get a response. And Section officials had been on the alert throughout the design process for anything to which sensitive southerners might object. Until they received the photograph of the finished mural just prior to installation, nothing offensive had been found. It is possible that Cadmus made Pocahontas so nubile and put so much emphasis on the backside of the foreground Indian as tests of how far he could go. If so, he had been disappointed. No one objected to a certain amount of exposed flesh on Indians. But in that supposedly final rendering, Cadmus had clad one regal savage, his front to the audience, in a loin piece made of fox skins. As he prepares to strike, the brave stays his prey, Captain John Smith, with his left foot. Thus the fox skin is prominently thrust forward just below Pocahontas' suggestively placed hand. But the picture as it is today is quite respectable compared to the one Cadmus was required to touch up. The fox's head, with the long and pointed nose, was a plausible, though furry, representation of the Indian's private parts. After a protracted correspondence in which the artist pretended not to know what Rowan objected to, the fox-head penis was removed, but the tail remains.[24]

Everywhere an Indian greets the people who will drive him from his home, everywhere he signs a treaty that will eventually be broken, he displays his backside. In Augusta, each wary Indian wears a garment that only partially covers the buttocks. In his original design for the Christiansburg, Virginia, Post Office, John De-Groot, Jr., presented his buffalo-shooting Indians properly breech-clothed (Figure 69). By the time he finished the mural, the loincloths had virtually disappeared. For his Morganton, North Carolina, mural of Indians greeting arriving Spaniards, Dean Cornwell included one full-length figure in the foreground, facing the Spaniards so that his back is to the post office lobby. Dutifully wearing his leather leggings, he displays his muscular backside. And so it goes. Southern mural Indians are either clad in full Plains Indians' cool-weather costumes, or they expose more than their ancestors ever exposed.

24. See Marling, *Wall-to-Wall America*, 282–89, for details of the controversy about the Richmond Parcel Post murals by Cadmus and Jared French.

69 / John DeGroot, Jr., *Great Road*, Christiansburg, Va., 1939

Although only the Indians were permitted actual nakedness in the stifling southern summer, the fascination with backsides extends to blacks and white women as well. Often it is a matter of arranging a black figure so that his tight pants show off the muscles he has accumulated doing work the white man would not deign to do. Equally often, a woman of either race in the foreground turns her back to pick something off the ground. And occasionally, a horse's backside takes the place of a human. For example, Peter De Anna's original design for Belmont, North Carolina, was rejected. He had depicted an industrious Indian encampment: women tanning hides; women hauling grain, men planting and storing it; others building a dwelling. And in the right foreground, one Indian turns his back to the audience as he tests the strength of a bow. His exposed rear end would not provide a pleasant prospect for the viewer. De Anna's completed mural is the same design but the matter is different. This time it is a cavalry encampment at play. Where the Indian hut was under construction, now is an army tent. Where the storage house was, now is a large boulder. Where Indians planted corn and gutted a deer, now a cavalryman prepares a meal and officers examine charts. Where Indian women braided mats, cavalrymen arm-wrestle. And where the Indian bowman exposed his backside to the post office lobby, now a white cavalry horse does likewise.

Black backsides were just as acceptable as those of Indians and horses. The winning design for Newton, Mississippi, was a montage of modern Mississippi industry (Figure 70). The design was arranged so that it extended quite far down the wall on each side of

70 / Franklin and Mary Boggs, design for Newton, Miss.

the postmaster's door. In the left foreground, a 4-H boy is awarded a blue ribbon for his heifer, and behind him other 4-H children, one of them female, tend their cattle entries. Behind them and moving toward the center, a white man loads newly milled lumber onto a flatbed truck. In the upper-left-hand corner, a sign reads "REA Co-op," and as if to prove REA is indeed active in Newton, a row of electric poles recedes into the background through a field of stumps. At the center right is a cotton gin, and, just as the left side of the mural had featured whites, the whole right side of the mural features blacks.

Even here, however, a white foreman with a clipboard keeps track of the various activities of five black men. One stands atop a pile of sacks of meal, his pronounced buttocks to the audience, and reaches for a sack carried by another man. The face of the carrier is hidden, his load improbably balanced on his right shoulder by his left hand. His right hand grabs his back as if he were in the last throes of lumbago. Below them, one black's body is arranged in an exaggerated *s*, and the one in front, also *s*-shaped, wears strange garments. The pants are rolled up to his knees, and over that he sports a knee-length white loincloth. Markedly exaggerated lips, a receding forehead, and a board balanced on his head complete the impression that, not quite evolved to the present state of the human race, he performs some kind of primitive African ritual. And still lower on the picture's plane is a man in a loose-fitting sleeveless shirt, again suggesting some exotic and primitive garment. He struggles to lift three boards and pokes his derriere suggestively toward the viewer. All the white figures in the mural stand straight and tall; every black bends, either as if in struggle or as if in a ceremonial dance.

The Section wrote Franklin and Mary Boggs that it was impressed with their design, but it did have reservations: "Your design was regarded as a handsome solution . . . , but it was felt that further study was needed in the lower right hand section. The Negroes seem overdrawn in their distorted postures. This would not be so noticeable if it were not true of all of them. It is particularly suggested that the one in the lowest part of the mural be restudied and redrawn."[25] The Boggses did do further study, and they must have concluded that if they adjusted only that figure in the lowest part of the design, it would be acceptable. They turned the board-carrying black around to face the audience, but if anything, his posture is more distorted. It is difficult to believe that the artists could convert a scale model drawing (two inches to the foot) into a mural of over one hundred square feet without changing any details, but the Boggses did it (Figure 71). The completed and installed mural differs from the design only in the one figure; everything else looks the same. The result is a very attractive design with what could have been excessively formal balance offset by the fact that horizontals and verticals dominate the left side of the panel while a zigzag motif counterbalances them on the right.

Blacks did not protest the representation of themselves in the Newton mural, and they did not protest the one in Tallulah, Louisiana, either, though the postmaster observed: "There has been quite a bit of comment both pro and con in regards to [the mural]," he wrote. "It is quite amusing to watch the colored people, and listen to their comments."[26]

25. Rowan to Mr. and Mrs. Frank Boggs, June 17, 1941, in Newton, Mississippi, file, RG 121, NA.

26. R. M. Almond to Treasury Department, August 2, 1938, in Tallulah, Louisiana, file, RG 121, NA.

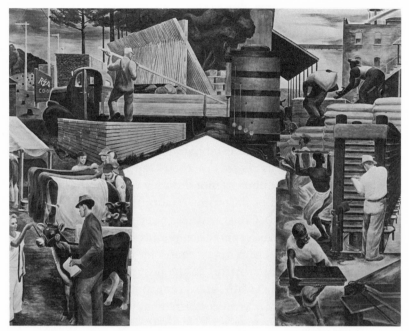

71 / Franklin and Mary Boggs, *Economic Life in Newton,* Newton, Miss., 1941

During the 1960s when blacks demonstrated, even rioted for their constitutional rights, they did so in the regions where dialogue between the white power structure and the black community had begun, areas in which wide-scale employment, unionization, and a better-than-average black standard of living suggested that all the rights of American citizenship were indeed possible for blacks. Protests seldom occurred where blacks were most oppressed, areas in which the few past concessions suggested that few were likely in the future. Riots occurred in Detroit, in Harlem, in Watts; sit-ins and bus boycotts happened in Atlanta and Jackson— not in small towns, not in the rural South. In the rural areas, voter registration drives, whether they were conducted by whites or blacks, could not convince the majority of blacks that either registering or voting would do any good. That the black community organized in St. Joseph, Missouri, in the 1940s suggests that the dream of blacks "earning" full citizenship had come nearer to realization there than in the Deep South. Where blacks knew that protest was useless, they did not bother to protest. Even though murals elsewhere depicted blacks in less-than-flattering terms, St. Joseph was the only place they voiced any organized opposition.

It was not until the mid-1970s that black organizations objected to the representation of blacks as banjo-playing children in Jackson, Mississippi (Figure 63), as the exclusive pickers of cotton in Columbus, Mississippi (Figure 1), and as primitive tribesmen in Sylvester, Georgia (Figure 47). The protest was no more effective in removing offending murals than the one in St. Joseph had been. But at least this time, the establishment argued that the murals should be preserved as records of an art movement. They neither called the protests groundless, nor did they contend that the representation was factual or flattering. And in the 1970s, the protests were not total losses. Consciousness was raised. Postal patrons who may hitherto have accepted the pictures as accurate representations now know there is more than one interpretation. Blacks confidently point out to visitors in the post office lobbies the misrepresentations on the wall. The attention of people, black and white, in towns where protests occurred has been called to the murals themselves, and a new pride in their significance as historic artifacts now runs through the South. As a result, murals in several locations have been restored, though restoration in the South lags far behind that in the rest of the country.[27]

One suspects that often the apparent racism in the murals was not racism in fact, but rather a way for artists designing under heavy restriction to say something poignant, to infuse lyricism into their works. There is, indeed, something lyrical about the zigzag arrangement of the skewed black bodies in the Newton, Mississippi, mural. It is more interesting than the stiff straight backs of the blond children at the other side of the mural. And some southern murals are infused with the tragedy of the black American experience. In the mural for Tallulah, Louisiana, about which the blacks' comments so amused the postmaster, the bodies

27. NAACP protests in Sylvester, Georgia; Wynne, Arkansas; Jackson, Mississippi; and other southern communities have probably awakened local blacks to both the misrepresentation in and the historic value of the murals. Information about how widespread NAACP protests are is scarce, as such protests are kept out of notoriously conservative southern small-town papers. The Jackson protest led by a white lawyer, however, reached local news media, and though the mural is preserved as an artifact, it is now draped and shown only to those who ask.

of black flood-fighters reflect centuries of struggle and the resulting exhaustion.

In May, 1927, Tallulah was among the many Mississippi River communities practically destroyed by the biggest flood on record. Not until 1937, the year Francesca Negueloua was commissioned to paint a mural for that post office, did the river behave so boisterously again, and by that time new flood-control measures offered a bit more protection. But Tallulah remembered that first flood with more pride than regret. In July, 1927, the *Atlantic Monthly* had published an article about Tallulah during the flood; it was written by local resident Helen Murphy. In the aftermath of the more recent flood, Negueloua chose the decade-old article as inspiration for her mural. Murphy had begun her article, organized as a diary, with an account of the work blacks did to stem the flood:

> I saw huge trucks filled to "standing room only" with Negroes going to work on the levee. They were shouting, laughing, chewing tobacco and swearing, but going cheerfully to delve in the muck and the danger, driving heavy piles, tying willow mattresses, filling countless thousands of sacks with earth to top the already high levee crest.
>
> How our men—white and black, even the high-school boys—have toiled, day and night, through these horrible weeks! Everything known to engineering ingenuity is being done to hold back the sullen, swollen river which looms above us sixty feet on the Vicksburg gauge.

Even after those accolades to black workers, however, Murphy commented that "Negroes, though often irresponsible, are never unresponsive."[28] Any suspicion that racism in the 1930s was confined to southerners is thereby demolished: that statement was published with no disclaimer in a national magazine aimed at intellectuals. Even so, if Negueloua agreed with Murphy, she did not let it show in her mural. She chose to portray black men and white men working side by side to reinforce the levee with sandbags. Although blacks dominate the picture, there is no white foreman, no white engineer. Some of the blacks, though, have a tragic demeanor lacking in any of the whites. In the left background, a black woman comes out of an endangered cabin with a tray full of refreshments for the workers. To the right, three blacks lug sandbags where they are needed farther down the levee. In the middle ground is a 1920s

28. Helen Murphy, "Overflow Notes," *Atlantic Monthly*, CXL (July, 1927), 223.

vintage truck from which workers haul the heavy bags. In the foreground, a white man and a black one labor to put other bags in place. Although a bit of creeping muddy water can be glimpsed in the lower-right-hand corner, the angle of the picture is such that viewers are farther up the levee, presumably safe because the white and the black work so well together.

Although the black man works alongside the white at the same task, there is a difference in the way they hold their bodies. The white is just putting down his burden, and from the way he squats on one knee and lifts the elbow of the opposite arm, it is clear that, whatever he was doing a moment before and whatever he will do in the next, at this moment he exerts little physical effort. The implication is that his burden is light, his movements swift—an allegory for the southern white male who, after the flood recedes, can resume his life of liberty, plenty, and self-assurance. The black rests on his knees and bends to set down, or to lift, a sandbag. Both hands reach to grasp the bag at either end, the palms and fingers turned out. His head is bent, and his attitude is one of prayer, of faith in a higher power, in contrast with the faith in himself demonstrated by the white. The impression is that the black man's burdens are so heavy that the release of a single hundred-pound sandbag will not be noticed. So it is with the three men in the upper-right-hand corner. Their backs bend as if they were accustomed to such loads. Their burdens are heavy, but the viewer can see that the real burden is neither sandbag nor flood, that this particular trial is only one in a series that does not stop.

The blacks of Tallulah were probably not impervious to the implications. One white citizen who wrote the Section a letter of gratitude for the mural made a point of the fact that "the negroes throng here to see the mural."[29] Those throngs must have recognized that the real burdens carried by Negueloua's blacks are not the sandbags but the ambiguous compliments of those who, like Helen Murphy, sing praises to black loyalty and industry on one page and then categorically assert black irresponsibility on the next one. Those who, like Helen Murphy, speak of the unspeakable suffering of their friends whose two-storied columned homes and spring planting are lost in the flood, and then are charmed by the quaintness of homeless blacks camped on the levee. Such secure,

29. Tallulah citizen to Rowan, August 12, 1938, in Tallulah, Louisiana, file.

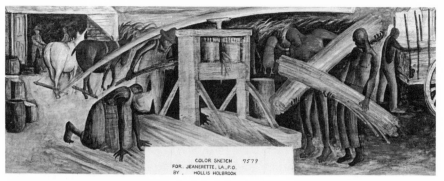

72 / Hollis Holbrook, cartoon for Jeanerette, La., 1941

dry whites can then be warmed by the fact that blacks "though often irresponsible, are never unresponsive."

The "man of sorrows" did not appear only in the Tallulah mural. For Jeanerette, Louisiana, Hollis Holbrook designed a mural on the subject of sugarcane, and the theme is at least as much black tragedy as it is sugar milling (Figure 72). A cane mill composed of right angles and diagonals sits at the center of the wall. Around it are arranged curved lines and bent figures. Mules attached to the mill by a sweeping arched beam provide power to operate it, and black workers carrying long arcing sheaves of cane feed it. Although the workers are strong, their shoulders slope down from their necks, and their faces bend toward the ground. In the left foreground, a black woman bends, presumably to pick up another armload of cane. Her position is precisely the same as that of the black levee worker in the Tallulah mural. She bends under invisible burdens, and her head is bowed in an attitude of prayer. Her hands rest flat on the cane, fingers outward. At the moment she holds no load, and the position of her hands suggests that they rest on the cane rather than reach for it. The load she carries could not be weighed on a scale, and cane is not what bends her back and tugs at her shoulders.

For Dardanelle, Arkansas, Ludwig Mactarian painted *Cotton Growing, Manufacture, and Export,* a mural comprising three vignettes. At the left, white men work in a modern, all-electric cotton mill, so modern, in fact, that the two men can handle as much spinning as once required many women. At the right, whites mechanically load cotton through a vacuum tube onto a modern streamlined riverboat. And in the center middle-ground—in front of a clean, neat modern gin; a load of cotton pulled by a truck with an internal combustion engine, not mules; and a long, fast-moving freight train—white men pick cotton. In the foreground, just over the postmaster's door, the only life-sized figure is a muscular black man balancing a basket of cotton on his broad shoulders. A basket of cotton is not heavy, and yet this brawny male bends under the weight of this one. His face expresses deep contemplation, and lines around his eyes and nose suggest worry. Here may well be a representation of the effects of modernization on the South.

Although Mactarian may not have intended a social message in his representation, depression was not the only cause of unemployment in the South. Technology had much to do with it. Increasing automation made it possible for fewer and fewer workers to accomplish the same amount of work, especially in the cotton mills. Millowners could cut losses suffered during the depression by using more machines and hiring fewer people. One man could oversee operations that, a few years before, twenty men and women were needed to perform. While the greater responsibility increased the tension for the workers who remained, the rest were out of work completely. Thus, unemployed whites competed for the janitorial and cotton-picking jobs once the province of blacks. At the same time, if we are to believe Mactarian's picture, modern methods of shiploading made such work palatable to whites. And so at the focal point of the Dardanelle mural is the victim of modernization in the cotton industry. Soon, perhaps, the mechanical cotton picker would obviate even the need for such capable men to carry the cotton from the fields.

In H. Amiard Oberteuffer's original design for Vicksburg, Mississippi, we see a similar possibly unwitting story of the blacks' struggle. The mural presents a montage of Mississippi River activity typical of Vicksburg (Figure 12). But local residents had objected to the prevalence of blacks in the design; therefore, the artist was ordered by the Section to substitute whites for many of her black workers. She obeyed, and the result depicts a dilemma similar to the one in Dardanelle. All across the massive canvas, white men gather stone for building, supervise dock work, board passenger steamers, weigh cotton, and work in agriculture. In the left foreground, a white teacher consults with white children who are equipped with books, paper, desks, and toys. The blacks remaining in the picture pick cotton and twiddle idle thumbs. Balancing the outdoor schoolroom scene are a black woman, hands in her lap, and three children. One child holds the smallest one, and all look to the female adult. For what? Books, toys—the equipment to grow and learn? Whatever it is, she cannot provide it. She avoids the children's eyes, a thoroughly bemused expression on her face. And in the lower-right-hand corner, walking out of the mural into the post office, is the same man who dominates the Dardanelle mural. Apparently worried, needing the same well-developed muscles and broad shoulders to carry the weight of a world in which he is not needed, he avoids the eyes of the children and the woman as well.

At least occasionally, there seems to have been recognition that blacks' experience in the South might be as tragic as it was paintable. And it could be that in a couple of southern murals, the artists recognized the greater tragedy of the southeastern Indian. Those who first saw the English landing at what is now Augusta are aware (if we can trust the look in their eyes) that the event bodes no good for them. And if the Indian in Beata Beach Porter's mural for Monticello, Georgia, failed to recognize the fateful implications for his people of the activities he watched whites performing, he certainly seemed amazed at the speed with which they did it (Figure 73). In one of the busier, darker, most confusing, and least attractive murals in the South, Porter painted an Indian protected by lush foliage watching the whites take over his land. In a text edited by the Section, she described the mural:

> [Monticello] was built on a rise of land selected for the several springs surrounding it. One spring was set aside for public use and this served as a watering place and center for the simple social life of the early settlers. Here paused wagon loads of people who had come to find new homes. Here, too, the trader, returning with his pack of furs, halted on the edge of the wilderness. This spot was also one of the stations of the post on

73 / Beata Beach Porter, *Early Monticello*, Monticello, Ga., 1938

the stagecoach route which linked the Savannah River with the Chattahoochee. Here horses were changed and the travelers dined and rested at the Inn which stood on the site of the present Post Office. An Indian of the friendly tribe of Southern Creeks, returned to fish the yet clear waters of those days watches passively and prophetically the influx of new holders of the land of many creeks.[30]

Whether the last uncapitalized word in that description refers to the springs or the area's original tribal inhabitants is unclear, but that the land had new holders is abundantly evident. The dominant figure in this mural and the only one immediately recognizable without close scrutiny is the Indian. Wearing only a band to hold his hair out of his eyes, he sits, his back to the viewer, water spilling from his forgotten jug. His shoulders are not bent under the weight of what he sees, and his face may or may not display lines of worry. The spring is in the center of the picture and about it, in no recognizable design, is all manner of activity: oxen and people drinking from the same trough, men plowing, a beaver building a dam. In the right-corner background is indeed the inn on the spot where the post office now stands. Horses rear, stagecoaches plod uphill, women do their laundry, snakes crawl, children play, and in one corner a dark, apelike figure crouches hugging something to its breast. Whether it is indeed an ape lost far from Africa, a slave waiting to be acculturated, or another Indian is not apparent. And through and around it all is a swirl of foliage/brush strokes that tends to hide rather than highlight the action.

If these two southern murals seem sympathetic to the Indians' plight, those that glorify Indians and render them impervious to the danger to their way of life abound. In 1818, the Michael Dickson family escaped an Indian massacre in Tennessee with only a few possessions and a flatboat. Sometime later, they arrived at the Chickasaw village of Chief Tuscumbia, where for five dollars and two poleaxes they purchased a large tract of land and became the first white settlers in what is now Tuscumbia, Alabama. For that post office, Jack McMillen painted a mural commemorating this event (Figure 40). In a frieze across the front of the panel is the boat with a few boxes, kegs, and, most prominently displayed, the fam-

30. "Mural Painting by Beata Beach Porter," in "Biographical Data File," Entry 136, RG 121, NA.

ily shotgun. Mr. Dickson propels the boat with a pole, the two older boys work paddles and Mrs. Dickson holds the baby while another son peers with the family dog at the greeting party onshore.

In the background between two lush forests is the wigwam village. And at the extreme right are three Indians. The one standing lifts his hand in greeting, apparently unaware that his compatriots upstream had probably felt forced to use violence in order to drive the white settlers from their land. The Indians are armed, but, like the Dicksons' gun, their spears and bows are at rest. Nobody anticipates having to use weapons. Like most Indians in the South, these are upright and regal. It would never do to suggest that they were associated with tragedy.

Why southern murals almost invariably degraded the black man and never presented the Indian as less than regal is a subject for conjecture. One possible answer is that southerners' racism was so well known and so much vilified, they wanted to counter that they were not racist, just aware of the inferiority of blacks. Most southerners—indeed, most Americans—would have denied that they were racist. They would have explained, like Helen Murphy of Tallulah, Louisiana, that while Negroes were charming and useful, they were a childlike race in need of white guidance to achieve a place in this country and in need of white care until they did. Northerners, they would explain, did not understand these things. But the southerner's relationship to the Indian was not too different from the southerner's relationship to the black. Most Indians had left years before for Indian Territory, where, according to the WPA guides and school textbooks, they had established good, middle-class communities with their own churches, schools, and social events. Thus southerners could acknowledge the worth of the noble savage without having to pay the price of sharing their bounty with him or learning anything about his values.

Another possible reason has to do with the fact that meetings to sign treaties and perform land transactions were between aristocratic Indians and aristocratic whites. Some southeastern Indians adopted a white way of life. Not only did the Indians already practice agriculture before the whites discovered them; they taught early settlers to grow the first southern cash crop, tobacco, and they introduced the white world to corn, pumpkins, beans, and squash. They taught the settlers to make many of the renowned staples of the southern diet—grits, hominy, and cornbread among them.[31] And they adapted readily to capitalism, as Captain John Smith learned during the "first business deal in Isle of Wight County," and as Michael Dickson was grateful for when he settled in Tuscumbia. But there was more—the well-heeled southeastern Indians, the ones who managed to drive hard bargains with white capitalists, took up the legendary southern way of life: they bought, raised, worked, and traded black slaves. They built traditional "southern mansions," and they worked traditional southern plantations.[32] Of course, the Indians who did that were few, but so were the whites who did. Out of 2,776 Cherokee heads of family in Alabama, Georgia, North Carolina, and Tennessee in 1835, over 10 percent, or 209, owned slaves.[33] Not a bad showing. Possibly enough to have convinced white slave-owners that Indians were more like them than blacks were.

Whatever the reason, painters of southeastern Indian murals did not depict Indians as suffering individuals, and they did not emphasize imagined childlike qualities as they did with the blacks. For Blakely, Georgia, D. Putnam Brinley painted *The Land Is Bought from the Indians* (Figure 74). Although he was apparently unaware that the Indians had a tribal name, Brinley painted them as worthy associates. The Indians in the picture wear tribal dress, and, as usual, it is not accurate. Although the trees are laden with foliage, the Indians are swathed in blankets. But then the Americans wear coats and hats, too. Perhaps that was Brinley's interpretation of business dress for the Indians. The chief is taller than the American representative with whom he deals, and all about them other Indians and other Americans stand in similar postures and on similar planes. The Indians are to be trusted in this picture—and respected.

The only recorded local comment on the Blakely mural was the standard postmaster's letter that it was properly installed and added to post office decor. Such lack of notice indicates that the mural's content probably met with local concepts of how trading was done with the Indians. Neither was there any comment on

31. Hudson, *The Southeastern Indians*, 498.
32. Very little documentary evidence of the extent of the slave-owning Indian aristocracy survives, but that regarding the biggest slaveholders is collected in R. Halliburton, Jr., *Red Over Black: Black Slavery Among the Cherokee Indians* (Westport, Conn., 1977).
33. *Ibid.*, 191 (Table 5).

74 / D. Putnam Brinley, *The Land Is Bought from the Indians*, Blakely, Ga., 1938

Douglass Crockwell's mural, *The Signing of the Treaty of Dancing Rabbit*, for Macon, Mississippi. The negotiations for this treaty in 1830, which ceded to Mississippi the land on which Macon now stands and about a third of the present state as well, were described in the WPA guide to Mississippi:

> The first conference was held Sept. 18, 1830. Sixty Choctaw leaders seated themselves in a horseshoe on the ground. Facing them, seated on a fallen log, were the Government agents, John Eaton, William Coffee, and the interpreter, John Pitchlyn. Among the Indians, a group of seven of the oldest women of the tribe squatted, muttering their disapproval throughout the deliberations. During the first day Government agents dominated the council. Only one Indian, Killahota, a young half-breed, addressed the gathering. He spoke in favor of the treaty, and the grunts and other signs of disapproval that had greeted the speeches of the white men swelled in volume as he spoke. At one point an old squaw, unable to control her indignation, rose and made a lunge at Killahota with a knife. For several weeks the negotiations proceeded. Every half-breed present advocated capitulation to the demands of the white men, and every full-blood Indian opposed it.[34]

A compromise treaty was finally reached in which the Choctaw who wished to stay in Mississippi were promised government protection—protection that was not granted until shortly before the FWP's *Mississippi* was written.

Crockwell could have read the FWP account, or he could have used the same sources. However he prepared, he had done his homework. Everything in the painting fits the quoted description: government agents on the log, the half circle of tribesmen and women. At the right, a young brave who must be Killahota delivers his unpopular speech. And just behind him on the ground, her pendulous breasts indicating her advanced age, sits an old Indian woman—

34. Federal Writers Project, *Mississippi*, 369.

undoubtedly the one who lunged for the speaker. It seems important to the writer that his readers know that *real* Indians, *i.e.*, full-blooded ones, did not approve the treaty. Indians were worthy associates, and they were not the type who would trade their land for "trinkets and whiskey," the bribes brought by the government. In the mural, it is not clear who will prevail—the Indians are on a better than equal footing with the government—one of their number speaking, the objects for trade spurned on the ground. If they are to be humiliated, it will not be in front of post office patrons.

Not only are Indians worthy traders; they are worthy foe as well. In the several southern murals that depict Indians at war with whites, the tribesmen are still regal and dignified. They never cower at the superior might of the whites, just as Confederate soldiers never bowed to the superior might of the Yankees; neither are they bowed by the prospect of life after defeat. For Cuthbert, Georgia, Carlo Ciampaglia created *The Last Indian Troubles in Randolph County in 1836*. The mural depicts a time just before removal when Indians, desperate to save their land for themselves, attacked the fort at what is now Cuthbert.

In the right background, smoke billows from the fort, which the white man's enemy set on fire. In the foreground, a dashing cavalry officer on a white merry-go-round horse points with his sword toward the danger in the right half of the mural. Behind him, legions of unmounted men await the command to charge. One infantryman aims an anachronistic rifle toward the enemy. In the center foreground, a wounded cavalryman is tended by a buckskin-clad scout. And on the left, most of them armed only with bows and arrows—there is one musket—are the Indians. In the scale of the picture, they appear not more than ten or fifteen feet from the Americans. But they neither hide nor bolt. Outnumbered at least two to one, they stand, nude and ready to fight. One has to know from other sources that the whites won. Nothing in this mural betrays who the heroes are. The Indians and the whites are equally valiant and equally dignified.

For Greensboro, Georgia, Carson Davenport was persuaded by an overbearing local historian to paint an early Indian massacre, though the Section usually tried to avoid overly violent scenes. In this one, there is no question who the heroes and who the enemies are. White settlers dominate the foreground. One is mortally wounded, and a bereaved mother holds her fatherless child while she examines the body. In the background, Indians ravish women, drag them about by the hair, take slaves—commit all sorts of atrocities. But the whole time, they look glamorously dignified. They will not submit without a struggle. Although the whites are the sympathetic figures, it looks as if the reds are winning. And their bodies are more beautiful than those of the overdressed white figures.

A few artists seem to have been so enamored of the physical beauty attributed to Indian bodies that they painted half-naked Indians where none was called for. When Bert Mullins was commissioned to paint a scene about Zachary Taylor for the Campbellsville, Kentucky, Post Office, he chose Taylor's tenure in Florida to quell the Seminoles (Figure 75). In the center of the mural, Taylor sits behind a table, studying maps and charts. About him foot soldiers set up camp. Two cavalry officers and one horse study the maps with him. The weapons for his detachment are neatly stacked against some luggage on the left, and on the right is a lone Seminole. Perhaps he is the resident translator, but the only other reason for his inclusion is his regal bearing. He need not be covered with unsightly clothing as are the other figures.

75 / Bert Mullins, *General Zachary Taylor in the Everglades*, Campbellsville, Ky., 1940

When Indian subjects did not present themselves, some artists seemed to be unwilling to relinquish the opportunity to paint impossibly regal tribal figures and, thus, chose to use blacks. In 1940, Alice Flint was asked to design for the Adel, Georgia, Post Office. In his appointment letter, Rowan cautioned her to paint something "appropriate to and reflective of the locale of Adel rather than to undertake another of the historical coach themes." He did not feel, he said, that it was "fair for you to go on record as a painter of highly decorative stage coaches." Flint replied that he had seen a single series of coach sketches in preparation for a single painting of stagecoaches.[35] It could be that Flint took Rowan's reference to "stage coaches" too literally and missed his reference to generic coaches, or it could be that she forgot the two other murals she had painted for the Section. In 1938, she had done for Fairfield, Connecticut, a mural of three highly decorative, stylized coaches. And in 1939, for Arabi, Louisiana, she had painted a single antique coach, richly decorated for Mardi Gras, as were the horses that pulled it. At any rate, Flint's coach-bedecked past is significant only for what it reveals about her penchant for linear design. This time, she chose to take the postmaster's suggestion and paint a plantation scene. At least that is what she thought she was doing.[36]

Actually, what Alice Flint considered a plantation scene would not have been recognizable as such to anyone in central Georgia in 1941. She was a decorative painter, and all of her mural designs were stylized and linear, forming a sort of wide border across the post office walls. She had written that she was interested in the early Spanish and French history of Georgia, which was not, she guessed, appropriate for Adel's part of Georgia. She was right. Any Continental influence in Georgia was confined to the coast around Savannah. Apparently, she never really relinquished the idea. What she painted was a row of six blacks, each carrying a colorful package on his head, each wearing some sort of colorful tribal "skirt" about his middle, and each naked from the waist up—except for a few earrings (Figure 76). Between the distinctively African blacks the viewer can see myriad tropical flowers growing just behind them. And in the background is a row of wrought-iron-decorated

35. Rowan to Alice Flint, July 10, 1940, Flint to Rowan, July 26, 1940, both in Adel, Georgia, file, RG 121, NA.
36. Flint to Rowan, April 30, 1941, *ibid.*

76 / Alice Flint, *Plantation Scene*, Adel, Ga., 1941

buildings such as might be seen in Savannah or New Orleans but never in Adel. The panel is finished in shades of blue and rose, contrasting with the black of the main figures and the blue green of the leaves.

The design is altogether attractive. It just bears no relationship to the American scene or to the southern scene as the rural South expected it to be. Flint's inspiration came from something she had read about plantation owners fleeing to the coast to escape yellow fever and having slaves carry their luggage—hence a plantation scene. And the desire to paint lovely dark-colored bodies that afflicted many creators of southern murals took control. But none of that had any interest for the people of Adel, and D. F. Bruton, the postmaster, had to write: "I am sorry that there is no newspaper comments that I can furnish you. The general public was looking forward to the installation of a mural that depicted something of the background of this section of Georgia, and I am sorry to advise that there has been much comment on the mural, but the general opinion is that the subject matter is not what would be expected in this section. All comment is that the colors are beautiful."[37]

Those who painted the South were eager to paint the southern minorities. They could exercise a bit more freedom and give freer range to their imaginations with nonwhite subjects, and they need not worry about offending the white establishment as they did when they tried to get creative about poverty in the rural South. Whites would accept without complaint unrealistic interpreta-

37. D. F. Bruton to Rowan, April 14, 1941, *ibid.*

tions of blacks and reds so long as they did not suggest that the power structure was mistaken in its preconceived notions. And it was seldom that artists encountered members of those races with enough self-confidence and enough organization to protest what they saw on the post office walls. As long as artists remained in the real South with their questionable interpretations, they succeeded. When they painted for a true border area, such as St. Joseph, Missouri, they encountered the same insistence on accurate detail, the same fear of Yankee and government condescension from blacks that they found in the South from whites.

VI / THE UNVANQUISHED: OR THE SOUTH
WAS NEVER DOWN

In the summer of 1755, settler Mary Draper Ingles was captured by the Shawnee and taken far from her mountain home near what is now Radford, Virginia. After living for a time with her Indian captors, she learned that the Shawnee planned to attack the settlers. As the story goes, she escaped and made her way 850 miles back home to warn her kinsmen and fellow pioneers. Having saved the fledgling community, she lived a long and productive life as mother to generations of the town's prominent citizens.[1]

Late in the eighteenth century, Daniel Boone, already well known as an explorer, a leader, and a frontiersman, was perhaps somewhere near the present city of Bowling Green. At the same time, a group of explorers and hunters known as the Kentucky Long Hunters (because of the duration of their expeditions) was investigating the area. The Long Hunters, we are told, heard an animal sound that, unlike those they were familiar with, never moved. The brave woodsmen set out to track down this new and strange fauna in the new and strange territory. They managed, undetected, to surprise the beast in its lair. What they found was their hero, Daniel Boone, sprawled on top of a knoll on a deer-skin bed, singing lustily and happily to himself.[2]

J. E. B. Stuart, Confederate cavalry officer, in 1862, led a daring secret raid miles around Union General McClellan's army menacing Petersburg, Virginia, in order to bring Robert E. Lee news of the enemy's strength and position. To get to their destination, Stuart's

1. Although Mary Draper Ingles was a historical figure, much of her story belongs to folklore. Accounts vary with the source and the purpose of the telling. Ironically, the most reliable account is *Follow the River*, a novel by James Alexander Thom (New York, 1981), because it is based on research and attempts to correlate all available sources. The only other widely circulated account is John P. Hale, *Trans-Allegheny Pioneers: Historical Sketches of the First White Settlements West of the Alleghenies*, ed. Harold J. Dudley (1887; 3rd ed. Raleigh, 1971), in which the story occupies much of the first 85 pages.

2. Boone's biographer John Bakeless, cited in Edward Laning to Edward Rowan, April 22, 1941, Bowling Green, Kentucky, file, Entry 133, Record Group 121, NA.

1,200 cavalry had to cross the Chickahominy River without using the bridges held by McClellan. Because Union troops were close, the need for quiet was acute. Consequently, rather than ford the stream on their horses, the cavalry, we are told, stripped and led the animals across. Stuart reached Lee, and at that point Confederate forces had no reason to think the raid might be in vain.[3]

On April 4, 1865, when Union troops had surrounded Richmond, the Confederate capital, and Jefferson Davis had deserted the city, leaving residents nothing but his advice to evacuate, several business and residential blocks of the city burned to the ground. During the uncontrolled fire, as residents fled, there was much pillage and perhaps some rape. Accounts of the cause of the blaze vary. Some Virginia schoolchildren in the 1930s learned that Yankees burned it. Others are told that Confederates burned the city so that Yankees could not make use of it. Another version is that a fire meant only to destroy Confederate munitions burned out of control, and the great destruction was the result of accident spurred by weather conditions. Perhaps the most colorful story is that a small fire started accidentally near Confederate stores of alcoholic beverages. Some eyewitnesses reported that Confederates, fearing that discouraged soldiers in the process of evacuation would take advantage of the confusion to raid the stores, ordered the stores destroyed. The result in this version was more—not less—access to the liquor. But later versions insist that Virginia rabble, knowing that the city was without law and order, looted the liquor stores and, faced with such plenty, were careless about spillage. And the booze running in the gutters spread the fire and ignited respectable parts of the city. Except for the tale that the Yankees burned the city—they did not arrive until after the destruction—all versions contain some truth. Whatever the cause of the fire, the result was even more confusion and greater loss in the evacuation than might otherwise have been the case.[4]

3. David Herbert Donald, *Liberty and Union* (Lexington, Mass., 1978), 223; Jared French to Edward Rowan, September 29, 1937, in Richmond, Virginia, Parcel Post, file, RG 121, NA.

4. See Virginius Dabney, *Virginia: The New Dominion* (Garden City, N.Y., 1971), 350–51; Maurice Duke and Daniel P. Jordan, *A Richmond Reader, 1733–1983* (Chapel Hill, 1983); John Fiske, *Old Virginia and Her Neighbors* (2 vols.; Boston, 1901); Adolf A. Hoehling and Mary Hoehling, *The Day Richmond Died* (San Diego, 1981); William J. Kimball, *Starve or Fall: Richmond and Its People, 1861–1865* (Ann Arbor, 1978), 198–200; Earle Lutz, *A Richmond Album: A Pictoral Chronicle*

And what have these four apparently disparate events in the history of the American South in common? They were subjects that southerners, having begged for local history in their murals, objected to on their post office walls. They were also subjects that the Section considered so appropriate that it was willing to foist them on the citizens despite local protest.

Southerners, many would claim, have been so entrenched in their history that they long kept the American god Progress at bay. Whatever the actual effect of this commitment to history, citizens throughout the South wanted historical themes in their post office murals. A large and vocal group of Paducah, Kentucky, citizens, for example, were adamantly opposed to the contemporary mural that showed local industry with all its pollutants and ugly forms. The only way the Section could mollify them—in that instance, the Section chose to mollify—was to require the artist to design a second mural with a historical subject. Yet, some months later, when Julien Binford, local artist selected by the Section to decorate a Richmond post office, proposed to immortalize the burning of Richmond, he was greeted with protest. And when Alexander B. Clayton of Chevy Chase, Maryland, submitted his sketch *The Return of Mary Ingles* for the approval of Radford, Virginia, local citizens who had originally suggested the subject, they reversed their opinion and asked him to paint something that would "do justice to the natural beauty of this section of the country."[5] In Petersburg, Virginia, even after artist Jared French painted pants on J. E. B. Stuart's cavalrymen and let them swim the Chickahominy clothed, the local news media and civic organizations, spearheaded by the Daughters and the Sons of the Confederacy, found the mural intolerable. And certain citizens of Bowling Green, Kentucky, never made their peace with the 160-square-foot rendition of their state's most famous hero enjoying himself in Kentucky's lush and teeming forest. Even in mollified Paducah, though some citizens were happy with Pennsylvania artist John F. Folinsbee's depiction of the city a century before, others never became reconciled to the fact

---

of an Historic City's Outstanding Events and Places (Richmond, 1937); Louis D. Rubin, Jr., *Virginia: A Bicentennial History* (New York, 1977); and Mary Newton Standard, *Richmond: Its People and Its Story* (Philadelphia, 1923), 206–209.

5. "Mural Painting for the Radford Post Office," unattributed statement, stamped by the Section, June 9, 1942, in Radford, Virginia, file, RG 121, NA.

that their mural did not depict General George Rogers Clark's contribution to the civilization of the nation.

It would have been well for the Section of Fine Arts to look more closely at the history of the South and the South's attitude toward its history before approving any artist's historical presentation. It would have been well for the Section to examine closely the characteristics and the subject matter of the historical murals that were well received. And, of course, it would have behooved them, as well as the artists, to take into consideration the characteristics of the particular community into which they wished to place the mural.

It is tempting to try to study southern culture without consideration of the War Between the States. One might wish that the twentieth-century South could be seen as a regional variation on American culture without taking into account the region's nineteenth-century history. But it cannot be done. The nation that tires of reading about that war and its effect on the South, and the nation that never wearies of chuckling because southerners supposedly still fight that war, may wish that the effect of that war on the South had been exaggerated. But in the 1930s, perhaps even today, the consequences of that conflict remained with the South and the southerner. However much we may suspect today that slavery in the South would have collapsed of its own weight, however much we may realize that the one-crop agricultural system carried in its very practice the means of its own destruction, that the majority of white southerners even then struggled for a decent standard of living, that the landed aristocracy was a small minority whose wealth and whose claim to aristocratic heritage both had precarious bases. However much we know these things, we know too that the prosperous, bucolic, singing, aristocratic South was a dream not of the South alone but of the nation.[6] And we know that not only did that war call into question the antebellum southern system and change its face forever; it left the once-powerful South the black sheep of the national family—and an impoverished one, at that.

In the early days of the nation, southern leaders held the highest offices in the land—president, secretary of state, and chief justice—about two-thirds of the time. Right up to the onset of that

6. See William R. Taylor, *Cavalier and Yankee: The Old South and American National Character* (Cambridge, Mass., 1979).

war, nonsouthern Republicans and Democrats alike complained of the political stranglehold the South had on the law-making bodies.[7] Even when war came, even when hot-blooded young men supposedly scrambled to the adventure of battle, southern leaders and gray-bearded patriarchs often felt that northern actions left the South no choice but to secede and fight. Both Robert E. Lee and Jefferson Davis are said to have counseled compromise and to have abhorred the idea of a nation divided. Only when events over which nobody had complete control, each of which most politicians saw as designed to maintain one nation, seemed to force the South to form a separate nation and the North to go to war did the two sections of the country fight.

And when surrender was at hand, the most charismatic of southern leaders, Robert E. Lee himself, counseled absolute surrender—not the military surrender often forced on a country that intends to maintain its national identity, but absolute surrender, surrender to become a part of the enemy nation.[8] Most southerners cherish the belief that Lee devoted the rest of his life to an unsuccessful attempt to lead the South toward a peaceful reintegration with that nation despite ideological differences. And, in the 1930s, southerners believed that it was the North that kept them from completely reintegrating.

When we chuckle at the southerner during the 1930s who refers to the Civil War as "The War," we forget that for the southeastern part of this country, it was "The War." We tend to forget that for the American South, that war and especially its aftermath loom as the cause of every economic and social evil. However much the South in the 1930s revered its war heroes and immortalized their deeds, it was and is reconstruction—the re-construction brought about by the war and the Emancipation Proclamation and the Reconstruction that followed—that the South continued to fight. By the 1880s, Thomas Nelson Page was writing from Virginia immensely popu-

7. See Donald, *Liberty and Union*, Chaps. 1–4; Peter N. Carroll and David W. Noble, *The Restless Centuries* (Minneapolis, 1973), Chap. 17; and Paul H. Buck, *The Road to Reunion: 1865–1900* (Boston, 1937), Preface.

8. In *The Marble Man: Robert E. Lee and his Image in American Society* (New York, 1977), Thomas L. Connelly explicates the evolution of Lee's image since the Civil War. He shows Lee as an enduring national hero, and he cites evidence that during the depression Lee was viewed as one who loved the Union above all else, who fought for the South because honor left him no choice, and who maintained his honor in the face of defeat.

lar books that kept alive for the nation the melody of the Old South. And by the 1930s, Stark Young in *So Red the Rose* wrote of grizzled southern patriarchs who stuck philosophically, at least, to the Union. William Faulkner peopled the novels he set in the days of the Civil War with Confederate heroes who regularly deserted to see that the crops were planted, with plucky women who battled Yankees as individuals bent on plunder rather than as representatives of an enemy nation, and with men and women for whom the war was only a chance for adventure—not a cause worth dying for.

And, of course, Margaret Mitchell did not write of a South that wished to continue the rivalry. She wrote of a Georgia willing time and again to accept any restrictions placed on it in order to become once again a fully integrated segment of the nation. Half of *Gone With the Wind* tells of Georgia's repeated frustration when it was treated as a lesser part of the nation. In the 1939 movie, the best-remembered and most-publicized portions tell of the Dream South, the gaudy and easy antebellum South.[9] But most of the film and its less-remembered parts are set against a background of the South's efforts to reconstruct itself in its own image, as opposed to being reconstructed by outsiders. And popular audiences throughout the nation, particularly in the South, regarded Mitchell's tale, in the book and as rendered in the movie, as the true story of the South's struggle.

What the South in the 1930s wanted to remember of that war was the fantasy that a beautiful way of life had been lost and that southerners, forced to fight their own compatriots, did so bravely and with chivalry. What the South in the 1930s wanted to remember of its history was its respected and powerful position in the nation long before the war. But Julien Binford, a native Virginian, had the poor taste to propose a picture for a Richmond post office of Richmond being burned and of southern people ignominiously fleeing.

To give Binford credit, the burning of Richmond as a subject was not his idea. The Section of Fine Arts put him up to it. Rowan had been committed to a painting of that tragedy since he had sponsored the decoration of the Richmond Parcel Post building several years earlier. In 1937, Paul Cadmus announced his intention to

9. Edward D. C. Campbell, Jr., *The Celluloid South: Hollywood and the Southern Myth* (Knoxville, 1981), 130–40.

paint the burning of Richmond. Rowan was enthusiastic, counseling only that Cadmus, and Jared French, who was to paint a mural for the other end of the lobby, not refer to the pair "as an allegory of war and peace. We are not interested in sponsoring the glorification of war and I will have several things to tell you about this verbally." Neither we nor Paul Cadmus ever learned what Rowan intended to say. This time, other members of the Section got to Rowan before a sketch was submitted. In a letter several weeks later, Rowan said: "Some question has been raised in this office as to whether or not subject matter 'Dawn—April 3, 1865' for the Richmond . . . mural might not create unfavorable sectional feeling and prejudice."[10]

Although he may have been mistaken about the actual emotions a painting of the burning of Richmond might arouse, Rowan made no mistake about Richmond's reluctance to immortalize its distress on the walls of a federal building. Richmond had no desire to be reminded in its daily routine of mailing and receiving mail that it had not always been a valued part of the Union. But Rowan liked the subject, and late in 1942, he suggested that Julien Binford design a mural based on the event. By that time, all available federal funds had been channeled into the war effort, Edward Bruce had died, and the Section's staff had shrunk so that no one was left to remind Rowan of its controversial nature. Besides, Binford was a native Virginian, and he had the approval of the director of the Virginia Museum, Tom Colt, whom both Binford and Rowan seemed to forget was unpopular with Virginians.[11] Rowan wrote to Colt, telling him that the Section found the design "lively and entertaining."[12]

Because of the straitened condition of the Section and because of the pressure to get as many post office walls as possible decorated before war sentiment called a halt to the whole project, no competition was held to select a painter for the Richmond–Saunders Branch Post Office. Binford was selected on the basis of his commendable performance in the Harrisonburg, Virginia, competition. He was not, however, the only possible native-born painter. Binford had

10. Rowan to Paul Cadmus, April 29, June 17, 1937, both in Richmond, Virginia, Parcel Post, file.

11. Theresa Pollak to Rowan, April 23, 1936, in Petersburg, Virginia, file, RG 121, NA. She recommends Tom Colt to chair the Petersburg competition.

12. Rowan to Tom Colt, April 21, 1942, in Richmond, Virginia, Saunders Branch, file, RG 121, NA.

some national reputation. That meant that, despite his personal resonance with southern people, his painting was probably not what they preferred. Virginians could be proud of their local painter without wishing to see his work displayed where they conducted their daily business. Edmund Archer, whose reputation outside Virginia was negligible, probably understood better what people of the South wanted.

Archer had decorated the Hopewell, Virginia, Post Office with a mural that gave immense satisfaction to the local population, and he had been given no reason to believe that the Section was not equally satisfied. Archer knew that painters were occasionally appointed on the basis of satisfactory work in another community close to the one needing an artist. So, in 1940, before Binford's appointment, Archer offered his services for the Saunders Branch and enclosed a description of the mural he would paint. Rowan dutifully submitted the idea to the then fully staffed Section, and he supported Archer when he called Archer's Hopewell mural "rather architectural in its conception." But with less restraint, after he was certain the rest of the Section did not favor Archer's appointment, he confided, in a penciled addendum in the margin, that he "loathe[d] the life figure on the right." In his reply, Forbes Watson open-mindedly stated: "The [Archer] scheme sounds intelligent & would probably please the citizens of Richmond, but I find Archer's work unpleasantly cold. To me it is even obnoxious."[13]

What is it that so pleased the people of Hopewell and would probably please the citizens of Richmond as well but that left members of the Section so cold? Feeling as they did that reconstruction of the South by the rest of the country had begun in 1865—or maybe even 1860—and continued in 1941, southerners wanted the decorations in their public buildings to illustrate that the South had been a part of the Union long before many of the regions that seemed to wish to see the South further reconstructed and to reflect the taste and way of life for which the South had received positive national attention.

In the late 1930s, southerners, eager as they were for northern capital and for recognition as a part of the nation, still resented and feared efforts from the outside to tell them how to fashion their

13. Rowan to Edward Bruce, Forbes Watson, Inslee Hopper, and Maria Ealand, Memorandum, March 26, 1940, *ibid.*

New South. Garet Garrett's article in the *Saturday Evening Post,* suggesting from the East ways in which the South might turn native resources into cash industries, was greeted with suspicion and anger. And the Roosevelt administration's 1938 study of the South's particular economic woes brought unpleasant publicity. Furthermore, Congress was apparently vacillating on funding such New Deal projects in the South as a second TVA dam in eastern Kentucky. Southerners doubted the New Deal's sincerity in help-ing the South to climb out of its economic morass.[14]

Even in 1940, after the TVA had proven that it could provide electricity for southerners cheaper than local power companies could and after the WPA had made good its promise that funds would be channeled into the southern states, southern newspapers had ambivalent reactions to those Yankee enterprises. Although they welcomed the capital, the jobs, and the cheap access to the Good Life, they were aware that the ideas and money for those enterprises emanated from Washington and that many of the local administrators even for the TVA, which strove for grass-roots con-nections, were modern-day "carpetbaggers." Every little scandal associated with either agency brought renewed newspaper accounts of suspicion that the federal government could not do anything honest for the South. If southerners were this suspicious of pro-grams that most of the nation welcomed without question and that undoubtedly aided the South, they were likely also to look askance at styles of art fostered by the federal government and practiced by artists in New York.[15]

14. A blow-by-blow account of one-southern city's impression of federal vacilla-tion over whether or not to build the TVA Gilbertson Dam (today, Kentucky Dam) near Paducah can be found in the Paducah *Sun-Democrat*, January-March, 1939. At-titudes toward the New Deal changed as Congress wavered.

15. See Jonathan Daniels, *A Southerner Discovers the South* (New York, 1938), for an impressionistic examination of southern attitudes toward the TVA. South-erners in the 1930s were ambivalent about New Deal operations, and the evidence is in southern newspapers, which sang praises to the influx of federal money one day, criticized handouts and make-work jobs another, and gleefully reported any hint of a scandal in the ranks still another. These tendencies were observed in: Abbeville (La.) *Progress*, 1938–39; Atlanta *Constitution*, October-December, 1935, and October-December, 1939; Atlanta *Journal*, October-December, 1939; Birming-ham *News*, July-December, 1935; Conyers (Ga.) *Times and Rockdale Record*, 1936–40; Louisville *Courier-Journal*, March, 1938; Meridian (Miss.) *Star*, 1939–40; Nash-ville *Banner*, 1938; New Orleans *Morning Tribune*, August-October, 1938; New Orleans *Times-Picayune*, March-April, 1938; Okolona (Miss.) *Messenger*, 1936–40;

The moneyed inhabitants of the South, few though they were, had always been supporters of Art. Thomas Jefferson and George Washington, for example, were confirmed collectors of the works of well-known European artists and of Americans who had achieved an international reputation, such as Benjamin West. They commissioned portraits of themselves and their ancestors, often by Americans, but invariably in the grand manner of seventeenth- and eighteenth-century European portrait painters. And in the twentieth century, southerners willingly supported only museums devoted to collecting and exhibiting artworks that were internationally known.

Contemporary art was shown on occasion in the South, but a show of American scene painting in 1938 drew more schoolchildren than it did unescorted adult connoisseurs, despite a favorable review by the Richmond *Times-Dispatch*. As an offshoot and imitator of European aristocracy, the southern art world did not take to much that was modern in art or American in flavor.[16] Southern tastemakers appreciated beauty, and their conception of beauty could not be found in the mundane subjects and crowded canvases of Thomas Hart Benton and John Steuart Curry, much less in those of Yankee artists of whom they had never even heard but who painted in similar styles. Naturally, then, they would rarely care for art favored by Washington bureaucrats and practiced by New York residents. Many Iowans delighted to have Grant Wood painting gentle satires of their foibles, and people in Wisconsin were proud to have Curry at their state university. Kansans thronged to see the murals Curry painted on the walls of their capitol. Regional

---

Owensboro (Ky.) *Daily Messenger*, 1938; Paducah (Ky.) *Sun-Democrat*, 1939; Petersburg (Va.) *Progress-Index*, October-December, 1937; Richmond *Planet*, 1937–39; Richmond *Times-Dispatch*, March, 1938; Tuskegee (Ala.) *News*, 1935–39; Winston County Journal (Louisville, Miss.), 1938.

16. Richmond *Times-Dispatch*, March 13, 1938, p. 16, and March 20, 1938, p. 3. Babbette Fromme, *Curator's Choice: An Introduction to the Art Museums of the U.S., Southern Edition* (New York, 1981), cites highlights of collections throughout the South, and always, it seems, a reputed minor Renaissance or seventeenth-century piece gets higher billing than does a modern work even by a major artist. In *Treasures in the Virginia Museum* (Richmond, 1974), only European works are illustrated (except for Mary Cassatt) and those are no later than nineteenth century and usually much earlier. Stark Young, in his historical novel *So Red the Rose* (New York, 1934), emphasizes the collections of "old masters" with which those who pretended to aristocracy marked their status.

artists in the South, however, usually had to leave to find an audience for their art—unless, of course, they painted sentimental scenes of the "darky" at play.

On the other hand, the works of academic European artists of centuries past found a ready home in the South and as much support as the economically bereaved region could muster. In the 1930s the South still admired aristocracy and had not relinquished the idea that one existed, an aristocracy to which anybody could aspire.[17] Therefore, that which was classical and Continental always had a home in the region. Aristocracy in the South was never confined to the privileged few, who were themselves descendants of at best second sons who sought their fortune in an unknown land and, more likely, commoners who managed to get to the unsettled regions first and take the greatest acreage of uncultivated land. Scarlett O'Hara's father was, after all, an immigrant Irishman. Daniel Boone was pioneer stock who made his name hunting, exploring, and squatting on unclaimed land. Yet any Kentucky female who could find the remotest connection to the Boone family counted herself among the gentry.[18]

The South, like the rest of the nation, valued the log cabin myth about worthy people of humble origins who could become prominent and prosperous citizens. For many southerners, however, to reach the top was to obliterate through manner and action vestiges of a rude background. The difference between southern and nonsouthern ideas of achievement is illustrated in the Kentucky monuments to Abraham Lincoln and Jefferson Davis, presidents during the war. The monument to Lincoln reflects the northern and midwestern ideal of retaining folk wisdom and folk virtue as guides to exercising power. A reconstructed log cabin encased in imposing but functional concrete marks Lincoln's birthplace near Harrods-

17. Wilbur Cash, *The Mind of the South* (1941; New York, 1969), and Carl Bridenbaugh, *Myths and Realities: Societies of the Colonial South* (Baton Rouge, 1952), discuss the humble origins of most of the "Old Southern Families." In the chapter entitled "Thou Shalt Be Kings No Matter Who Begat Thee" of Florence King's only slightly facetious popular examination of southern social mores, *Southern Ladies and Gentlemen* (New York, 1975), we see a believable and reasonably accurate account of the southern quest for ancestry, thus aristocracy.

18. In *The Cavalier in Virginia Fiction* (Baton Rouge, 1985), Ritchie Devon Watson, Jr., supplies historical background and documentation for the infatuation with the concept of aristocracy that informs Virginia fiction in all eras. Much other southern fiction reveals that the same infatuation permeates the South.

burg, Kentucky. Not a hundred miles away near Fairview stands the 351-foot obelisk that marks the site of Davis' birth, replacing his log cabin origin with the idea of high birth and even higher destiny. Here, governing is based on *noblesse oblige.* Perhaps perceiving that Davis had small chance of rising to southern prominence otherwise, his brother gave him a plantation in Mississippi; thus the younger Davis could enter southern politics as an aristocrat. Apparently ownership of land and slaves—and perhaps a president's daughter to wive—was all that was required of a southerner to be aristocratic. The obelisk is reminiscent of the Washington Monument and of the academic styles that characterized most District of Columbia monuments until the 1930s. And despite Huey Long's ultramodern Louisiana capitol, the obelisk represented the idea of leadership that most influential southerners retained through the decade of the Great Depression. Southerners respected the ancient, the tried in monuments and in art.

In Edmund Archer, the residents of Hopewell, Virginia, had found a living artist who painted what they had learned was good art in the time-honored academic tradition. The subject of Archer's mural *Captain Francis Eppes Making Friends with the Appomattox Indians* reminds citizens of "the youngest of Virginia cities but one of the oldest communities" that southerners were making friends with Indians when Elizabethan clothes were still in style and thus that the South was instrumental in building the nation (Figure 77).[19] The mural proclaims, too, that Hopewell itself was not really a product of the new industrial South that alien northerners imposed on gentility but an ancient bastion of the New World. And it does so in a painting style that Hopewell people, and presumably Richmond people as well, recognize as having a respectable history. Archer borrowed composition from fifteenth-century Italian masters and figures from twentieth-century motion pictures.[20]

In this mural an exceedingly handsome Elizabethan captain, Francis Eppes, stretches across his hat, a tiny inlet of the Atlantic Ocean, and Indian utensils to clasp hands with an equally handsome—and equally European—Appomattox Indian. Using his free hand to maintain his balance, Eppes manages also to point to a ship

19. Federal Writers Project, *Virginia: A Guide to the Old Dominion* (New York, 1940), 378.

20. On Archer's style and composition, see Karal Ann Marling, *Wall-to-Wall America* (Minneapolis, 1982), 309–12.

77 / Edmund Archer, *Captain Francis Eppes Making Friends with the Appomattox Indians*, Hopewell, Va., 1939

laden with those who will deprive the Indian of his home. The Appomattox with the face of Errol Flynn and the body of Adonis indicates with an unstrung bow clutched in his free hand a welcoming party of his statuesque countrymen. The message for Hopewell is that their city is important enough to be decorated by an American great master and that no Yankee need apply for the job.

But Rowan and company could never decide whether they wished to please the population or their own taste, and doing both was frequently a problem. When John Folinsbee designed for Paducah, Kentucky, a mural of the contemporary railroad yards featuring much machinery and still more smoke, citizens were distraught (Figure 78). Their city, rich in history and natural beauty, was to be represented only by its ugliest and most humdrum industrial endeavors, and Paducah, after all, was, if anything, a river city. The railroads were recent intruders. But there was hope. Residents could not stop the installation of one "modern" industrial mural, but the building was to have two murals. Could they, representatives of fourteen different civic organizations wrote to the Section, have in the second mural a depiction of the city's history and its river? [21]

21. Paducah Garden Club to Rear Admiral C. J. Peoples, Director of Procurement, November 17, 1938, Mrs. Marshall Puryear to Peoples, November 18, 1938, Mrs. Louett Marshall to Peoples, November 18, 1938, Martha Grassham Pursell to Peoples, March 5, 1939, Mrs. Marshall Puryear to Edward Rowan, March 9, 1939, S. A. Fowler to Fourth Assistant Post Master General, September 3, 1941, all in Paducah, Kentucky, file, RG 121, NA; "Women Push Fight for Historic Mural in Paducah Courthouse," Louisville *Courier-Journal*, November 25, 1938, clipping, and many more, *ibid.*

78 / John F. Folinsbee, design for Paducah, Ky.

The ladies of the garden clubs and the men of the Rotary were not without suggestions for appropriate subjects—General George Rogers Clark's brief stop on one of Paducah's Ohio River islands on his westward trek to subdue the Indians, and his brother William Clark's participation in the city's founding when he was instrumental in changing the settlement's name from Wilmington to Paducah. Some cosmopolitan citizens, notably Paducah author Irvin S. Cobb, objected to George Rogers Clark as subject. Clark, he wrote, "only passed the town before there was any town and came no nearer to it than Owen's Island." Besides, he could be claimed by any number of communities across the nation.[22] But Cobb's national experience got in the way of his southern origin. He no longer saw with a southerner's eyes. What he missed is that the very fact that Clark could be claimed by many communities in many different regions made his brief encounter attractive to Paducans. As southerners from a state that did not secede but in a section of Kentucky that fought for the South, they were anxious to assert what they had in common with the nation as a whole. They asked that their federal building's walls proclaim that their city was part of the Union and had been long before sectional strife threatened.

Paducah's demand for a historical subject whose connection with their city was tenuous at best is not unique. The residents of Campbellsville, Kentucky, seat of Taylor County, were pleased with and grateful for their mural of the state's agriculture. They were happy with Kentucky artist Bert Mullins, who had made two expensive trips to Campbellsville in search of subject matter and who brought with him no dangerous Yankee ideas. They were flattered that a town no larger than theirs was considered worthy of a federal artwork at all.[23] *But,* some of them wrote wistfully in their grateful letters to the Section and to Mullins, it would be nice to have a mural with a historical theme. That was early in 1938; enthusiasm for the Treasury art project was still high, not only in the government's art enclave, but on Capitol Hill as well. Funds were not skimpy, and those who controlled the purse strings were easy to convince. Thus, later that same year, Mullins was instructed to

22. Irvin S. Cobb to Rowan, March 23, 1939, *ibid.*
23. Campbellsville *News-Journal*, August 18, 1938, clipping, in Campbellsville, Kentucky, file, RG 121, NA.

make still another trip to Campbellsville to find material for a second mural with a historical theme for the other end of the post office lobby. When he went, he found that the people of Taylor County wanted a mural featuring Zachary Taylor, for whom their county was named.

So far as the records show, Taylor probably never set foot in Taylor County. Although he grew up near Louisville, he was born in Virginia and spent his adult life nearly everywhere else. If he ever visited the site of Campbellsville, he did nothing of historic significance there. But Rowan and the Section were so buoyed by Campbellsville's humble attitude, and by finding a southern artist who could please them and the community, they approved any request. Mullins rendered a scene of General Taylor on campaign in the Florida Everglades, and Campbellsvilleans were delighted (Figure 75).

Zachary Taylor fought the Black Hawk Indians, subdued the Seminoles in Florida, served in the Southwest Territory, led a campaign into Mexico, became president of the United States, and his daughter married Jefferson Davis, who had been born in Kentucky. His image on the post office wall in Taylor County, Kentucky, assured Campbellsvilleans that they were part of national history. His daughter's alliance with the president of the Confederate States of America assured them that there never had been too great a split between the two warring factions of the country and that the split in their own state had not been too serious. Their need for a historical representation was satisfied by a picture of a man who had no direct contact with their community.

The Section's prosperity was short-lived, however, and Paducans, two hundred miles away, were not grateful for federal attention. Rather, they *demanded* history for their Federal Building's walls. And their attitude toward Folinsbee was the condescension reserved for hired labor. Thus the Section was not so well disposed toward them late in 1939 as it had been toward Campbellsville in 1938, and perhaps it searched for ways to show Paducah citizens how uninformed and naïve they were.

An uneasy compromise was reached, however, in a mural featuring G. R. Clark's brother, William. As a subject, William Clark met Paducah's requirements, but Folinsbee's depiction of him did not (Figure 79). The mural—Clark leaning on a rail fence in front of a historic inn—was placed on the wall with the approval of the Louis-

79 / John F. Folinsbee, *Early Town,* Paducah, Ky., 1939

ville *Courier-Journal* as well as the local paper. But the staunch supporters of "history painting" first made sure Rowan knew that neither the figure of Clark nor the landscape had the heroic dimensions they required for complete satisfaction. And they made sure he knew that no Yankee could understand Paducah. A local commercial artist who had a well defined sense of the place, they wrote, could have made a more acceptable mural.[24] Edmund Archer could undoubtedly have pleased the people of Paducah, as he could the people of Richmond, and they would certainly have been less suspicious of polite, humble Bert Mullins.

In the case of the Richmond–Saunders Branch, Archer, who Forbes Watson was sure would please the citizens but whose work he found obnoxious and whose life figures Rowan loathed, lost out to an artist with whom the Section felt at home. And Archer's design, which "sound[ed] intelligent" to Watson and which would have emphasized southern unity with the nation rather than its brief separation and defeat, lost to one that Rowan should have known would arouse objections.

It is not necessarily a foregone conclusion that any painting of the burning of Richmond would arouse the ire of all the citizens of that city. They were offended at dangerous misconceptions in captions for the Currier and Ives prints of that event.[25] But many southern textbooks contained Mathew Brady's photographs of Civil War destruction, and Virginia textbooks featured latter-day artistic imitations of J. M. W. Turner's burning London rendered in black and white. But when Binford's sketch was published, it had people in it. Not the anonymous throng crowding across a distant bridge of Currier and Ives. Not the soulless and unpeopled ruins of Brady. Not the every-city conflagration of Turner's imitators—but real people who would be painted on the post office walls larger than life (Figure 80).

One Richmond citizen who failed to appreciate Binford's artistry and who thought the subject might work if it were treated correctly, offered to help. He told of a nineteenth-century Richmond artist who "drew a picture on the spot portraying the people . . .

24. See letters and articles from Paducah *Sun-Democrat,* September 12, 1939, in Paducah, Kentucky, file.

25. Julien Binford to Mrs. Charles E. Bolling, May 12, 1942, in Richmond–Saunders Branch, file.

80 / Julien Binford, design for Richmond—Saunders Branch

whose homes had been destroyed, in Capitol Square . . . with what they had saved of their belongings about them. . . . It seems to me an adaptation of this scene would be very much more appropriate for the proposed mural."[26] Such an adaptation surely would have been appropriate. According to the description, Richmond's finer citizens had apparently been allowed to clean up before posing with their saved belongings, and the artist carefully rendered them in all their dignity.

Julien Binford, on the other hand, had taken the liberty of show-ing them in a state of confusion and dishabille. Like Paducah's Irvin S. Cobb, Binford had traveled enough that cosmopolitan expe-rience was added to his genuinely southern sensibility. He was born in Virginia and currently lived near Richmond, and he took a profound interest in the South and what it meant to be a south-erner. Usually, that would have ensured the success of a Section artist commissioned to paint for the South. But Binford saw and painted things in a broader perspective than, say, an Archer who had moved out of the South but remained of the South.

Binford reasoned that people suddenly forced to flee both an en-emy army and a raging fire would find themselves less than com-posed. And as a Richmond citizen, he was aware of local tales of confusion and lawlessness associated with the fire. He seems, how-

26. A. B. Upshan to Rowan, April 22, 1942, *ibid.*

ever, to have forgotten that what southerners say of themselves among themselves is not for proclamation to outsiders. He seems to have forgotten, too, the defensiveness with which southerners, alert to alien efforts to reconstruct them and to deny them their autonomy, protect their image as a genteel society. In his confusion about his place as a Virginian and his equally valid place as a citizen of the 1941 art world, Binford created his sketch. Its artistic merit was unquestioned. Then Tom Colt, apparently unaware of the Section's policy against premature publication, the general population's inability to read preliminary black-and-white sketches, and his own lack of judgment where southern public relations were concerned, got Binford's permission to publish the initial sketch *The Great Richmond Fire* in the Richmond *Times-Dispatch*. Colt announced that the artist would accept local suggestions for revision. And suggestions he got. Richmond citizens were confronted with such a picture of themselves as they would never have permitted outsiders to see.

In the center foreground is the flower of southern womanhood, naked in the middle of a city street, one arm raised in a vain effort to protect herself from imminent trampling by a frightened horse. To her right, a fully clothed black woman sprawls hopelessly directly under the horse's feet. At the left of the sketch, a black man's wheelbarrow is laden with the unlikely cargo of a devastated white woman. On a stoop above her, a woman of undistinguishable color holds a bundle, which might be a baby or a collection of household belongings, out to a black man. A soldier rides into the picture's background on an excited horse, and at the extreme right, a southern gentleman who should have known better flies through the air—propelled by what, is unclear. Nothing in the published sketch suggests that the confused state of affairs results from a fire, though Binford made clear in letters to the Section that when he added color, the sky would show clearly that a fire raged in the background.[27]

The scene is one that might be expected in such a devastating situation in any other part of the country, and it is, as Rowan commented when he accepted it and told Binford to develop his color sketch, "lively and entertaining." It is not, however, representative of the South in any situation, crisis or otherwise, as southerners

27. Binford to Rowan, September 9, 1942, *ibid.*

wished outsiders to see it. The extensive published controversy centered on the white woman's nudity and the possibility that the woman on the stoop might represent a black looter. Tom Colt revealed once again his inability to understand the community in which he had come to live: "The fundamental basis of the smoke is the bright flame burning over the mere idea of a nude woman in the middle of a Richmond street. . . . And I am inclined to believe that, if we put a bit of sackcloth on her, it would probably be wise and would certainly extinguish the one real flame of protest." People who are unsure how to comment on art or how to express their own vague misgivings about an unsavory confrontation can retreat into specific comments on superficial particulars. It is much more difficult to analyze a culture's reaction to a depiction of its own less acceptable history. Nevertheless, in a letter to Binford, one local woman made a good stab at it:

> If the walls of public buildings are to [be] decorated with mural paintings, these should depict historical events that may stir the imagination and lend inspiration to those who look upon them.
>
> The youth of today are bearing the burdens, seeing the tragedy and suffering the agonies of war and to many the future holds no hope. Should we not do all we can to blot out tragic memories?
>
> Richmond is rich in its history from the time the settlers first came and planted the cross upon the hill high above the ancient river.[28]

Virginius Dabney, editor of the *Times-Dispatch*, later the author of his own history of Richmond, on the other hand, did protest only the nude and the figure who could be mistaken for a black looter. It seems that Richmond was concerned that blacks not be wrongfully accused of misconduct during the fire, when they all knew that *their Negroes* had behaved appropriately and loyally during the event. But he, like Binford and Cobb, had absorbed experiences that made his outlook more cosmopolitan. Like Colt, he believed that were the nude to be clothed and the "looter" to be painted white, all controversy would die.[29]

Binford undertook to defend himself in a lengthy correspondence with Richmond citizens in the "Voice of the People" column of the

---

28. Tom Colt to Rowan, April 27, 1942, Mrs. Charles E. Bolling to Binford, April 25, 1942, both *ibid.*

29. "Murals and Nude Ladies," Richmond *Times-Dispatch*, April 25, 1942, editorial page, clipping, *ibid.*

Times-Dispatch and did it admirably. He patiently explained that he only wanted to tell the truth in the picture. And he explained that the causes of the fire as well as the bad press it had received were irrelevant. It was a tragedy in Richmond's history comparable to the last days of Pompeii and the destruction of Atlantis.[30] But he missed the point: the truth alone is not adequate unless it protects the South from outside condescension. Replies to his letters indicate both support (from nonsoutherners passing through, local blacks, and Dabney) and opposition.[31] The blacks were convinced that Richmond whites were mistaken in their interpretation of the figure on the stoop. One of Binford's black neighbors wrote:

> I am sure you have misinterpreted the picture in the left hand corner [of the presumed black looter]. . . . I am a neighbor and friend of Mr. Binford. I feel that from his daily walk in life, his actions with us, "his Negro neighbors," he is also a dear friend to us. . . . He co-operates with us in the uplifting of our race in any respect we ask of him, and things we don't ask he gives his part voluntarily for school, church, sickness and health. . . . From the idea of your write-up, those who don't know Mr. Binford would class him as a Negro discriminator, but he is not. Remember, Mr. Editor, "Man looks at the outward appearances, but God looks at the heart." I can't see Mr. Binford's heart but by his daily walk he is a friend to the Negro.

Binford's friendship with the blacks had worked to mutual benefit, and now they came to his defense. Once during the depression he heard that a neighboring black Baptist church needed a mural for its baptistry. Binford responded by trading his talent for whatever produce the Baptists could spare. *Life* magazine reported that he was supplied with "beets, jelly, corn, potatoes, chickens, enough to last the Binfords all winter."[32]

Several other people wrote in defense of Binford's design in April and May, 1942, but many more wrote against it. And several of these

30. James Birchfield, "History in the Nude" (April 28, 1942), Ulysse Desportes, "A Bare Back's Beauty" (April 28, 1942), Michael J. Engel, "The Binford Mural" (May 8, 1942), Marcia Silvette, "Binford's Good Right Arm" (May 19, 1942), Richmond *Times-Dispatch* clippings, all *ibid.*; Virginius Dabney to Edward Rowan, May 19, 1942, *ibid.*

31. Julien Binford, "Apotheosis of the Nude" (May 5, 1942), Binford, "Episcopal Eyes and Nudes" (May 16, 1942), Richmond *Times-Dispatch* clippings, both *ibid.*; Binford to Mrs. Charles E. Bolling, May 12, 1942, *ibid.*

32. "Voice of the People," Richmond *Times-Dispatch*, May 3, 1942, clipping, *ibid.*; "River Jordan Mural," *Life*, November 16, 1942, pp. 138–40.

81 / Julien Binford, revised design for Richmond–Saunders Branch

attacks received a long and detailed defense from Binford. Binford was so articulate, as a matter of fact, that Tom Colt wrote Rowan: "The discussion here, however, has been unique in that the artist has made complete, tempered and effective replies to criticism, so much so that he has clearly answered the . . . criticisms enumerated in my letter and it now appears to me that the public is largely with him."[33] All that Colt said was true except that what "the public" thought of Binford the man and Binford the locally celebrated artist was irrelevant. The public had never been against Binford. It was against the federal government's idea of good art for post office walls, and it was against a painting of the great Richmond fire.

We get our clue to the real nature of the objections to the mural after Binford conceded to drape the center female and made clear that the woman on the stoop is white and that she is handing a baby to a trusted black retainer so that it will be safe as she makes good her own escape (Figure 81). The new design was published, and the furor continued. So we know that Richmond protested something else. The fact that the most vocal protesters were the Daughters and the Sons of the Confederacy suggests that the central objection has something to do with the Civil War. And the sources of Binford's support—Dabney, Colt, and other outlanders passing through—indicate that the problem has more to do with a particular Richmond sensibility than with anything else. It is just

33. Colt to Rowan, June 10, 1942, in Richmond–Saunders Branch, file.

plain undignified to depict a scene of horror and disgrace from the city's past, and it is unfair to remind those Yankees once again that nineteenth-century southerners did not always comport themselves admirably.

Binford knew Richmond history, and he knew that it extended into the past far beyond 1865. But Rowan was so enthusiastic about the subject, and Binford had become so committed to a design of which he may have been justly proud, he failed to gauge the sensibility of his constituency. Occasionally, Yankee artists who came to southern towns to listen and to learn had a better chance to please the local folk than did southern artists who, like Binford, were more committed to art than to the voice of the people. William Dean Fausett, born in Utah and a resident of New York during the 1930s, spent several months in Augusta, Georgia, and he worked with local historian Mrs. Bryan Cumming to arrive at a subject for his mural. The subject they chose was everything a southern city needed to remind itself and everyone else that Georgia had an early and productive part in founding the nation and had done so decorously.

Fausett's mural of James Oglethorpe, founder of the Georgia colony, greeting the Indians who met him at the site later to become Augusta received widely demonstrated public approval (Figure 67). Not only did the Augusta *Herald* publish several articles about the project in process and on completion, but a local show of Fausett's works featured the uninstalled mural. And Augustans were eager that not only would what Fausett termed "the nicest and most influential people in Augusta" get to enjoy the show, but so would the ordinary Augustans who only dreamed of being nice and influential. When the paper announced the show, society editor Virginia Fleming made clear that it was for everyone: "Knowing how art conscious the Augusta public has become, and how appreciative it is, those in charge have arranged for the showing, . . . to be given free of admission."[34] Although, like Binford, Fausett graced the central foreground of his mural with a nude woman—in a much less dignified pose, at that—his picture kept the support of

34. William Dean Fausett to Rowan, October 15, 1938, *ibid.*; "Paints Post Office Mural" (October 16, 1938), "Dean Fausett is Prominent Young Artist of U.S." (October 20, 1938), "Gossip," by Virginia Fleming (October 21, 1938), "Dean Fausett's Mural Shown Yesterday at Art Club Preview" (October 24, 1938), Augusta *Herald* clippings, all in Augusta, Georgia, file, RG 121, NA.

Augustans because it did not fly in the face of southern dignity. His Indian nude was clearly not a member of the white aristocracy.

But Mary Draper Ingles of the territory that became Radford, Virginia, was, if not a member of that aristocracy, a founder of it. And the Boones of Kentucky still claim aristocratic status by virtue of their illustrious, if buckskin-clad, ancestor. Images of either person could remind local citizens as well as nonsouthern America of the comparative age of the South and of its vital part in building the country that now seemed to deny its importance. And yet images of both figures were rejected in no uncertain terms by local citizens. Despite the Section's (by this time, Rowan's) continued insistence, Richmond won its battle to keep the fire off the post office walls. How Binford proceeded with his mural between June, 1942, and August, 1943, is unrecorded. Perhaps local citizens continued to work for a change in subject in their own indirect fashion while Binford continued to defend the truth of his depiction. On August 25, 1943, everybody involved was spared further confrontation. In the face of the sudden and absolute termination of the Section of Fine Arts so that all available funds could go to the war effort, Binford received the following message from the commissioner of public buildings: "The Commissioner now deems it expedient and necessary on behalf of the United States indefinitely to defer the balance of the work under the contract and to terminate your services in connection therewith." Binford was deemed to "have satisfactorily performed all work required for the completion of the preliminary design and the full size cartoon and delivered the latter with photograph and negative to the Government." Thus he was paid for 45 percent of his commission and dismissed forthwith.[35] Citizens of Richmond were saved from doing daily business in plain view of an undignified and distressed 1865 citizenry by a veritable deus ex machina. Those in Radford, Virginia, and Bowling Green, Kentucky, were not.

When, early in 1942, Alexander B. Clayton was appointed to paint a mural for the Radford Post Office, Rowan asked historian D. A. Cannaday of the local teachers' college for suggestions on subjects. Cannaday replied that he had no authority in the matter but that he would be pleased to convene a committee composed of

35. Commissioner of Public Buildings to Binford, August 25, 1943, in Richmond–Saunders Branch, file.

himself, the postmaster, and the mayor to advise Clayton. This he did, and, with the approval of William Ingles, locally prominent descendant of Mary Ingles, they proposed a depiction of her return from Shawnee captivity. According to his agreement with them, Clayton submitted a copy of his cartoon for their approval. He failed to get it. The committee politely detested the cartoon and suggested a scene involving a local ferry or some scene that would pay homage to the local natural beauty. In June, Rowan received a letter from Clayton, saying, "I can't understand why such a bone of contention is made over the subject matter not only because it was suggested to me by several Radford people, including the postmaster & Mr. Cannaday, but also because it does seem the most unique & indigenous piece of history."[36]

One need only to look at the cartoon submitted to the committee and to Mary Ingles' descendant, for whom that descent meant membership in the aristocracy, to surmise reasons for their rejection (Figure 82). The annals of American history are replete with stories of women who, having been forced to live with Indians, were rejected as ruined when they returned to civilization. Often, in early America a woman with such experiences as these women presumably had was deemed unworthy to sleep with heroic American men or to bear wholesome American children. That Mary Ingles had returned from captivity to raise a family whose descendants still lived in Radford was cherished local history, but the Radford establishment had probably never considered the condition in which she returned. Even the information Clayton received from the local committee seems to lose sight of her 850-mile trek in favor of the last few miles of her journey after she was rescued, as any southern lady should be, by one Adam Harmon.[37]

The cartoon the committee saw does not show a lady properly dressed and escorted by an American knight in shining armor. Instead it depicts a woefully bedraggled woman, shod in Indian sandals, uncombed hair matted over her shoulders, alone and unprotected. She staggers toward a poor representation of American

36. John Cannaday to Rowan, January 13, 1942, Alexander Clayton to Rowan, June 2, 1942, both in Radford, Virginia, file.

37. The attitude toward the escaped female captive in captivity narratives ranges from the marking of the captive as sullied for life to making her an absolute heroine, but some Radford citizens seem to have seen implications of the former in Clayton's sketch.

82 / Alexander B. Clayton, cartoon for Radford, Va., 1941

manhood. The two men she staggers toward, one of whom must be local hero Adam Harmon, crouch in the shelter of a tree, their discomfiture so great that their mouths hang open and their rifles practically drop from their hands.

And what of the natural beauty of the area? In the distance a log cabin is set at a rakish tilt. It is more appropriate as a setting for *Tobacco Road* than as a representation of the industry and artistry of pioneer forebears. In the center foreground, a tree has been carelessly chopped to bits and left in the path for Ingles to trip over. Pines struggle to stay alive as they grow horizontally out of rocky cliff faces, and there seems to be as much dead wood as there is healthy forest. The committee members were ill equipped to imagine what definitive lines, living color, and careful draftsmanship could do for the finished product. And, though we can never know what prompted William Ingles' rejection of the sketch, we can surmise that he just could not face the implications for his great-grandmother if she returned from the Indians in such a state. Surviving members of the Ingles family still protect her reputation from "mistaken" interpretations. When her own son wrote the story of her captivity and escape, he did not mention the child she bore while in captivity and deserted in order to escape and warn the settlement.[38]

None of Rowan's sympathy, however, went to the committee or to the Ingles descendants: "I feel the local advice is developing into something of a real burden for the artist." But he would try to mol-

38. Roberta Ingles Steele and Andrew Lewis Ingles (eds.), *Escape from Indian Captivity: The Story of Mary Draper Ingles and Son Thomas Ingles* (Radford, Va., 1982), is the account written by Mary Ingles' son. I am also indebted to Grace Toney Edwards, Director of Appalachian Studies, Radford University, for further information on family and community folklore regarding the Ingles story.

lify them, without giving up a subject to which he was committed. Rowan, it seems, despite his own predisposition toward circumlocution, was unaware of the tradition in which many southerners will go to great lengths not to say directly and precisely what they mean and to even greater lengths to avoid uttering what they perceive to be a direct insult. The southern predilection for indirection is difficult to document, but examples from popular literature of the South during the 1930s, demonstrate that southern citizens know that propriety prohibits saying what one means. In *Gone With the Wind* when Margaret Mitchell describes the ideal of southern antebellum womanhood, she tells us that Scarlett O'Hara has learned that "above all, you never said what you really thought about anything, any more than they [other people] said what they really thought." And in Medora Field Perkerson's popular 1938 detective novel, *Who Killed Aunt Maggie?*, the main character remarks to a male Yankee transplanted to Georgia, "You become more Southern every day. I never know any more whether to believe you or not."[39]

Rowan opted to take at face value the Radford committee's polite complaint that the design did not do justice to local natural beauty. He thought that if Clayton would just put a beautiful background behind his bedraggled and misused Mary Ingles and his startled and impotent men, the local patriarchs would be satisfied: "I do believe it will be possible for you to take the suggestion of the local committee in reproducing in your mural a reflection of the natural beauty of the section of the country. I am convinced that those who reviewed the color sketches are not in the habit of reading preliminary sketches."[40]

True, they were not accustomed to preliminary sketches, but neither were they in the habit of telling an artist that they thought his main figure atrocious. And they probably could not accept that ravished creature as a beloved female ancestor. That might imply that she lived with the Indians, made good her escape, and returned to them in such a condition as would have ruined her for union with any southern gentleman. And yet, they had William Ingles

39. Rowan to Clayton, May 5, 1942, in Radford, Virginia, file; Margaret Mitchell, *Gone With the Wind* (1936; New York, 1975), 160–61; Medora Field Perkerson, *Who Killed Aunt Maggie?* (New York, 1938), 213.
40. Rowan to Clayton, May 5, 1942, in Radford, Virginia, file.

sitting among them to prove that she had done so. When they suggested the topic, they could not have imagined the interpretation by a contemporary artist bent on presenting the American scene in all its marvelous, and sometimes seamy, variety.

And so, on June 9, 1942, having been shown a more finished color sketch of Clayton's proposed mural, the committee prepared a report to send to the Section in which they recounted the history of the mural venture and what they considered to be federal disregard of their wishes in the matter. The new sketch, it seemed, "appealed neither to the Postmaster nor to Mr. Ingles, who is a direct descendant of Mary Draper Ingles, nor to the professors of history at the college, nor to any of the other people of the community who were consulted." Radford would, the committee stated, rather have no mural than the one submitted, but in their conclusion they revealed their intense desire still to have art decoration for the post office: "As far as time is concerned the committee is willing to wait any length of time in order to secure a satisfactory work."[41]

But Clayton had accepted a position as a topographic draftsman with the navy, and the Section itself found time at a premium. The Section head and its chief liaison with the government power structure had been dead some months, and Rowan found his budget and his staff cut daily and drastically. Despite the pending dissolution of the Section and local protest, the mural of Mary Ingles' return did go up. To give Clayton credit, the color rendition does include something of the beauty of the region, and color softens the harsh reality of Mary Ingles' travail (Figure 83). But Clayton changed his figures not a whit. We have no records of how the mural was accepted in 1942, but today it is acknowledged with ambivalence at best. While the Radford postmaster is proud to have his lobby graced with the artwork, other people in Radford either do not know of its existence or refuse to acknowledge it. One postal employee of twenty years, though he works daily in the mural's presence, claims not to have known of its existence, and the owner of the bookstore next door, to whom inquirers about the mural are directed for information on Mary Ingles, acts surprised when visitors mention the mural. Although the tale is alive in books, in an outdoor drama that has played every summer since 1969, and in the

41. "Mural Painting for the Radford Post Office, June 9, 1942," *ibid.*

83 / Alexander B. Clayton, *Mary Ingles Returns from Captivity*, Radford, Va., 1942
Photo by Richard H. Beckham

continued preservation efforts of the Ingles family, the mural apparently still rankles local citizens—unless, of course, they really do not know about it.[42]

Memphis artist John H. Fyfe was appointed to do the Magnolia, Mississippi, mural early in 1939. When residents requested that he paint a scene from the early days of Pike County, he understood what they meant: they wanted a scene to remind post office patrons that Magnolia had been a part of the Union long before sectional strife and one that would emphasize the South's ability to handle its own problems. Fyfe located a historical situation that demonstrated not only Magnolia's place far in antebellum history but its loyalty to the Union as well. In addition, his subject was as unique and indigenous to Magnolia as Mary Ingles' escape was to Radford. And yet in the image of a Fourth of July celebration at Sheriff Bacot's, there is no suggestion that Magnolia residents had not always been so proper and refined as they were in the Year of our Lord 1939.

It seems that in the very early nineteenth century, a much-beloved local sheriff was given to inviting all residents of the fledgling town to his land to celebrate Independence Day with a picnic. And what better way to refute negative publicity about the South's economic plight than to show a fifteen-foot table, every inch laden with food and beverage? So laden, in fact, that it all would not fit. Around the tables are firkins of fruit and kegs of beverage (Figure 84).

Fyfe's successful mural does not make the mistake Clayton's did in attempting to render any specific local personage. Although the bounty may have been Sheriff Bacot's, he is nowhere to be seen. In-

42. Interviews with Radford postal worker and bookstore owner, August, 1985.

84 / John H. Fyfe, *July 4th Celebration at Sheriff Labon Bacot's,* Magnolia, Miss., 1939

stead, we have a picture filled with industrious men, women, and children on holiday—no traces of soil erosion or irresponsible deforestation. Only plowed fields, healthy trees, and a table bearing hams and joints and cheeses and cider and milk—and perhaps a little carefully corked corn liquor. Although these people, because they have not been in Pike County long enough to build imposing homesteads, appear to live in log cabins, their cabins are ramrod straight with nary a chink for air to leak through.

A Greensboro, Georgia, historian proudly reported that settlers there "began erecting log huts in which to make their homes until they could build more comfortable houses."[43] Thus he acknowledged the necessity for primitive dwellings while assuring people of the 1930s that the sturdy frame and brick houses of prosperous farmers were not long in coming. Similarly, the early log dwellings of Magnolia residents imply that, unlike their midwestern counterparts nearly a century later, these potential members of Mississippi's gentry would not live for years in log cabins. They would soon build more comfortable, not to say imposing, residences. One is reminded once again of the contrast between northern Republican Abe Lincoln's reputation in contemporary America and that of southern Democrat Jefferson Davis. Where Lincoln supporters call attention to their candidate's log cabin boyhood, those who re-

43. *Herald-Journal,* October 6, 1939, clipping, in Greensboro, Georgia, file, RG 121, NA. Although Greensboro historian T. B. Rice seems to be faintly comic, he is cited several times in Arthur Raper, *Preface to Peasantry: A Tale of Two Black Belt Counties* (Chapel Hill, 1936), as a source for early folk history in Greene County, Georgia.

member Jeff Davis, president of the nation where landowners automatically became army officers, preserve his aristocratic condition and seldom mention his Kentucky log cabin background.

Like the people of Campbellsville, Kentucky, those of Magnolia were grateful for the mural their government had given them. Led by their postmaster C. E. Bilbo, undoubtedly in a sinecure provided for him by his illustrious kinsman and hero of the working class, Theodore Bilbo, they were so effusive and humble in their gratitude that their government felt constrained to give them more. Fyfe was forthwith commissioned to do two smaller vignettes on the same theme to complement the mural.[44]

Small-town residents had other ways to get their post office decorated twice. If the custodian of local history were male, he stood a good chance of getting his wishes fulfilled, regardless of what the Section and the artist wished to do—usually through a barrage of prose. After writing Rowan upwards of fifty pages of flowery and excessively polite prose, J. William Slemons of Salisbury, Maryland, won for Salisbury residents not only historical murals they could live with but local support for a building in which to house the Salisbury Historical Society, of which he was president and the only male member. And T. B. Rice, historian of Greensboro, Georgia, so overwhelmed the Section with veiled charges of breach of promise and three-page, single-spaced letters that his town was granted a second mural with a historical subject, and they labeled it with the long-discarded spelling of the town's name, Greenesborough.

Once he had convinced the government and artist Jacob Getlar Smith that Salisbury should have a mural reflecting specific local social history, Slemons detailed precisely how the murals should look, down to the precise costume each figure should wear. Protesting that he was sacrificing artistic integrity and that historical murals were irrelevant, Smith complied with the committee's recommendations. Like the committee in Radford, the Salisbury group could not read preliminary sketches. Thus, Smith faced more criticism and the Section more prose when the sketches were submitted for Slemons' approval. At that point, however, the problem was easily solved. The artists had only to put a fine, glossy finish on his pictures of the town bell-ringer in Salisbury's early days and

44. Rowan to J. H. Fyfe, March 18, 1939, in Magnolia, Mississippi, file, RG 121, NA.

the wharf from which sailed the steamers bound for Baltimore to convince Slemons and Salisbury residents that what they saw on the post office wall was authentic history. Unfortunately, Smith got no credit for prostituting himself with what amounted to commercial art.

When the historical society building was dedicated and the picture unveiled in a day-long community celebration, Rowan was invited to speak, but Smith's name was not even mentioned. And Rowan was required to take second billing to Salisbury's own J. William Slemons. Rowan made the 150-mile trip from Washington to Salisbury to make a speech, though Slemons had warned him that it could be no more than five minutes long because the day would be so full of activities. Slemons, as the keynote speaker, was not only permitted to speak much longer; great chunks of his speech were published in the Salisbury *Times,* which only mentioned Rowan's name.[45]

At least in Salisbury, the Section got some recognition for its part in paying for the mural. In Greensboro, T. B. Rice took all the credit. "The scene," he wrote in his weekly newspaper column on Greensboro history, "will be depicted in a mural that is now complete and will be installed in the new Post Office during the week of October 1 to 7 [1940]." No mention of the Section or of artist Carson Davenport then or in the report of the mural's installation a week later.[46]

But Davenport deserved no credit, according to Rice. A good southern boy who should have known better, he visited Greensboro in search of material. He was hosted and escorted by Rice, who undoubtedly regaled him with local history the whole time. And what did he do when he returned to Danville, Virginia? He drew a picture of cotton picking in Georgia. One can hardly blame Greensboro residents if they did not want another cotton-picking scene just like all the others throughout the South—particularly since Greene County, of which Greensboro was the seat, had recently been singled out by Arthur Raper for his acclaimed book, *Preface to Peasantry,* as his example of the devastating effects of

45. Salisbury *Times,* September 18, 1939, clipping, in Salisbury, Maryland, file, RG 121, NA.

46. Dr. T. B. Rice, "Greensboro at 1, 73 and 153 Years of Age," September 30, 1939, and "How a Yankee Newspaper Man Saw Greensboro in 1865," October 6, 1939, clippings, both in Greensboro, Georgia, file.

the one-crop system in the rural South. But Rice's real objection was that he had told the press what the subject was to be. Not only had he leaked the incorrect news to the Greensboro *Herald-Journal*, but he "had released the information to Ralph Smith, the Washington correspondent for The Atlanta Journal, and he 'told the world' what the mural would be, therefore, any change in the subject would subject me to ridicule."[47]

Fearful of statewide, perhaps even nationwide, ridicule, Rice "took the matter up with . . . [Congressman] Paul Brown." Congressman Brown, according to Rice, was "somewhat appeased by a vague promise of the massacre scene to be painted later; but that promise hinges on the little word 'if.'" And that little word *if* did not appease the aging T. B. Rice: "I haven't many more years to live, and I do not care to spend a part of that time in explaining to the public why I lied about the picture, to be, in the new Greenesborough Post Office; but that is exactly what will happen if the cotton picking scene precedes the subject I have been telling the public about."[48]

The Section and Carson Davenport already knew what it was to have Rice defending himself to them. They did not want Atlanta and much of the state of Georgia burdened with Rice's laborious and irate explanations that he had not, in fact, lied to them; rather, he had been betrayed by the Treasury Section of Fine Arts and Congressman Brown's willingness to take *if* for an answer. But the Section could not admit to being brought to its knees by an insignificant local historian. Therefore, Davenport was put to work painting not one but two murals for Greensboro, Georgia—one of Georgians picking cotton; another of an infamous 1787 massacre by Indians of good Greensboro whites. Still, that was not enough for Rice: "Now for one other request—not overlooking the original spelling of GREENESBOROUGH—: I would like for your department to print on cardboard, in bold type, a copy of Governor Mathews' letter to the President, telling of the destruction of Greenesborough; also a brief description of the scene depicted, put it in a nice frame and have it fastened to the wall, just under the picture, so that those who see it can interpret the scene depicted."[49]

47. Rice to Rowan, January 23, 1939, in Greensboro, Georgia, file.
48. *Ibid.*
49. Rice to Rowan, March 11, 1939, *ibid.*

One wonders, with enough local history that Rice could devote a weekly column to it, why he was so committed to a picture showing death and devastation. In the hard-won picture are dead and dying white men, with faces and hairstyles such as one associates with Renaissance paintings of Jesus Christ, falling into the post office lobby. Creek Indians, later banished to Alabama, run rampant over white women and children. One buckskin-clad white male in the left foreground, so overcome by the enormity of it all, lowers his musket and turns from the Indians he fights to gaze wistfully toward the cotton picking at the other end of the lobby. In the background, a large contingent of Georgia soldiers march, arms shouldered, to deliver a few "guilty" Creek to the Greene County authorities. The troops are apparently oblivious to the woman being dragged by the hair—or scalped—almost at their feet. Couldn't a few of these well-armed soldiers, the viewer wonders, be detached to help the struggling civilians defend their homes and persons? But the massacre was history, and it did demonstrate to Greensboro citizens that their forebears were making Georgia safe for democracy long before the Yankees invaded. And if the town had survived that destruction in 1787, it could surely survive the devastation of cotton tenancy and the boll weevil in the 1930s.

It was invariably dangerous for the Section to tangle with a local historian. The man who had made as his avocation—and sometimes his vocation as well—the unearthing and preservation of obscure local history would not be thwarted. And when he brought his congressman into the controversy, he was bound to win his point.

The people of Russellville, Alabama, were not offered a second mural as a reward for their gratitude. Their tiny post office just could not support two 9-by-12 wall paintings; and besides, they only became grateful after they had apparently forced the Section to abide by their wishes. The Federal Writers' Project guide to Alabama had little to say about the tiny city except that a War of 1812 major had found the land at the site to be exceedingly fertile. But twentieth-century Russellville inhabitants knew the town had a history that would place it squarely in the center of industrial America. They might be a farming community in 1937, but in 1817, Russellville, as the home of the first iron furnace in the state of Alabama, had played an important role in the development of industry in the South. John M. Clark, Franklin County representative of the Natchez Trace Association, knew that his constituents would not be pleased with a humdrum "modern" farm scene. Russellville had a history after all. Thus in August, 1937, he wrote his congressman:

> The people of Russellville protest the acceptance of the subject submitted.
>
> The first iron furnace built in Alabama was erected in 1817 a few miles out from this town. It was there the iron and steel industry in Alabama had its birth. It is the one point of *great historic value* in this vicinity. It is *that* that we want in our mural.
>
> . . . We know the Bee Hive shape of all charcoal furnaces erected at that date. We know that this furnace and forge were motivated by water power through a race that still exists. We know they used a five hundred pound hammer to shape the pig—we still have the hammer. We know the ore was collected by slave labor and hauled in ox carts to the furnace . . . and we have the records where it sold . . . for one hundred dollars per ton. The rock wall foundation of the warehouse still stands along the creek bank . . . here is a site of great historic value that is rapidly disappearing.
>
> We insist that an Artist can give a magnificent conception of the true appearance of the old furnace.[50]

Clark's opinion was backed by urgent telegrams to the Section from more organizations interested in the preservation of local history than one would have thought Russellville could support, and each organization sent night letters to Congressman W. B. Bankhead as well.[51] An as-yet-unjaded Ed Rowan was eager to please, and besides, anytime a congressman got in on the act, the community was likely to win on subject matter. He wrote the artist suggesting that he "seriously consider the matter in question and see if your capabilities will not permit you to create a design which you, as an artist, can approve of and which will also meet with the approval of Dr. Clark and his group." Fortunately, the commissioned artist was Conrad Albrizzio, a talented artist from Louisiana. His idea of art was in harmony with the Section's, but he was, under

50. Federal Writers Project, *Alabama: A Guide to the Deep South* (New York, 1941), 354; Dr. J. M. Clark to Hon. W. B. Bankhead, August 19, 1937, in Russellville, Alabama, file, RG 121, NA.

51. Russellville Study Club, Mrs. W. L. Chenault, Pres., to Edward Rowan, August 21–22, 1937, is a sample of several identical night letters Rowan received, each from a different organization with a different female president, *ibid.*

85 / Conrad Albrizzio, *Shipment of First Iron Produced in Russellville*, Russellville, Ala., 1937
Photo by Richard H. Beckham

duress, willing to please local people in order to make some money. Reluctantly explaining that there was no way a vertical furnace could be artistically presented on a horizontal post office wall, he gave up his "genuinely artistic" ideas and replaced them with drawings of the furnace, hammer, slaves, oxen, and all.[52]

The result was a singularly unlovely mural (Figure 85). The furnace rises in the center middle-ground behind rather unlikely hills. Slaves labor in the foreground and in the background. The water-wheel is clearly visible behind the furnace, and at the extreme left a gigantic covered wagon looms over the hills. One suspects that the size of the wagon and the strange hill formation are Albrizzio's effort to provide perspective for the furnace, a pale blob in the center. The result, however, is a confusion of sizes and shapes. The most sympathetic object in the picture is the ox in the left foreground, his head larger even than the wagon he pulls. From his position, crowded behind the picture's frame and with no place to pull his wagon, he gazes into the lobby, where he might have room to stretch his legs. It is difficult to see how anyone could be comfortable with him around. But the town's inhabitants and its postal employees are not only comfortable with him; he has become an especial favorite.[53]

52. Rowan to Albrizzio, August 31, 1937, Albrizzio to Rowan, August 26, 1937, both *ibid.*
53. Conversation with postal patrons and postmaster, Russellville, Ala., August, 1981.

In 1938 the people of Russellville were proud that the one item of great historical value in the vicinity was immortalized, and they remain so today. Perhaps the reason no one in Russellville was disturbed by the strange composition is that they had the chance to see it in process. Albrizzio did for the little Alabama town one of the few true fresco murals in the South. When a community feels a part of the process of making a monument, they are less likely to be critical of the product. The very fact that Albrizzio lodged in the town and created the picture before their eyes gave them a sense of propriety they might not have felt had he merely brought a finished canvas to install.

But the main reason Russellvilleans were and are so pleased with their mural is that its theme is so appropriate to the community. One would think that the image of Daniel Boone would have been equally appropriate for a mural in Bowling Green, Kentucky. His connection with Bowling Green was similar to Zachary Taylor's with Campbellsville and George Rogers Clark's with Paducah. And, like Taylor and Clark, he was a national figure—more important, actually, than either of them. It was he who had opened a gateway to the West, not a latter-day man-made arch in St. Louis, but a natural gap in the Cumberland Mountains that enabled pioneers to settle not only Kentucky but, ultimately, to make their way over the Oregon Trail and fulfill manifest destiny. And the gap had turned the "Dark and Bloody Ground" into the "Land of Milk and Honey." It was through his legendary accomplishments that Kentucky Indians were subdued and the way was opened for Kentucky to become the fifteenth state.

Unlike Mary Ingles' image, Boone's had been scrutinized from every angle and, by the late 1930s, was well defined and unimpeachable. He was dead and a hero long before Kentuckians had to face any question of whether to stay with the Union or leave it. He was not associated with any event humiliating to Kentuckians as the great Richmond fire was to Virginians, and any slight claim to descent from him rendered any Kentuckian a New World aristocrat.

Besides all that, when Ward Lockwood had selected Boone as the subject for his Lexington, Kentucky, mural, all expectations were realized. Although a nationally known painter of the American scene, Lockwood knew how to deal with the residents. And since the Lexington commission was important, he was paid enough to warrant careful research into the local sensibility. Before he even went to Kentucky, he considered "a great many different ideas for the subject matter, allegory, contemporary scenes and history." He decided on a historical theme because he perceived such to "be the most satisfactory from the viewpoint of the Section, the people of Lexington and [him]self." He was indeed in a rare and fortunate position when that which would satisfy him would also please the Section and the people of the community for whom he would paint. Lockwood was also sensitive enough to choose an incident from Boone's life that would not only leave his reputation untarnished but would lend itself to an especially heroic representation:

> The sketch illustrates the arrival of Daniel Boone, who composed the party of Virginia settlers that explored the country around what is now Lexington, Kentucky, in 1769. Here is a quotation from Stewart Edward White's "Daniel Boone; Wilderness Scout"—: "They had come out (on a mountain promontory) opposite one of the headwaters of the Kentucky River. Immediately at their feet, of course, rolled the billows of the lesser ranges and the foothills, but creeping out from that and rising to the horizon opposite their eyes lay a rich and beautiful country of forests, of low hills and vales and vast level plain. . . . Long they stood leaning on their rifles, gazing in a muse of speculation or anticipations. Perhaps it was from this point that Boone received his inspiration that he was ordained by God to open an empire to a people."[54]

Once he had a sure-fire topic for his mural, Lockwood still traveled to Lexington, where he surveyed the mural space and hired a professional plasterer to prepare the wall and an experienced decorator to install the mural under the artist's own supervision. Then, so that he was certain to depict Boone as heroically as Kentuckians did in their minds, he asked for the advice of C. Frank Dunn, secretary of the Daniel Boone Bicentennial Commission. And finally, not to be criticized for inaccurate detail, Lockwood visited the Frankfort, Kentucky, museum where he could view and sketch Boone's actual rifle and other personal artifacts.

The picture Lockwood painted of Boone was literally larger than life (Figure 86). Unlike Albrizzio in Russellville, Lockwood had a vertical space for a vertical subject. Stretching nearly twelve feet above the spectator seats, his companions surrounding him, as awed by the discovery as he is but much less aware of its implica-

54. Ward Lockwood to Rowan, December 9, 1937, in Lexington, Kentucky, file, RG 121, NA.

86 / Ward Lockwood, *Daniel Boone's Arrival in Kentucky,* Lexington, Ky., 1938
Photo by Richard H. Beckham

tions, Boone surveys the bounteous countryside that will guarantee his exaltation by posterity. His eyes are dreamy, but his feet are planted squarely on the ground. He is the American hero, godlike in his vision, common sense his guide. And his possibilities are not limited by any immediate responsibility for women or children.[55] Only men accompany him into the wilderness. Lockwood's Boone had neither time nor inclination for tall tales, romping with wild beasts, or singing to himself. He was a man of destiny, and Lexington, Kentucky, was that destiny.

For Bowling Green, Kentucky, Edward Laning also selected Daniel Boone as the subject. Although this mural did not call forth the mutinous winds the murals of Radford and Richmond–Saunders Branch did, it was less than warmly received. In the first place, Boone's exploration had been farther east in Kentucky. In the second, it is one thing to tell amusing anecdotes about a hero's common humanity around the pot-bellied stove. It is quite another to render a hero quite human for all posterity to see on the post office walls. In Laning's painting, Boone rests on his back atop the door to the post office (Figure 87). The painted background suggests the door to be a very small knoll exposed on all sides. The Long Hunters have been able to get within a foot or two of him undetected. In the sweltering Kentucky summer, both Boone and the Long Hunters wear fur caps and other clothing appropriate to a Minnesota spring. Boone's rifle lies a foot or so from his body, its stock toward his feet. And he sings to a cardinal, fully as large as Boone's own head, who has no more sense of impending danger than Dan'l does. Mary T. Moore, librarian of the Kentucky Collection at Western Kentucky State Teachers College in Bowling Green, stated the sentiments of the community:

> Mr. Laning could well spend a little time studying scout traits, hunter's rules for handling guns—and birds. All these points were brought out in newspaper criticisms before, when the original cut was published. Mr. Laning evidently felt that artistic license excused these errors in a realistic picture of Boone. . . . Boone and the cardinal both must have been under the spell of Kentucky moonshine to have been so unaware of the dangers surrounding them!

55. Robert Jewett and John Shelton Lawrence, *The American Monomyth* (Garden City, N.Y., 1977), convincingly argue that in the popular media the American hero who becomes entangled with women or family renders himself unfit to guide America toward its destiny.

87 / Edward Laning, *The Long Hunters Discover Daniel Boone*, Bowling Green, Ky., 1942

. . . When we are lucky enough to get other murals, we will hope to get an artist who knows Kentuckians—and an out-of-doors man, also. We will be glad, maybe, that Mr. Laning's attempt has been placed in an out-of-the-way wall.[56]

One hopes that before Laning attempted another mural of a local hero for local folk, he took a lesson from Ward Lockwood, who did his homework thoroughly, or from John H. Fyfe, who might counsel him to avoid direct representation of historical personages.

Southerners in the 1930s had had enough of outsiders telling them who they were, what they should be, and how to deal with their problems. They wished the outside to listen to them. If they

56. Mary T. Moore to Harold W. Sublett, Postmaster, January 20, 1942, in Bowling Green, Kentucky, file, RG 121, NA.

had read Wilbur J. Cash's 1941 interpretation of southern history in terms of guilt, they would have found that as absurd as Daniel Boone's rifle stock being toward his feet. They were not guilty; they were unheard. Had they had access to C. Vann Woodward's *Burden of Southern History* (1960), they might have pondered his interpretation of their history a little longer before they laughed it off. It is true that having lost a war made the southern sensibility in the 1930s different from that of any other American region. But the loss of the war was not what burdened them—not when they contemplated permanent decorations for the post office walls. They were burdened by what they perceived to be the rest of the country's reluctance to let them back into the Union and to recognize that their history preceded 1860 by more than two centuries. They wanted to be rid of federal condescension. When they asked for southern artists, it was not that they wanted people who better understood their difference from the rest of America. They hoped that artists from the South would recognize the South's rightful place in the national culture.

What southerners in the 1930s wanted was to be freed from the burden of their unique history and to share the bountiful and victorious history of the rest of the country. They had not discovered cultural plurality and they had no desire to. The southern coasts had been the first American frontier, and southern land had been the virgin territory in the seventeenth century. The South had produced American heroes in great numbers and its allegiance was to the American dream. What they asked of the Section of Fine Arts was that it appoint artists for historical murals who sensed all that and who would provide them with enduring reminders of their place in American culture.

CODA / ALL'S WELL THAT PROMISES
TO END WELL

The stranger who drives south on US 84 into Enterprise, Alabama, and asks directions to the railroad depot (recently converted into a community museum) will be told to turn right at the Boll Weevil. Upon asking the whereabouts of the post office, the stranger is told to drive straight on past the Boll Weevil, and it will be in the first block on the right. Inquiring for the public library, the puzzled driver is instructed to circle the Boll Weevil and proceed up the street to the left. Very confusing for the first-time visitor, especially since on that same US 84 is a restaurant called the Boll Weevil, and it's in the middle of the block.

At first the traveling stranger is likely to consider the whole town addled. The boll weevil is an unattractive insect whose cotton-consuming habits were responsible for a great many of the South's ills between 1910 and 1929, and it continued to wreak devastation over much of cotton country through the 1930s. Besides that, it is too small for the passing motorist to see, let alone negotiate a turn around. The confused tourist eventually figures out that the neo-Greek monument in the geographic center of the town must be the landmark to which local directions refer. That statue of a goddess, holding above her head an insect on a platter, is the point about which the town revolves geographically, economically, and socially.

For years the only enemies of cotton in the South were the earth itself, which simply refused to work after many years of unrequited cotton growing; the weather, which cooperated with cotton growers to produce an abundant harvest in only about three out of every ten years; and the fluctuating cotton market. Then, late in the nineteenth century, the Mexican boll weevil made the trek across the Rio Grande into the Texas cotton fields. Gradually, the insect worked its way eastward across the southern United States until 1915, when he destroyed 60 percent of the cotton crop in Alabama's Coffee County, of which Enterprise was and is the metropolis. The next year the boll weevil destroyed more than two-thirds of the crop, but in 1917, facing a similar disaster, the Enterprise community decided to do something about it.[1]

In the early 1830s, early settlers of the Enterprise area had attempted to practice what the *Progressive Farmer* in 1939 was to call "two-armed farming." That is, they had raised livestock along with food crops, but the piney woods were ill suited to grazing and, like just about everyone else in the South, Coffee County settlers soon turned to the crop mythically associated with instant cash—cotton. And also like just about everyone else in the South, very few made a decent living at it. Years passed with Coffee County farmers prospering occasionally but more often eking out a living. Until the coming of the boll weevil. The insidious little pest chewed away at the cotton plants and at Coffee County chances for prosperity at the same time. When planters could not earn a living raising cotton, neither could storekeepers, bankers, gin operators, or anybody else. But in 1917, unlike many other southerners, Coffee County farmers gave up on King Cotton and looked elsewhere. They invested in corn, potatoes, sugarcane, and hay. And by that time, the land was sufficiently cleared that they could return to livestock as well. All these agricultural endeavors, we are told, flourished, but the big cash crop turned out to be peanuts—so big that Enterprise soon labeled itself the Peanut Capital of the World. Even during the Depression, when the whole South suffered, Enterprise residents raised a variety of food crops and claimed to have been less devastated than were their Alabama neighbors. And citizens of the greater Enterprise area had learned an all-important lesson in getting along in the agrarian South—diversified farming.

The town early realized the importance of its new agricultural diversity and thus in 1919, with contributions from local businesses and individuals, it erected its monument in the town center: a neoclassical lady atop a pedestal holding, on a platter above her head, a very large wrought-iron boll weevil. On the base of the monument are inscribed the words:

1. Information about Enterprise and its Boll Weevil Monument is derived from Richard C. Adams (ed.), *The Enterprise Centennial: An Affectionate History,* Official Program of the Centennial Celebration of the City of Enterprise, Alabama (1982); a chamber of commerce brochure, "Boll Weevil Monument: The Only Monument In The World Glorifying a Pest"; and conversations with local citizens on a visit to Enterprise in August, 1983.

In Profound Appreciation
Of the Boll Weevil
And What it Has Done
As the Herald of Prosperity
This Monument Was Erected
By the Citizens of
Enterprise, Coffee County, Alabama

The monument celebrates the pest that taught local farmers a lesson the rest of the South was much slower to learn. And its presence is so well known—it earned a place in *The Book of Lists* as the world's only monument to a pest—that locals just assume a guest to the town will understand directions to "turn right at the Boll Weevil." It was this monument around which, in 1940, Virginia artist Paul Arlt designed his mural for the Enterprise Post Office (Figure 88). In his mural, Arlt celebrated everything the town's booster club and chamber of commerce still promote about Enterprise, and he celebrated the ordinary people as well. The visitor who goes east around the monument will find the public library— in the building that once was the New Deal post office. And inside Arlt's mural is just where it was installed during the Section's heyday. Except that now, with the sunshine yellow library walls reflecting the midday sun and the removal of the wall of post office grilles that crowded it, the picture shows up even better than it did when it adorned a post office.

Fancying themselves more prosperous, more progressive, more

88 / Paul Arlt, *Saturday in Enterprise*, Enterprise, Ala., 1941

open-minded than were residents of other southern small towns, citizens of Enterprise had no need to clamor for a historical wall painting in their post office; they were pleased with the present. Feeling as they did, that their town was second to no other, that the results of their hard work were visible in the bustle around them, they had no need to demonstrate in their mural that agriculture and industry did indeed exist in Enterprise. Since the bustling town center was much more beautiful to prosperous citizens than was the surrounding countryside, which only served to contribute to Enterprise's prosperity, they had no need for landscapes. In a South that often needed assurance that it was indeed a part of a great nation, a South that Jonathan Daniels suggested was to the United States what the Negro was to the South, Enterprise needed no such assurance. After all, practically a carload of Enterprise School Days brand peanut butter was shipped to the remote regions of the country every day.[2] It was the home of Coffee County Homesteads, the first resettlement project of its kind in the county. Coffee County was already equipped to grow its own food when much of the South struggled to do so on ravished land. Thus Arlt chose to depict a "typical" Saturday afternoon half-holiday in Enterprise.

The Enterprise mural demonstrates that Enterprise is a modern, thriving, commercial city. It suggests that the Saturday half-holiday, for which labor unions negotiated in the 1930s, was a reality for blacks and whites in Enterprise, that people had money to spend on trifles, and that the town itself was more than commonly attractive. In the center, of course, is the boll-weevil-bearing Greek woman high atop her pedestal. The focal point of an attractively faced brick pavement obviously radiating from her base, she has been turned so that, though she faces the viewer, the downtown's most distinctive building is clearly visible. Immediately to her back, on the corner, is a building lower but longer than the others, its nine classically arched windows and doors providing a more fitting backdrop for her than would the others with their false fronts and wrought-iron balconies. Those others, each housing a thriving Enterprise business, stretch down the two main streets, which intersect at the statue, each tiny building a different pastel hue—blue,

2. Jonathan Daniels, *A Southerner Discovers the South* (New York, 1938), 345; Federal Writers Project, *Alabama: A Guide to the Deep South* (New York, 1941), 361.

amber, ecru, salmon, coral. For some reason, the Section allowed Arlt to break one of its hard and fast rules. Not only are the buildings copied from actual Enterprise structures; they are labeled with the names of actual Enterprise businesses. The viewer can see a Coca-Cola sign, advertising another southern commercial success story, on the front of the City Cafe. One can see Perlman's dry goods emporium and the Ford garage, and one can see *Sal*, the first syllable in the name of another local establishment.

To show the world that, though it had only four thousand or so citizens, Enterprise was indeed modern and progressive, there is that Ford garage and many diagonally parked vehicles—coupes, sedans, and pickup trucks. In the actual 1930s, reports one nostalgic citizen, the sounds of bells attached to mule-drawn wagons signaled, among other things, ice and milk deliveries six days a week and mail twice daily.[3] But in Arlt's modern community, the internal combustion engines need not contend with such old-fashioned conveyances. Only motor vehicles gather round the Boll Weevil monument. After all, Enterprise had had public electricity since 1903, a movie theater since 1905, and automobiles since the local doctor purchased one in 1904.[4] And that automobile was only the beginning. Just above the statue's head, as if to illustrate how closely agriculture, industry, and technology work together in Enterprise, hangs the town stoplight—not the variety with only red and green, but a fully modern apparatus complete with yellow caution light.

The people of Arlt's *Saturday in Enterprise*, however, are what make the mural live. Men, women, and children, all well dressed, gather in the main intersection to chat, to observe, to court or they move across it to shop. Saturday is a casual time: few of the men wear coats, some have their collars open. The farmers wear traditional overalls and straw hats. The townsmen wear suspenders unless they are young blades in pleated trousers. Two men, one black, one white, lean on the fence surrounding the Boll Weevil and people-watch, suggesting that in Enterprise, at least, blacks have "earned the right" to relax with the white folks of a Saturday, though the black does his watching from behind the statue while the white

---

3. "Recollections," paragraphs by Mrs. Fred Ray, Mrs. Fred Kelley, and Mr. and Mrs. Burney Reese as told to Rhonda Reese, in Adams (ed.), *The Enterprise Centennial*, n.p.

4. "Annual Highlights and Sidelights," *ibid.*, n.p.

leans against the fence on the audience's side. Under a lamppost in the right middle-ground, a dashing black man and saucy black woman appear to be making their Saturday night plans. As a matter of fact, the middle ground seems to be the designated area for blacks in Enterprise. They dress like the whites, their activities are the same as the whites'. They have the same half-holiday, the same money to spend downtown on Saturday, but they do not have the foreground. As usual, in the mural South, they are outnumbered by whites (about three to one here), but they are as modern and prosperous as their white neighbors are.

The whites have the foreground. All the people in this picture stand or strut in jaunty positions. All appear to be happy to be who they are, and doing what they do, but the whites have the foreground. A small overall-clad boy sells peanuts—boiled, of course—to a gaily dressed, package-laden woman and her husband, who digs deep into his pocket for money to buy one more frippery before they trundle home with their purchases. And on the other side of the square, the only person in the whole picture who does not seem delighted with her immediate lot is the girl child who tugs her mother toward the peanut vendor. Wearing Mary Jane shoes, a starched pink dress, and a bow in her brown sausage curls, the child is distinctly unhappy with her mother, who clearly intends to go in a different direction.

Enterprise, at least in Paul Arlt's mural, is the paradigm of the progressive southern small city, or the Platonic ideal that informs earthly representations of the ideal South. In 1935, Howard Odum had completed his monumental *Southern Regions of the United States*, in which he reported that though the South lagged behind the rest of the United States, southern growth in agriculture, education, industry, and economy had outstripped that of any other region. He concluded with the hope that the southern states, armed with new agricultural and technical knowledge, the help of a beneficent federal government, and agreement among themselves to plan for the future, would cooperate in a twelve-year plan to bring the South into parity with the rest of the nation.[5]

In the 1930s South, murals abounded celebrating the region's history—the great men who had grown up in the South, those other

5. Howard W. Odum, *Southern Regions of the United States* (Chapel Hill, 1936), argues throughout for regional planning in the South, but it is in the final chapter, "Toward Regional Planning," that he actually outlines a plan.

great men whose lives had touched the South, the wars the South had helped to win, the technological developments that had emanated from the South, and the treaties by which the South was wrested from older tribes of Americans. And there were the murals with more general historical themes—the settling of the South and the carving of a culture out of wilderness, the nostalgic views of the genteel way of life for which, rightly or wrongly, the South was given credit, steam-propelled river traffic, hoop skirts and top hats, buckskins and loincloths, mansions, wigwams and log cabins. And murals abounded that celebrated work in the cotton fields, at saw-mills and cotton mills, with livestock and sugarcane. Very serious pictures of southerners, these, wherein no worker had time to smile or money to purchase boiled peanuts. Southern workers—indeed, those in the nation, as far as post office murals were concerned—were so busy that they had no time to smile or enjoy leisure.

The past was celebrated in the murals, as was the present, but relatively few looked to the future—except perhaps obliquely in the ones that demonstrated how adversity had been overcome and thus suggested that present adversity would also disappear. Even fewer dared to suggest that leisure was an aspect of that future. The Enterprise mural was one. Although it was set in the present, the present is composed in part of future hopes—the young peanut salesman and the female child who pulls toward him might be the future entrepreneur and his genteel wife. The Saturday afternoon gaiety and confidence were more a dream for the future than a present reality. Even the prosperity in 1940 Enterprise was more a fantasy of future times based on wise past decisions than it was an actual reality for a town that, despite its reluctance to say so, was still climbing out of the depression and deprivation. The emphasis in Enterprise was pride in the past, the present, but, most of all, the future.

Hope for the future was also what buoyed citizens of Starke, Florida. Faced with two possibilities for murals based in the present, Starke's postmaster requested one that promised well-being in the future. Early in 1941, Elizabeth Terrell was invited to design a mural for Starke's post office. Despite the fact that much of Florida, even in the 1930s, was cosmopolitan rather than regional—both coasts were home as much to tourists as to Floridians—Starke, in the north central part of the peninsula, was southern. Its industry was turpentine, a staple that served much of the piney woods South, and Terrell's first inspiration was to do "a dramatic mural . . . from the subject of turpentine, depicting the chipping of the trees and the distillation of the sap against a background of Florida pines."[6]

In the meantime, another subject presented itself, and so did a second artist. It seems that in 1940, Camp Albert H. Blanding, seven miles east of Starke, had been converted from a sleepy National Guard camp into one of the nation's largest army training centers and as such was burgeoning into "Florida's third largest city."[7] The more startling growth, however, was in Starke. The influx of more than five thousand workers associated with the camp had more than quadrupled Starke's normal population of fifteen hundred. The town was so full that even an empty room above the post office had been fitted with cots and converted into a dormitory. Not to be outdone by the opportunists who always follow army installations, artist Sahl Swarz, who had been drafted and was stationed at Camp Blanding, wrote to a Section official about his own inspiration for a decoration appropriate to Starke's post office. "It occurred to me," he wrote, "that perhaps some New York artist may be invited to submit a design [Terrell was a New York artist] who has never been there, or who wouldn't come all the way down just to look at the Starke Post Office." He continued:

> No amount of research work in the New York Public Library could reveal the true character of Starke today. It has been converted from a quiet hamlet handling local farm and other produce such as turpentine . . . into a soldiers boom town. This all has been a windfall to the residents of Starke, who invariably are running shops and beer halls catering to the needs and pleasure of the service men.
>
> Being a part of all this, I realized that I had right at hand the material and the inspiration for the decoration of this particular Post Office.[8]

And with his letter Swarz sent his design. A taller-than-life soldier marches into the post office lobby. He is flanked by vignettes of pack-laden soldiers off on bivouac, soldiers firing howitzers and

6. Elizabeth Terrell to Postmaster, May 27, 1941, in Starke, Florida, file, Record Group 121, National Archives.

7. Lowell Clucas, "Defense Comes to Our Town," *Saturday Evening Post,* March 15, 1941, p. 13. All information on Camp Blanding's effects on Starke are taken from this article.

8. Sahl Swarz to Inslee Hopper, July 4, 1941, in Starke, Florida, file.

other cumbersome artillery, soldiers sitting at a bar, and soldiers entering an establishment labeled "Army Store"—presumably the PX. None of it except perhaps the six tall pines at the left and right extremities of the design and the bar that would spew forth drunken and rowdy soldiers had anything at all to do with the town of Starke. Even so, by July, 1941, Washington was abuzz with the possibility that the country would have to be defended, and the design struck the Section as a marvelous idea. Rowan, always the bureaucrat, was less enthusiastic about the red tape involved in overturning Terrell's appointment, but he compromised by suggesting that Terrell adopt the army camp motif for her design.

Swarz was correct when he suggested that "no amount of research work in the New York Public Library could reveal the true character of Starke today," but in her trip to the New York Public Library or from her own subscription to the *Saturday Evening Post*, Terrell had learned things about Starke that no amount of Saturday night bar-hopping could teach a soldier-artist. When the Section suggested that she submit a design based on Starke's proximity to Camp Blanding, Terrell quoted from a *Post* article to demonstrate why she would not use a military design for Starke:

> Unfortunately for Starke, Camp Blanding was designated a major defense project. . . . Now in the hue and cry of larger cities asking for Government aid in meeting housing problems and the like, Starke's plea for help has not been heard.
>
> An overtaxed sewer system is threatening an epidemic. The county and city jails are jammed. Rents have trebled and quadrupled. Money is being made hand over fist, it is true, but when you ask a local citizen how the boom has affected the lives of the residents he answers, "Lives? We don't have lives any more!" . . .
>
> Three-for-a-dime photographers, fortunetellers, dart-game, shooting-gallery and bowling alley operators set up their noisy emporiums around town. Gaunt country fiddlers, accordion players, the halt, the lame and the blind lined Call Street, Starke's main thoroughfare. Juke joints appeared over-night along roads dotted with hitch-hikers. Laborers drank themselves silly on pay-envelope cash and were packed like sardines into City Jailer Ben Rowe's four-man jail.[9]

9. Terrell to Edward Rowan, August 2, 1941, *ibid.* Terrell's quotation from Clucas accurately reflects the timbre of the article and the words are accurate. They are, however, a composite of statements scattered throughout the six-page article.

Not the stuff of which gratefully received post office murals are made. It was true that the military installation had brought unprecedented, even undreamed of, wealth into the area, but that was not an unmixed blessing. Merchants and vendors of services were getting rich, but not all of them liked the sacrifice that entailed: lack of time to spend with friends and family, constant noise and crowding, even loss of personal privacy as every citizen in Starke was pressed to take in boarders. And the wealth was not evenly distributed. Funds for services—schools, teachers, sewers, law enforcement officers, new housing—were usually not forthcoming and when they were available, there was nobody to hire to do the work. Everybody was employed by the government at Camp Blanding. Postmaster Fred Stump had his own problems. The *Post* reported that he had lost fifteen pounds the first three weeks handling the additional postal responsibility. It seems logical that he would not be eager to have the event commemorated on the wall over his door.

Terrell consulted Stump with her idea of what for the contemporary boom town was a picture from the past, the comparatively bucolic turpentine industry. He rejected that with a countersuggestion that would hark to the future, and not one that celebrated the military invasion either. Stump wanted a picture of reforestation— as important for Starke as armament was for the country, a drive that continued quietly in spite of the hustle and bustle of camp followers and inadequate housing. And Terrell's sensitivity resonated with Stump's choice; it had to do with Starke's future and the future of the South: "There is the chance that a mural of army life might not be applicable to Starke beyond the period of National Emergency. This section of the country from early days has depended mainly upon the distillation of turpentine, which commodity in turn is dependent upon the proper care and maintenance of the pine forests. Reforestation has been a vital problem in the South due to early destructive methods used to obtain the sap."[10]

Reforestation was indeed working well for Starke and Bradford County. Even in 1941, there were more of the pine trees on which the locals depended for their livelihood than there had been twenty years before, and the work continued. Terrell followed the post-

10. Terrell to Rowan, August 2, 1941, in Starke, Florida, file.

master's advice and designed a mural of reforestation that was gratefully received by the local paper: "Connoisseurs of art may see much more in the picture; but the average Bradford countian can easily discern workmen grubbing and burning stumps from old dead pines, and planting small pine saplings, so that future generations may 'rise up and call them blessed.' He may also see deer wandering around, presaging a national park with vast animal preserves."[11]

Depicting the community's monument to the pest that had brought about contemporary hopes for a prosperous future was the way one artist painted the future of a southern town. Showing quiet efforts to preserve the life and livelihood of a town after the end of a temporary scourge was another. And a third way to remind local residents of a promising future was to refer to a departed citizen who had become a monument in his own right because of his contributions to a town's future welfare. Such a mural was the subject of John T. Robertson's decoration for Nashville, Arkansas. Robertson's first idea was to do something with the folklore of the Arkansas Traveler. The artist did his research in the community, however, and he learned that residents wanted a mural grounded in their rapidly growing peach industry. In response to their wishes, the artist designed a mural that would show harvesting, spraying for pests, and planting new peach trees—a distinct salute to the prosperity to come.

When the Arkansas Nashvillians saw the design, they were pleased. They did, however, want something added. They asked their artist if he could include a portrait of Bert Johnson, the father of the peach industry in Arkansas. There was only one problem: Bert Johnson was dead. Trying to paint a recognizable portrait of a dead man from photographs caused Robertson some trepidation, especially since the particular photo he was offered had been taken the day of Johnson's death, but Robertson decided to try it to please his constituency. It seems that in late summer of 1938, Johnson had gone to Little Rock to send a basket of peaches by plane to President Roosevelt. He was photographed with the peaches at the airport. The peaches reached their destination, but on the way home, Bert Johnson was killed in an automobile crash. Memorial

11. "Beautiful Mural in Postoffice," unidentified clipping, n.d., in Starke, Florida, file.

89 / John T. Robertson, *Peach Growing*, Nashville, Ark., 1939

services were held for him at the 1939 peach festival shortly before Nashville's mural was installed.[12]

The mural in Nashville, Arkansas, is a fitting memorial to the father of the Arkansas peach industry, but more than that, it is a declaration of faith in the future of Arkansas peaches (Figure 89). The middle ground is filled with an endless peach orchard; the time is before the advent of spring foliage. Sturdy Arkansas men spray the trees with insecticide coursing through hoses attached to a blatantly "modern" technical apparatus. In the right foreground are several boxes brimming with ripe, juicy, pest-free peaches. Just behind them, two men pick this year's crop from a tree laden with the fruit. One of the pickers is himself a testament to the future. Not only is he virile, intent, and industrious; he is exceedingly young and has many years of peach raising ahead of him. At the other side of the mural, Bert Johnson plants a tree with the help of another young Arkansas farmer who will tend it after Johnson is gone.

The people of Nashville were delighted with the picture, and Robertson was delighted with the people: 90 percent of them, he reported, recognized the portrait, and both the local newspaper and the Texarkana *Gazette* carried stories on the mural. Not all artists who tried to paint portraits from photographs of the dead, however, were so successful. But then not all of them were as willing as Robertson was to try an obvious likeness. When Anne Poor con-

12. John T. Robertson to Rowan, November 25, 1938, August 8, 1939, both in Nashville, Arkansas, file, RG 121, NA.

tracted to paint the sweet potato industry for Gleason, Tennessee, she also agreed to include a portrait of the late "father" of sweet potato culture in the area. What neither the Section nor Gleason had counted on was her theory that "in mural decoration it was sometimes just as well to leave portraits more or less generalized in harmony with the other figures in the painting."[13] At least that is how she explained to the postmaster his inability to recognize Mr. Hawks in the completed mural.

The explanation must have worked because the postmaster and the town were pleased with their mural—a situation that could so easily have had another outcome during the early years of the war. Often, communities resented the government's spending money on murals when everything should go to the war effort. Gleason, however, shared with Starke, Florida, the desire to express faith in the community's future after the war was over. The mural cele-brates the shipping of the sweet potatoes, a particularly festive time in Gleason. In the background, protecting the town from out-side intrusion (whether Yankees or Germans), is a rendering of the actual Gleason railroad depot, sketched from life. And in front of it are many people involved in the sweet potato industry. The num-ber of young men is surprising, in the midst of a war, perhaps a sug-gestion that they would come home to raise the crop again. A more explicit reference to the future is the number of children in the pic-ture. At two different points in the design, girl children watch while their mothers work. And an equal number of preteen boys chat with the workers or themselves lift baskets of sweet potatoes. The dominant figure in the picture is at the extreme right. He of course is Mr. Hawks, and there is indeed an otherworldly quality about him as he passes on the lore of his calling to a younger man who kneels before him. For some reason, perhaps because she lived in New York, though it is late spring when the tubers are shipped, Poor has populated her picture with unfoliated trees. But that did not bother the locals—they were happy. The cash crop is indeed foliated, and the most unusual feature of the mural is that it is framed by a design of lushly producing sweet potato vines.

Agriculture and reforestation were important to the South, but the government's most ambitious investment in the South's future,

13. Anne Poor to Rowan, November 27, 1942, in Gleason, Tennessee, file, RG 121, NA.

and one that promoted the other two, was the Tennessee Valley Authority. The TVA was a project about which the South was ambivalent. When everything went well, most southerners were grateful; when there was scandal or when some particular dam project threatened to disrupt people's lives, then the TVA became the biggest carpetbagging scheme of the century. Howard Odum remarked: "In terminology the Valley and its Authority have ranged from the greatest national experiment in social and economic reconstruction to the pork barrel de luxe, 'a river basin draining the seven states, an authority draining forty-eight states.' The experiment is of the essence of Americanism; it is the quintessence of unamericanism. To the North it is sometimes seen as regional favoritism; to the South it has at times been characterized as federal dictation; yet in both North and South, it has appeared most often as a great and hopeful portent in the American scene."[14]

Whatever the politics, whatever the suspicions of the TVA, few seem to have had so many reservations that they refused to take advantage of the agency's flood control and conservation efforts, its offer of cheap electricity and its programs to control disease. Even so, relatively few murals expressly celebrated the TVA. Usually, if the TVA were alluded to in a mural, it was only that. A dam would be visible somewhere near the horizon (hidden in most southern murals) or wires to otherwise impoverished cabins would indicate that the REA, which brought TVA electricity to rural homes, was functioning. But three muralists created overt tributes to the TVA.

In Xavier Gonzales' finished creation for Huntsville, Alabama, one would be hard put to know that the subject was the TVA. In his initial design, the message is completely unintelligible (Figure 90). The first sketch, which was to go through five revisions before it was accepted, was judged by the Section to be more appropriate to a hotel lobby than to a federal building. The design is built around a frieze of symbolic figures such as the middle-aged female in transparent drapery who represents "Spiritual Values." She was apparently both too old and too symbolic for Rowan. He suggested that she should be "less lugubrious" and that she should be "a figure of great beauty and need not be associated with senility."[15] Next to

14. Odum, *Southern Regions of the United States*, 167.
15. Rowan to Xavier Gonzales, January 14, 1937, and undated draft [just before January 14, 1937], both in Huntsville, Alabama, file, RG 121, NA.

90 / Xavier Gonzales, design for Huntsville, Ala.

Spiritual Values but facing away from her is Mercury, his left arm outstretched and his left leg raised so high that he would surely fall except that his right hand rests on the shoulder of a less ethereal woman who shapes a vessel at a potter's wheel, "symbolizing the actual relationship between Art and Industry."[16] Beneath Mercury's toe, a figure of Agriculture laconically holds a leaf, revealed in later versions to be corn. In the crook of Mercury's knee, Industry lifts a mighty arm to hammer something glimmering on an anvil. In the center foreground sits Home, a concrete woman cradling a virtually unrecognizable lump of a baby. And in the center, a truly lugubrious woman, with melon breasts and a diaphanous costume, holds on her shoulder a container of fruit.

16. Information on the spiritual significance of this design is taken from "Prospectus for the Huntsville, Alabama, Court House and Post Office Mural Decoration," which Gonzales submitted with his design, after January 14, 1937, *ibid.*

The rest of the mural is more confusing than the figures. Above Mercury are symbols of contemporary technology—here a stylized airplane, there a skyscraper, elsewhere craggy cliffs and factory stacks. In the land and air part of the picture on the right, doves fly through a teardrop-shaped cloud and a square of starry sky represents night. The left side, the water side, is more interesting. Porpoises leap, water falls, waves heave, ships founder, rain rains, and gigantic droplets drop.

Rowan was gentle in his criticism; he had seen other work by Gonzales. He suggested that the central figures be put in a "less arbitrary setting." By the third attempt, Gonzales had anchored his grouping in less decorative and more recognizable forms. Gone were the mythical representations of the benefits of the TVA; they were replaced by dams, turbines, electrical towers, and—testimony to concrete realities—baskets of produce. He added a rampaging flood "in all its fury destroying everything in its path . . . only to be stopped by" not a TVA dam or a TVA floodwall but by "a hand of large proportions, which holds the sword of Justice." Of this image the artist wrote: "Allow me to say, that I am proud of using this symbol which so clearly expresses the function of justice as a protection of human life and property. All of this came into being because of a favorable decision of the Supreme Court toward this project." [17]

Perhaps—but to Rowan, the symbol was not all that clear. This design had to go and with it several things from the other one: Spiritual Values, for one, Mercury for another, and the airplane. Gonzales worked through two more designs before one was approved for the Huntsville Court House and Post Office (Figure 91). In number and arrangement, the figures in the final design are not too different from the originals. But they are much more "realistic." These figures are clearly people as earthlings know them. The baby could need changing at any minute. The woman will finish that pot and serve vegetables in it. Agriculture seriously examines a corn plant, and the smithy wields a practical hammer on a usable horseshoe. The woman in the center, now modestly clothed, holds on her shoulder a recognizable basket of produce. The background, too, is in the here and now. Fields, trees, and rock walls are clearly that. Not one but two TVA dams protect the figures from floods and

17. Gonzales to Rowan, January 25, 1937, *ibid.*

91 / Xavier Gonzales, *Tennessee Valley Authority*, Huntsville, Ala., 1937

provide cheap power. The waterway flowing from the mountains that block off the horizon is a recognizable Tennessee River, and amid the Huntsville factories is an accurate depiction of the First National Bank. Gonzales' interpretation of his creation has also descended from the sublime and ridiculous to the mundane and commonplace:

> The women represent work in the arts, motherhood and a happy home life, and the work of the young girl. One of the men is painted as he sits on a stump and holds two blades of a green corn stalk, symbolizing the growth of agriculture . . . by the scientific method. The blades are held in the hands of the man as if they were a book. Then the other male figure is painted as he holds a shop hammer in one hand, and a piece of iron on an anvil in the other. He symbolizes the activity in the various industries.
>
> Besides the five figures, a portion of the painting is devoted to the portrayal of farm fields in the valley, and to a few of the buildings in Huntsville. The land is painted in furrows with a series of curved lines representing the way to preserve farms from washing when they are

cultivated. . . . Outlining the top of the picture . . . is a dim line of mountainous territory, which enfolds the valley lands. One of the dams is painted as a reproduction of Wilson Dam. Huntsville buildings . . . in the picture . . . are The Times, Postoffice, First National Bank and others.[18]

Xavier Gonzales' mural tribute to the Tennessee Valley Authority in its final form did satisfy the people of Huntsville, Alabama, but the really successful statements of faith in a southern future with the TVA were in small towns. TVA murals for the Tennessee communities of Lenoir City and Newport received national recognition. That had to be a good sign for southern small towns that felt the sting of prejudice against the South and wished only to be a part of a growing nation.

Meriting only eight lines in the Federal Writers Project guide to Tennessee (not even one directing travelers to a sight worth seeing), Lenoir City must have been gratified when it was designated the Tennessee town for the Section's massive "Forty-eight States Competition," and even more gratified when the Chattanooga *Free Press* carried pictures of the new post office and reported that it would be "the repository for the winning mural in Tennessee."[19] Lenoir City Postmaster Harry M. Calloway took the time to write the government of his gratitude and his pleasure in the proposed subject, electrification. Then a conflict-of-interest controversy delayed the mural by nearly two years. It seems that the Tennessee winner, David Stone Martin, was employed by the TVA, which objected to his taking another government contract. There followed lengthy correspondence between Martin, the Section, the TVA, and several other government agencies until the TVA finally learned that Martin won his commission in a competition. That seemed to put a different light on things. The artist was apparently not moonlighting at all—he had won a contest.[20] Thus, finally, Martin was authorized to finish the Lenoir City mural.

18. "Hanging of Large Mural in U.S. Courtroom Finished: Tulane Art Professor Hangs His Job in Courtroom," Huntsville *Times,* October 24, 1937, clipping, *ibid.*

19. Federal Writers Project, *Tennessee: A Guide to the State* (New York, 1939), 305; "Lenoir City Mural Repository," Chattanooga *Free Press,* [1939], clipping, in Lenoir City, Tennessee, file, RG 121, NA.

20. The Lenoir City file in the National Archives is in disarray—apparently a problem that dates back to Section days, since the Archives very strictly preserves the original order of documents. Since much of this file is copied from letters not actually received in the Section and since other documents are undated, the exact

92 / David Stone Martin, *Electrification*, Lenoir City, Tenn., 1941

What appeared on the wall of the Lenoir City Post Office was a mural of strong Tennessee men putting up power lines so that electricity and all that its presence implied were assured for the future of rural Tennessee (Figure 92). Perpendicular scaffolds—shaped very like football goalposts—to support the lines and the transformers march to the picture's vanishing point in the distance. In the foreground, the scale of these supports and of the project to electrify the Tennessee Valley is clearly indicated as a workman prepares to set in motion the process that will raise a single structure many times his height. In the background, two minuscule figures grasp the other end of the rope with which the scaffold is to be raised and another operates the winch on which the line itself is wound. In the lower right corner, two workmen assemble transformers presumably to be mounted on the next support. And to be certain that viewers know this work is for the future, a woman and her son stroll along the line of poles. Despite the ten figures in the mural, the overall impression is clean, angular, mechanical. The TVA is a well-oiled machine that will continue to serve the area long after the present workmen have departed.

People in Lenoir City celebrated their mural—the Rotary Club, for instance, gave a banquet in honor of the artist and his wife. A chemistry professor at the University of Tennessee asked for the

order of the controversy is difficult to reconstruct. What is abundantly clear, however, is that Martin's having won his commission in competition was revealed late in the conflict because no one guessed that it would make a difference in the TVA's attitude. It is also not clear what position Martin had with the TVA. It does not seem that he served as an artist.

cartoon, which he wanted to display in his lab. And then when the mural was selected as a frontispiece in the nationally circulated *Public Utilities Fortnightly*, the residents must have felt that Lenoir City, at least, had finally been restored to the Union.[21]

Newport, Tennessee, just over half the size of Lenoir City, merited nearly a page in the FWP guide and more mural space as well. Situated in the Great Smoky Mountain foothills, its scenery was beautiful, and founded in 1789 (a century before Lenoir City), it offered several subjects for history paintings. Despite the town's historical possibilities, artist Minna Citron, appointed on the merit of her losing entry in the Vicksburg, Mississippi, competition, chose to paint the future. For a mere $650, a meager sum for a large work even in 1940, she painted the whole length of the wall above the post office grilles.[22]

In the long, narrow mural, a farmer on a futuristic tractor cultivates lushly producing fields, workmen in a richly appointed automated factory prepare canned food for market (probably vegetables canned by Stokely Brothers, who had their home office in Newport), cows fatten and relieve themselves at a futuristic carousel with an electronic apparatus to shovel excrement automatically, a sow feeds her recent litter, and a second farmer rides on the functional trailer of an even more elaborate tractor-cultivator rig driven by a third farmer just out of sight of the viewer. And above all the activity, automation, and progress hang TVA power lines. The numerous TVA towers march over the mountains. In the left background can be seen a TVA dam, and the Great Smoky Mountains protect it all from outside interference.

While the artist was in Newport installing her creation, she was entertained at the mayor's house and when she left, he wrote her a letter: "And too, I do not know when any 'furriner' (as the mountain people would say) has captured our hearts as you have. You have made many friends while here, and your interest in the people of this Section and the friendships made will further endear the murals to us. We shant forget your kindness and patience in explaining your work to all of us who asked so many questions."[23]

21. David Stone Martin to Edward Bruce, July 30, 1940, A. Knighton, Editorial Assistant, *Public Utilities Fortnightly* (offices in Washington, D.C.), to Forbes Watson, April 15, 1940, both in Lenoir City, Tennessee, file.
22. Federal Writers Project, *Tennessee*, 431.
23. Mayor of Newport to Minna Citron, November 11, 1940, in Newport, Tennessee, file, RG 121, NA. The letter was retyped for the Section file.

The mayor's words and the community's regard would have been reward enough for Minna Citron and for the Section; and the mural itself would have been enough for Newport. The mayor's letter and the mural expressed a town's satisfaction with its government and its confident attitude toward its future. But a second reward was to follow, one that both the town and the artist must have gloried in. There were important implications about the South's place in the nation when Citron's mural sketch was selected to illustrate a major magazine article by TVA director David E. Lilienthal. It could have been enough for Newport's mural to be featured alongside Lilienthal's article in *Survey Graphic: Magazine of Social Interpretation,* but the legend beneath the picture and the contents of the article said much that the South had been trying to say for years. The legend said: "The new face of the TVA region. Farms and industries show the effect of cheap electricity, refreshed soil, local enterprise."[24] The South had something to show the nation about prosperity.

In the first part of his article, Lilienthal both celebrated and vilified centralization. Government authority saw to it that everybody had the same rights and privileges. Centralization in business allowed the whole country to benefit from the same high quality in goods and services. In southern terms, Lilienthal was saying that with centralized planning and authority, the South did not need to play a secondary role, or as Erskine Caldwell had it, to accept the hand-me-down, to sit at second table: "And for the most part people enjoy the uniformity which the change has brought. Thanks to nationwide enterprises, window gazers can see the same goods displayed in similar windows from Maine to California; and everywhere in these United States people are reading the same magazines on the same day, listening to the same programs on the radio, or going to see the same movies. People like that." Southerners liked that. They read *Time, Life,* and the *Saturday Evening Post* just like other Americans. They thrilled to John Ford and David O. Selznick movies, and they listened with everybody else to "Amos 'n' Andy." They bought their radios and their clothes from Sears-Roebuck and Montgomery Ward. Centralized *authority* in the government and in business was a good thing. On the other hand, centralized *ad-*

24. David E. Lilienthal, "The TVA and Decentralization," *Survey Graphic,* June, 1940, pp. 336–37.

ministration, according to Lilienthal, was bad. It deprived citizens in a democracy of their democratic rights to self-control and to the benefits of their labor. "The people of this country have a right to demand their federal government guarantee to them the benefits of advancements in science and research; they have a right to demand protection from economic abuses beyond the power of their political units to control. And they have the further right to insist that the methods of administration used to carry out the very laws enacted for their individual welfare will not atrophy the human resources of their democracy."[25]

Centralized administration in government and business tended to weaken the ability of the administered to act on their own behalf. It allowed profits of the businesses to be siphoned into the central countinghouses and benefits of government projects to accrue to Washington. Enter the TVA: it guaranteed the rights available only through centralized authority, and as the first experiment in decentralized administration, it was putting the profits, the benefits where they belonged—in the states, in the communities, with the people. And more important to the citizens of Newport, Tennessee, and other parts of the South, the TVA was putting those benefits squarely in the South. "We must recognize," wrote Lilienthal, "that a central government, like a business empire centrally managed, is bound to suffer from lack of knowledge of local conditions and parochial customs. And when differences in local and regional customs are forgotten, statutes seem irrelevant or harsh."[26]

That is exactly why in the 1930s, such politicians as Huey Long, Theodore Bilbo, and Eugene ("Wild Man from Sugar Creek") Talmadge were so successful. When a federal government and Yankee capitalists forgot the differences in local and regional customs—or seemed to—voters looked for someone who would not forget because those local and regional customs were his own. And that is what the South tried to tell the Section of Fine Arts for seven years. When the Section appointed artists who were cognizant of local customs or who, like Minna Citron for Newport, Tennessee; Elizabeth Terrell for Starke, Florida; and Paul Arlt for Enterprise, Alabama, cared enough to learn them, when it made good on its expressed goal to decentralize administration of government art, the gentle

25. *Ibid.,* 335.
26. *Ibid.,* 336.

reconstruction implicit in government patronage of art for southern federal buildings successfully carried the message of the edify-
ing nature of fine American art to the byways of the South. Any
reconstruction has one foot in the present. The first Reconstruction of the South tried to stop (real or imagined) rebellion in the
South and to provide for the newly freed blacks. The second one
tried to do almost the same thing—to stop rebellion against the Supreme Court decisions in the 1950s and 1960s and to provide for
the newly integrated (legally, anyway) blacks. The gentle reconstruction in the 1930s was another story. Like the consensus historians and the myth-and-symbol students of American culture, it
often tried to assert that there were no cultural differences between
American regions that a good artist could not overcome with good
art. It tried to assert the cultural status quo while it lauded technological progress. While promoting different subjects for murals
in different regions, it often tried to ignore the more significant
local and regional customs that Lilienthal was concerned about.
And when it sent uninformed artists into regions with which they
were culturally at odds, it seemed to try once again to keep the
South out of the Union.

When, however, the Section of Fine Arts matched artist, theme,
and community, it asserted the other purpose of reconstruction.
Every reconstruction has one foot in the present, but the other foot
of every reconstruction is firmly planted in the future. When the
Section and the artists it hired painted pictures of a southern future
that was both American in every way but still cognizant of those
regional cultural differences, it made a tiny step toward a positive
and gentle reconstruction of the South. For De Witt, Arkansas,
William Traher painted a mural based both in the present and the
future, one that was cognizant of the pride and the prejudices of
the South (Figure 93). Before he began his mural, he got to know
the community and its culture. Selected on the basis of his competent entry in a Colorado mural competition, Traher traveled to De
Witt and lived there three weeks, "long enough to make piles of
sketches and to sound out the townspeople on their preferences
regarding the subject of the mural." During his visit, the artist
learned much about the town and he learned to respect its people
and its way of life. No efforts would he make at a jarring reconstruction of the South into the North's own image. Rather, when

93 / William Traher, *Portrait of Contemporary De Witt,* De Witt, Ark., 1941

he wrote of his plans for the mural, he made a statement that might have served as a model for those who would paint the South for the South—and for those who would appoint painters for the South:

> DeWitt is a farm community. . . . It is flat country—plains divided by dense woods like huge hedges. The town is built within such a wood. It is a placid place—more so than most small towns because it is southern, more so than most southern towns because it is in Arkansas. Then, too, no one can be boisterous nor busy in a forest. Even the dogs respect this mood. . . .
>
> And so should I. No dramatics, sweeping rhythms, struggling forms, nor violent contrast of design belong in a portrait of DeWitt. The extremely literal minded citizens will fail to understand and resent obvious distortion or simplification. Rather I must rely on quiet literal representation of significant subject matter, and the handsome texture and pattern of such commonplace things as weathered cabins and massed trees to make the mural interesting.[27]

Traher and the townspeople he consulted agreed on a portrait of contemporary De Witt, and Traher returned to Denver to work on his design. He decided on a series of three panels as opposed to the usual long narrow one, for architectural reasons, he said. It is possible that, because of the respect he had for De Witt, he was subconsciously inspired to keep certain aspects of the community's

27. William Traher to Rowan, July 5, 1940, in De Witt, Arkansas, file, RG 121, NA.

life completely separate. There is a panel for the white community, one for the black, and a third, separating the other two, for agriculture and industry. The whole design is clean, orderly, spare—and placid. Thus, Traher suggested the region's distinctive traits and, at the same time, a South with a technological and agricultural future not terribly different from the future on which the whole country placed its hopes. The possibilities for contemporary De Witt are limitless. So are they for the children Traher features in the mural.

And so were the possibilities for a South electrified by the TVA, enriched by two-armed farming and crop rotation, reconstructed by a central government willing to decentralize administration—a South being gently reconstructed from within as well as without.

APPENDIX / LOCATIONS OF SECTION ARTWORKS IN THE SOUTH

Every time I speak about the murals, some murals, or even one mural, whether the audience be scholars, art historians, or the general public, one question is bound to arise. That question is, "Where can I see some of these murals around here?" Assuming readers of this book are no less curious, I thought it wise to publish such a list, despite inevitable inaccuracies.

Any list of Section of Fine Arts artworks and their locations must, of necessity, have errors. The only list compiled during the short-lived existence of the agency (*American Art Annual*, 1941–42) was itself incomplete, since it covered only from the Section's beginnings until some indeterminate time early in 1940. While the list compiled by Karel Yasko during his tenure as "Counselor for the Fine Arts" in the General Services Administration (ending with his death in 1985) includes many of the projects after 1941, it misses some of the earlier works, many of the later ones, and in most cases, is not up to date on their contemporary whereabouts. Even the Section files themselves are incomplete for 1942 through 1943, when staff had been cut and the agency was rushing to complete commissioned works before its termination to make way for the war effort. While the list in Marlene Park and Gerald E. Markowitz, *Democratic Vistas: Post Offices and Public Art in the New Deal* (Philadelphia, 1984), represents excellent archival research, it is based on sources available in the District of Columbia and little fieldwork outside that area. Even so, they have unearthed some information that I have not. Rita Moroni, Postal Service Historian, is doing her best to track down the "final disposition" (present whereabouts) of New Deal Post Office artwork, but her resources are limited and she is often dependent on information supplied by itinerant researchers such as myself. As a matter of fact, I would appreciate hearing from anyone who knows anything about any of the murals including whether the one in your hometown is still there.

Meanwhile, this list represents my best knowledge of the locations and condition of the murals installed in the southern and border states. Unless otherwise stated, the work of art listed remains in the original building and the building is still the community's post office. An asterisk after the date indicates that I have personally verified the location and condition of the mural. Two asterisks indicate that the material relies on the research of Park and Markowitz.

Community	Artist	Date	Comments
Alabama			
Alexander City	Frank Epping	1941	Three terra-cotta reliefs
Atmore	Anne Goldthwaite	1938	
Bay Minette	Hilton Leech	1939	
Brewton	John Von Wicht	1939	Missing**
Enterprise	Paul Arlt	1941*	Mural remains in place; building is now public library
Eutaw	Robert Gwathmey	1941	
Fairfield	Frank and Mary Anderson	1938	
Fort Payne	Harwood Steiger	1938	
Haleyville	Hollis Holbrook	1940*	
Hartselle	Lee R. Warthen	1941	
Huntsville	Xavier Gonzales	1937*	
Luverne	Arthur Getz	1942	
Monroeville	A. L. Bairnsfeather	1939	
Montevallo	William S. McCall	1939	
Oneonta	Aldis B. Browne	1939	
Opp	Hans Mangelsdorf	1940	Wood relief
Ozark	Kelly Fitzpatrick	1938	
Phenix City	Kelly Fitzpatrick	1939	
Russellville	Conrad Albrizzio	1937*	
Scottsboro	Constance Ortmayer	1940	Plaster relief
Tuscumbia	Jack McMillen	1939	
Tuskegee	Anne Goldthwaite	1937	

Continued on next page

Community	Artist	Date	Comments
Arkansas			
Benton	Julius Woeltz	1942	Mural remains in place; building now Federal Building**
Berryville	Daniel Olney	1940	Sculpture
Clarksville	Mary May Purser	1939	Missing**
Dardanelle	Ludwig Mactarian	1939	
De Queen	Henry Simon	1942	
De Witt	William Traher	1941	
Heber Springs	H. Louis Freund	1939	
Lake Village	Avery Johnson	1941	
Magnolia	Joe Jones	1938	
Monticello	Berta Margoulies	1941	Three terra-cotta reliefs
Morrilton	Richard Sargent	1939	
Nashville	John T. Robertson	1939	
Osceola	Orville Carroll	1939*	
Paris	Joseph P. Vorst	1940	
Piggott	Dan Rhodes	1941	
Pocahontas	H. Louis Freund	1939	
Siloam Springs	Bertrand Adams	1940	
Springdale	Natalie Henry	1940	
Van Buren	E. Martin Hennings	1940	
Wynne	Ethel Magafan	1940*	
Florida			
Arcadia	Constance Ortmayer	1939	Sculpture
De Funiak Springs	Thomas I. Laughlin	1942	
Fort Pierce	Lucile Blanch	1938	
Jasper	Pietro Lazzari	1942	
Lake Wales	Denman Fink	1942	
Madison	George Snow Hill	1940	
Miami	Denman Fink	1940	
Court House	Alexander Sambugnac	1938	Two stone reliefs
Miami Beach	Charles R. Hardman	1940	

Continued on next page

Community	Artist	Date	Comments
Milton	George Snow Hill	1941	
Palm Beach	Charles Rosen	1938	Three panels
Perry	George Snow Hill	1938	
Sebring	Charles R. Knight	1942	Mural remains in place; building now city hall**
Starke	Elizabeth Terrell	1942	
Tallahassee	Edouard Buk Ulreich	1939	Eight panels
West Palm Beach	Stevan Dohanos	1940	Six panels; mural moved to new post office
Georgia			
Adel	Alice Flint	1941*	
Atlanta			
Techwood	Daniel Boza	1936	No longer extant
Homes Housing	Earl J. Neff	1937	No longer extant
Project	Ahron Ben-Schmuel	1936	Sculpture
University Homes Housing Project	Orville Carroll	1937	No longer extant
Augusta	William Dean Fausett	1939	
Blakely	D. Putnam Brinley	1938	
Cairo	Paul L. Gill	1938	
Cochran	Ilse Erythropel	1940*	Terra-cotta relief
College Park	Jack McMillen	1938	
Commerce	Philip Guston	1938*	
Conyers	Elizabeth Terrell	1940*	Mural moved to railroad station converted to community center
Cornelia	Charles T. Henry	1939*	
Cuthbert	Carlo Ciampaglia	1939	
Decatur	Paul Rohland	1938	
Eastman	Arthur E. Schmalz	1938*	
Gainesville	Daniel Boza	1936	
Greensboro	Carson Davenport	1939	
Hartwell	Orlin E. Clayton	1939	

Continued on next page

Community	Artist	Date	Comments
Jackson	Philip Evergood	1940*	
Jesup	David Hutchinson	1938	
Lawrenceville	Andree Ruellan	1942	Now at Fine Arts and Preservation, General Services Administration**
Louisville	Abraham Harriton	1941	
Lyons	Albino Manca	1942	Terra-cotta relief**
McRae	Oliver M. Baker	1939*	Missing
Manchester	Erwin Springweiler	1941	Mahogany relief
Monticello	Beata Beach Porter	1938*	
Pelham	Georgina Klitgard	1941	
Rockmart	Reuben Gambrell	1941	
Rome	Peter Blume	1943	
Summerville	Doris Lee	1939	
Swainsboro	Edna Reindel	1939	
Sylvania	Caroline S. Rohland	1941*	
Sylvester	Chester J. Tingler	1939*	
Vidalia	Daniel Celentano	1938	
Warrenton	Arnold Friedman	1940	
Winder	Marion Sanford	1939	Sculpture
Wrightsville	Earl N. Thorp	1940	Cast stone relief
Kentucky			
Anchorage	Loren R. Fisher	1942	
Berea	Frank Long	1940*	
Bowling Green P.O. and Court House	Edward Laning	1942	
Campbellsville	Bert Mullins	1940	Two murals; missing**
Corbin	Alice Dinneen	1940*	New P.O. mural in place in old P.O. converted to city offices
Covington P.O. and Court House	Carl L. Schmitz	1940	Limestone reliefs

Continued on next page

Community	Artist	Date	Comments
Elizabethtown		*	Mural remains in place; building now municipal library
Flemingsburg	Lucile Blanch	1943	
Fort Thomas	Lucienne Bloch	1942	
Greenville	Allan Gould	1940	Six panels
Hardinsburg	Nathaniel Koffman	1942	
Hickman	William L. Bunn	1940	
Hodgenville	Schomer Lichtner	1943	
Jenkins	F. Jean Thalinger	1943	Terra-cotta reliefs
Lexington Court House	Ward Lockwood	1938*	
Louisville	Frank Long	1937*	New P.O. Ten murals in place in old P.O. converted to Federal Office Building
	Orville Carroll	1937	Mentioned on 1941 list; unable to locate murals or records of them
	Henry M. Mayer	1936	
Morehead	Frank Long	1939*	New P.O. Mural remains in old building with protected status; future tenants must leave it in place
Morganfield	Bert Mullins	1939	
Paducah	John Folinsbee	1939	Two murals
Pineville	Edward B. Fern	1942	
Princeton	Robert Purdy	1939	
Springfield	Richard Davis	1941*	Limestone reliefs
Williamsburg	Alois Fabrey	1939	
Williamstown	Romuald Kraus	1942	Terra-cotta relief
Louisiana			
Abbeville	Louis Raynaud	1939*	
Arabi	Alice Flint	1939	
Arcadia	Allison B. Curry	1942	

Continued on next page

Community	Artist	Date	Comments
Bunkie	Caroline Rohland	1939	
Covington	Xavier Gonzales	1939	
De Ridder	Conrad Albrizzio	1936	
Eunice	Laura B. Lewis	1941*	
Ferriday	Stuart R. Purser	1941*	
Gretna	Stuart R. Purser	1939	
Hammond	Xavier Gonzales	1937	Removed**
Haynesville	Joseph Pistey, Jr.	1939	
Jeanerette	Hollis Holbrook	1941	
Lake Providence	Ethel Edwards	1942	
Leesville	Duncan Ferguson	1939	Terra-cotta relief
Many	Julius Struppeck	1941	Sculpture
New Orleans			
Federal Office	Gifford Proctor	1941	Sculpture
Building	Karl Lang	1942	Limestone relief
	Armin A. Scheler	1941	Limestone relief
Oakdale	Harry Lane	1939	
Rayville	Elsie Driggs	1939	
St. Martinville	Minetta Good	1940*	New P.O. Four wall decorations removed when old P.O. closed; wherabouts unknown
Tallulah	Francesca Negueloua	1938*	Mural removed; building now city Welfare Building
Ville Platte	Paul Rohland	1939	
Vivian	John Tatschl	1941	Three walnut reliefs
Winnsboro	Datus F. Myers	1939	
Maryland			
Aberdeen	Henri Brenner	1938	Sculpture
Baltimore			
Catonsville	Avery Johnson	1942*	Several panels; undergoing restoration
Branch			
Bel Air	William Calfee	1938	
Bethesda	Robert F. Gates	1939	

Continued on next page

Community	Artist	Date	Comments
Elkton	Alexander Clayton	1941	In storage**
Ellicott City	Peter DeAnna	1942*	Two panels
Hagerstown	Frank Long	1938*	Three panels
Hyattsville	Eugene Kingman	1938	
Laurel	Mitchell Jamieson	1939	
Pocomoke City	Perna Krick	1940	
Rockville	Judson Smith	1939	
Salisbury	Jacob Getlar Smith	1939*	Two murals
Silver Spring	Nikolai Cikovsky	1937	
Towson	Nikolai Cikovsky	1939*	Series of murals
Upper Marlboro	Mitchell Jamieson	1938	
Mississippi			
Amory	John McCrady	1939*	
Batesville	Eve Kottgen	1942	
Bay St. Louis	Louis Raynaud	1938*	New P.O.; mural remains in old building with protected status; future tenants must leave it in place
Booneville	Stefan Hirsch	1943*	
Carthage	Peter Dalton	1941	
Columbus	Beulah Bettersworth	1940*	
Forest	Julien Binford	1941*	
Hazlehurst	Auriel Bessemer	1939	
Houston	Byron Burford, Jr.	1941	
Indianola	Beulah Bettersworth	1939	Destroyed**
Jackson P.O. and Court House	Simka Simkhovitch	1938*	Mural in courtroom; draped in late 1960s (content considered racially offensive)
Leland	Stuart R. Purser	1940	
Louisville	Karl Wolfe	1938*	
Macon	Douglass Crockwell	1944	

Continued on next page

Community	Artist	Date	Comments
Magnolia	John H. Fyfe	1939 1941	Two murals
New Albany	Robert Cleaver Purdy	1939*	
Newton	Franklin and Mary Boggs	1942*	
Okolona	Harold Egan	1939*	Fresco painted over decades ago
Pascagoula	Lorin Thompson	1939*	Mural moved to new P.O.
Picayune	Donald H. Robertson	1940	
Pontotoc	Joseph Pollet	1939*	
Ripley	George Aarons	1939*	Bas relief
Vicksburg P.O. and Court House	H. Amiard Oberteuffer	1939	Mural in courtroom
Missouri			
Bethany	Joseph P. Vorst	1942	
Canton	Jessie Hull Mayer	1940	
Cassville	Edward Winter	1941	Porcelain enamel murals
Charleston	Joe Jones	1939*	
Clinton	H. Louis Freund	1936	
Columbia	Edouard Buk Ulreich	1937	Two murals; removed**
Dexter	Joe Jones	1941	
Eldon	Frederick Shane	1941	Two murals
Fredericktown	James B. Turnbull	1939	
Higginsville	Jac T. Bowen	1942	
Jackson	James B. Turnbull	1940*	
La Plata	Emma L. Davis	1939	
Lee's Summit	Ted Gilien	1940	
Maplewood	Carl C. Mose	1942	Wood relief
Marceline	Joseph Meerts	1938	
Monett	James McCreery	1939	
Mt. Vernon	Joseph Meerts	1940	
Palmyra	James Penney	1942	

Continued on next page

Community	Artist	Date	Comments
Paris	Fred G. Carpenter	1940	
Pleasant Hill	Tom Lea	1939	
St. Joseph	Gustaf Dalstrom	1941*	Twelve panels
St. Louis	Edward Millman	1942	
	Mitchell Siporin	1942	
Clayton Branch	Daniel Rhodes	1942	Moved to Des Moines, Iowa**
University Branch	Trew Hocker	1940	
Wellston Station	Lumen Winter	1939	
Sullivan	Lawrence Adams	1942	
Union	James Penney	1941	
Vandalia	Joseph P. Vorst	1939	
Windsor	H. Louis Freund	1938	
North Carolina			
Albemarle	Louis Ribak	1939	
Beaufort	Simka Simkhovitch	1940	Four panels
Belmont	Peter De Anna	1940	
Boone	Alan Tomkins	1940	
Burlington	Arthur Bairnsfather	1940	
Canton	Sam Bell	1941	Seven terra-cotta reliefs
Chapel Hill	Dean Cornwell	1941	
Dunn	Paul Rudin	1939	Sculpture
Elkin	Anita Weschler	1939	Sculpture
Forest City	Duane Champlain	1939	Plaster relief
Gastonia	Francis Speight	1938	
Hamlet	Nena de Brennecke	1942	Three mahogany reliefs
Kings Mountain	Verona Burkhard	1941	
Laurinburg	Agnes Tait	1941*	Unceremoniously ripped from wall in early 1980s; resides in bad condition in National Museum of American Art Storage

Continued on next page

Community	Artist	Date	Comments
Leaksville	Ruth N. Greacen	1941	Sculpture
Lincolnton	Richard Jansen	1938	
Louisburg	Richard Kenah	1939	
Madison	Jean Watson	1940	
Marion	Bruno Piccirelli	1939	Sculpture
Mebane	Margaret C. Gates	1941	Destroyed; copy by Henry D. Rodd installed in 1964**
Mooresville	Alicia Weincek	1938	
Morganton	Dean Cornwell	1938	Two murals
New Bern	David Silvette	1938	Three murals
Red Springs	John DeGroot, Jr.	1941	Three murals
Reidsville	Gordon Samstag	1938	
Roanoke Rapids	Charles Ward	1938	Missing**
Rockingham	Edward Laning	1937	
Roxboro	Allan Gould	1938	Mural remains in place; building now Piedmont Technical Institute**
Sanford	Pietro Lazzari	1938	
Siler City	Maxwell B. Starr	1942	
Southern Pines	Joseph Presser	1943	
Wake Forest	Harold Egan	1941	
Wallace	G. Glen Newell	1941	
Warrenton	Alice Dineen	1938	
Weldon	Jean de Marco	1940	Plaster relief
Whiteville	Roy Schatt	1941	
Williamston	Philip Von Saltza	1940	
Wilmington	William F. Pfohl	1940	
	Thomas Lo Medico	1937	Eight plaster reliefs
South Carolina			
Aiken			
Court House	Stefan Hirsch	1938*	Mural in courtroom; draped when court is in session; specific visiting hours provided

Continued on next page

Community	Artist	Date	Comments
Anderson	Arthur Covey	1940*	Building converted for federal offices; mural remains but lower part has been covered and retouched by unknown hands
Bamberg	Dorothea Mierisch	1939*	
Batesburg	Irving A. Block	1941*	
Bishopville	Hans E. Prehn	1942*	
Chesterfield	Bruno Mankowski	1939*	Plaster relief
Clemson	John Carroll	1941*	New P.O. mural moved to Sikes Hall, Clemson University
Easley	Renzo Fenci	1942*	Terra-cotta relief; mural remains in place; building now Lyday Optometrics; Dr. Lyday pledges to preserve relief for posterity
Greer	Winfield R. Walkley	1940*	New P.O. Mural remains in building, now Greer City Hall
Kingstree	Arnold Friedman	1939*	
Mullins	Lee Gatch	1940*	Mural mysteriously disappeared
Summerville	Bernadine Custer	1939*	New P.O. Mural remains on original wall; building now Department of Public Works
Walterboro	Sheffield Kagy	1938*	New P.O. Mural on original wall; building now Cannaday Real Estate Agency
Ware Shoals	Alice R. Kindler	1939*	
Winnsboro	Auriel Bessemer	1938*	
Woodruff	Abraham Lishinsky	1940*	

Continued on next page

Community	Artist	Date	Comments
Tennessee			
Bolivar	Carl Nyquist	1941	
Camden	John H. Fyfe	1938	
Chattanooga			
P.O. and Court House	Hilton Leech	1937	
"New" P.O.	Leopold Scholz	1938	Sculpture
Clarksville	F. Luis Mora	1938	Destroyed**
Clinton	Horace Day	1940	
Columbia			
P.O. and	Henry Billings	1942	
Court House	Signey Waugh	1941	Sculpture
Crossville	Marion Greenwood	1940	
Dayton	Bertram Hartman	1939	
Decherd	Enea Biafora	1940	
Dickson	Edwin Boyd Johnson	1939	
Dresden	Minetta Good	1938	
Gleason	Anne Poor	1942	
Greenville			
P.O. and Court House	William Zorach	1940	Two wood reliefs
Jefferson City	Charles Child	1941	
Johnson City	Wendell Jones	1940	Missing**
La Follette	Dahlov Ipcar	1939	
Lenoir City	David Stone Martin	1940*	
Lewisburg	John H. R. Pickett	1938	
Lexington	Grace Greenwood	1940	
Livingston	Margaret C. Chisholm	1940	
McKenzie	Karl Oberteuffer	1938	
Manchester	Minna Citron	1942	
Mount Pleasant	Eugene Higgins	1942	
Nashville	Belle Kinney	1940	Sculpture; missing**
Newport	Minna Citron	1940	Now in DAR Museum**
Ripley	Marguerite Zorach	1940	

Continued on next page

Community	Artist	Date	Comments
Rockwood	Christian Heinrich	1939	Terra-cotta relief
Sweetwater	Thelma Martin		
Texas			
Alice	Warren Hunter	1939	
Alpine	Jose Moya del Pino	1940	
Alvin	Loren Mozley	1942	Building converted to new use; mural stored in basement**
Amarillo	Julius Woeltz	1941	Several panels remain in place; building converted to Federal Building
Anson	Jenne Magafan	1941	
Arlington	Otis Dozier	1941	
Big Spring	Peter Hurd	1938	Mural in place; building converted to public library**
Borger	Jose Aceves	1939	Mural now in Hutchinson County Museum**
Brady	Gordon K. Grant	1940	
Brownfield	Frank Mechau	1940	
Bryan	William Gordon Huff	1941	Plaster relief
Caldwell	Suzanne Scheuer	1939	
Canyon	Francis Ankrom	1938	Missing**
Center	Edward Chavez	1941	
Clifton	Ila McAfee	1941	
College Station	Victor Arnatoff	1938	Missing**
Conroe	Nicholas Lyon	1938	Destroyed**
Cooper	Lloyd Goff	1939	
Corpus Christi	Howard Cook	1941	Remains in original location; converted to Nueces County Courthouse**

Continued on next page

Community	Artist	Date	Comments
Dallas			
Parcel Post	Peter Hurd	1940	Two panels remain in original location; converted to Terminal Annex Building**
Decatur	Ray Strong	1939	
Eastland	Suzanne Scheuer	1938	
Edinburg	Ward Lockwood	1940*	Missing
El Campo	Milford Zornes	1940	In storage**
Electra	Allie Tennant	1940	Plaster reliefs
Elgin	Julius Woeltz	1940	
El Paso	Tom Lea	1938	Two panels
Farmersville	Jerry Bywaters	1941	
Fort Worth	Frank Mechau	1940	Three panels
Fredericksburg	Otis Dozier	1942	
Gatesville	Joe De Yong	1939	
Giddings	Otis Dozier	1939	
Goose Creek	Barse Miller	1938	
Graham	Alexandre Hogue	1939	
Hamilton	Ward Lockwood	1942	
Henderson	Paul Ninas	1937	Destroyed**
Hereford	Enid Bell	1941	Wood relief
Houston			
Federal	Jerry Bywaters	1941	Two panels
Building	Alexandre Hogue	1941	Two panels
	William McVey	1941	Sculpture
Jasper	Alexander Levin	1939	
Kaufman	Margaret A. Dobson	1939	Covered**
Kenedy	Charles Campbell	1939	
Kilgore	Xavier Gonzales	1941	Four panels
La Grange	Tom E. Lewis	1939	Missing**
Lamesa	Fletcher Martin	1940	Remains in original position; building converted to Federal Building**
Lampasas	Ethel Edwards	1940	

Continued on next page

Community	Artist	Date	Comments
Liberty	Howard Fisher	1939	
Linden	Victor Arnatoff	1939	
Livingston	Theodore Van Soelen	1941*	Two panels remain in original position; building converted to Police Department
Lockhart	John Law Walker	1939	
Mart	Jose Aceves	1939	
Mineola	Bernard Zakheim	1938	Destroyed**
Mission	Xavier Gonzales	1942	
Odessa	Tom Lea	1940	Moved to new post office**
Quanah	Jerry Bywaters	1938	
Ranger	Emil Bisttram	1939	
Robstown	Alice Reynolds	1941	
Rosenberg	William Dean Fausett	1941	Destroyed**
Rusk	Bernard Zakheim	1939	
San Antonio	Howard Cook	1939	Sixteen panels remain in original position; building converted to Federal Building
Seymour	Tom Lea	1942	
Smithville	Minette Teichmueller	1939	
Teague	Thomas M. Stell, Jr.	1940	
Trinity	Jerry Bywaters	1942	
Waco	Eugene F. Shonnard	1939	Wood reliefs
Wellington	Bernard Arnest	1940	
Virginia			
Altavista	Herman Maril	1940	
Appalachia	Lucile Blanch	1940	
Arlington	Auriel Bessemer	1940	Seven panels
Bassett	Walter Carnelli	1939	
Berryville	Edwin S. Lewis	1940	

Continued on next page

Community	Artist	Date	Comments
Bluefield	Richard Kenah	1942	
Chatham	Carson Davenport	1938	
Christiansburg	John DeGroot, Jr.	1939*	
Covington	Lenore Thomas	1939	Three terra-cotta reliefs
Emporia	Andree Ruellan	1941	
Harrisonburg	William H. Calfee	1943*	Four panels
Hopewell	Edmund Archer	1939	
Luray	Sheffield Kagy	1939	
Marion	Daniel Olney	1937	
Newport News P.O. and Court House	Mary B. Fowler	1943	Three terra-cotta reliefs
Orange	Arnold Friedman	1937	
Petersburg	William H. Calfee	1937*	
	Edwin S. Lewis	1937*	
Phoebus	William H. Calfee	1941	
Radford	Alexander B. Clayton	1942*	
Richmond			
Parcel	Paul Cadmus	1939	To be relocated in
Post	Jared French	1939	Richmond Federal Office Building**
Rocky Mount	Roy Hilton	1938	Three panels
Smithfield	William A. Cheever	1941	
Staunton	Florence Bessom	1940	Terra-cotta relief
Strasburg	Sarah Blakeslee	1938	
Stuart	John E. Costigan	1942	
Tazewell	William H. Calfee	1940	Two panels
Virginia Beach	John H. R. Pickett	1939	

INDEX